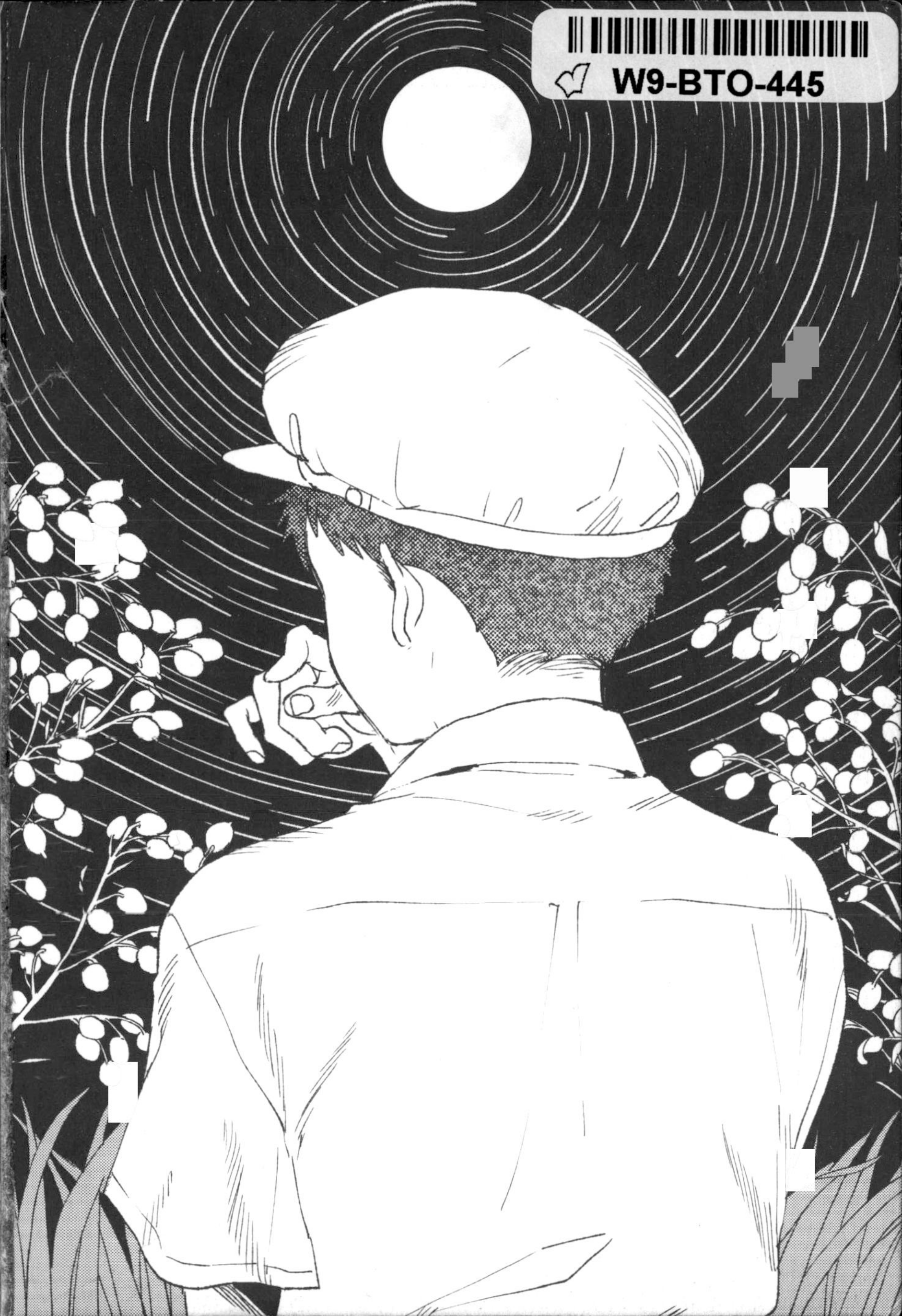

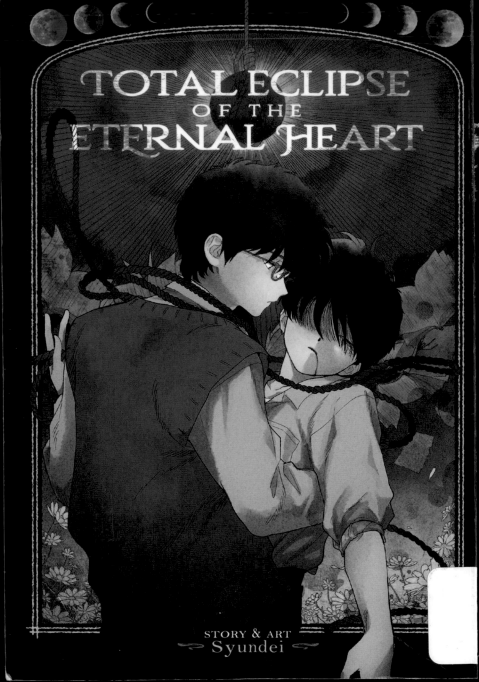

TOTAL ECLIPSE
OF THE
ETERNAL HEART

STORY & ART
Syundei

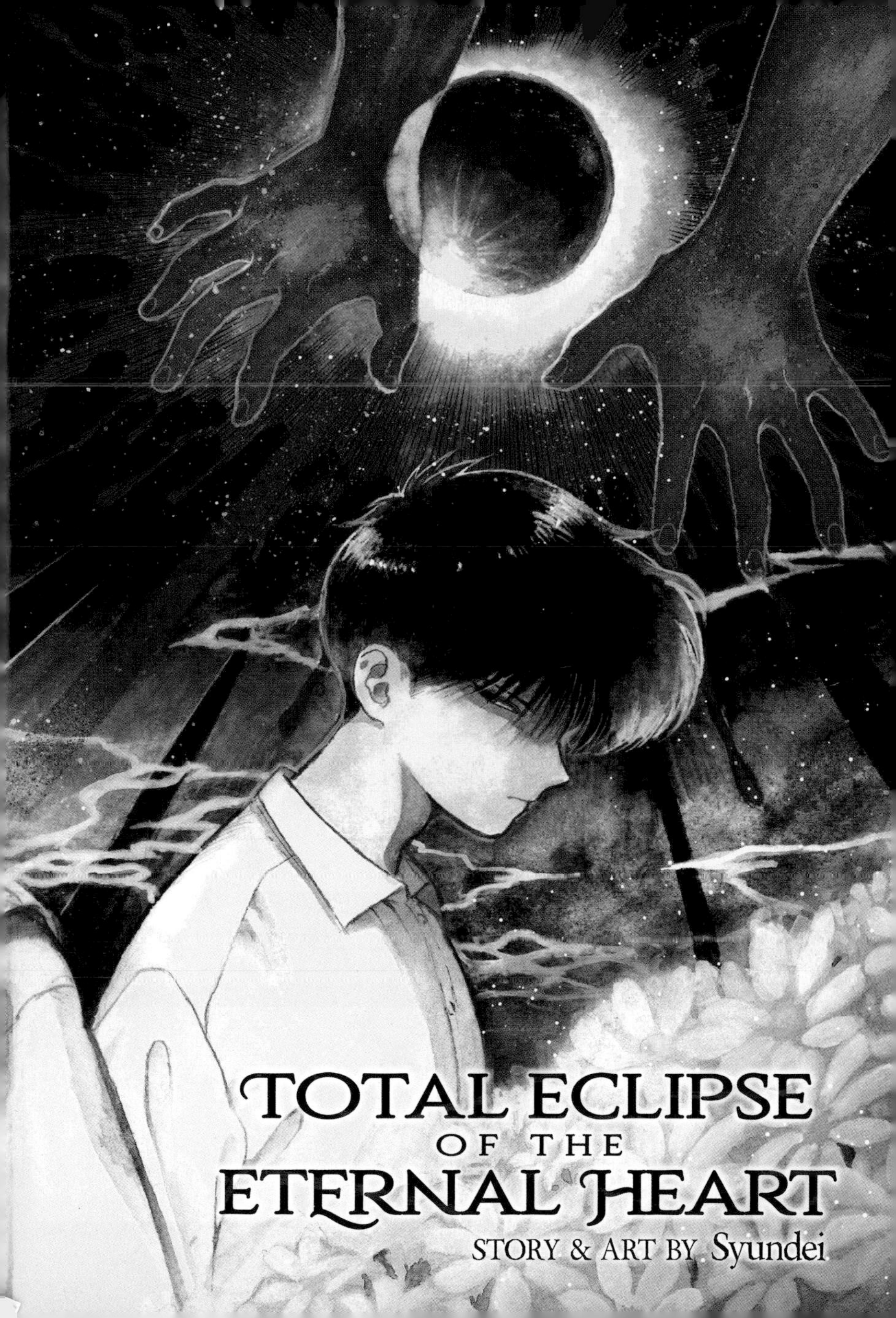
TOTAL ECLIPSE
OF THE
ETERNAL HEART
STORY & ART BY Syundei

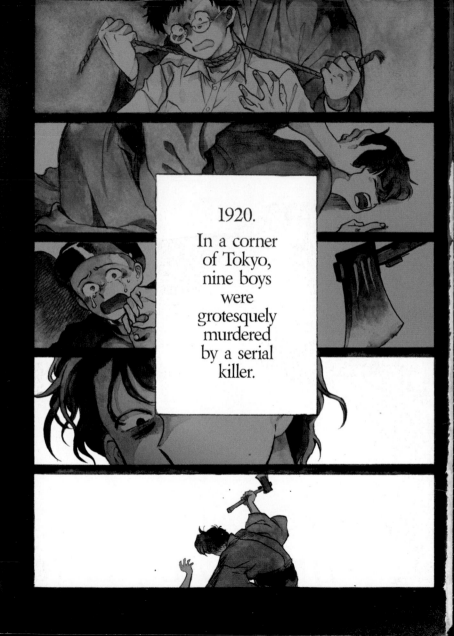

1920.

In a corner of Tokyo, nine boys were grotesquely murdered by a serial killer.

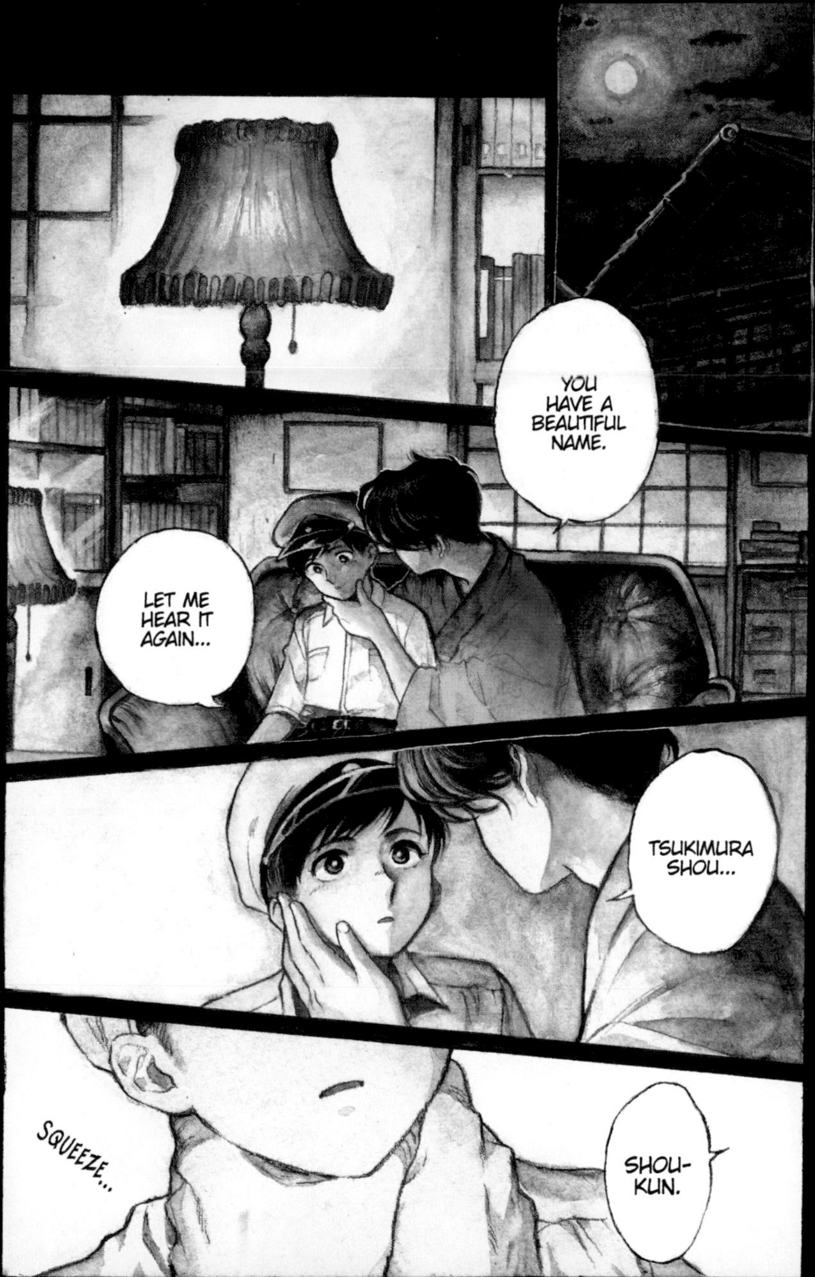
YOU HAVE A BEAUTIFUL NAME.
LET ME HEAR IT AGAIN...
TSUKIMURA SHOU...
SHOU-KUN.
SQUEEZE...

【Chapter 1】

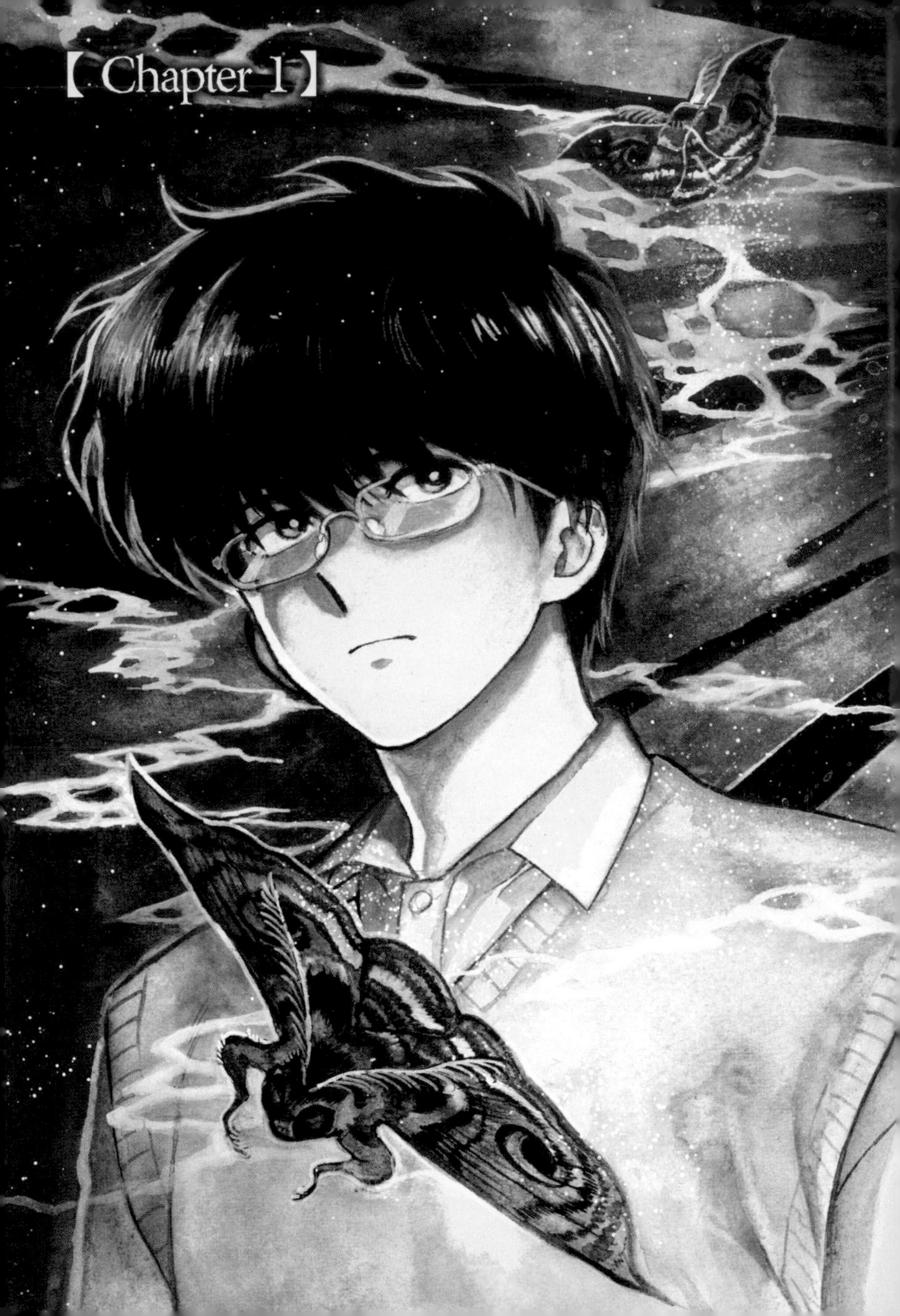

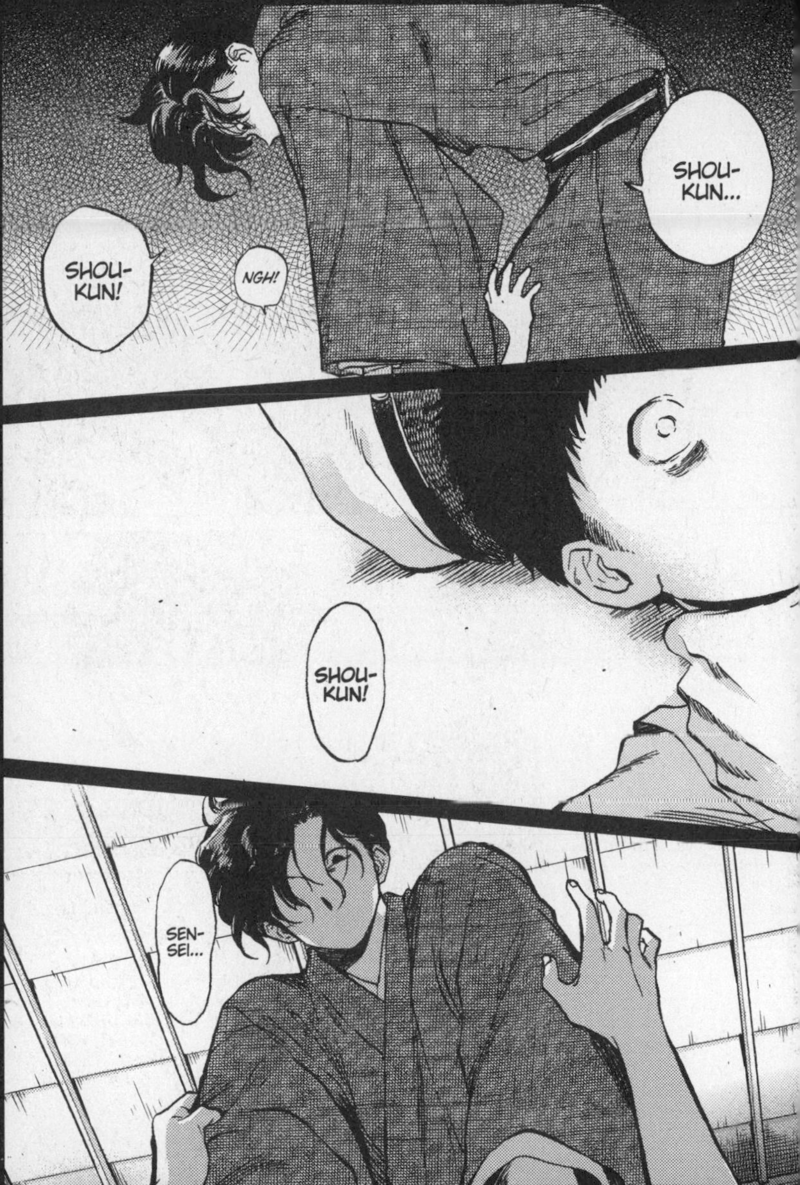
SHOU-
KUN...
NGH!
SHOU-
KUN!
SHOU-
KUN!
SEN-
SEI...

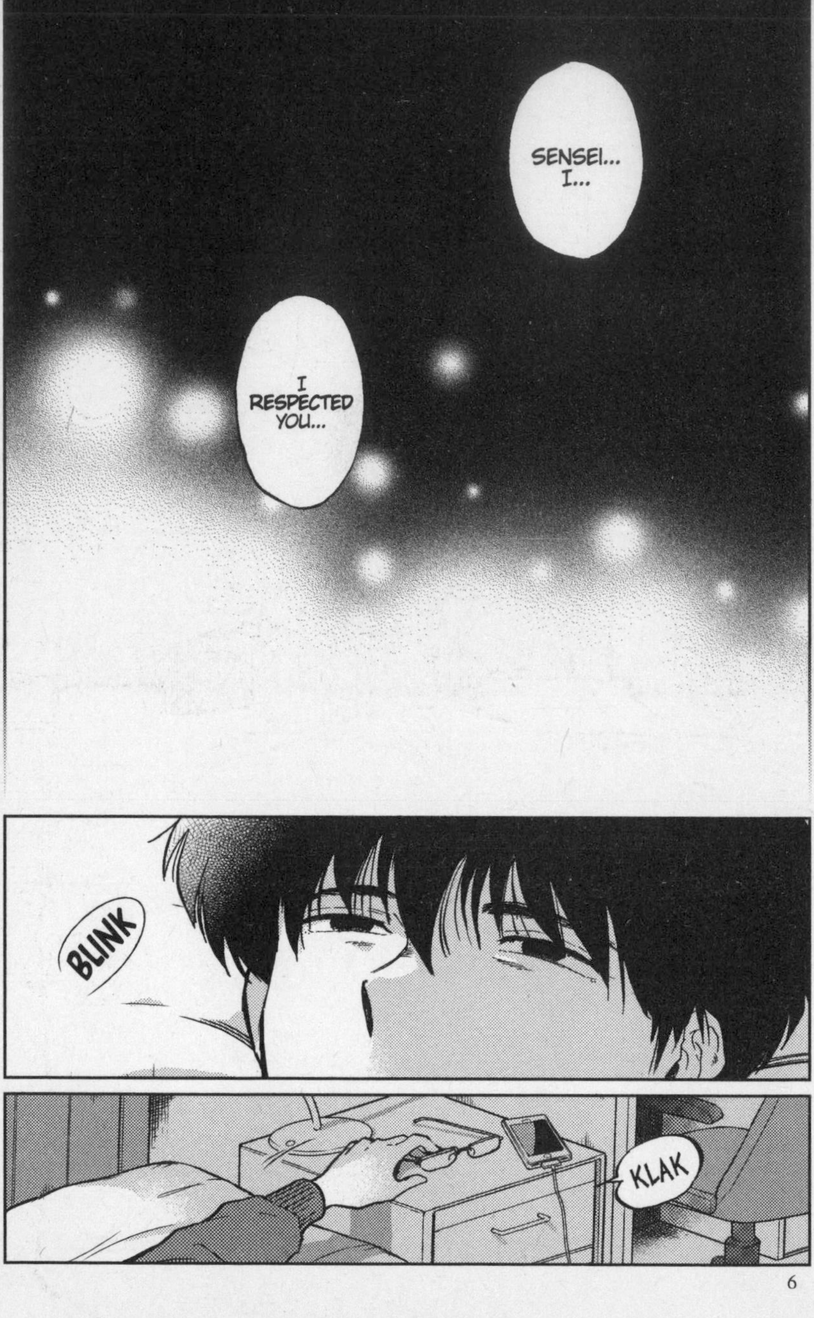
SENSEI... I...
I RESPECTED YOU...
BLINK
KLAK

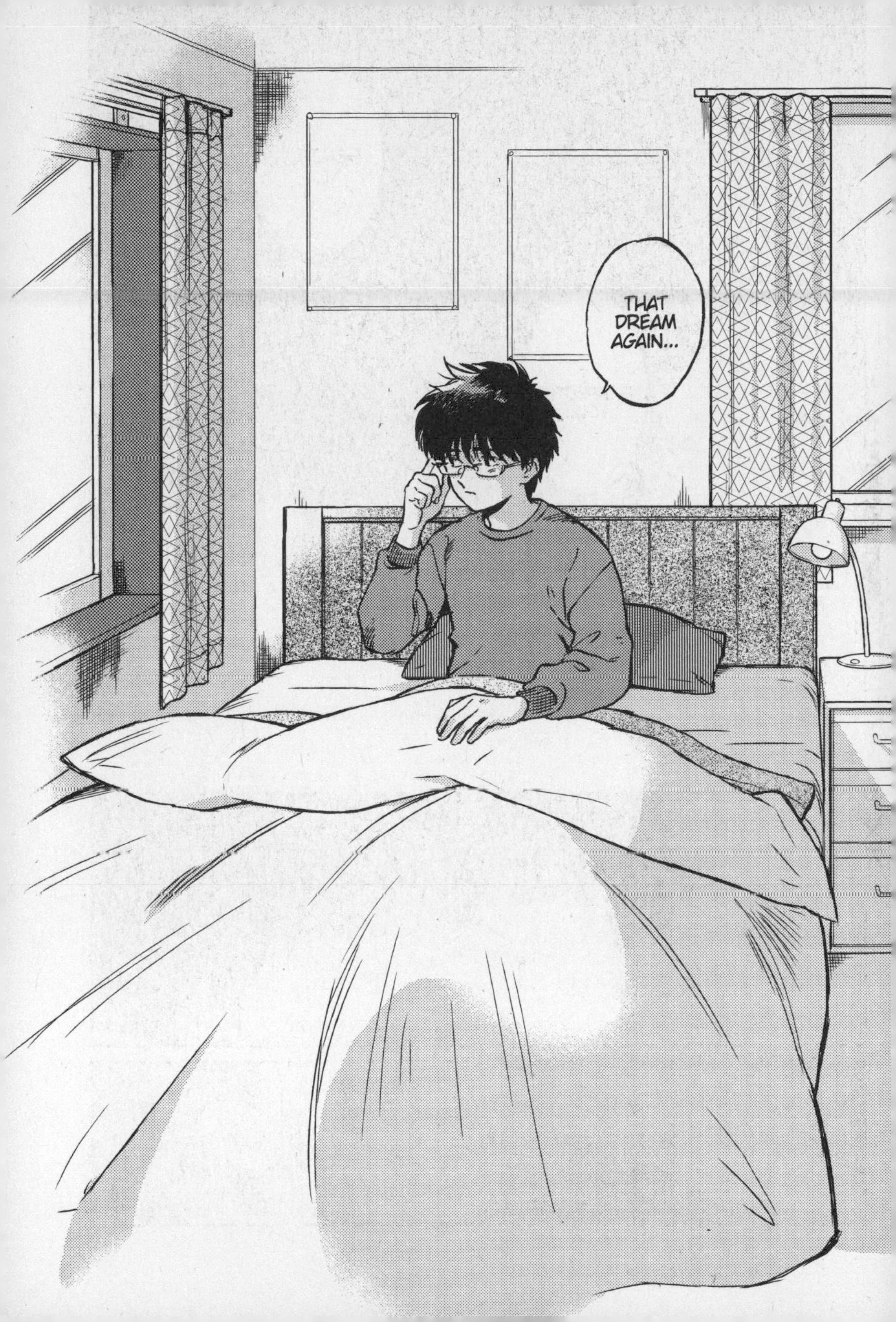
THAT DREAM AGAIN...

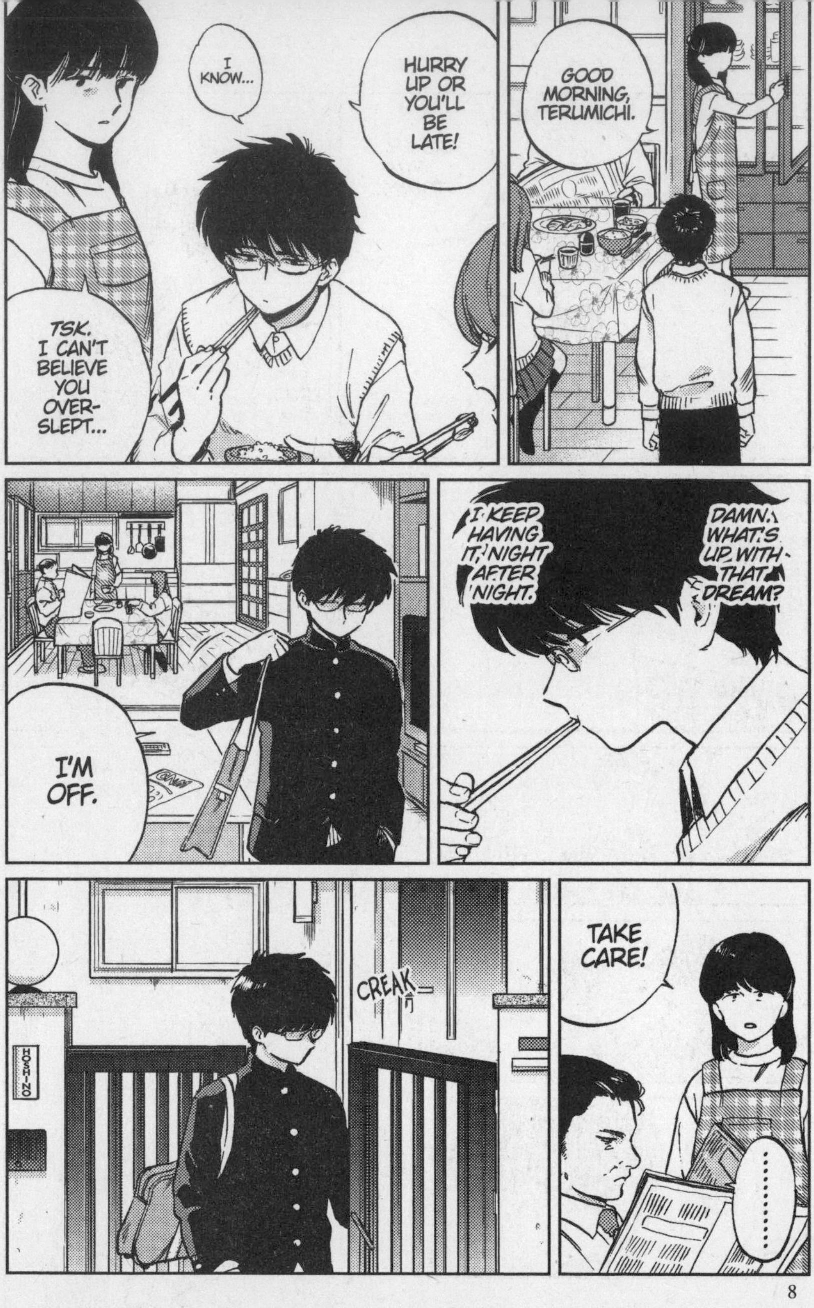
GOOD MORNING, TERUMICHI.
HURRY UP OR YOU'LL BE LATE!
I KNOW...
TSK. I CAN'T BELIEVE YOU OVER-SLEPT...
DAMN. WHAT'S UP WITH THAT DREAM?
I KEEP HAVING IT, NIGHT AFTER NIGHT.
I'M OFF.
TAKE CARE!
......
CREAK
HOSHINO

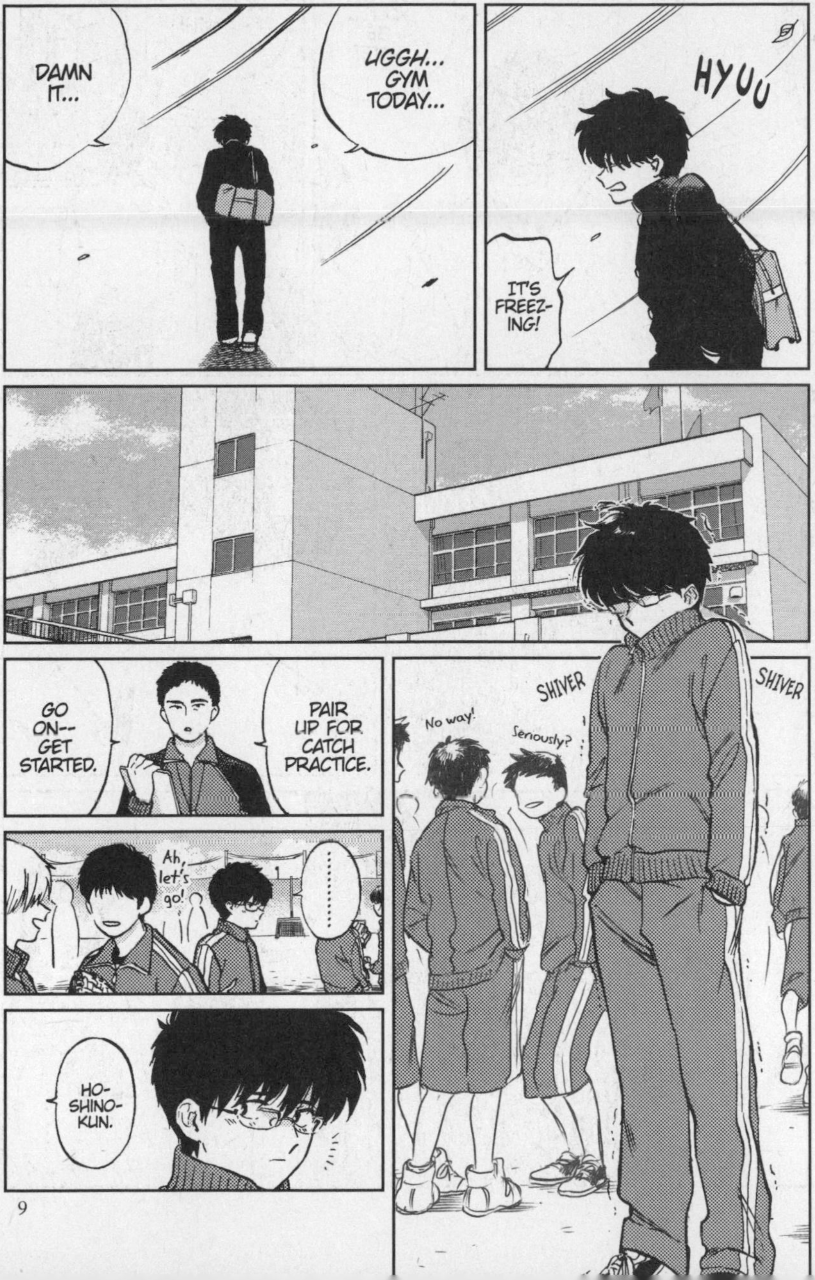
HYUU
IT'S FREEZ-ING!
UGGH... GYM TODAY...
DAMN IT...
SHIVER
SHIVER
Seriously?
No way!
PAIR UP FOR CATCH PRACTICE.
GO ON-- GET STARTED.
......
Ah, let's go!
HO-SHINO-KUN.

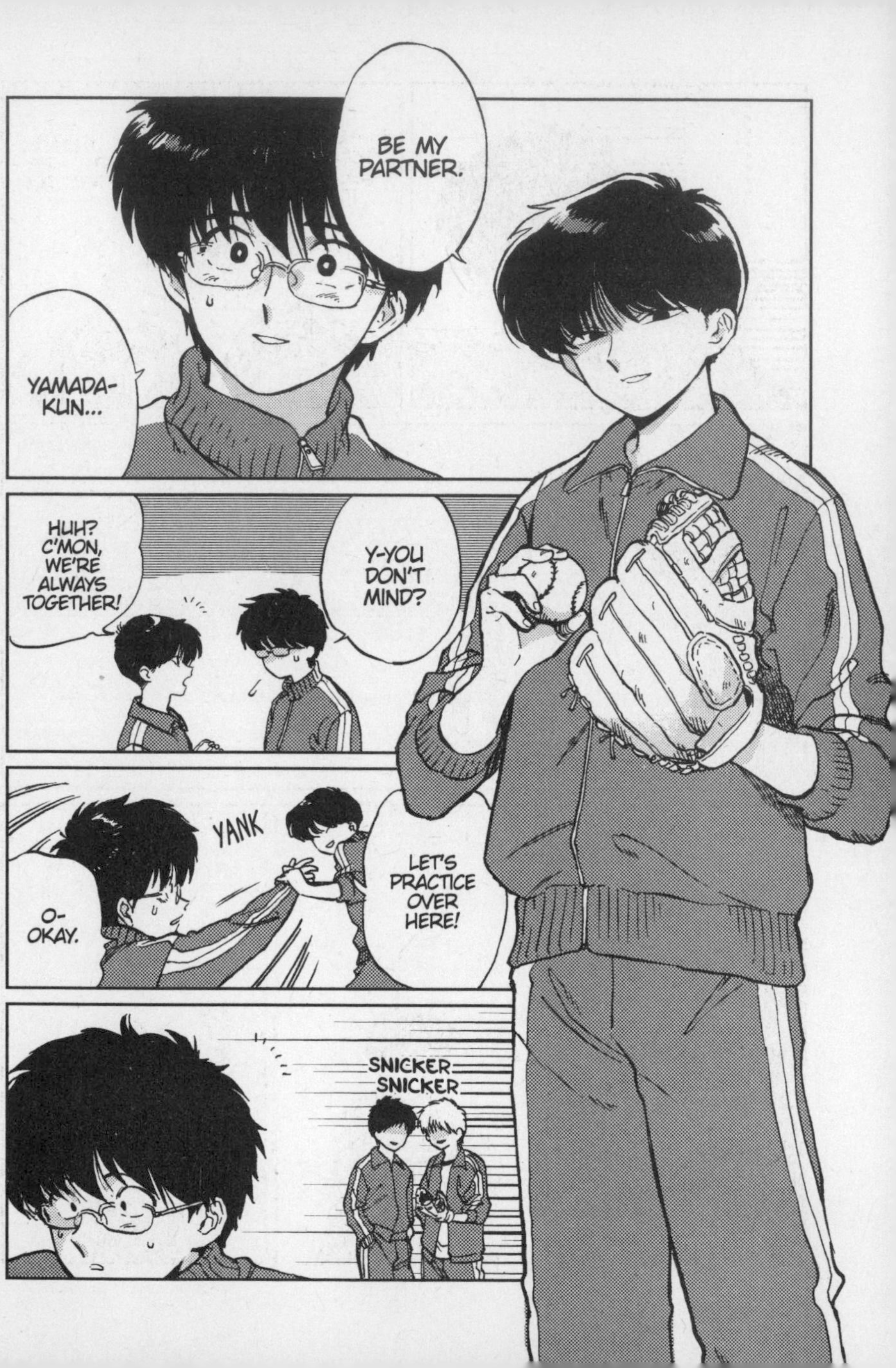
BE MY PARTNER.
YAMADA-KUN...
Y-YOU DON'T MIND?
HUH? C'MON, WE'RE ALWAYS TOGETHER!
LET'S PRACTICE OVER HERE!
YANK
O-OKAY.
SNICKER SNICKER

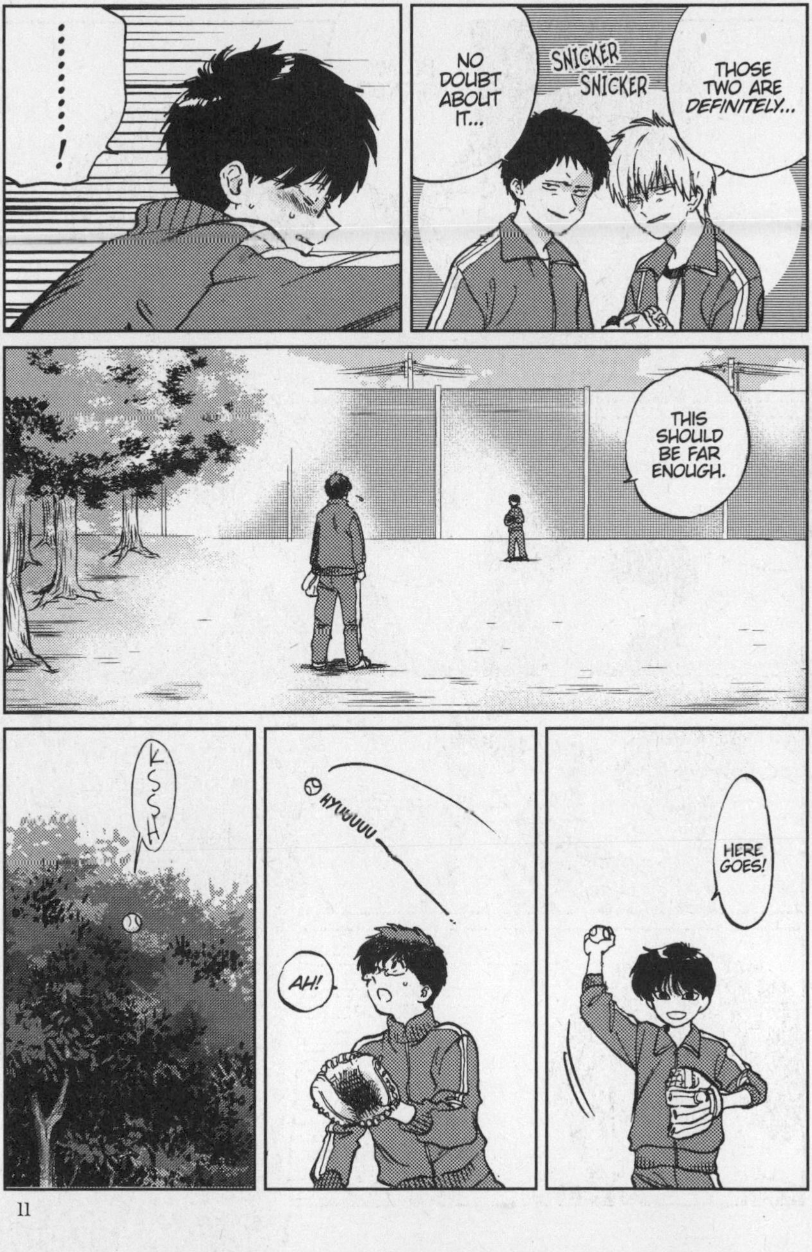
THOSE TWO ARE DEFINITELY...
SNICKER SNICKER
NO DOUBT ABOUT IT...
......!
THIS SHOULD BE FAR ENOUGH.
HERE GOES!
HYUUUUU
AH!
KSSH

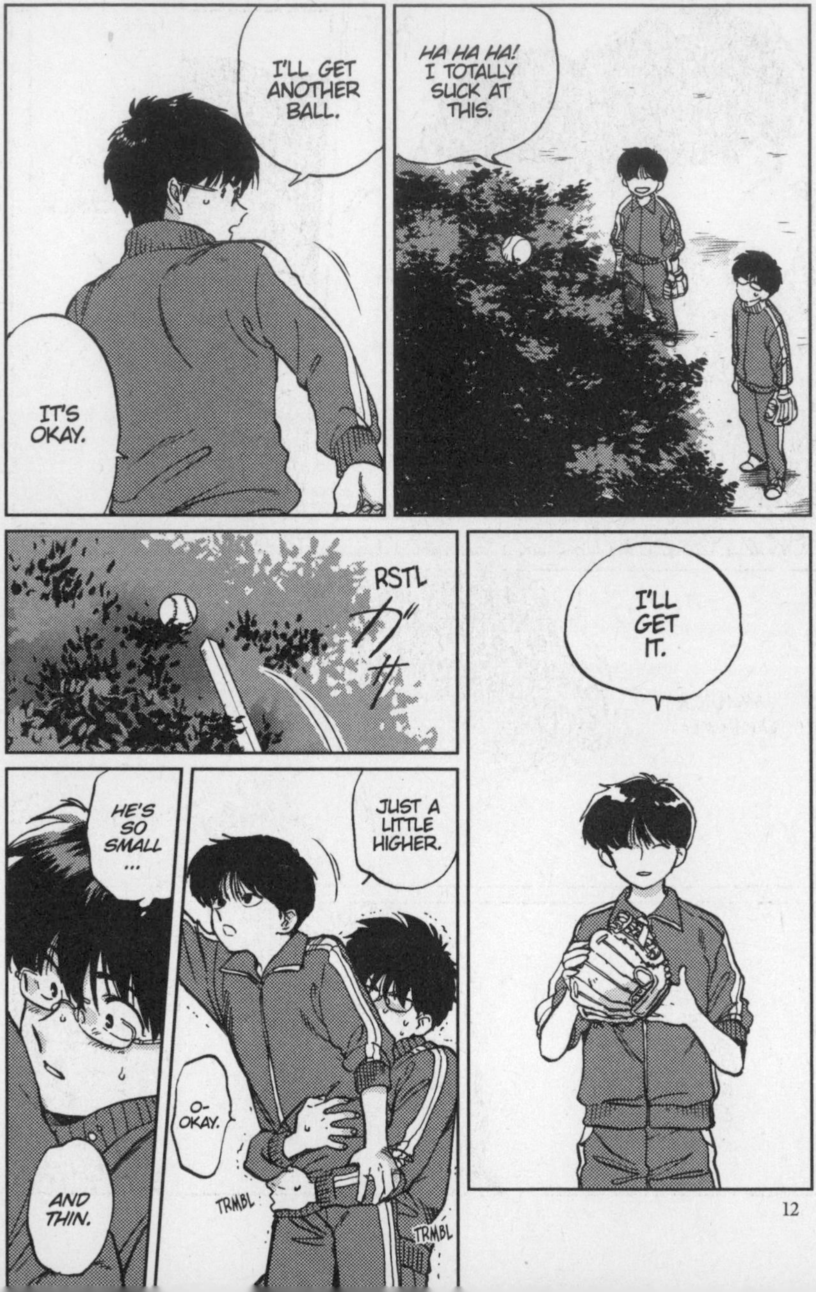
HA HA HA! I TOTALLY SUCK AT THIS.
I'LL GET ANOTHER BALL.
IT'S OKAY.
I'LL GET IT.
RSTL
JUST A LITTLE HIGHER.
O-OKAY.
TRMBL
TRMBL
HE'S SO SMALL ...
AND THIN.

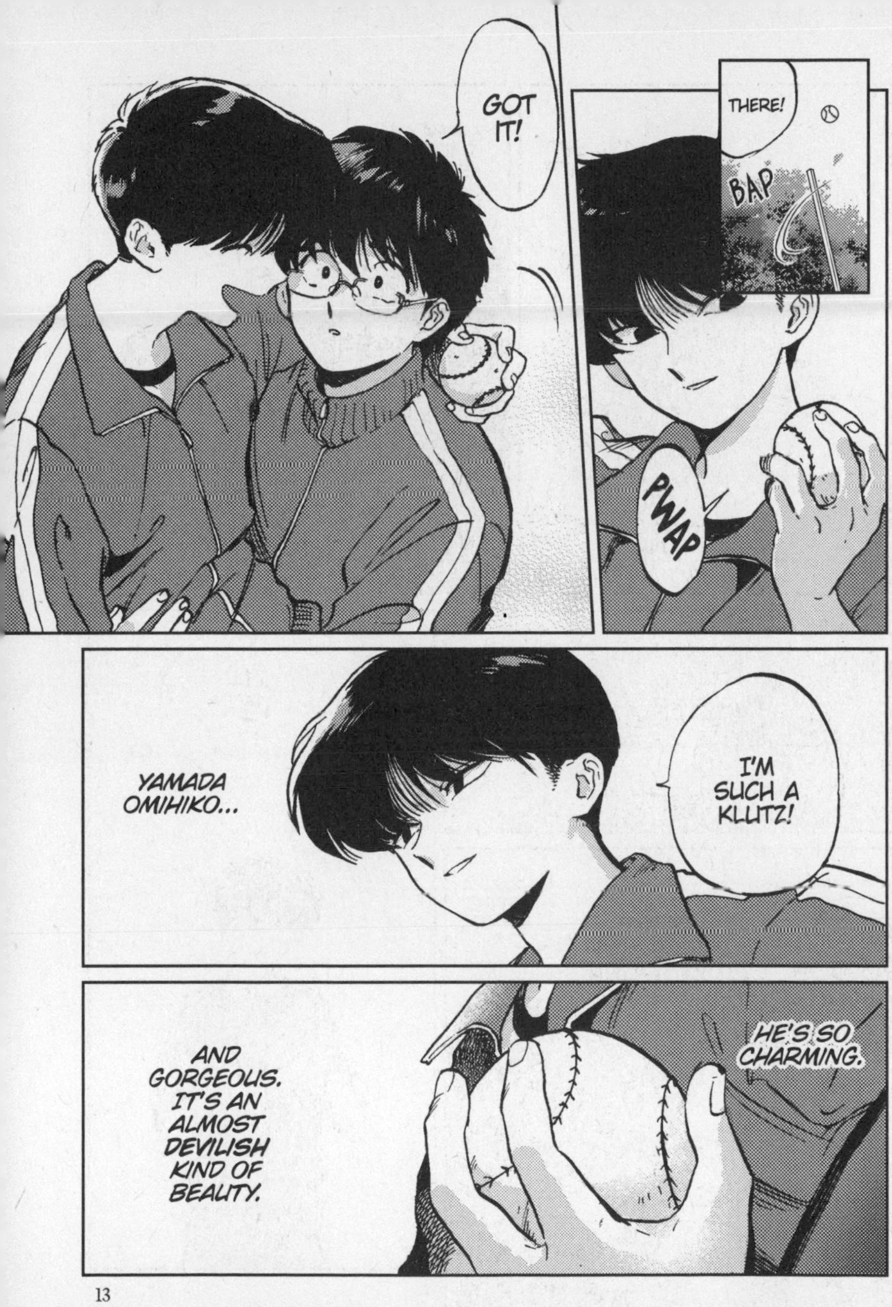
THERE!
BAP
PWAP
GOT IT!
I'M SUCH A KLUTZ!
YAMADA OMIHIKO...
HE'S SO CHARMING.
AND GORGEOUS. IT'S AN ALMOST DEVILISH KIND OF BEAUTY.

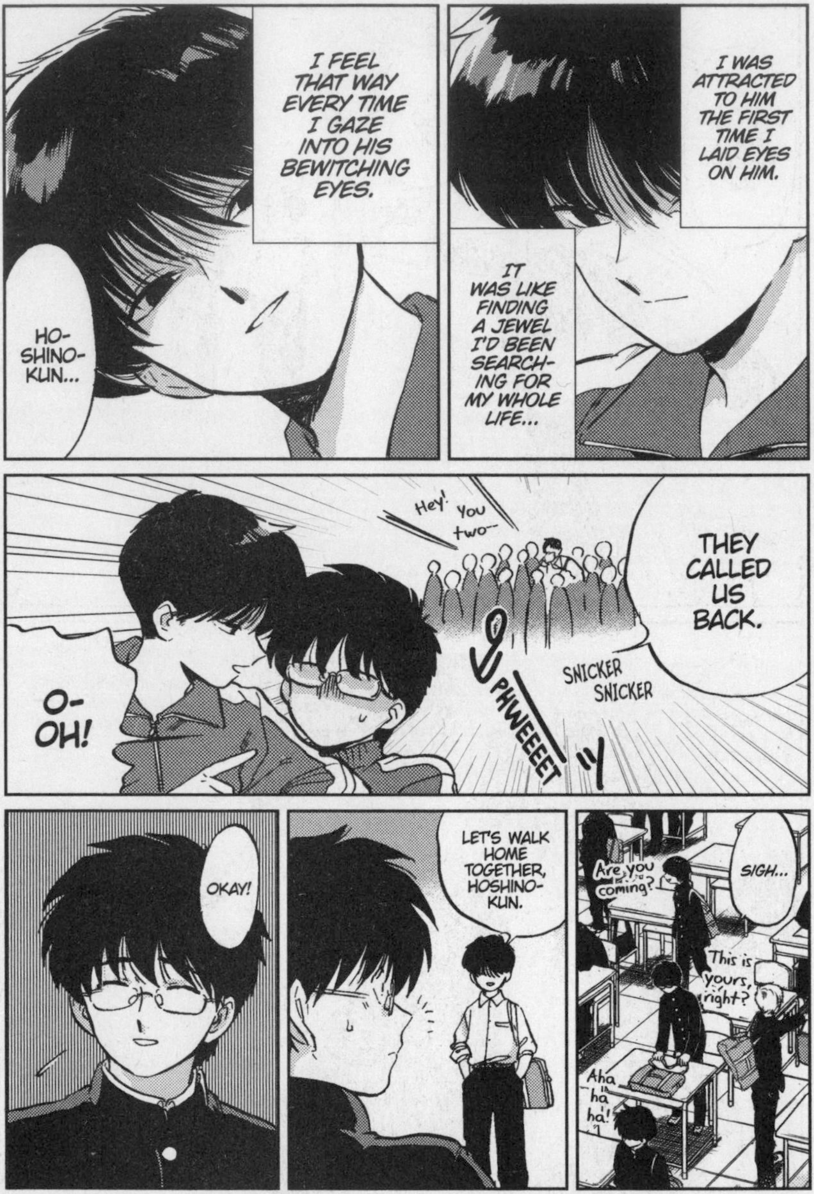
I WAS ATTRACTED TO HIM THE FIRST TIME I LAID EYES ON HIM.
IT WAS LIKE FINDING A JEWEL I'D BEEN SEARCHING FOR MY WHOLE LIFE...
I FEEL THAT WAY EVERY TIME I GAZE INTO HIS BEWITCHING EYES.
HO-SHINO-KUN...
THEY CALLED US BACK.
Hey! You two-
PHWEEEET
SNICKER SNICKER
O-OH!
SIGH...
Are you coming?
This is yours, right?
Aha ha ha!
LET'S WALK HOME TOGETHER, HOSHINO-KUN.
OKAY!

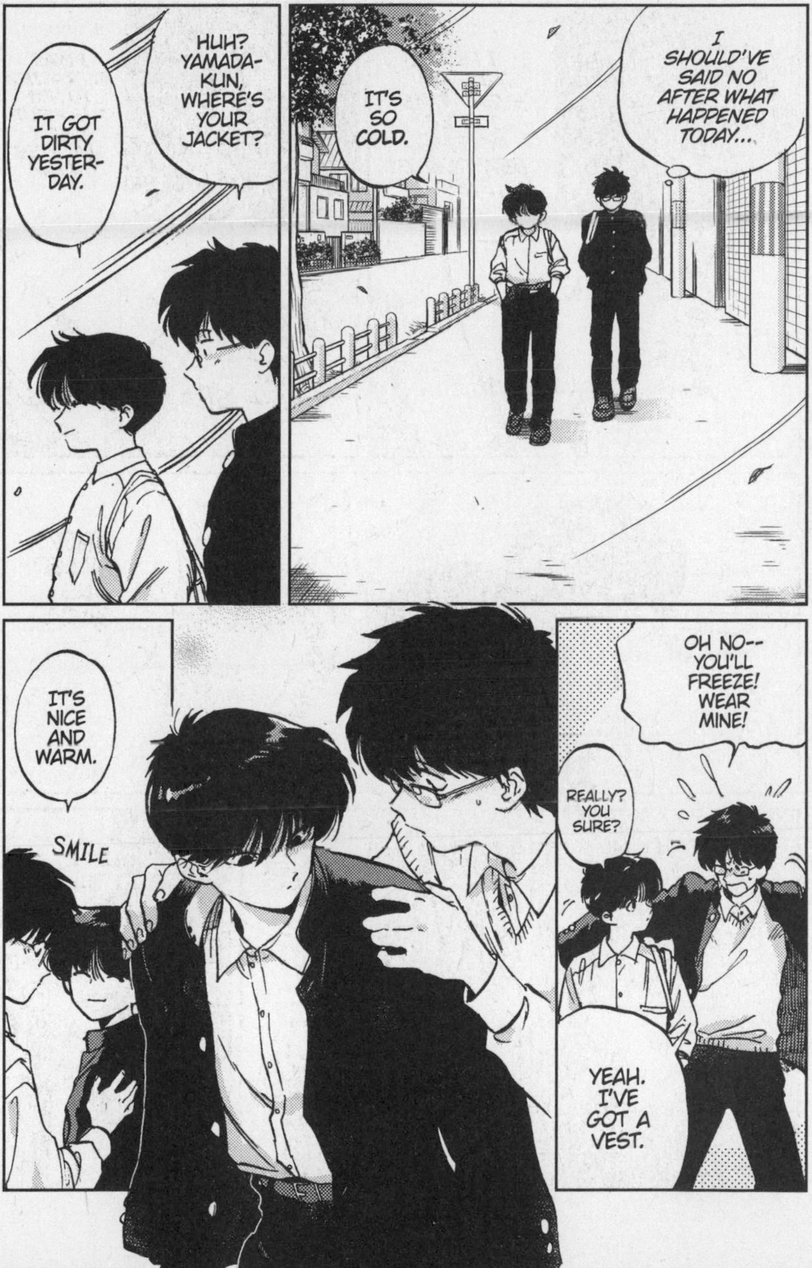
I SHOULD'VE SAID NO AFTER WHAT HAPPENED TODAY...
IT'S SO COLD.
HUH? YAMADA-KUN, WHERE'S YOUR JACKET?
IT GOT DIRTY YESTER-DAY.
OH NO-- YOU'LL FREEZE! WEAR MINE!
REALLY? YOU SURE?
YEAH. I'VE GOT A VEST.
IT'S NICE AND WARM.
SMILE

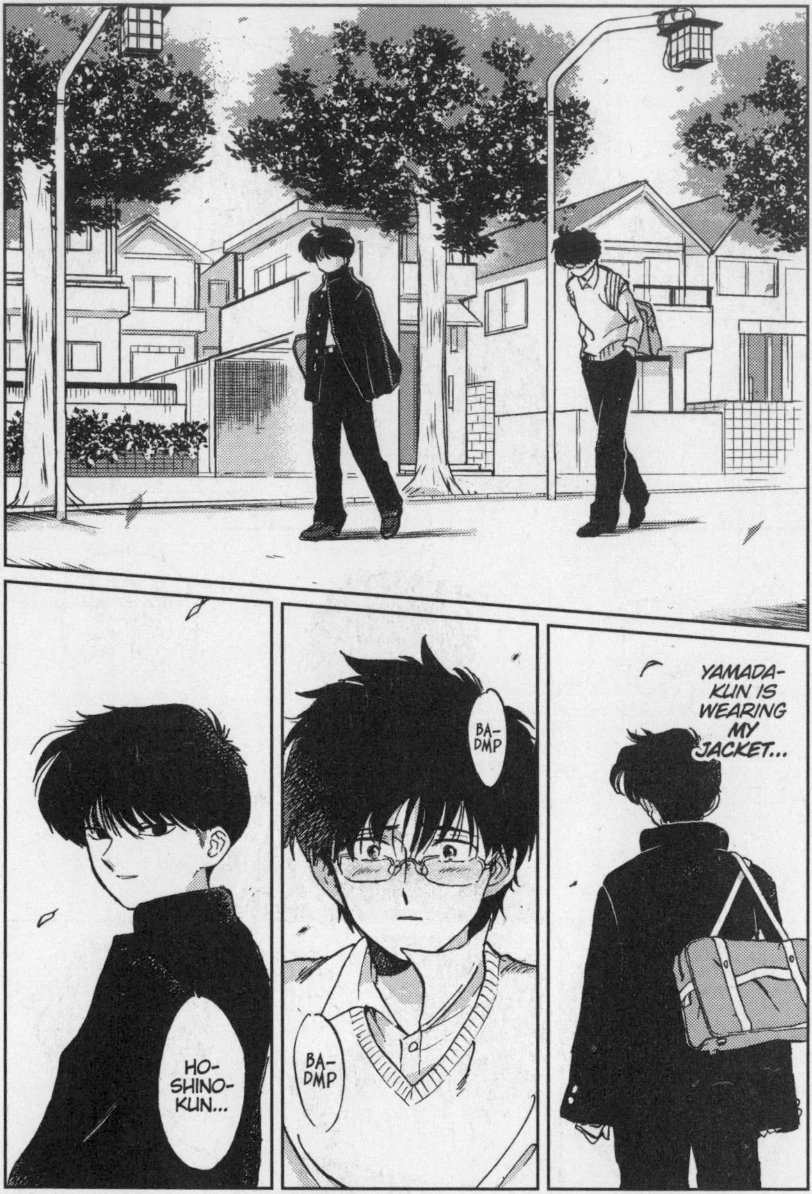
YAMADA-KUN IS WEARING MY JACKET...
BA-DMP
BA-DMP
HO-SHINO-KUN...

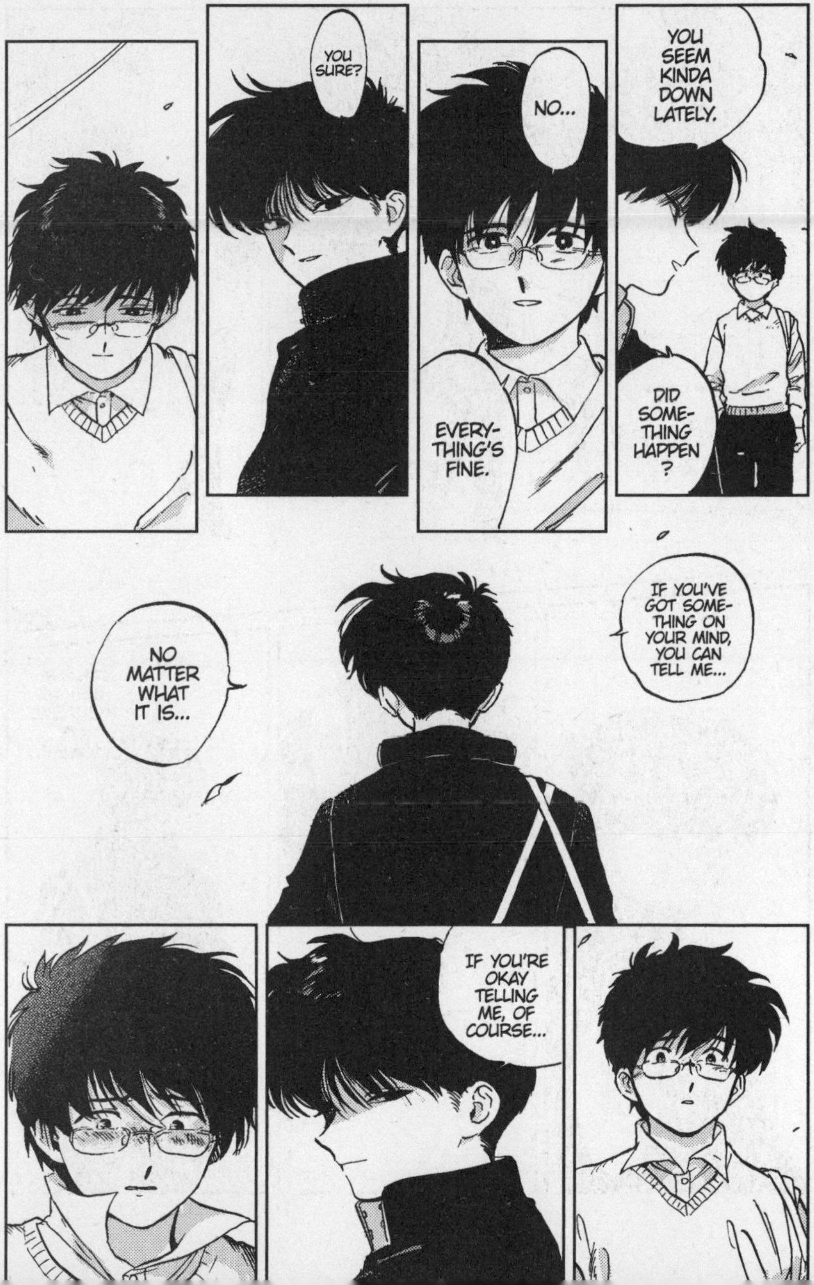
YOU SEEM KINDA DOWN LATELY.
DID SOMETHING HAPPEN?
NO...
EVERYTHING'S FINE.
YOU SURE?
IF YOU'VE GOT SOMETHING ON YOUR MIND, YOU CAN TELL ME...
NO MATTER WHAT IT IS...
IF YOU'RE OKAY TELLING ME, OF COURSE...

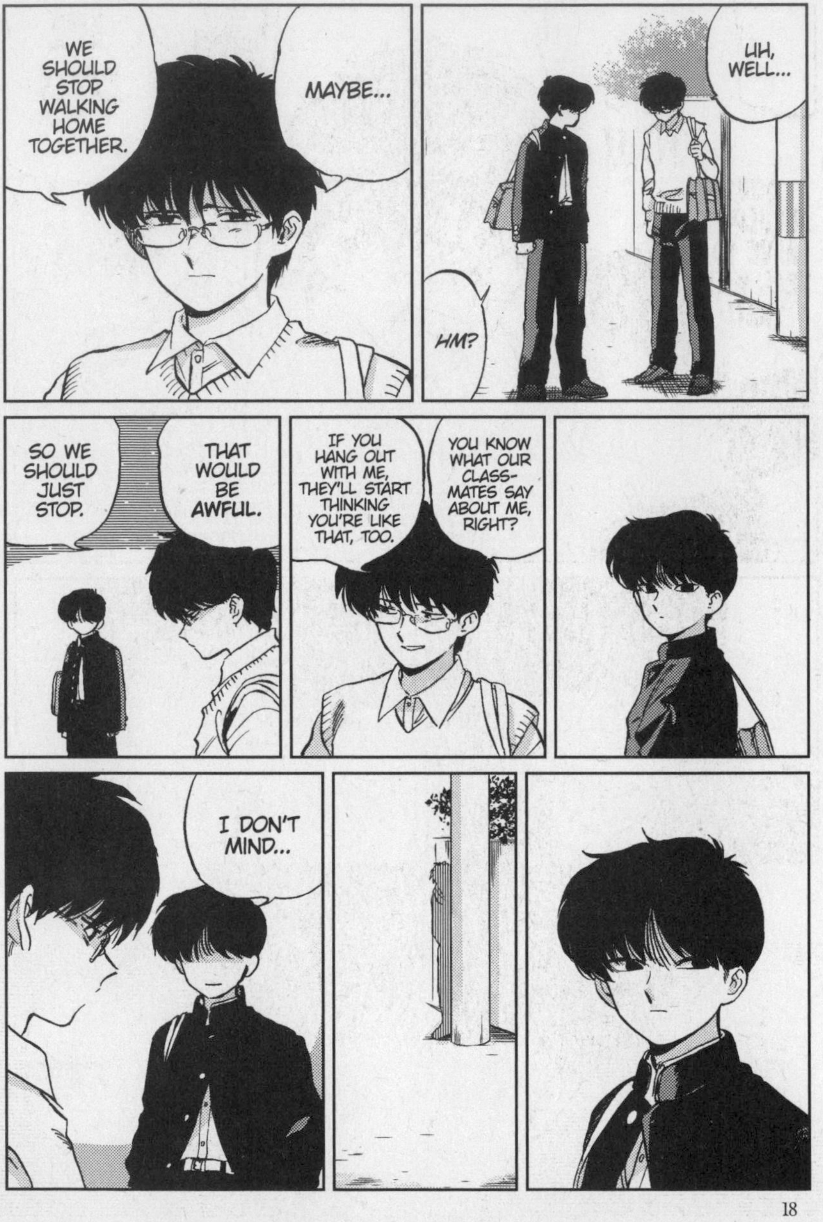
UH, WELL...
HM?
MAYBE...
WE SHOULD STOP WALKING HOME TOGETHER.
YOU KNOW WHAT OUR CLASS-MATES SAY ABOUT ME, RIGHT?
IF YOU HANG OUT WITH ME, THEY'LL START THINKING YOU'RE LIKE THAT, TOO.
THAT WOULD BE AWFUL.
SO WE SHOULD JUST STOP.
I DON'T MIND...

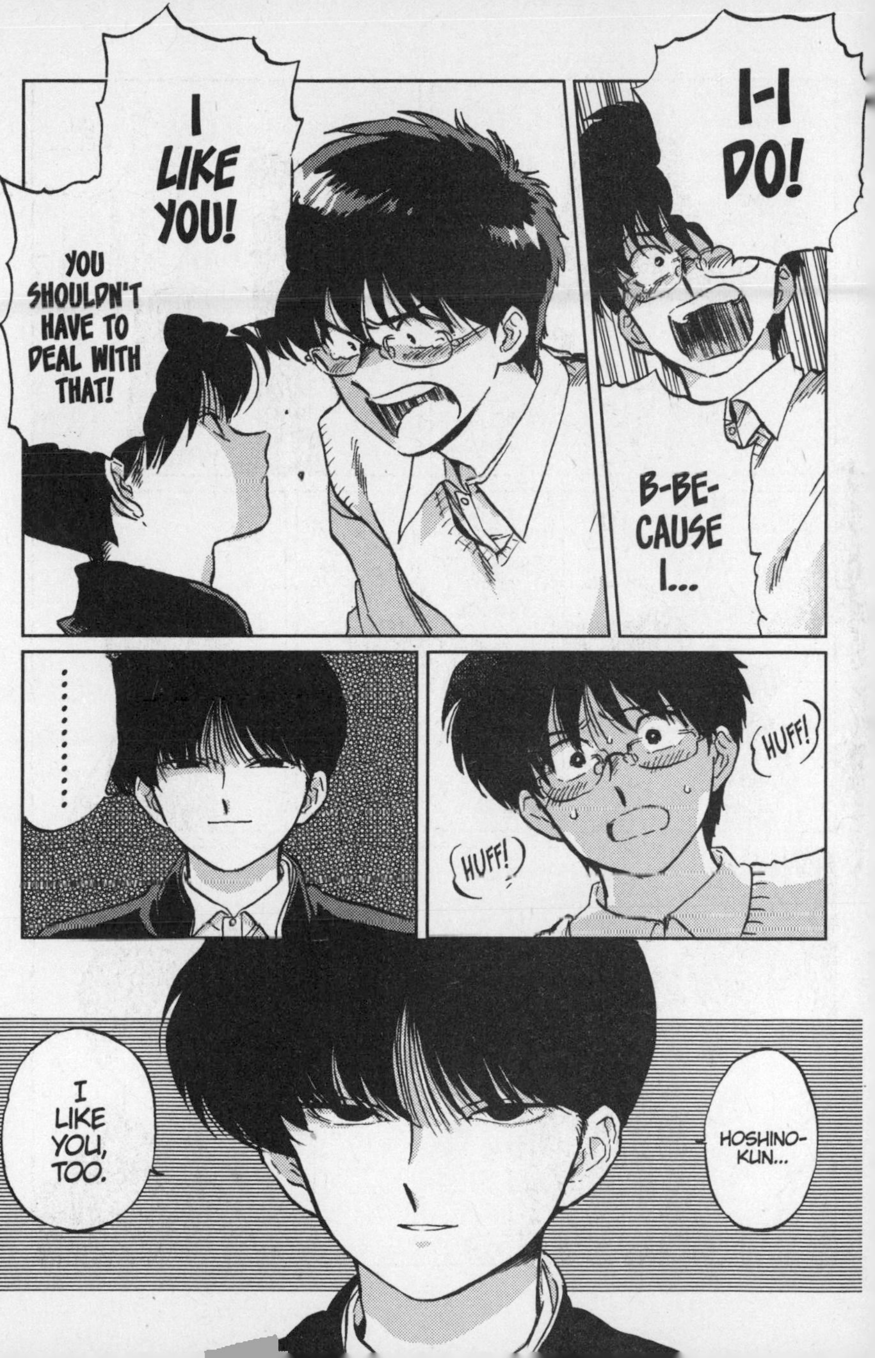
I-I DO!
B-BE-CAUSE I...
I LIKE YOU!
YOU SHOULDN'T HAVE TO DEAL WITH THAT!
HUFF!
HUFF!
......
HOSHINO-KUN...
I LIKE YOU, TOO.

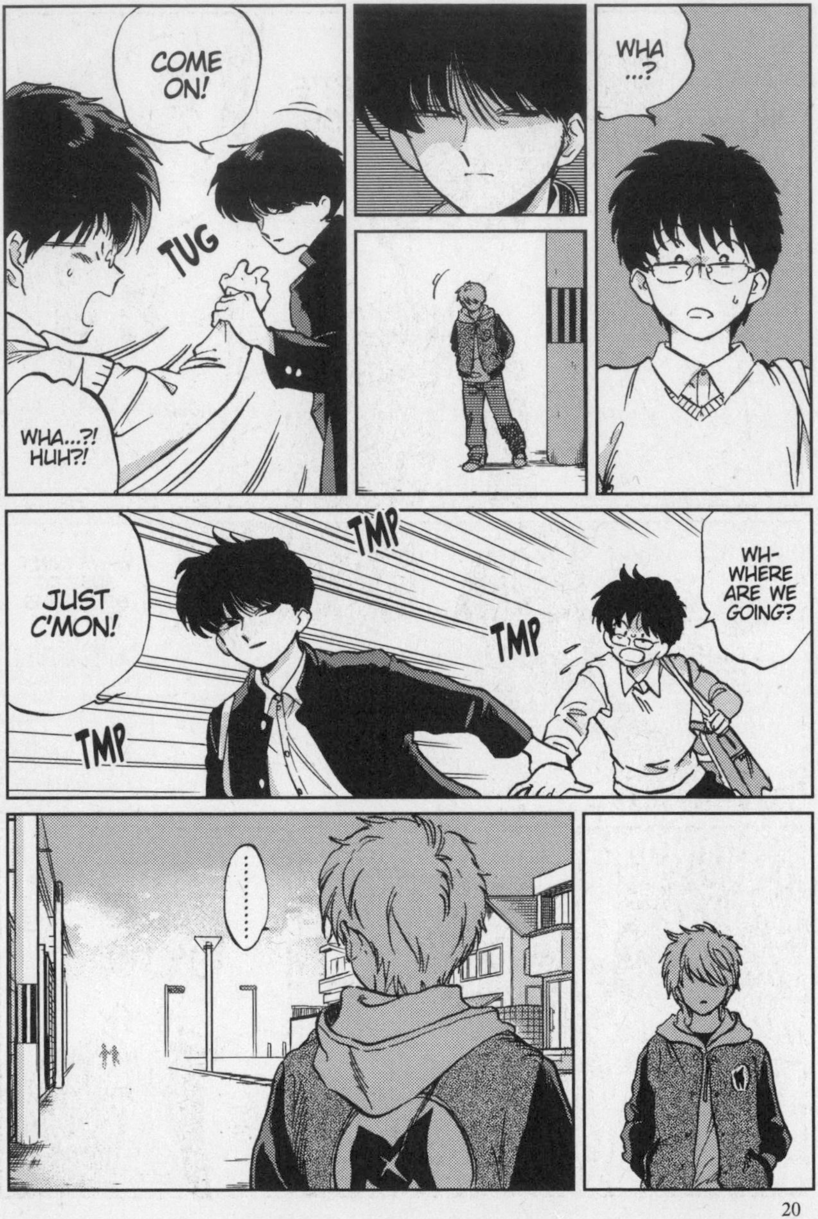
WHA ...?
COME ON!
TUG
WHA...?! HUH?!
WH- WHERE ARE WE GOING?
TMP
TMP
JUST C'MON!
TMP
......

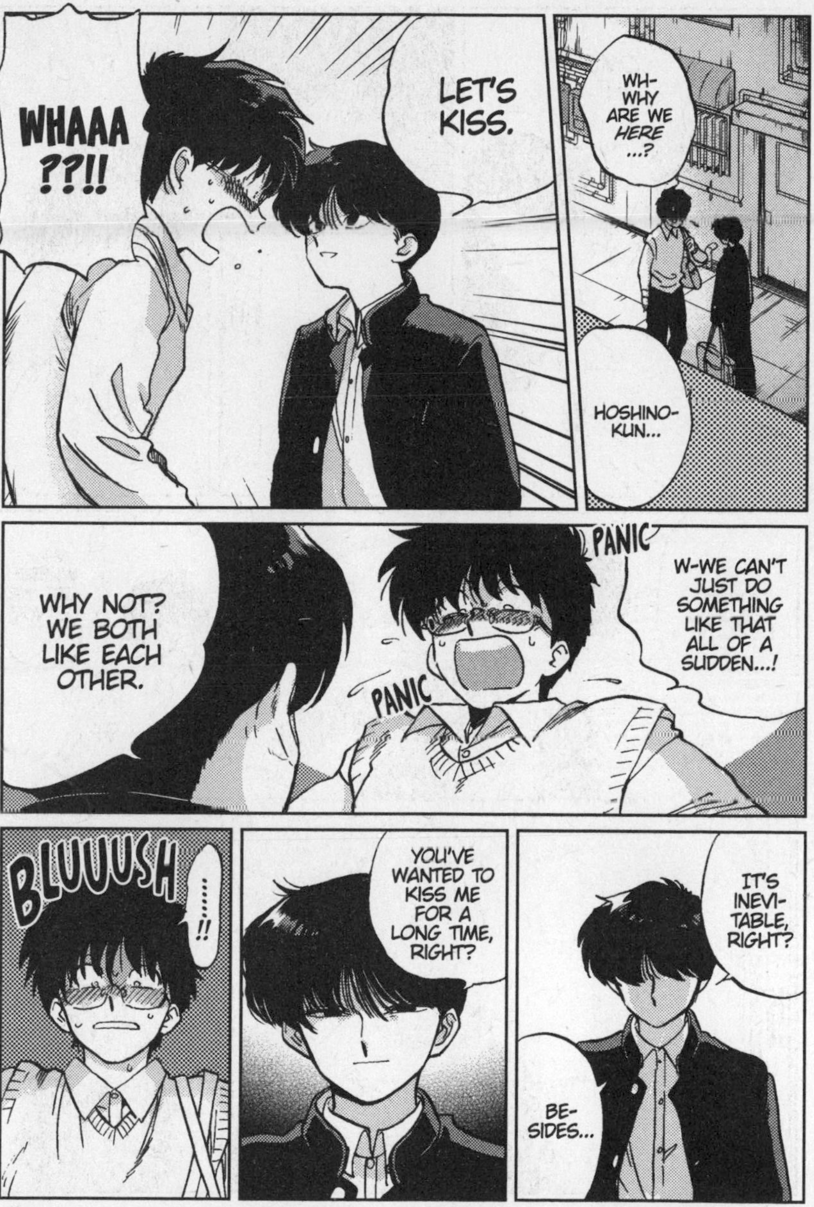
WH-WHY ARE WE HERE ...?
HOSHINO-KUN...
LET'S KISS.
WHAAA ??!!
PANIC
W-WE CAN'T JUST DO SOMETHING LIKE THAT ALL OF A SUDDEN...!
PANIC
WHY NOT? WE BOTH LIKE EACH OTHER.
IT'S INEVI-TABLE, RIGHT?
BE-SIDES...
YOU'VE WANTED TO KISS ME FOR A LONG TIME, RIGHT?
......!!
BLUUUSH

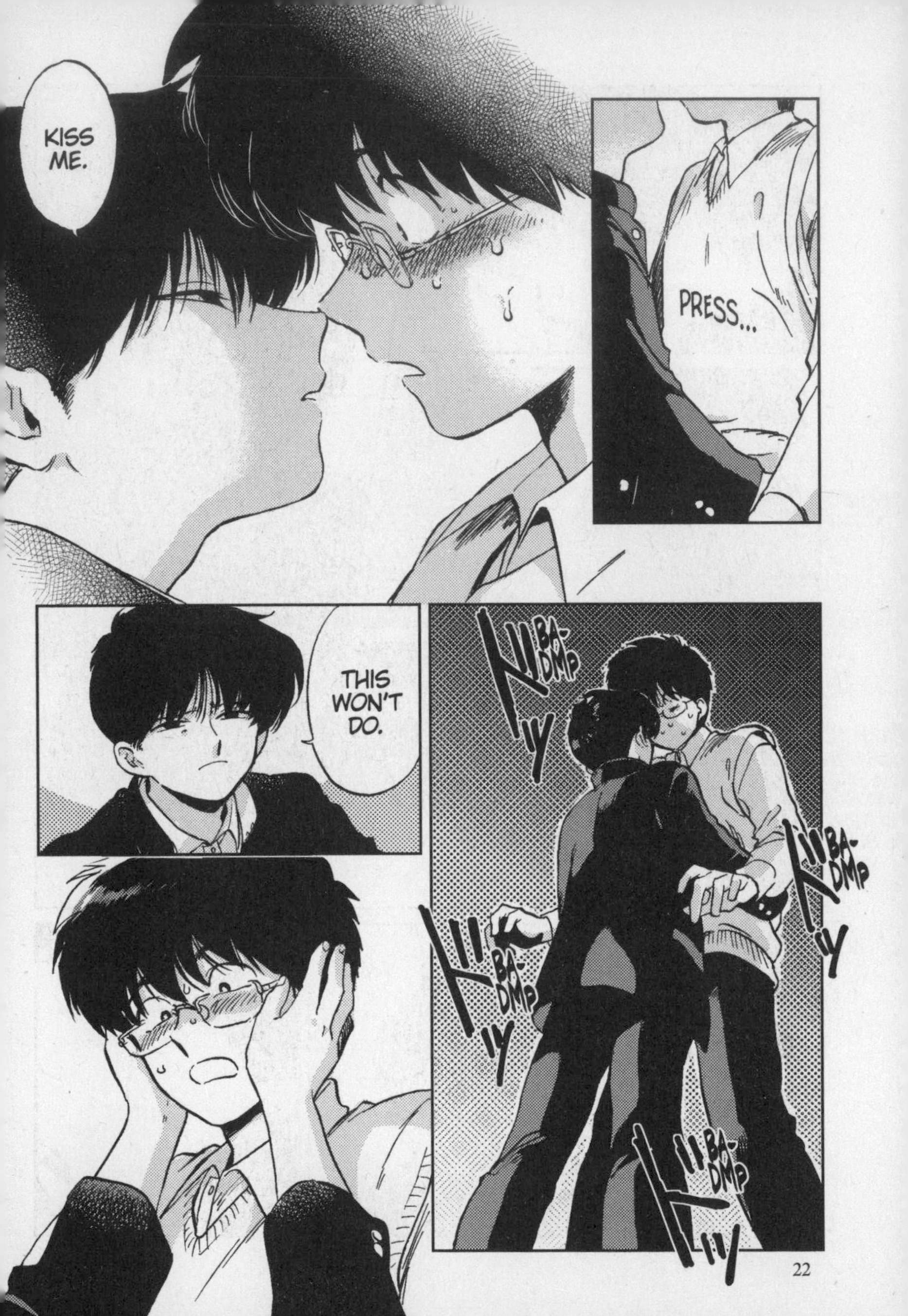
KISS ME.
PRESS...
BA-DMP
BA-DMP
BA-DMP
BA-DMP
THIS WON'T DO.

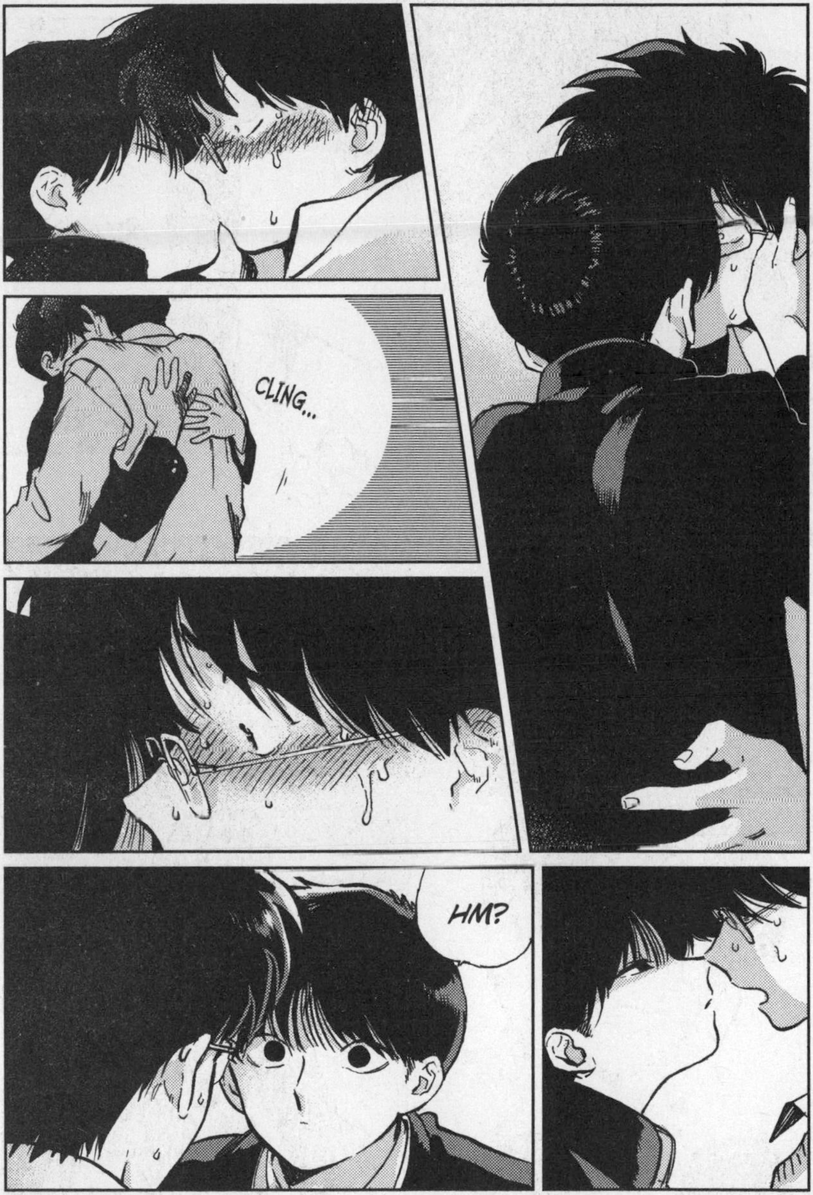
CLING...
HM?

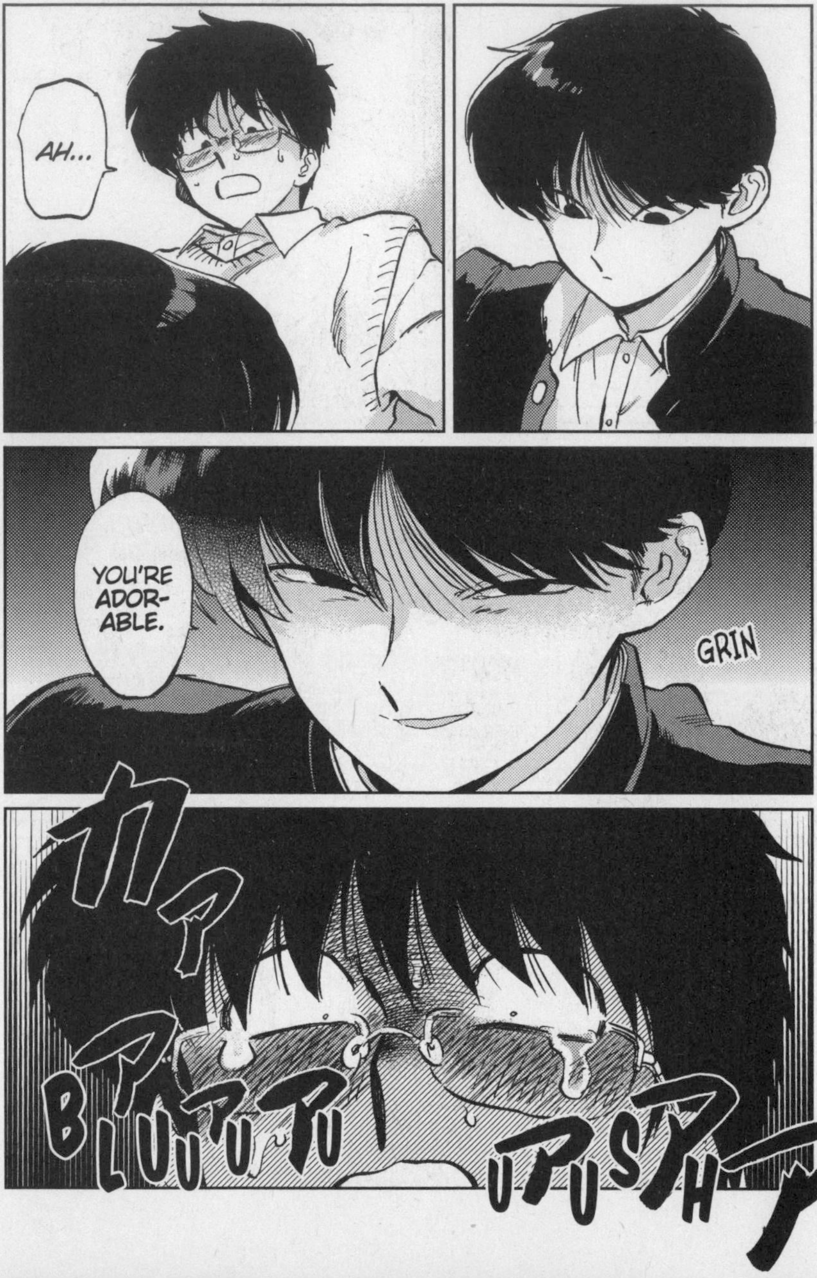
AH...
YOU'RE ADORABLE.
GRIN
BLUUUUUUSH

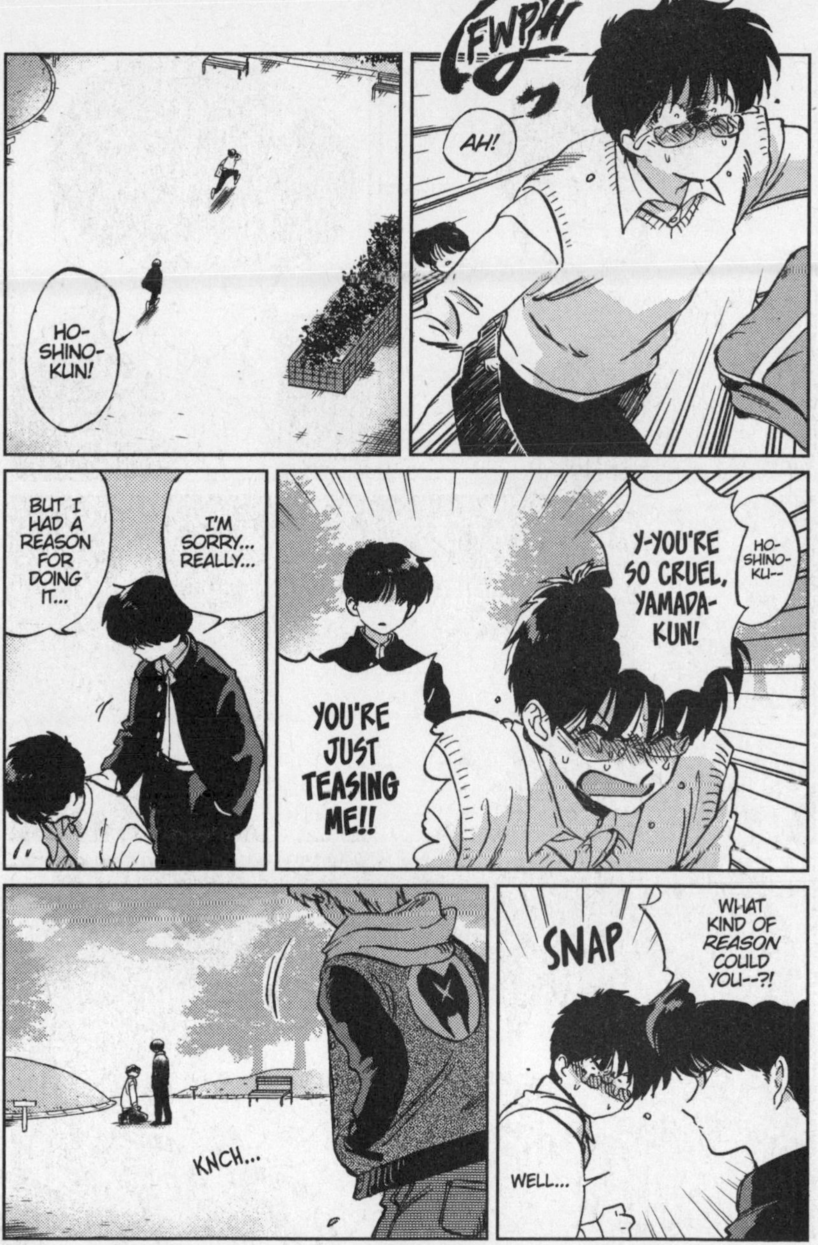
FWPAH
AH!
HO-SHINO-KUN!
HO-SHINO-KU--
Y-YOU'RE SO CRUEL, YAMADA-KUN!
YOU'RE JUST TEASING ME!!
I'M SORRY... REALLY...
BUT I HAD A REASON FOR DOING IT...
WHAT KIND OF *REASON* COULD YOU--?!
SNAP
WELL...
KNCH...

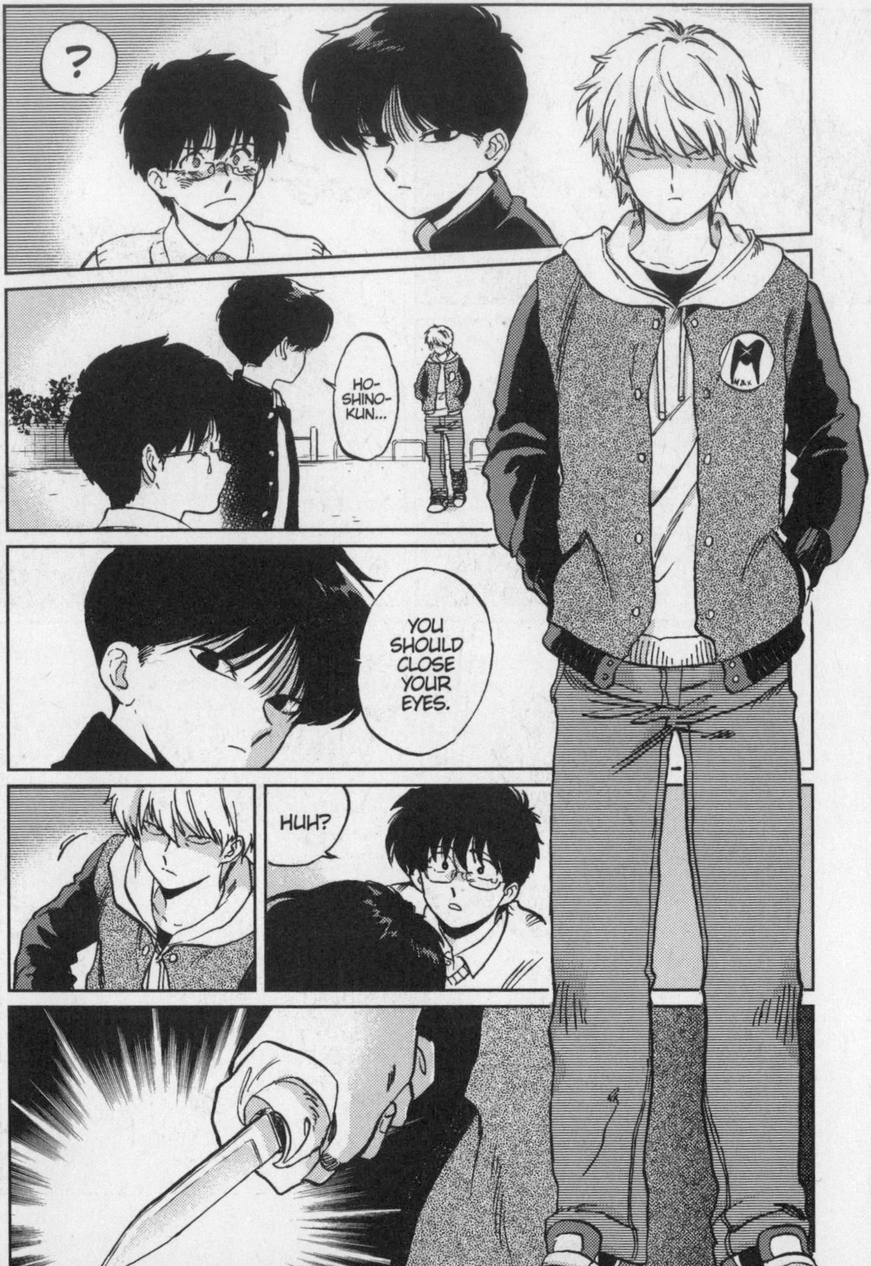
?
HO-SHINO-KUN...
YOU SHOULD CLOSE YOUR EYES.
HUH?

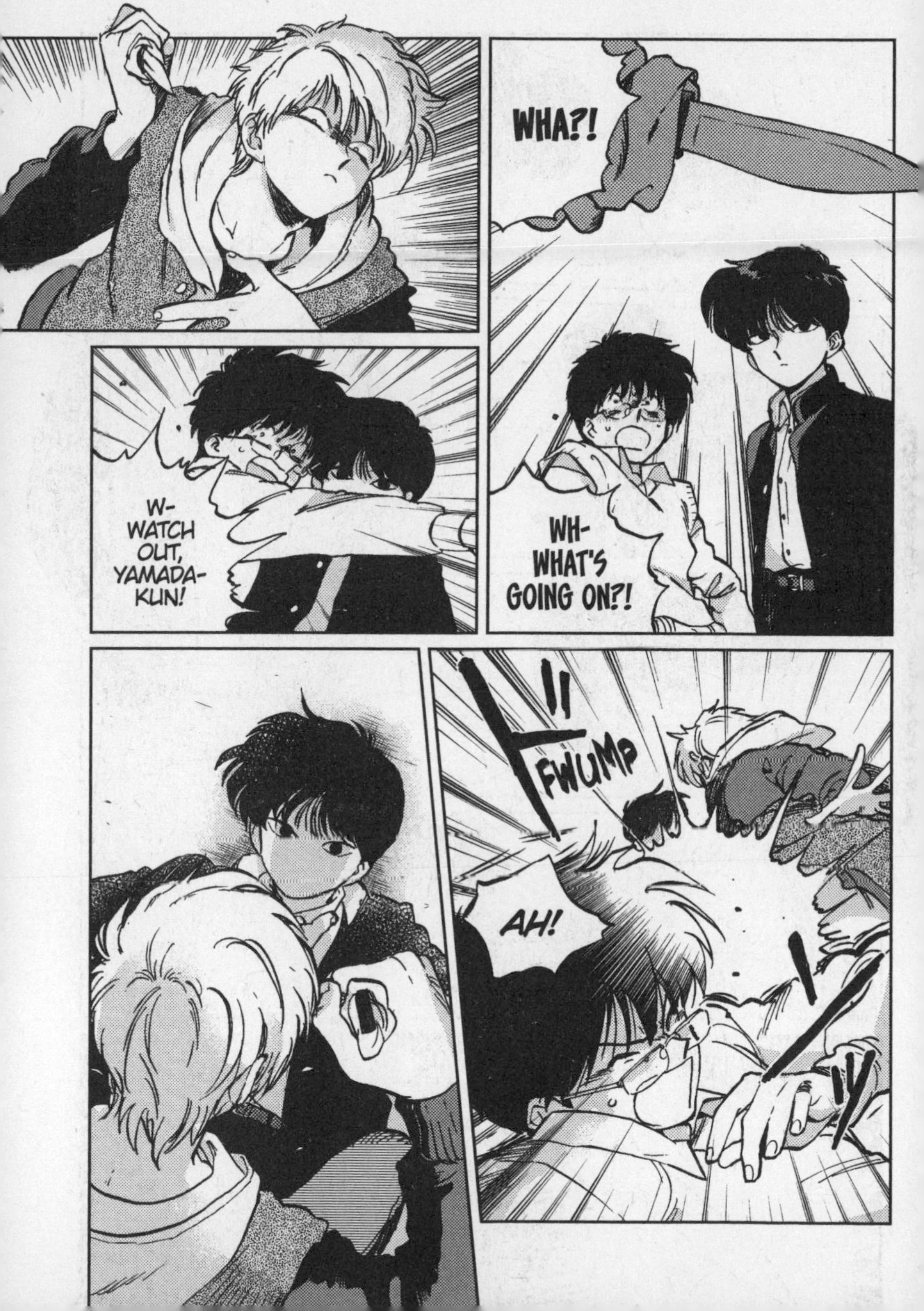
WHA?!
WH- WHAT'S GOING ON?!
W- WATCH OUT, YAMADA-KUN!
FWUMP
AH!

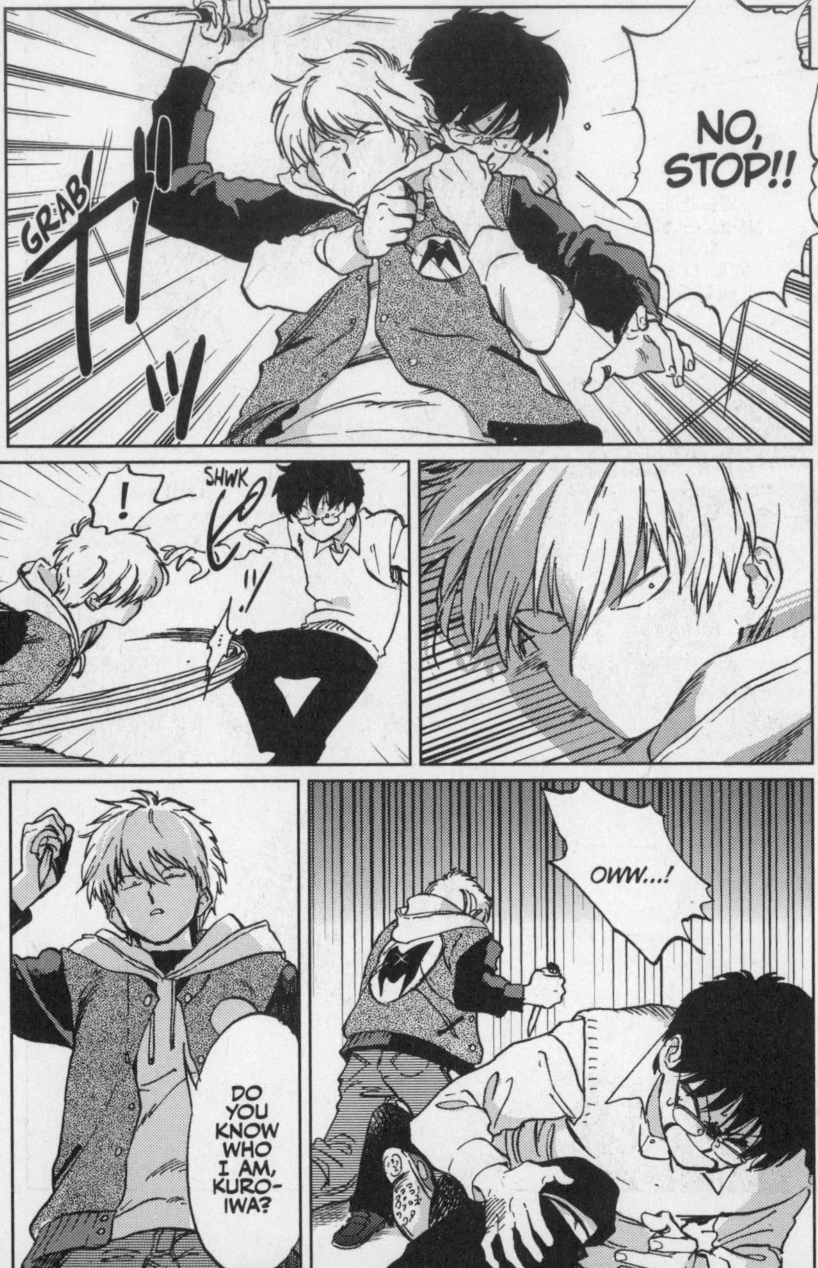
NO, STOP!!
GRAB
SHWK
!
OWW...!
DO YOU KNOW WHO I AM, KURO-IWA?

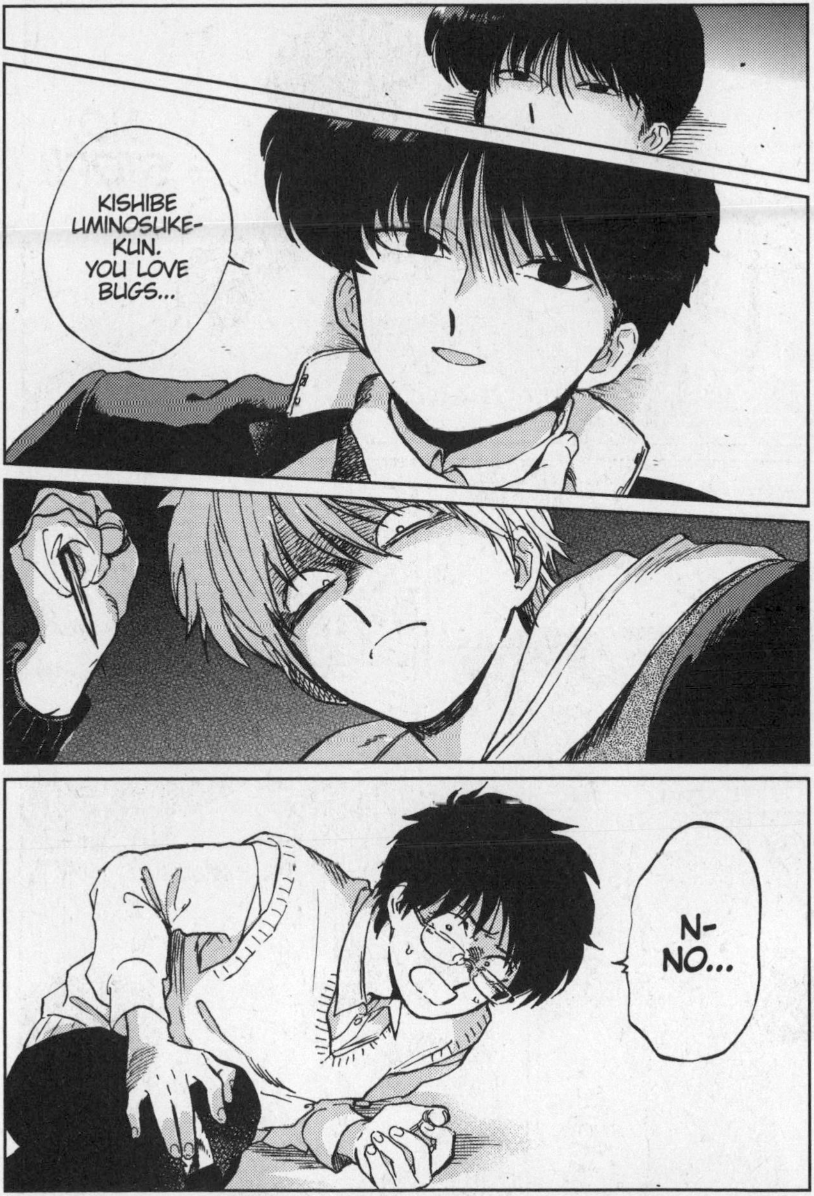
KISHIBE UMINOSUKE-KUN. YOU LOVE BUGS...
N-NO...

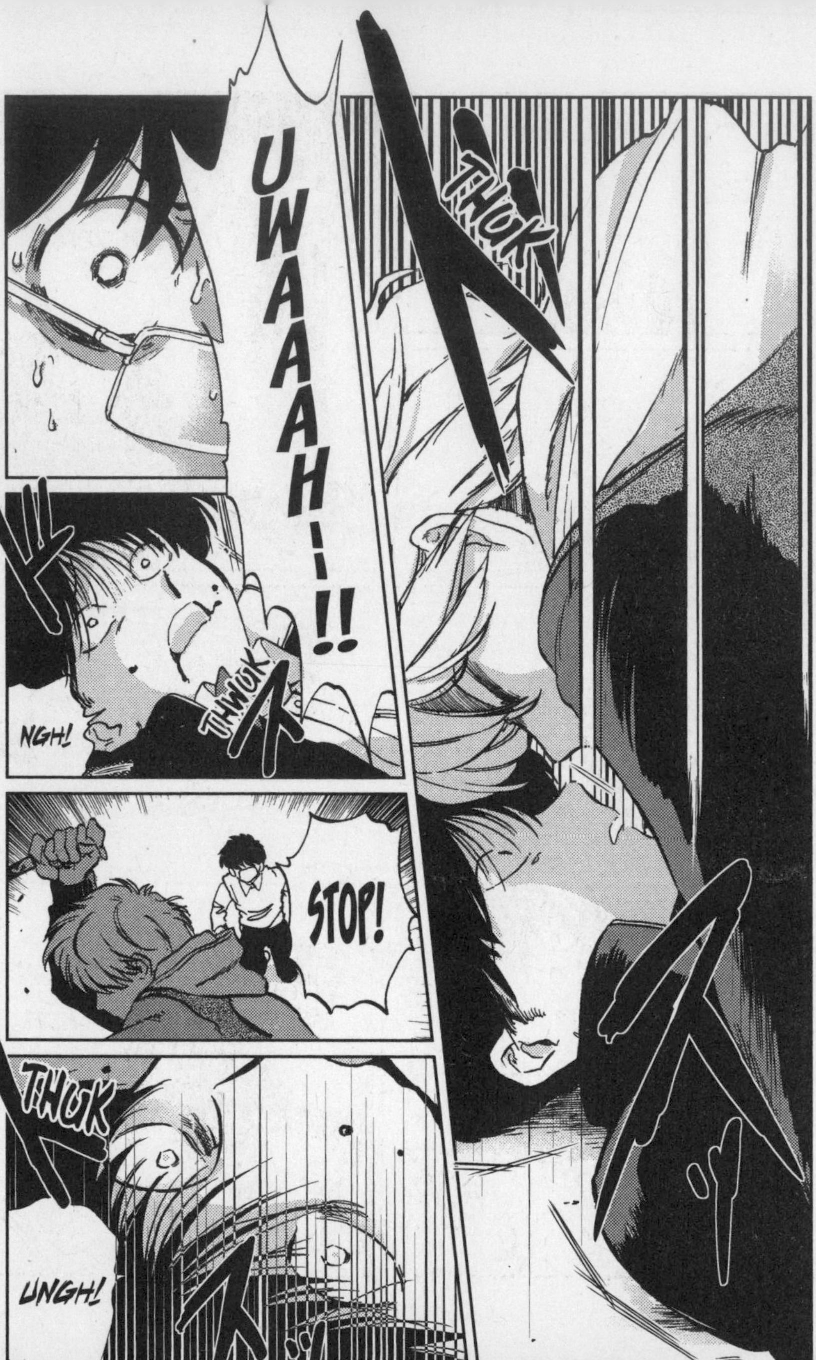
THUK
UWAAAH!!
THWUK
NGH!
STOP!
THUK
UNGH!

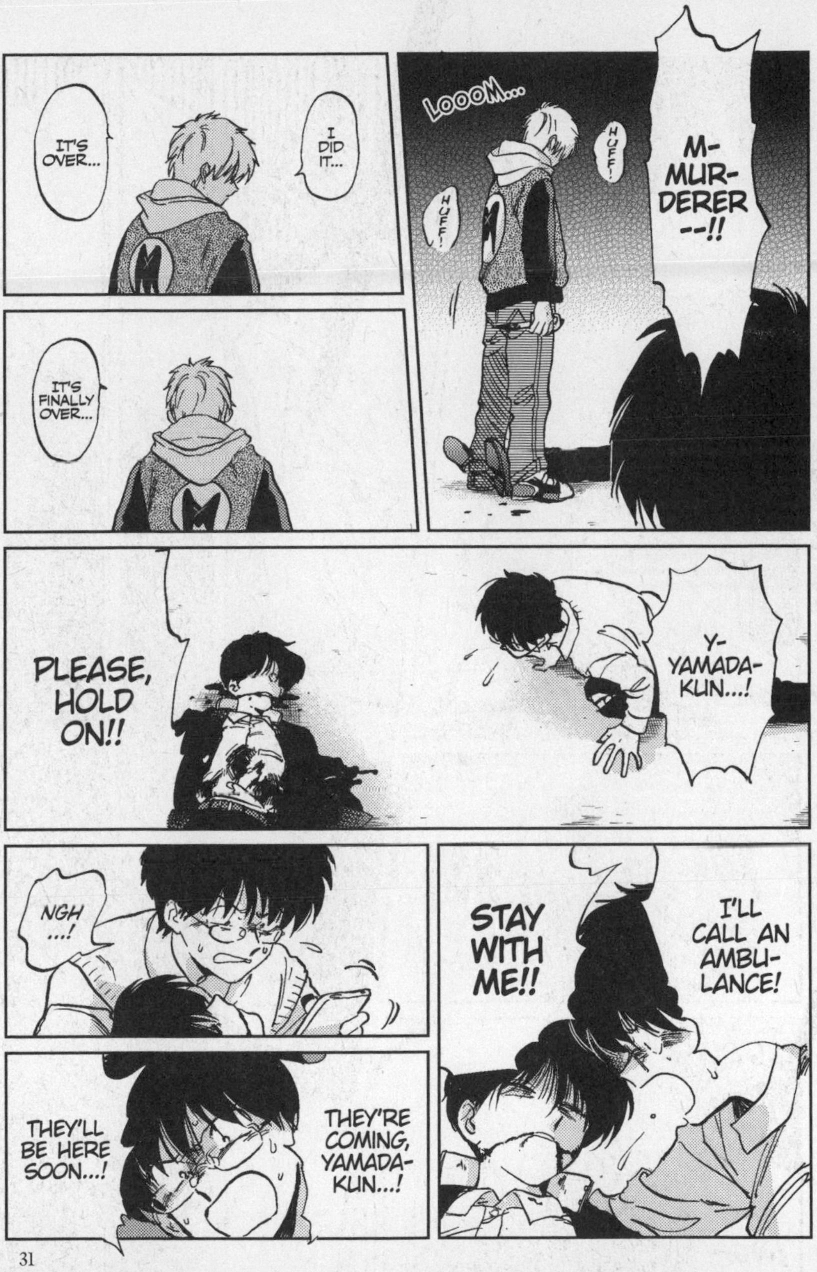
LOOOM...
HUFF!
HUFF!
M-MURDERER--!!
I DID IT...
IT'S OVER...
IT'S FINALLY OVER...
Y-YAMADA-KUN...!
PLEASE, HOLD ON!!
I'LL CALL AN AMBULANCE!
STAY WITH ME!!
NGH...!
THEY'RE COMING, YAMADA-KUN...!
THEY'LL BE HERE SOON...!

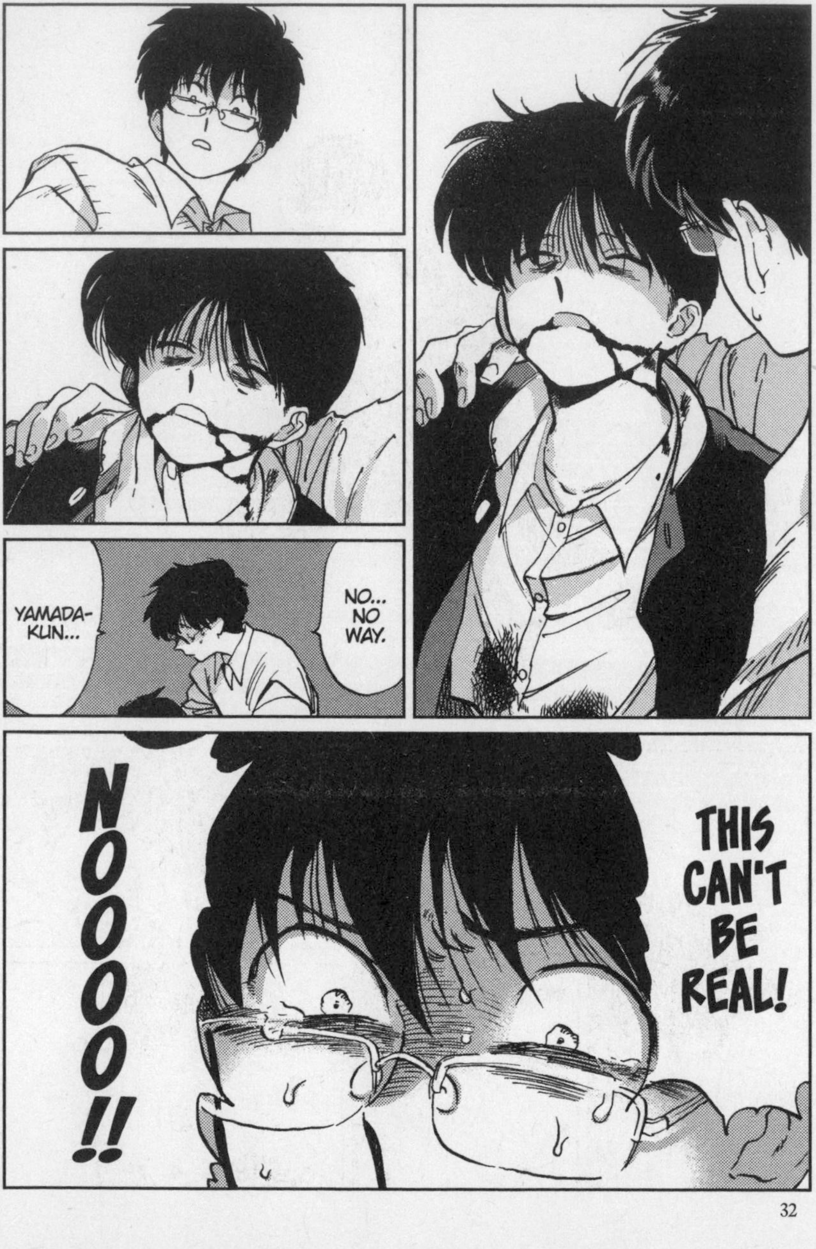
NO... NO WAY.
YAMADA-KUN...
THIS CAN'T BE REAL!
NOOOOO!!

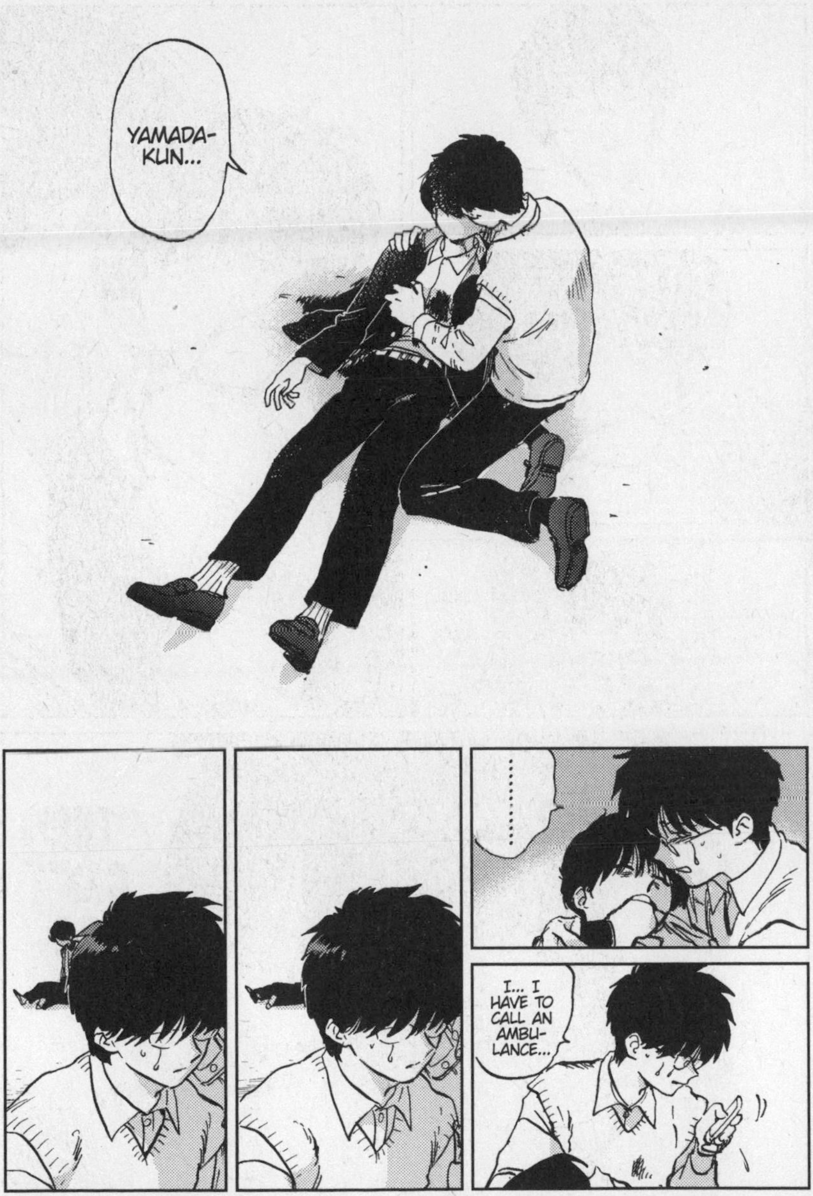
YAMADA-KUN...
......
I... I HAVE TO CALL AN AMBULANCE...

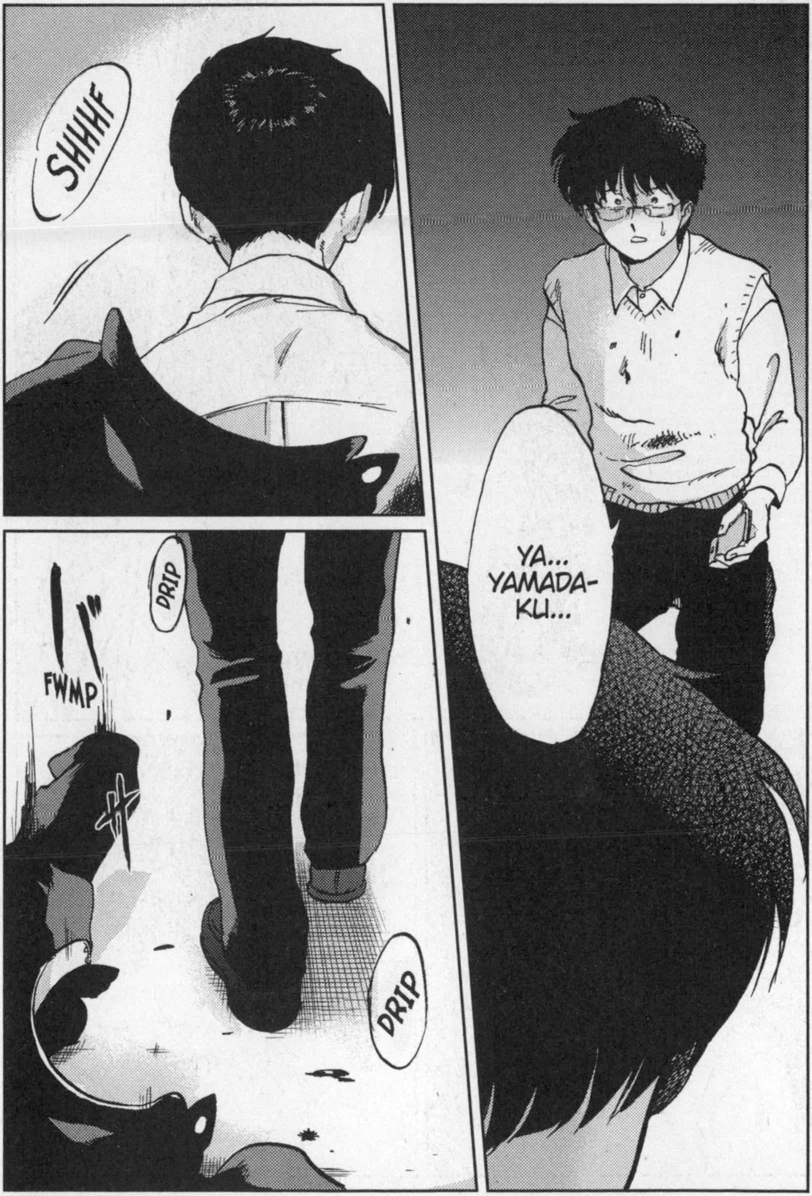
YA... YAMADA-KU...
SHHHF
DRIP
FWMP
DRIP

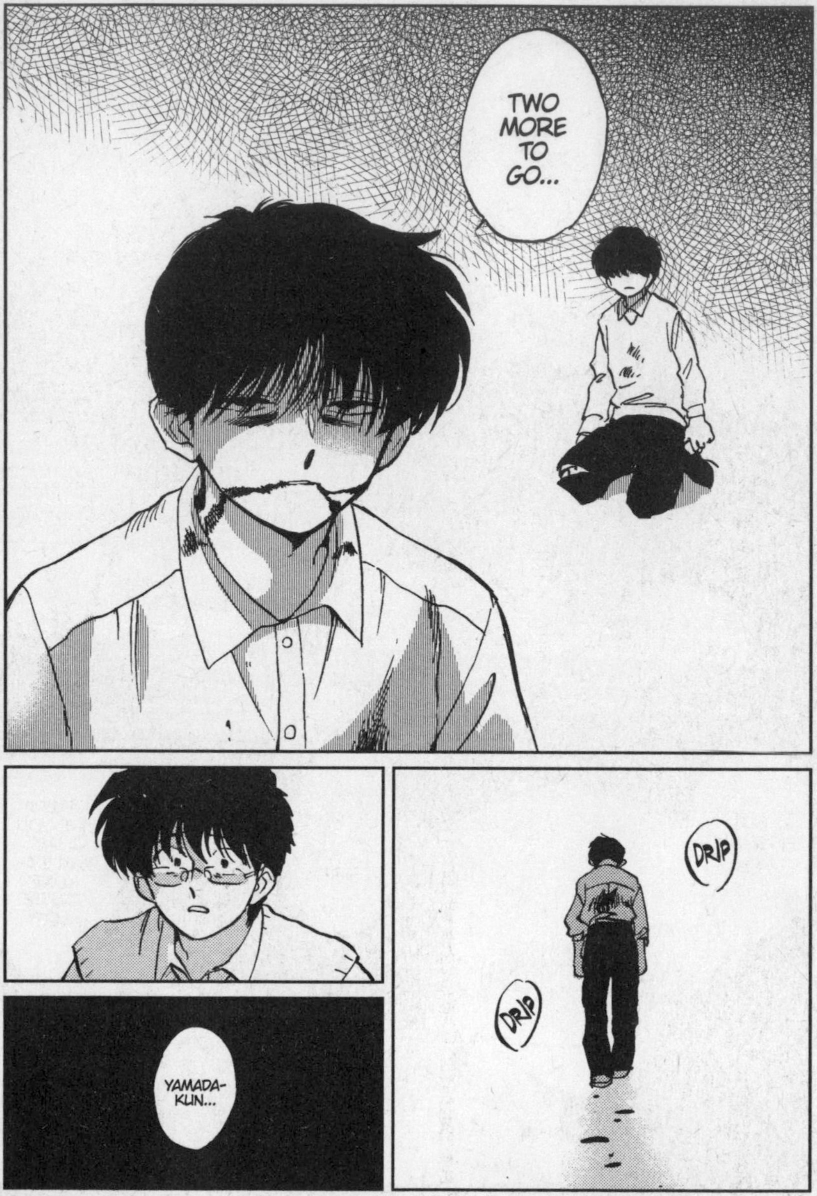
TWO MORE TO GO...
DRIP
DRIP
YAMADA-KUN...

【 Chapter 1 】END

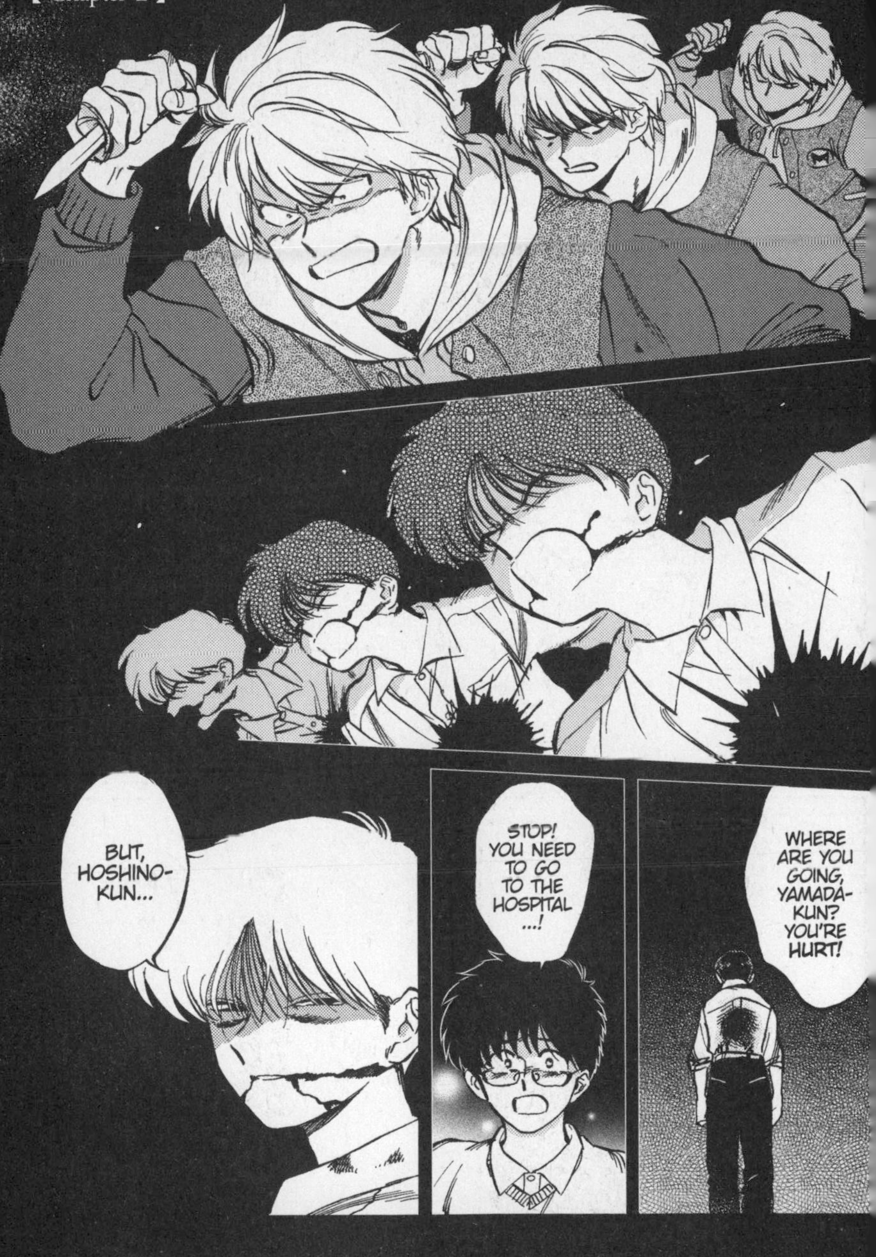
WHERE ARE YOU GOING, YAMADA-KUN? YOU'RE HURT!
STOP! YOU NEED TO GO TO THE HOSPITAL ...!
BUT, HOSHINO-KUN...
...

【 Chapter 2 】

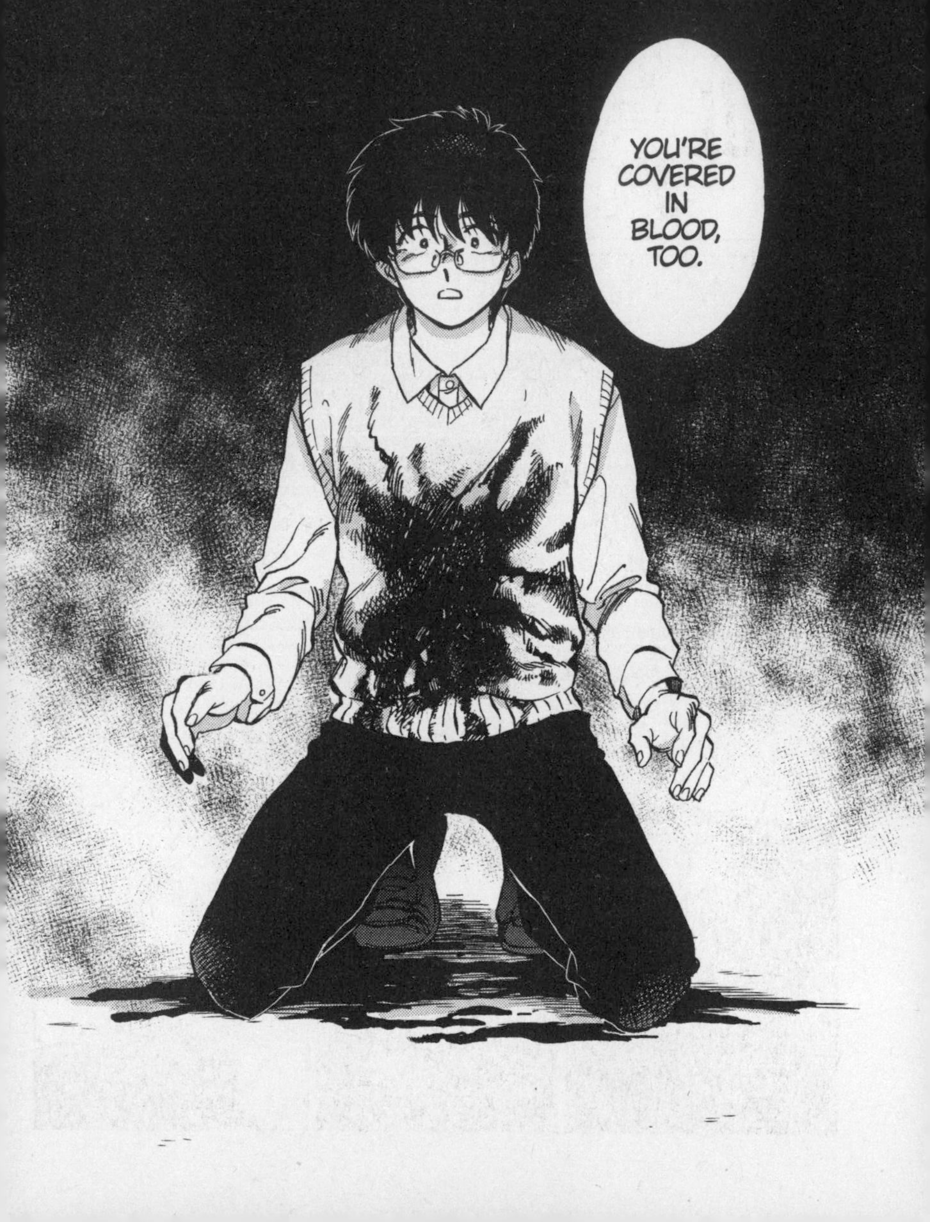
YOU'RE COVERED IN BLOOD, TOO.

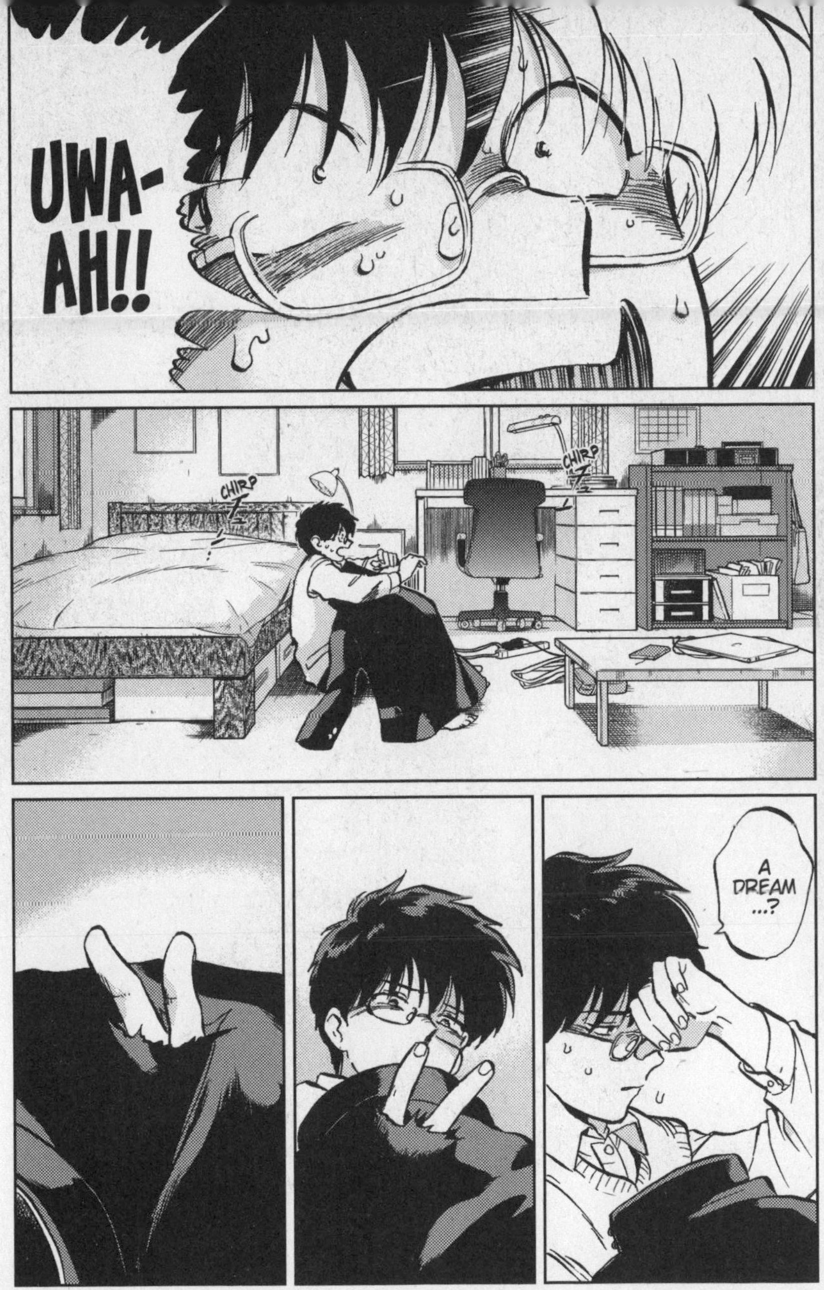
UWA-
AH!!
CHIRP
CHIRP
A DREAM ...?

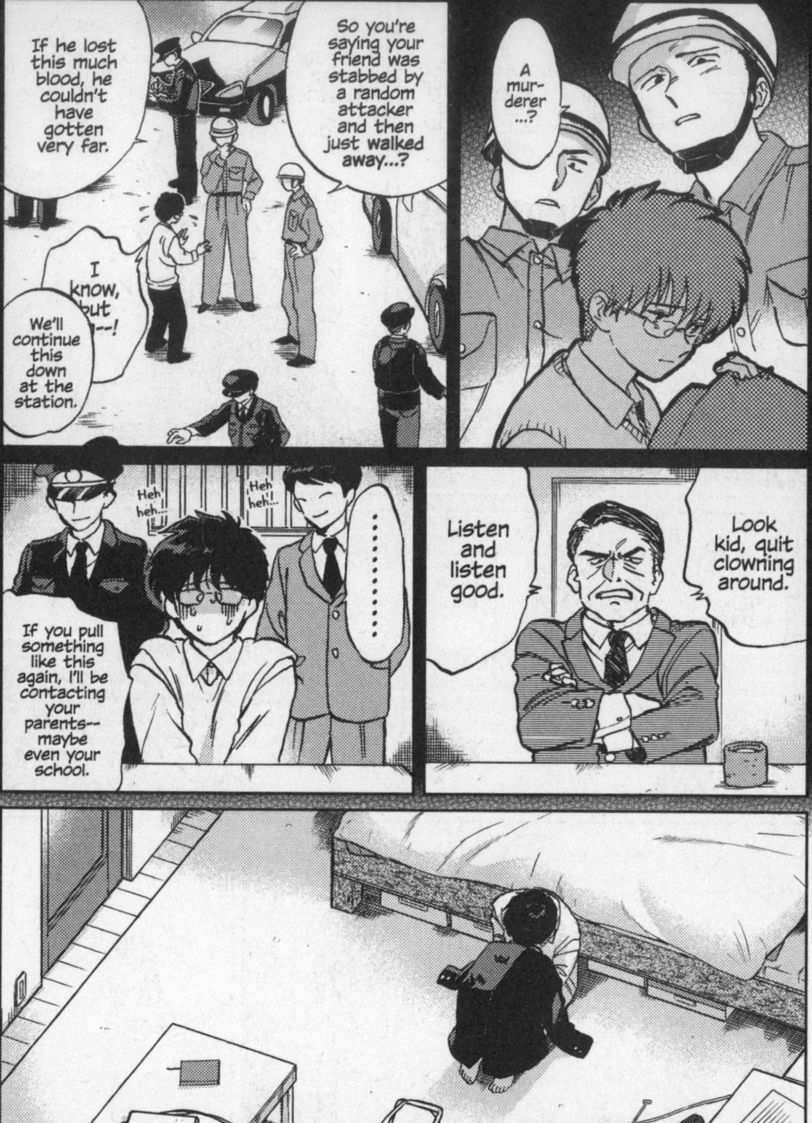
A murderer ...?
So you're saying your friend was stabbed by a random attacker and then just walked away...?
If he lost this much blood, he couldn't have gotten very far.
I know, but --!
We'll continue this down at the station.
Look kid, quit clowning around.
Listen and listen good.
Heh heh...!
Heh heh...
....
If you pull something like this again, I'll be contacting your parents-- maybe even your school.

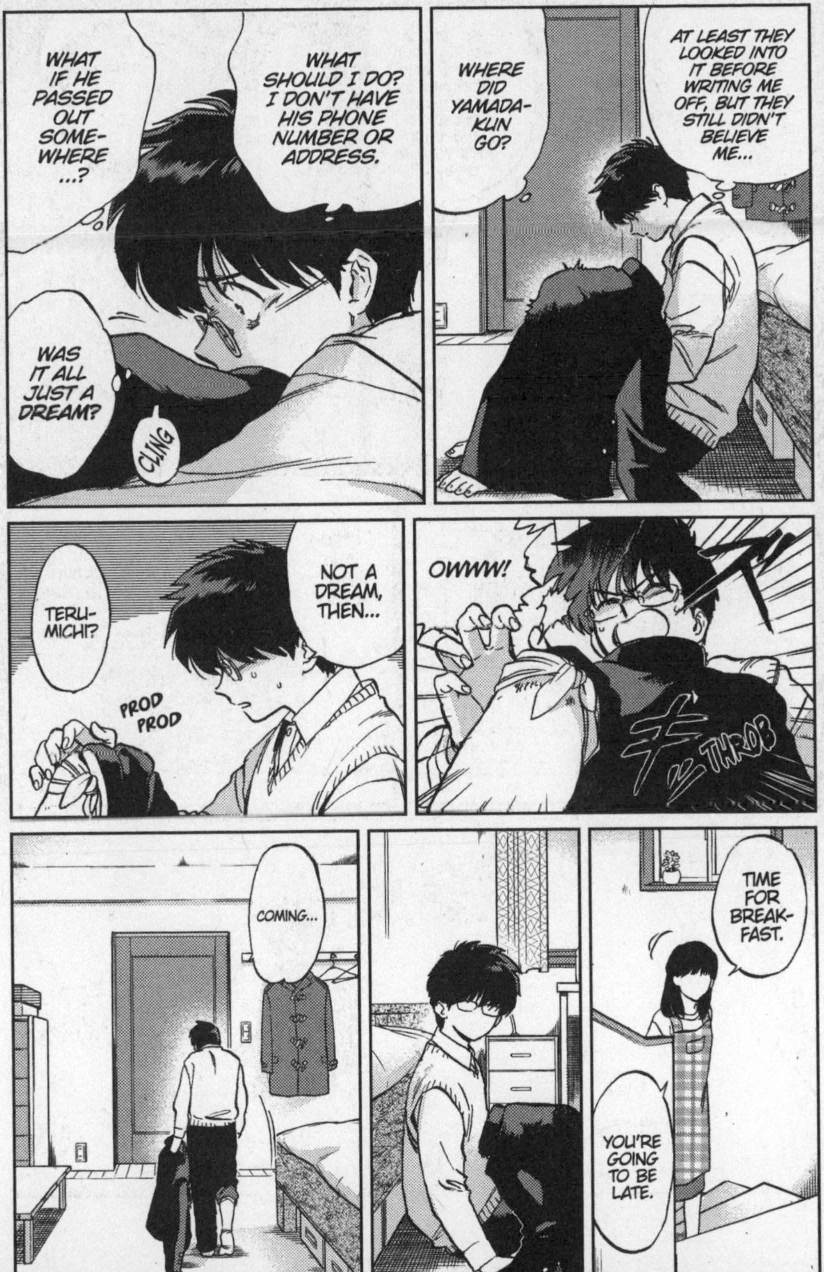
AT LEAST THEY LOOKED INTO IT BEFORE WRITING ME OFF, BUT THEY STILL DIDN'T BELIEVE ME...
WHERE DID YAMADA-KUN GO?
WHAT SHOULD I DO? I DON'T HAVE HIS PHONE NUMBER OR ADDRESS.
WHAT IF HE PASSED OUT SOME-WHERE ...?
WAS IT ALL JUST A DREAM?
CLING
OWWW!
THROB
NOT A DREAM, THEN...
TERU-MICHI?
PROD PROD
TIME FOR BREAK-FAST.
YOU'RE GOING TO BE LATE.
COMING...

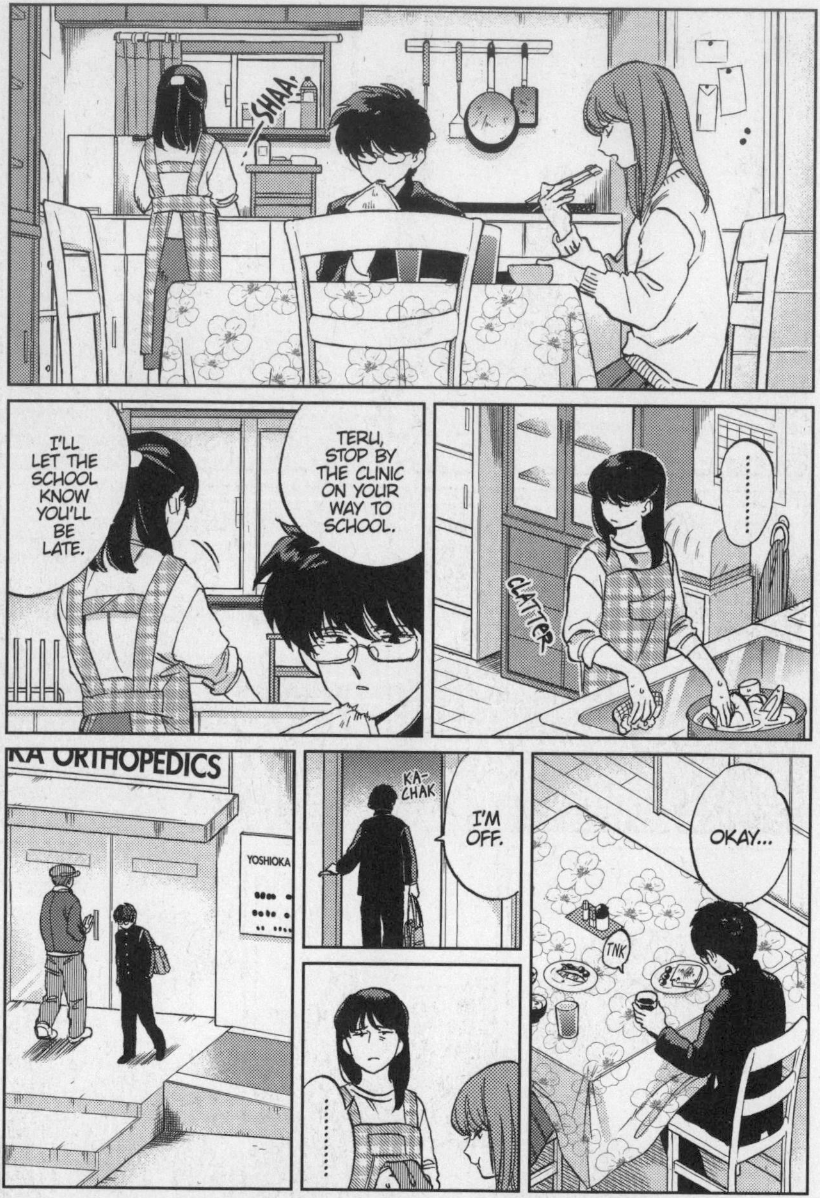
SHAA
......
CLATTER
TERU, STOP BY THE CLINIC ON YOUR WAY TO SCHOOL.
I'LL LET THE SCHOOL KNOW YOU'LL BE LATE.
OKAY...
TNK
KA-CHAK
I'M OFF.
......
KA ORTHOPEDICS
YOSHIOKA

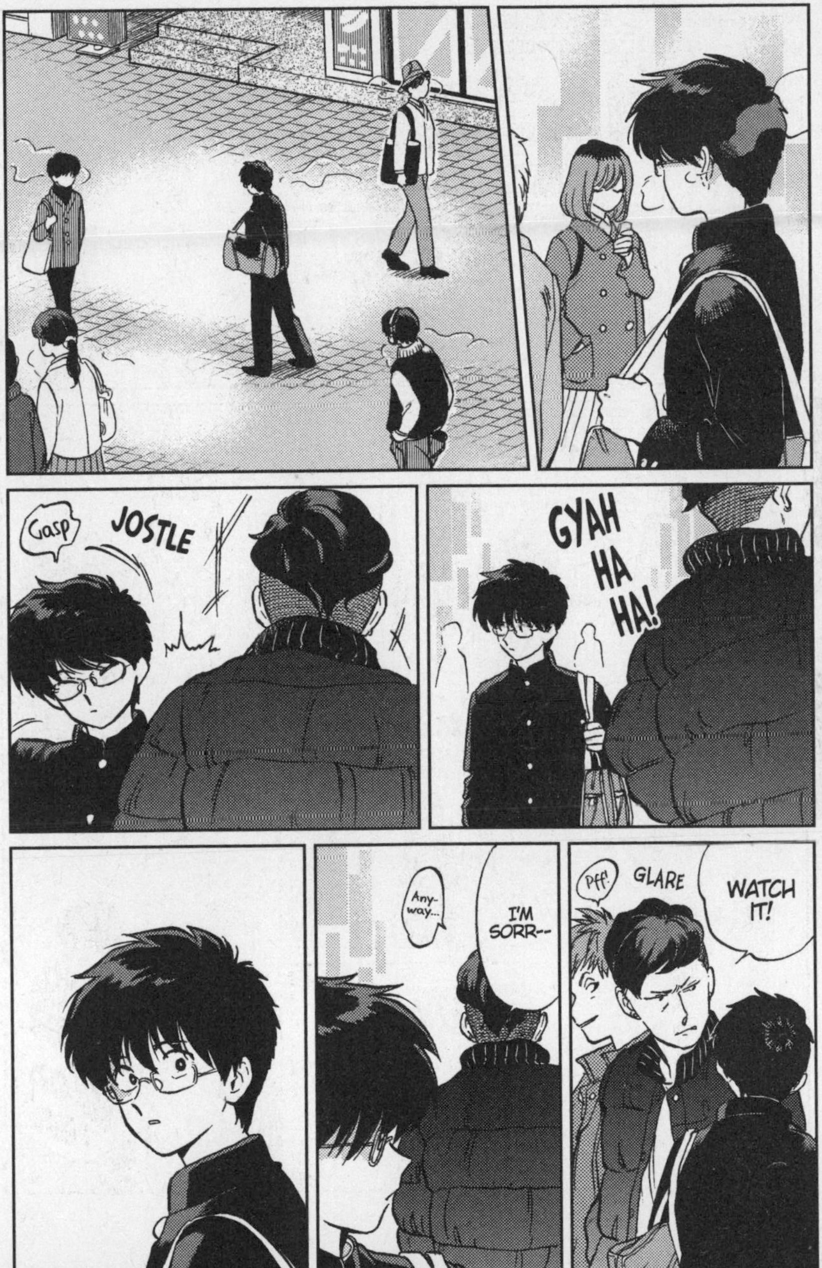
GYAH HA HA!
JOSTLE
Gasp
WATCH IT!
GLARE
Pff!
I'M SORR--
Any-way...

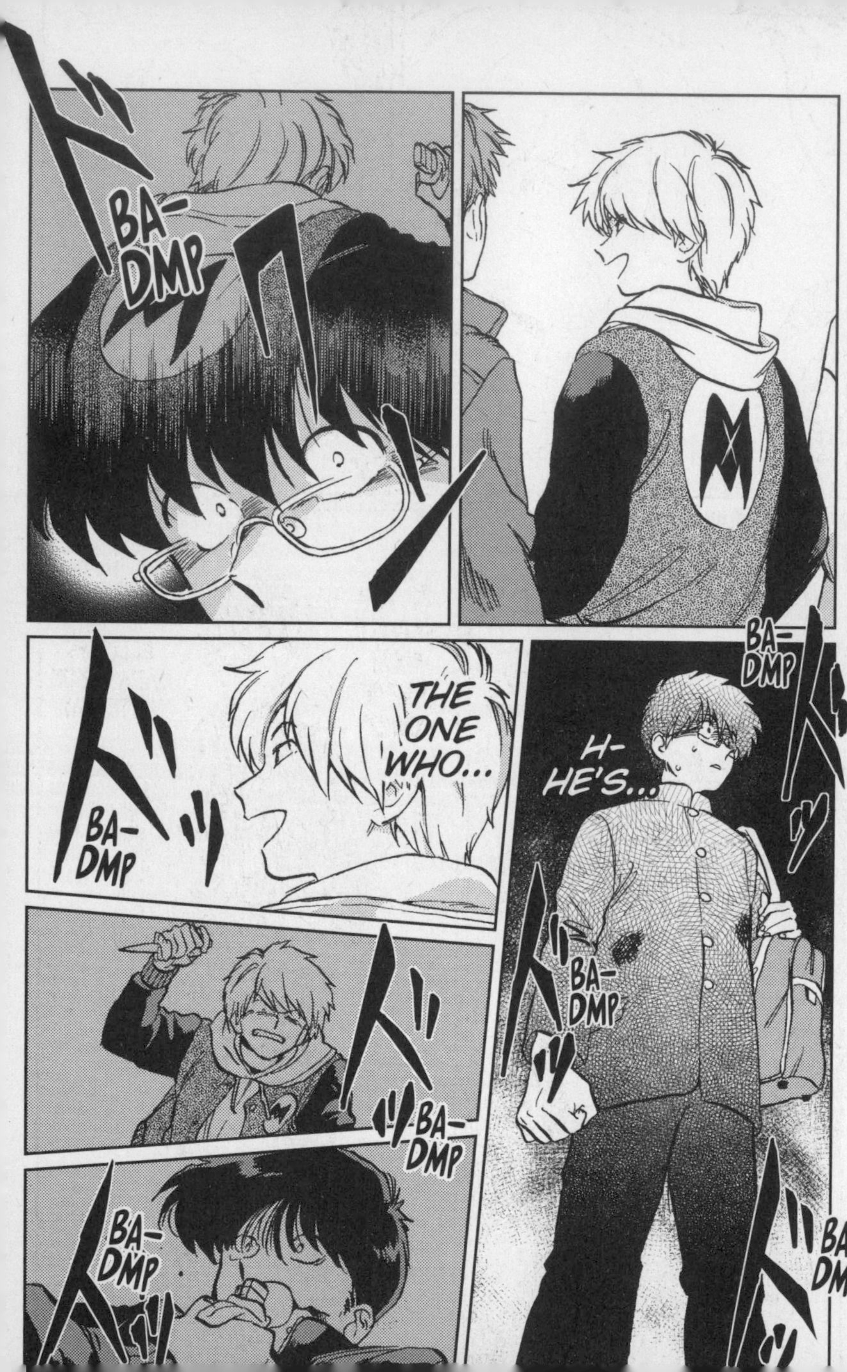
BA-DMP
BA-DMP
H-HE'S...
BA-DMP
BA-DMP
THE ONE WHO...
BA-DMP
BA-DMP
BA-DMP

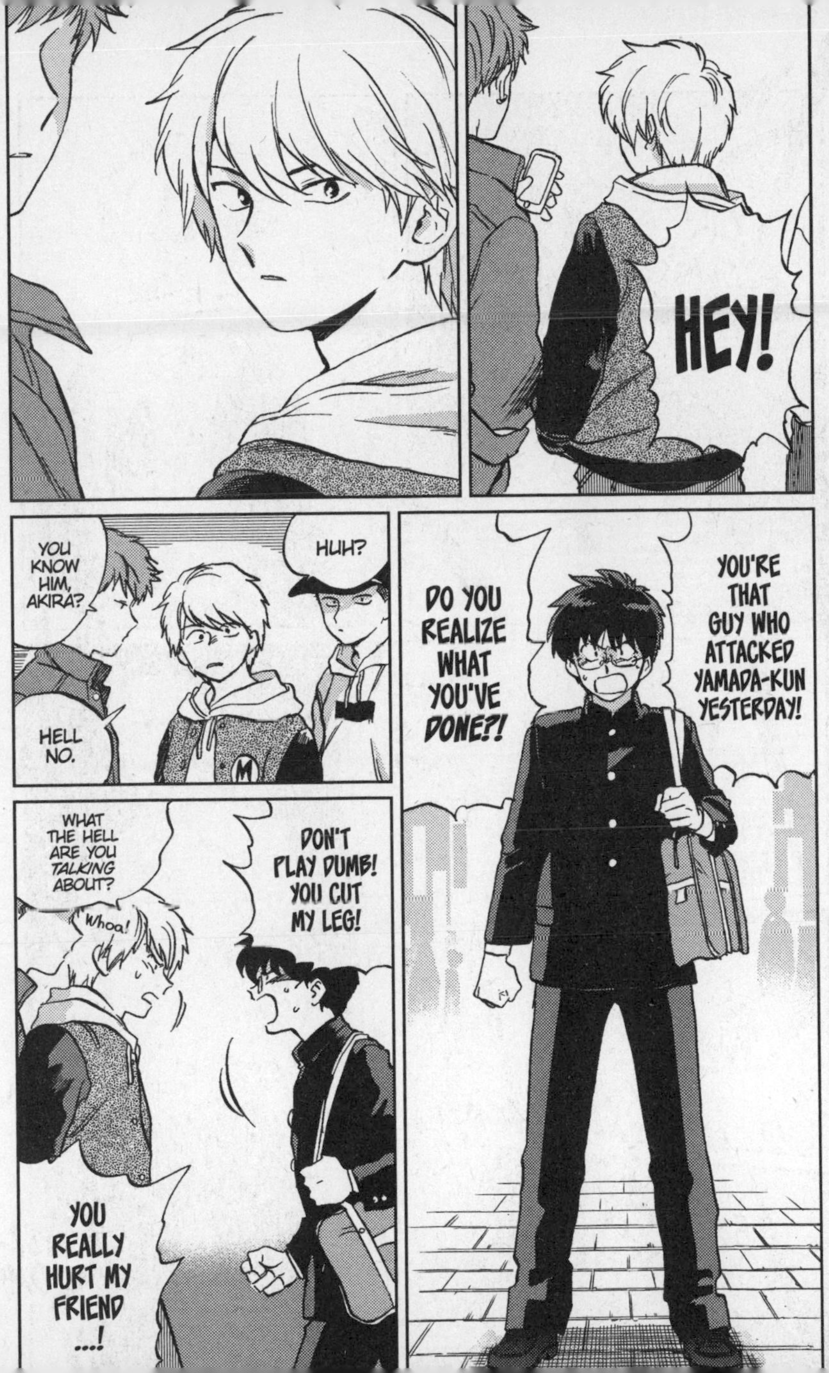
HEY!
YOU'RE THAT GUY WHO ATTACKED YAMADA-KUN YESTERDAY!
DO YOU REALIZE WHAT YOU'VE DONE?!
HUH?
YOU KNOW HIM, AKIRA?
HELL NO.
DON'T PLAY DUMB! YOU CUT MY LEG!
WHAT THE HELL ARE YOU *TALKING* ABOUT?
Whoa!
YOU REALLY HURT MY FRIEND ...!

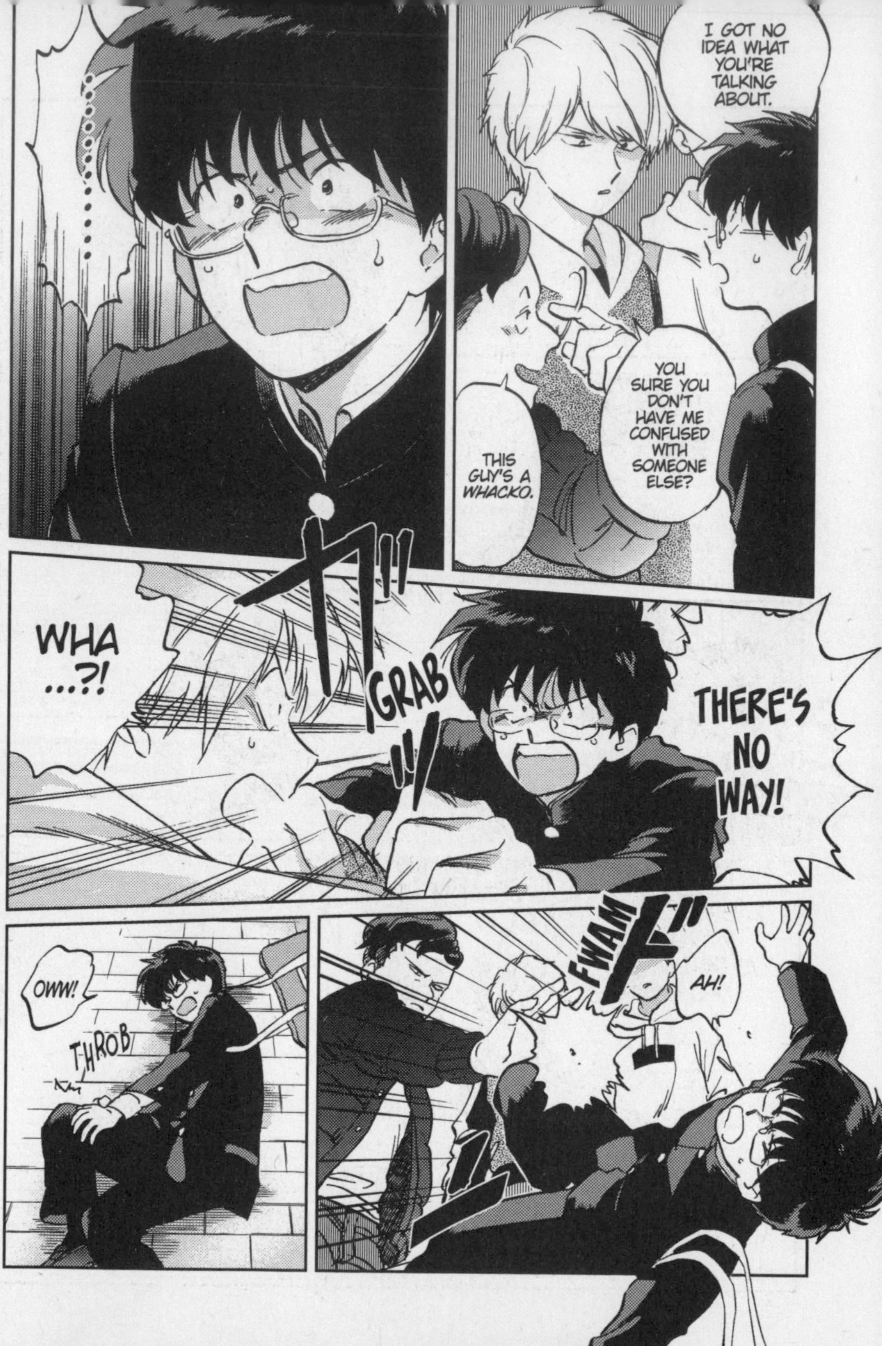
I GOT NO IDEA WHAT YOU'RE TALKING ABOUT.
YOU SURE YOU DON'T HAVE ME CONFUSED WITH SOMEONE ELSE?
THIS GUY'S A WHACKO.
THERE'S NO WAY!
GRAB
WHA ...?!
FWAM
AH!
OWW!
THROB

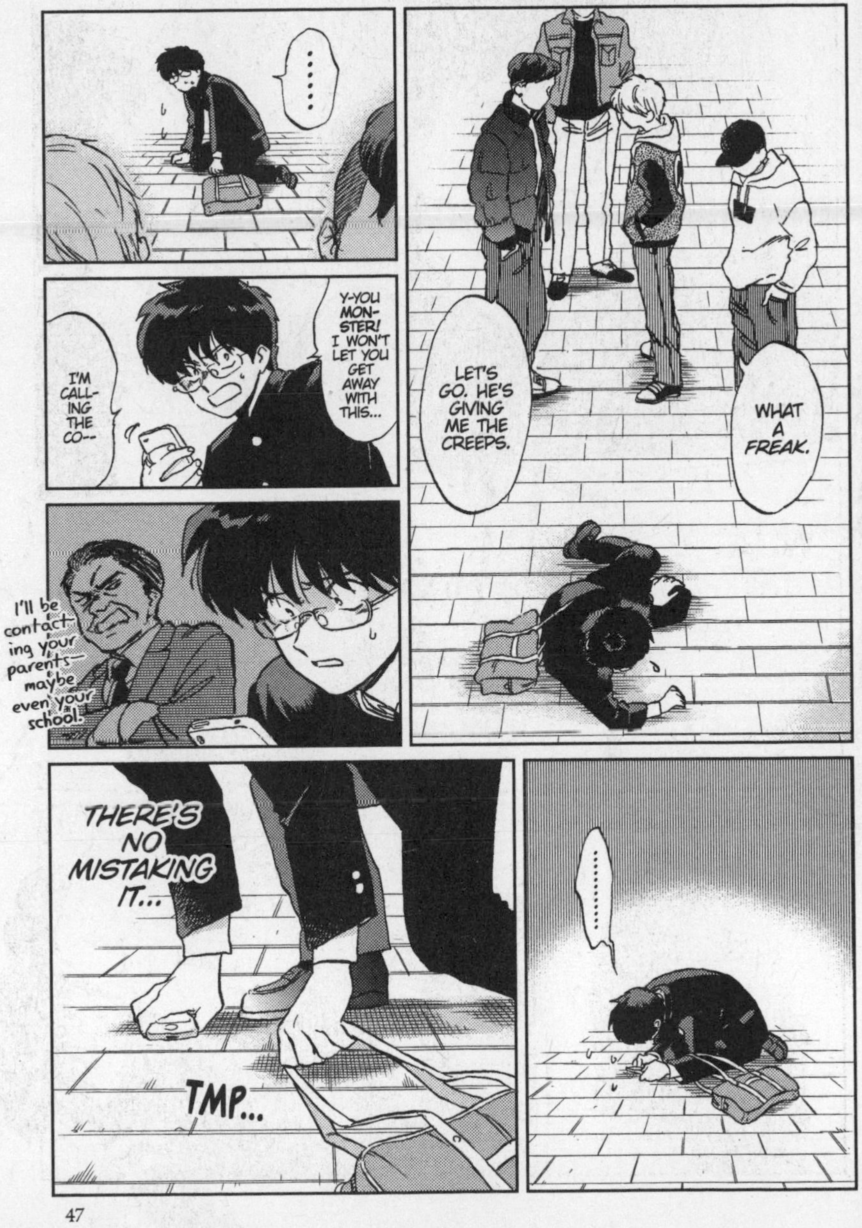
WHAT A FREAK.
LET'S GO. HE'S GIVING ME THE CREEPS.
......
Y-YOU MONSTER! I WON'T LET YOU GET AWAY WITH THIS...
I'M CALLING THE CO--
I'll be contacting your parents—maybe even your school.
......
THERE'S NO MISTAKING IT...
TMP...

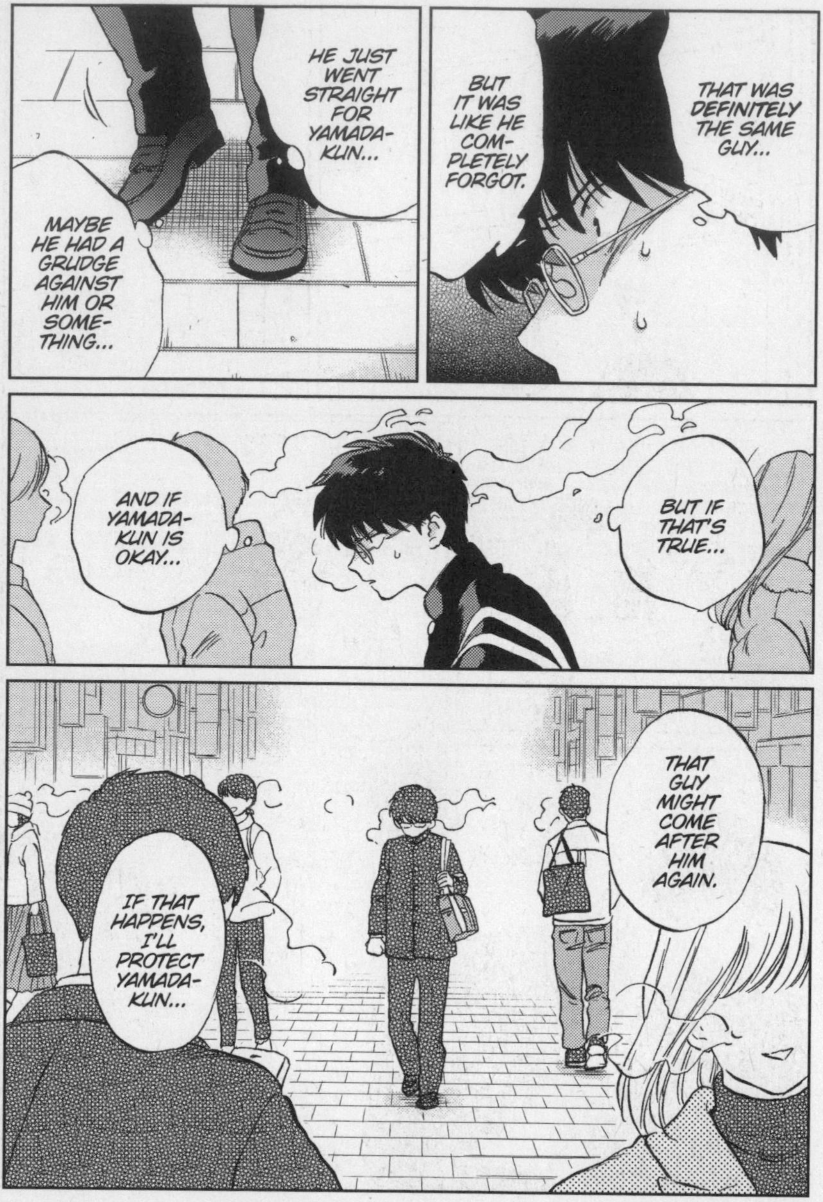
THAT WAS DEFINITELY THE SAME GUY...
BUT IT WAS LIKE HE COMPLETELY FORGOT.
HE JUST WENT STRAIGHT FOR YAMADA-KUN...
MAYBE HE HAD A GRUDGE AGAINST HIM OR SOMETHING...
BUT IF THAT'S TRUE...
AND IF YAMADA-KUN IS OKAY...
THAT GUY MIGHT COME AFTER HIM AGAIN.
IF THAT HAPPENS, I'LL PROTECT YAMADA-KUN...

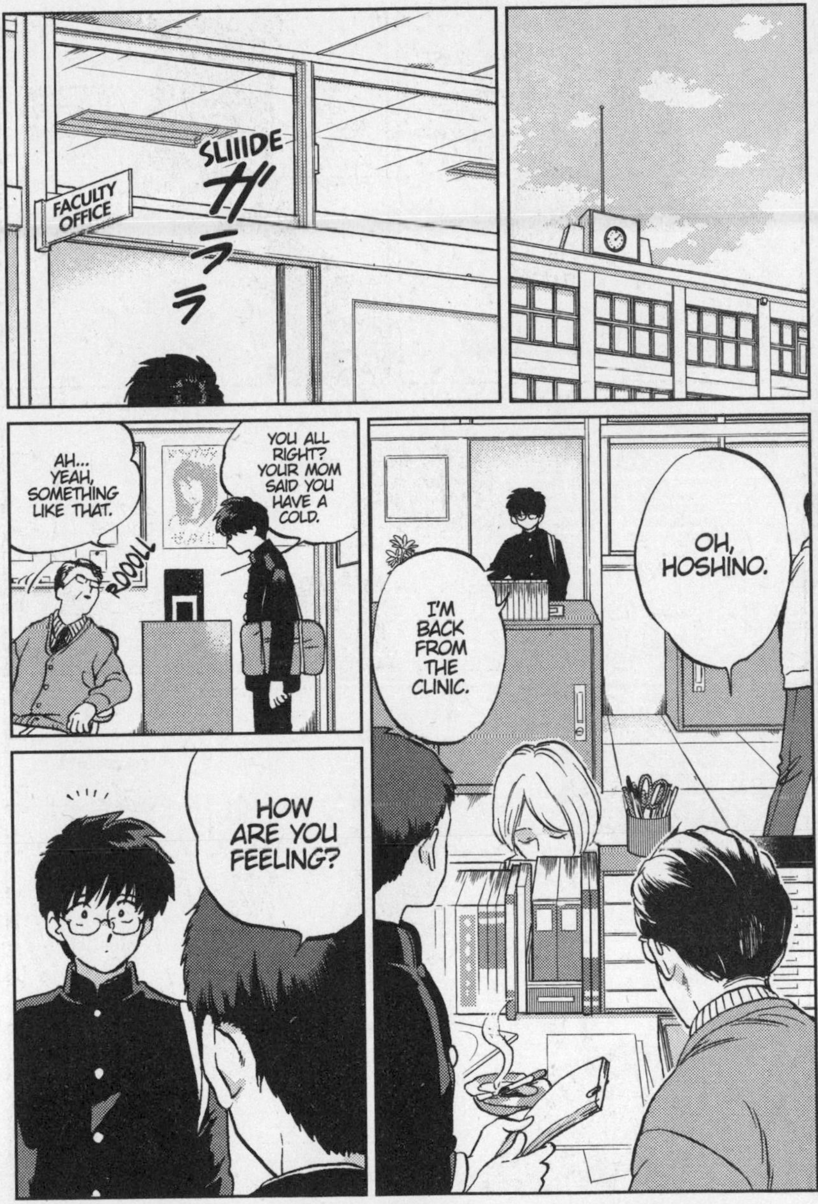
SLIIIDE
ガラララ
FACULTY OFFICE
OH, HOSHINO.
I'M BACK FROM THE CLINIC.
YOU ALL RIGHT? YOUR MOM SAID YOU HAVE A COLD.
AH... YEAH, SOMETHING LIKE THAT.
ROOOLL
HOW ARE YOU FEELING?

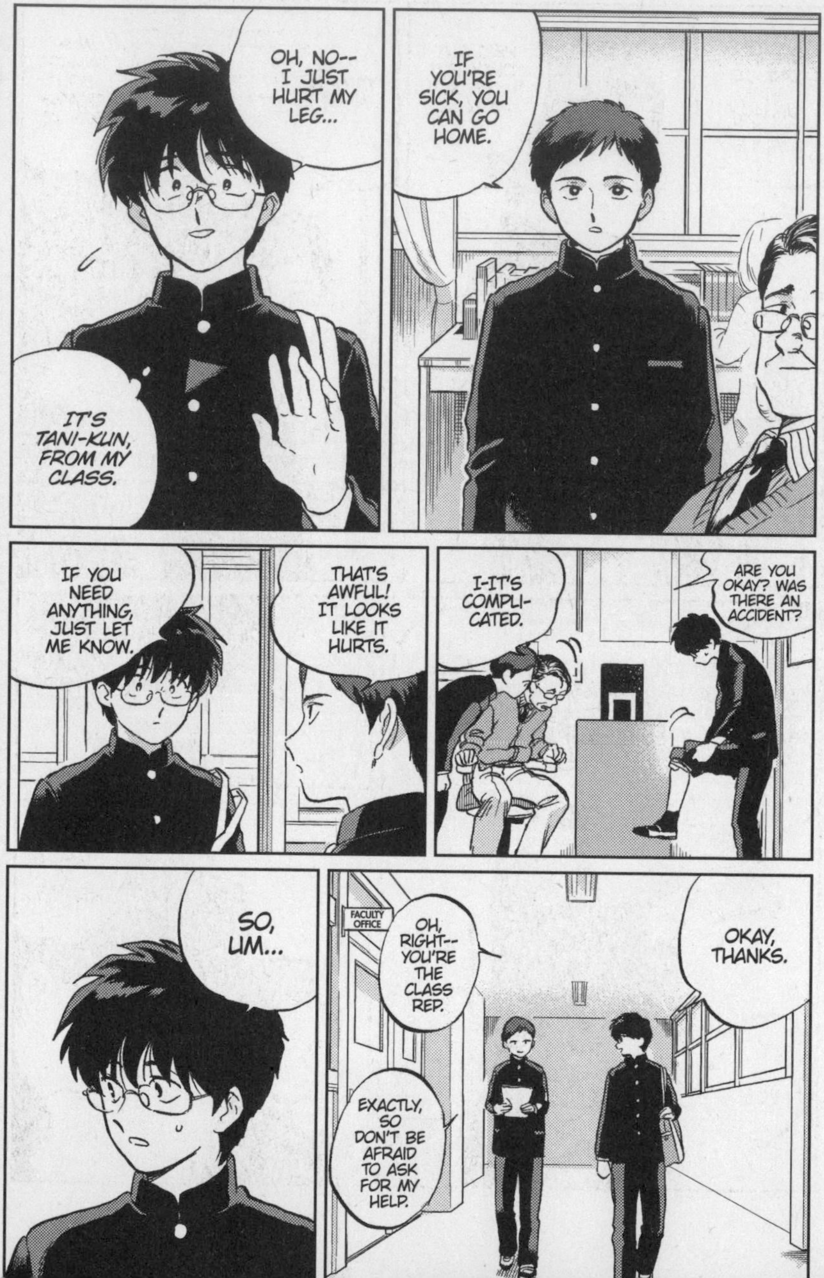
IF YOU'RE SICK, YOU CAN GO HOME.
OH, NO-- I JUST HURT MY LEG...
IT'S TANI-KUN, FROM MY CLASS.
ARE YOU OKAY? WAS THERE AN ACCIDENT?
I-IT'S COMPLICATED.
THAT'S AWFUL! IT LOOKS LIKE IT HURTS.
IF YOU NEED ANYTHING, JUST LET ME KNOW.
OKAY, THANKS.
FACULTY OFFICE
OH, RIGHT-- YOU'RE THE CLASS REP.
EXACTLY, SO DON'T BE AFRAID TO ASK FOR MY HELP.
SO, UM...

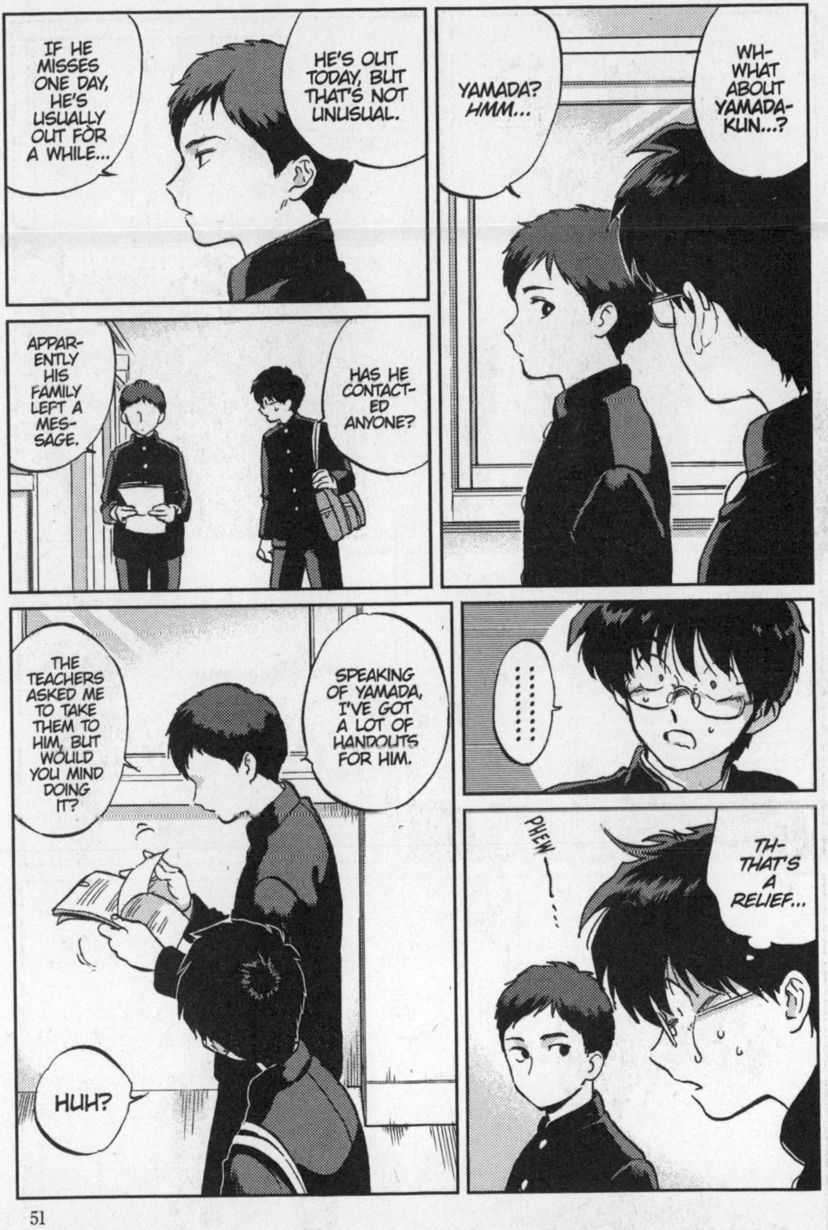
WH-WHAT ABOUT YAMADA-KUN...?
YAMADA? HMM...
HE'S OUT TODAY, BUT THAT'S NOT UNUSUAL.
IF HE MISSES ONE DAY, HE'S USUALLY OUT FOR A WHILE...
HAS HE CONTACTED ANYONE?
APPARENTLY HIS FAMILY LEFT A MESSAGE.
......
TH-THAT'S A RELIEF...
PHEW—...
SPEAKING OF YAMADA, I'VE GOT A LOT OF HANDOUTS FOR HIM.
THE TEACHERS ASKED ME TO TAKE THEM TO HIM, BUT WOULD YOU MIND DOING IT?
HUH?

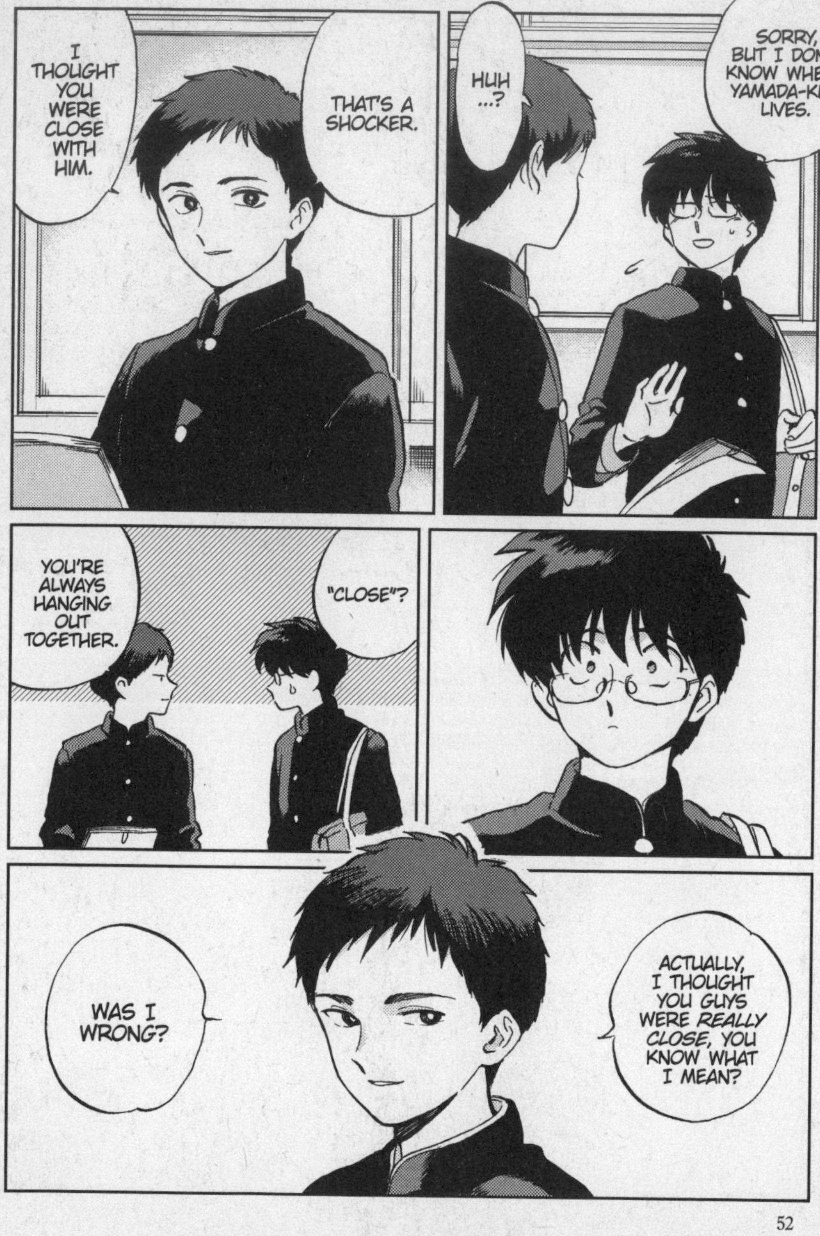
SORRY, BUT I DON'T KNOW WHERE YAMADA-KUN LIVES.
HUH ...?
THAT'S A SHOCKER.
I THOUGHT YOU WERE CLOSE WITH HIM.
"CLOSE"?
YOU'RE ALWAYS HANGING OUT TOGETHER.
ACTUALLY, I THOUGHT YOU GUYS WERE *REALLY CLOSE*, YOU KNOW WHAT I MEAN?
WAS I WRONG?

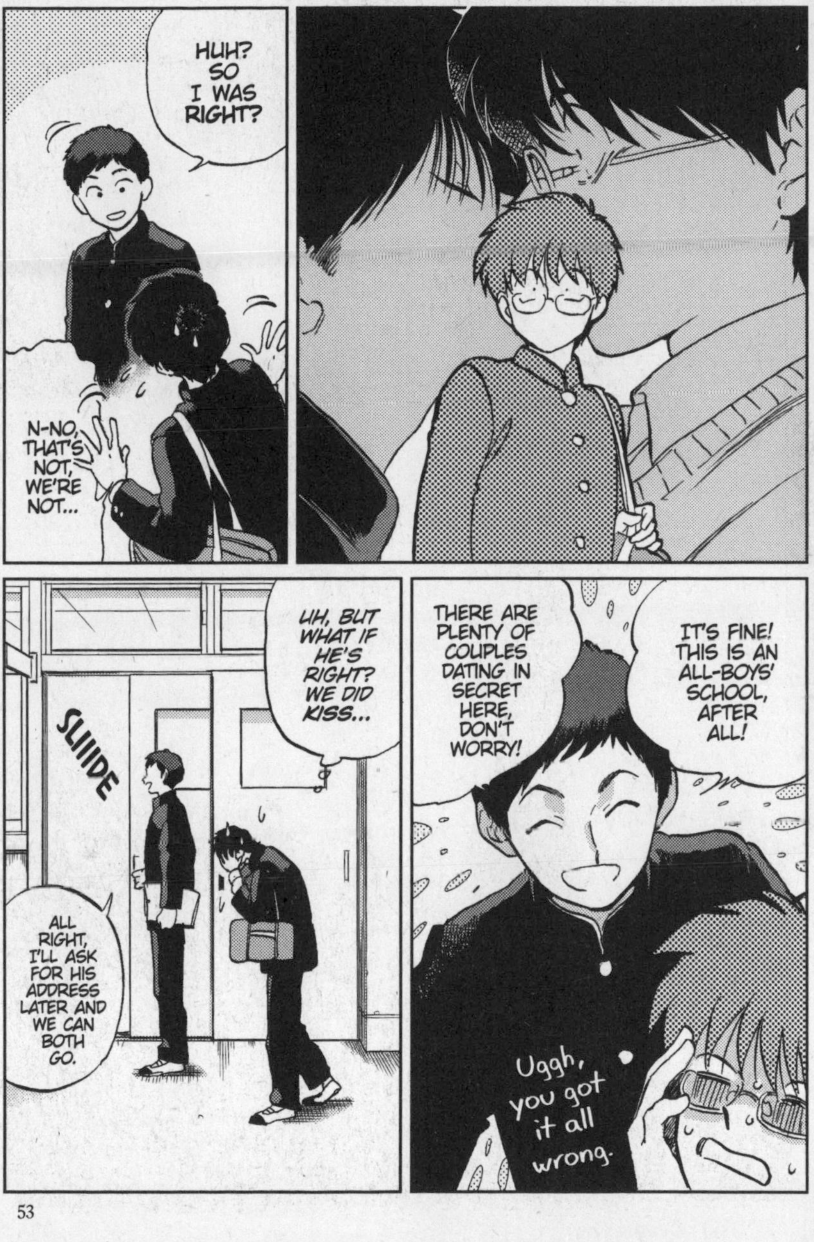
HUH? SO I WAS RIGHT?
N-NO, THAT'S NOT, WE'RE NOT...
IT'S FINE! THIS IS AN ALL-BOYS' SCHOOL, AFTER ALL!
THERE ARE PLENTY OF COUPLES DATING IN SECRET HERE, DON'T WORRY!
Uggh, you got it all wrong.
UH, BUT WHAT IF HE'S RIGHT? WE DID KISS...
SLIIIDE
ALL RIGHT, I'LL ASK FOR HIS ADDRESS LATER AND WE CAN BOTH GO.

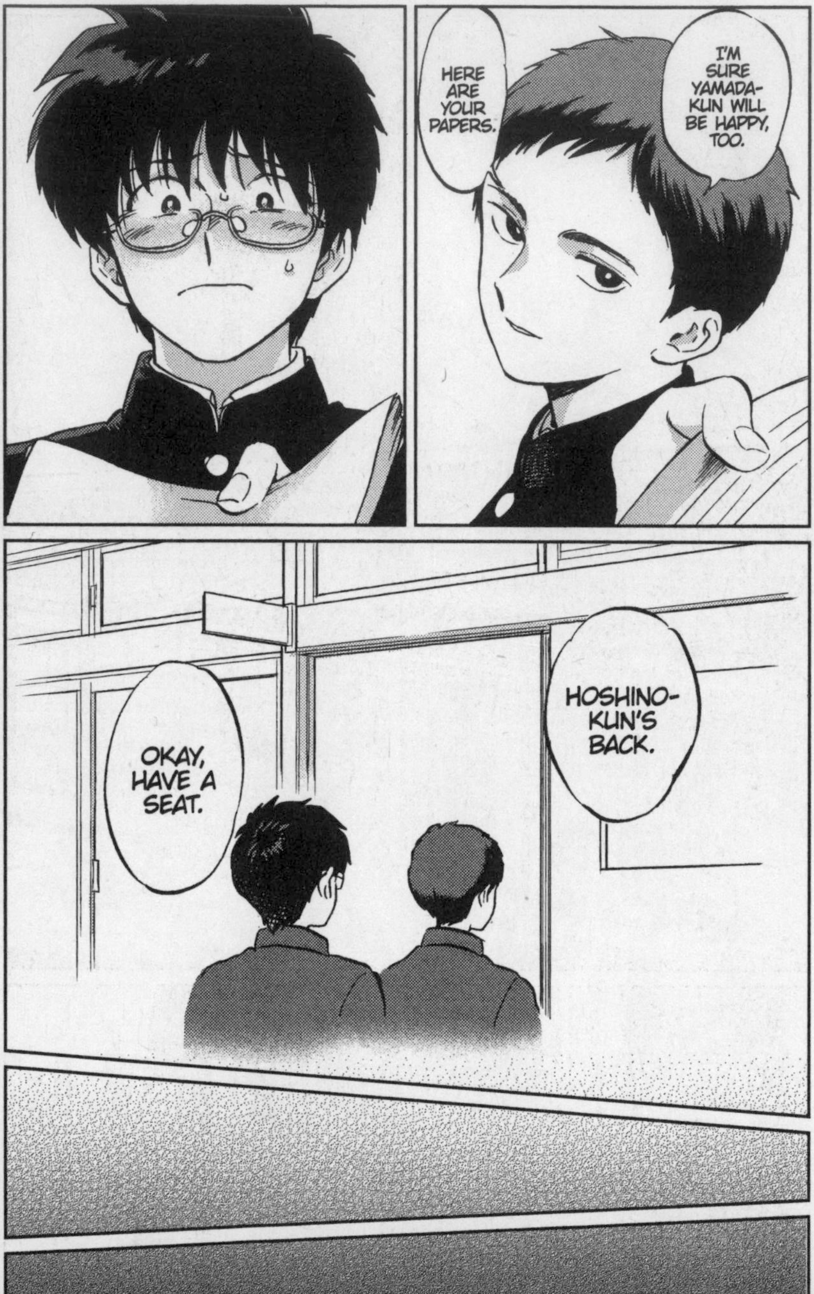
I'M SURE YAMADA-KUN WILL BE HAPPY, TOO.
HERE ARE YOUR PAPERS.
HOSHINO-KUN'S BACK.
OKAY, HAVE A SEAT.

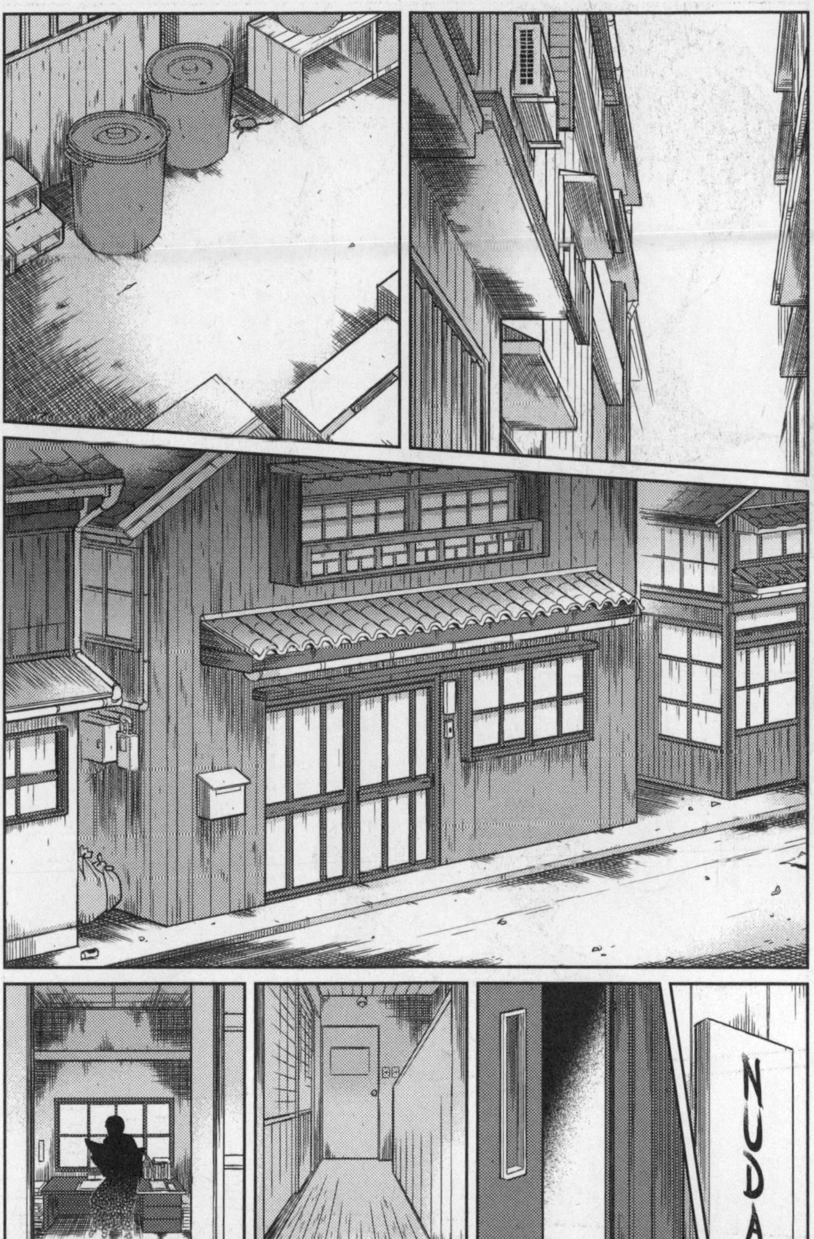
NUDA

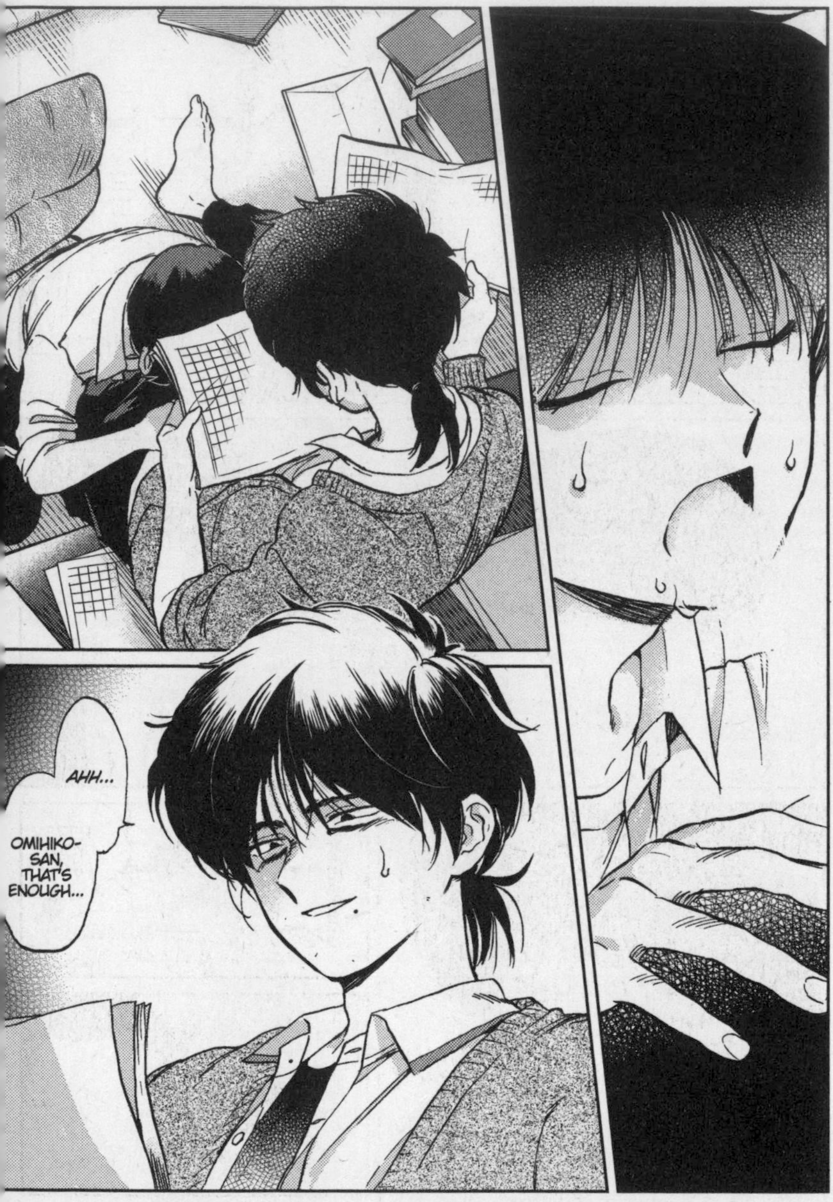
AHH...
OMIHIKO-SAN, THAT'S ENOUGH...

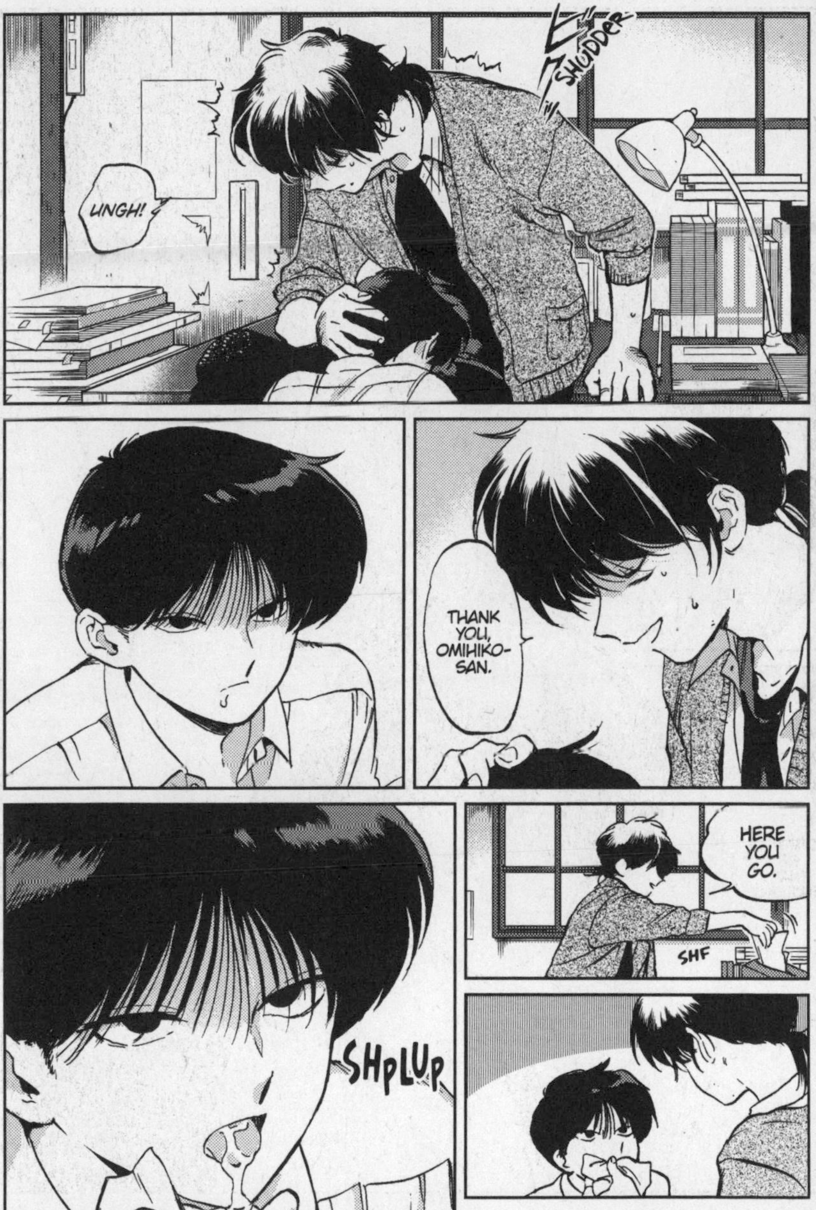
SHUDDER
UNGH!
THANK YOU, OMIHIKO-SAN.
HERE YOU GO.
SHF
SHPLUP

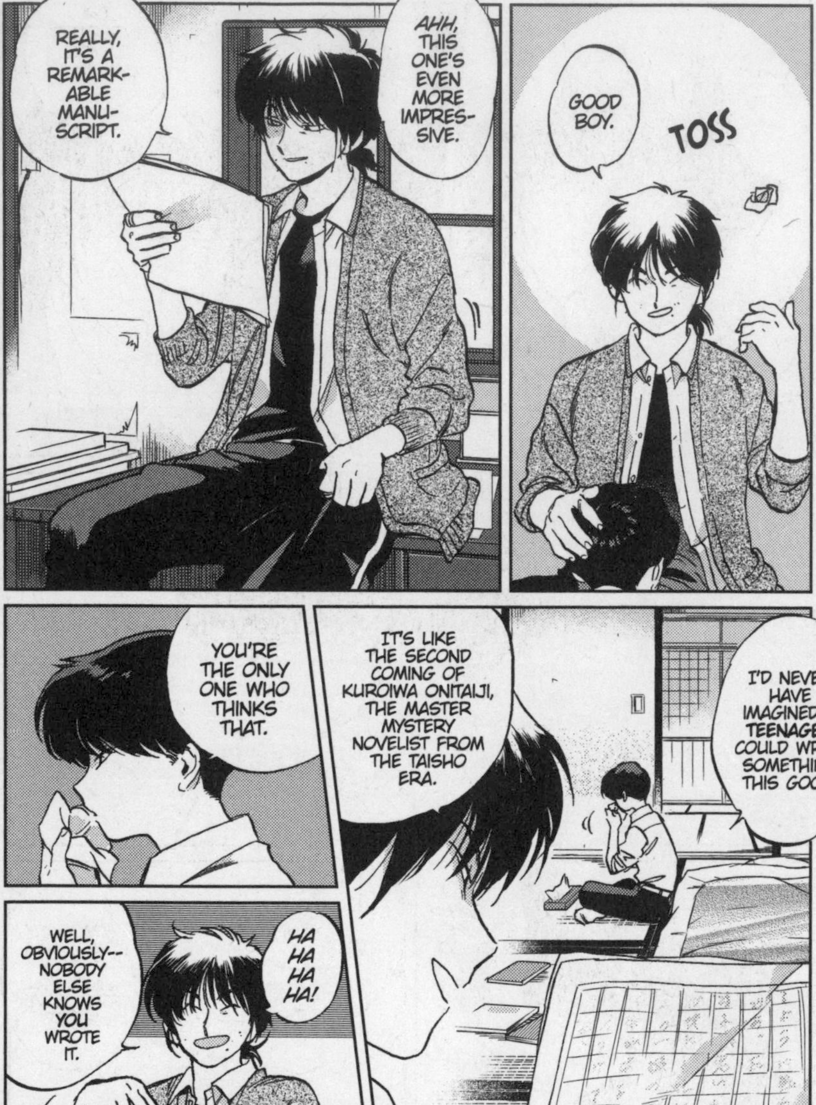
GOOD BOY.
TOSS
AHH, THIS ONE'S EVEN MORE IMPRES-SIVE.
REALLY, IT'S A REMARK-ABLE MANU-SCRIPT.
I'D NEVER HAVE IMAGINED A TEENAGER COULD WRITE SOMETHING THIS GOOD.
IT'S LIKE THE SECOND COMING OF KUROIWA ONITAIJI, THE MASTER MYSTERY NOVELIST FROM THE TAISHO ERA.
YOU'RE THE ONLY ONE WHO THINKS THAT.
HA HA HA HA!
WELL, OBVIOUSLY-- NOBODY ELSE KNOWS YOU WROTE IT.

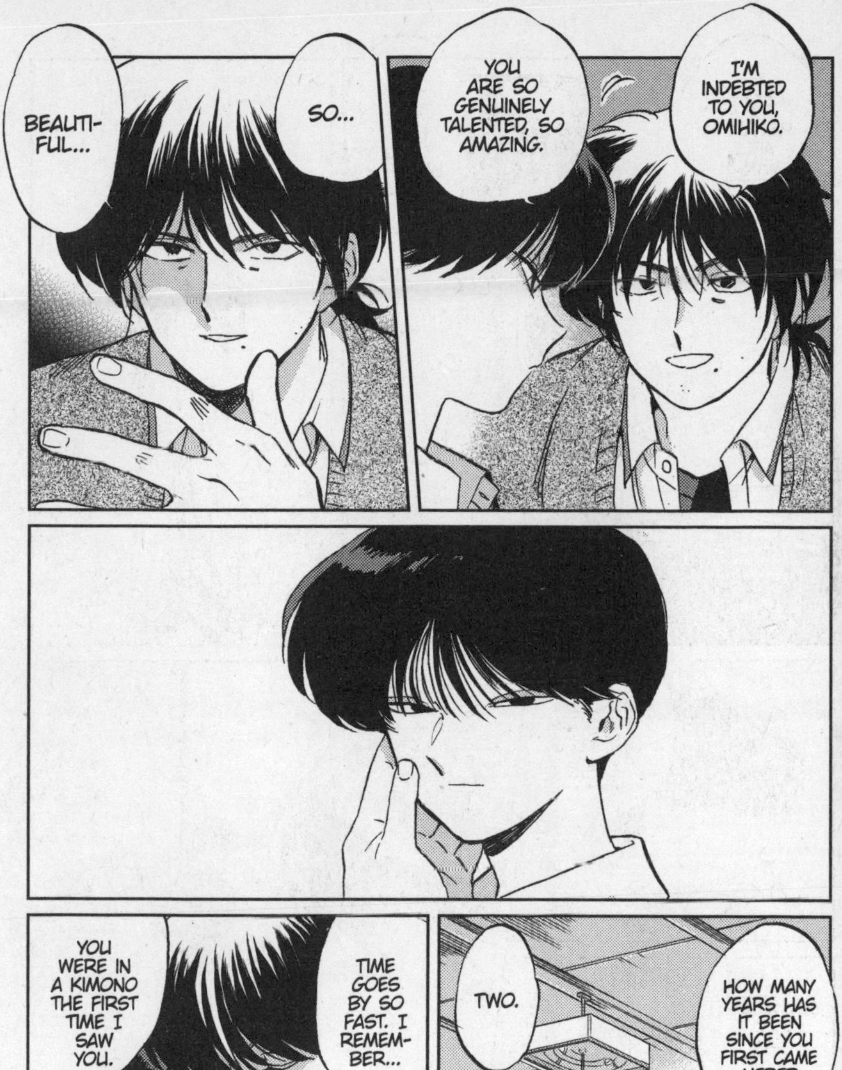
I'M INDEBTED TO YOU, OMIHIKO.
YOU ARE SO GENUINELY TALENTED, SO AMAZING.
SO...
BEAUTI-FUL...
HOW MANY YEARS HAS IT BEEN SINCE YOU FIRST CAME HERE?
TWO.
TIME GOES BY SO FAST. I REMEMBER...
YOU WERE IN A KIMONO THE FIRST TIME I SAW YOU.

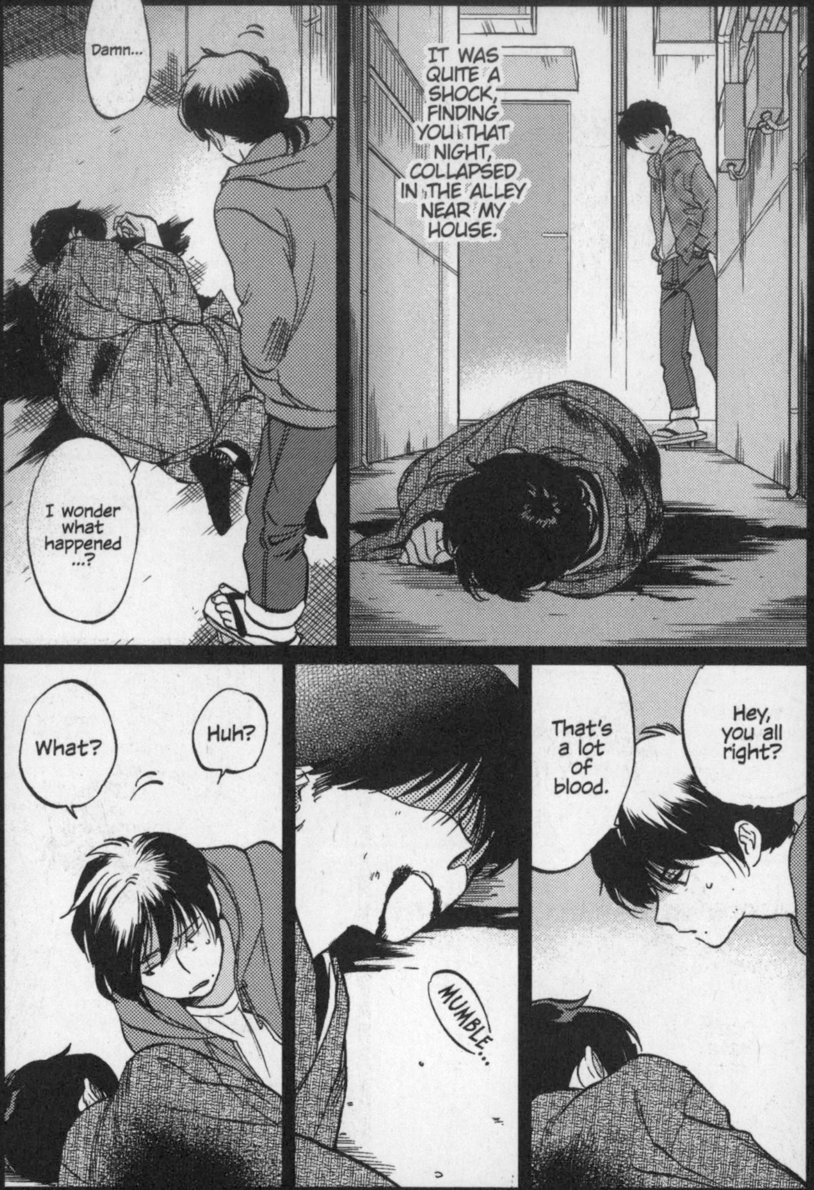
IT WAS QUITE A SHOCK, FINDING YOU THAT NIGHT, COLLAPSED IN THE ALLEY NEAR MY HOUSE.
Damn...
I wonder what happened ...?
Hey, you all right?
That's a lot of blood.
MUMBLE...
Huh?
What?

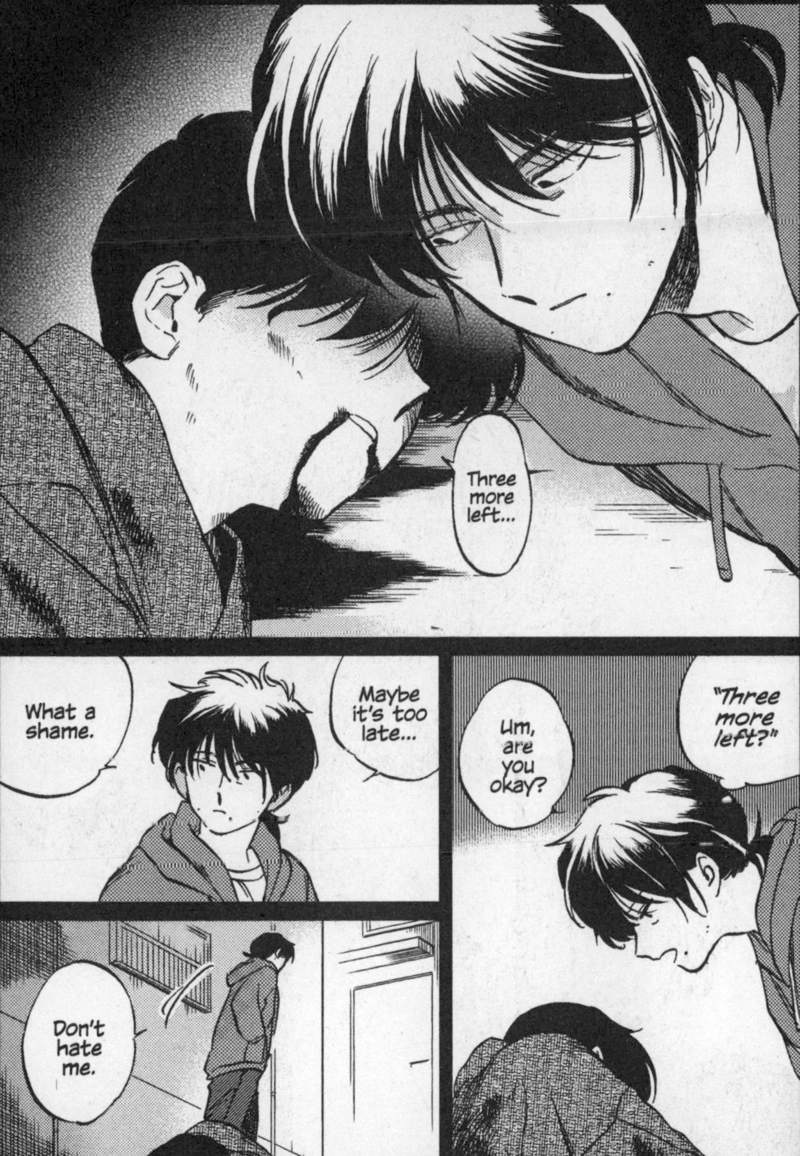
Three more left...
"Three more left?"
Um, are you okay?
Maybe it's too late...
What a shame.
Don't hate me.

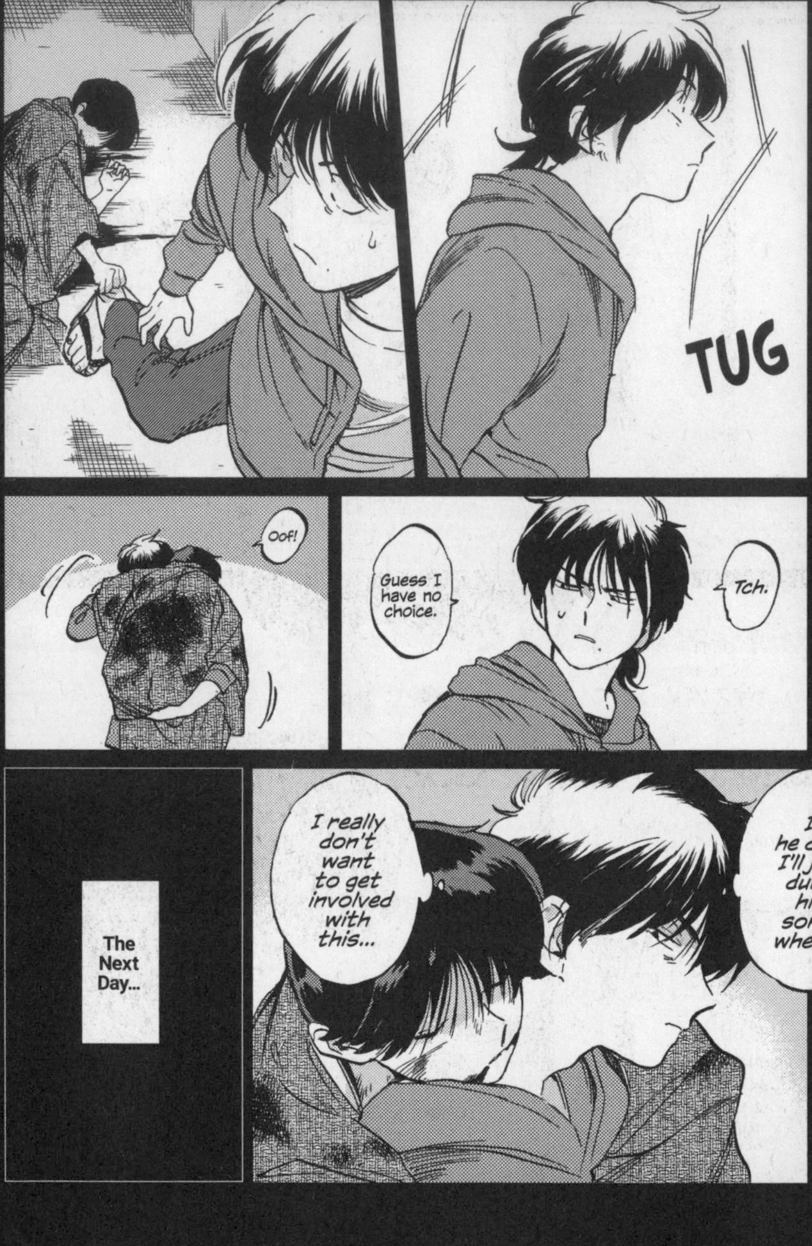
TUG
Tch.
Guess I have no choice.
Oof!
If he dies, I'll just dump him somewhere...
I really don't want to get involved with this...
The Next Day...

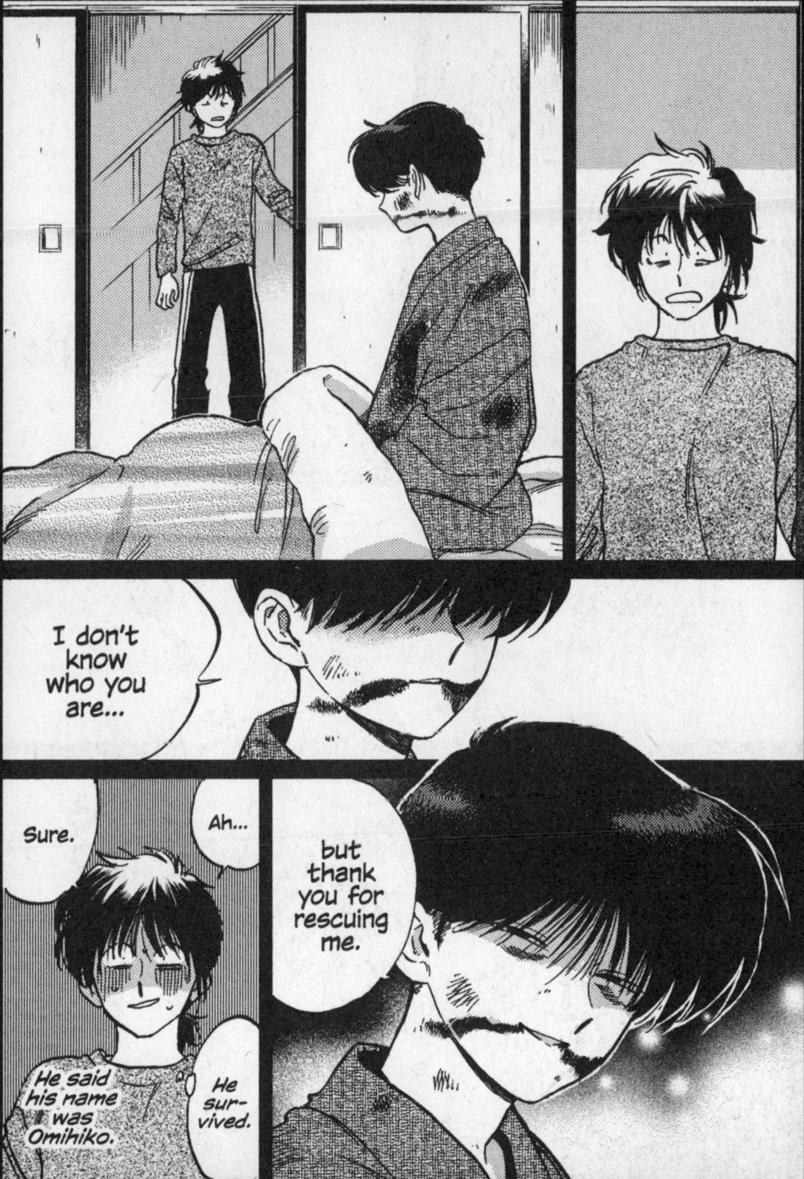
I don't know who you are...
but thank you for rescuing me.
Ah...
Sure.
He survived.
He said his name was Omihiko.

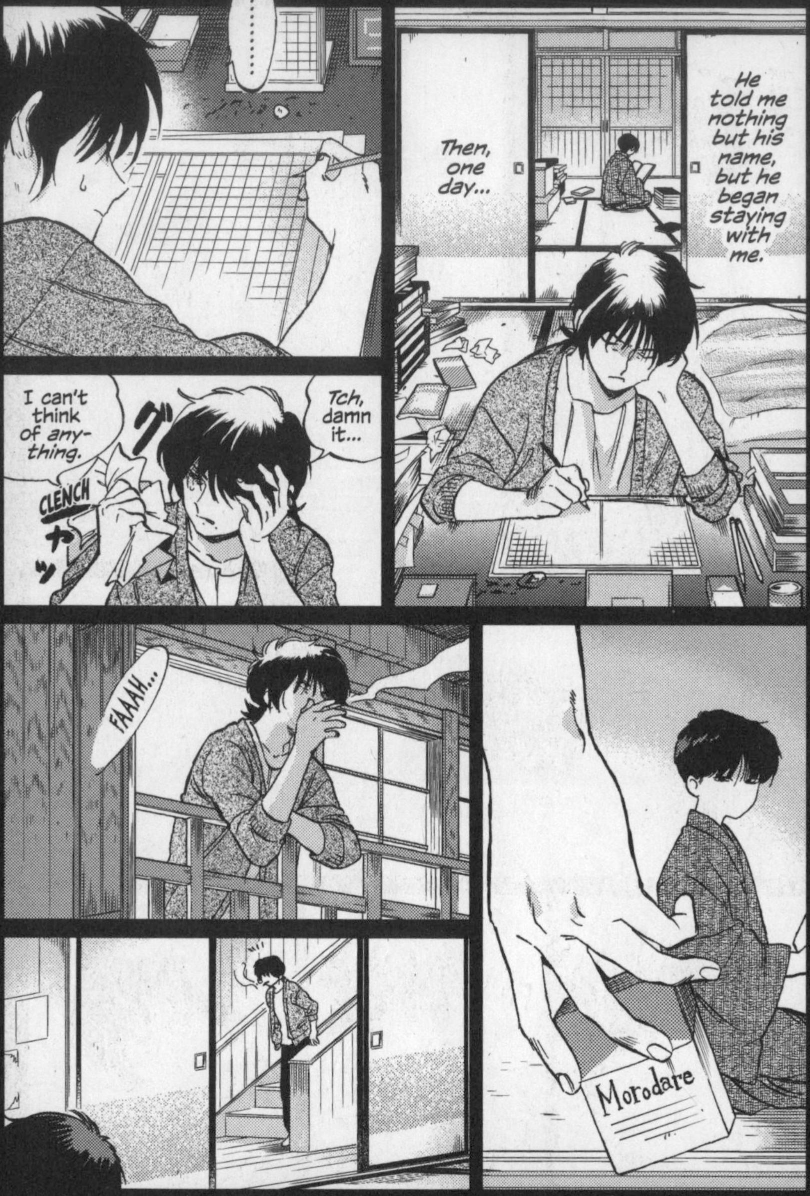
He told me nothing but his name, but he began staying with me.
Then, one day...
......
Tch, damn it...
I can't think of anything.
CLENCH
FAAAH...
Morodare

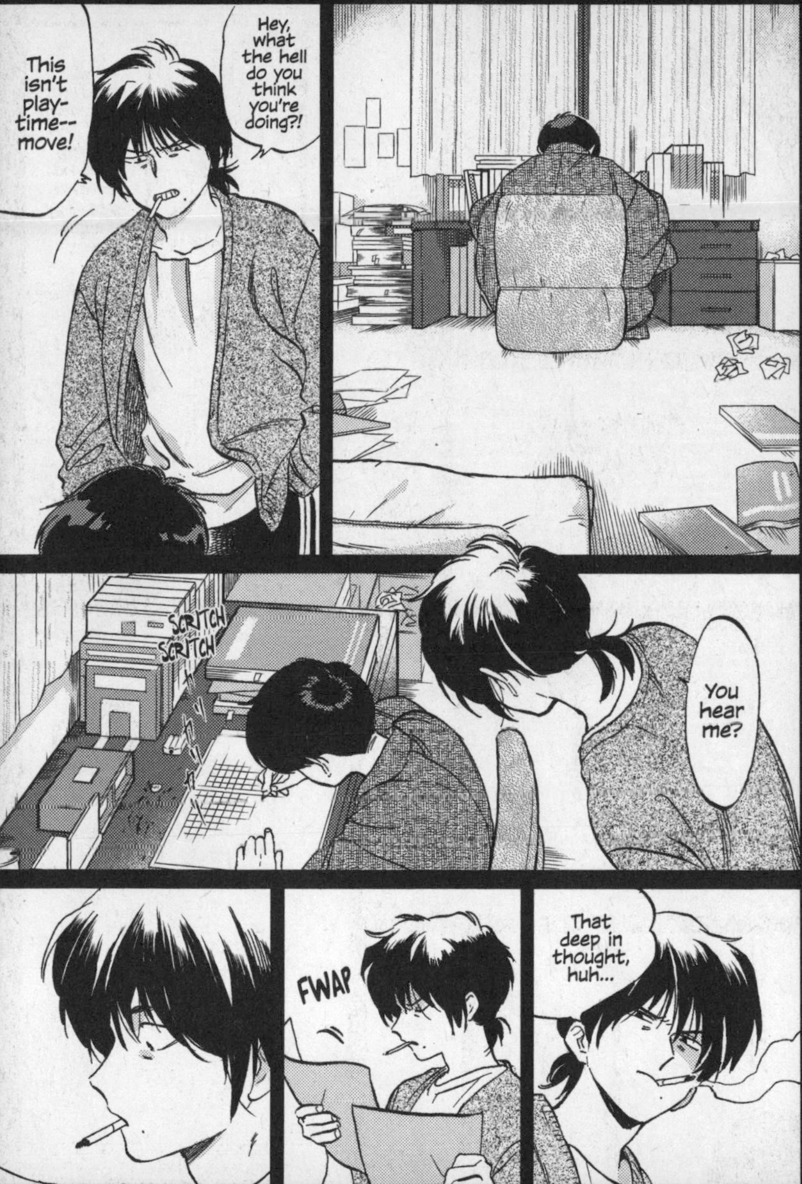
Hey, what the hell do you think you're doing?!
This isn't play-time--move!
You hear me?
SCRITCH SCRITCH
That deep in thought, huh...
FWAP

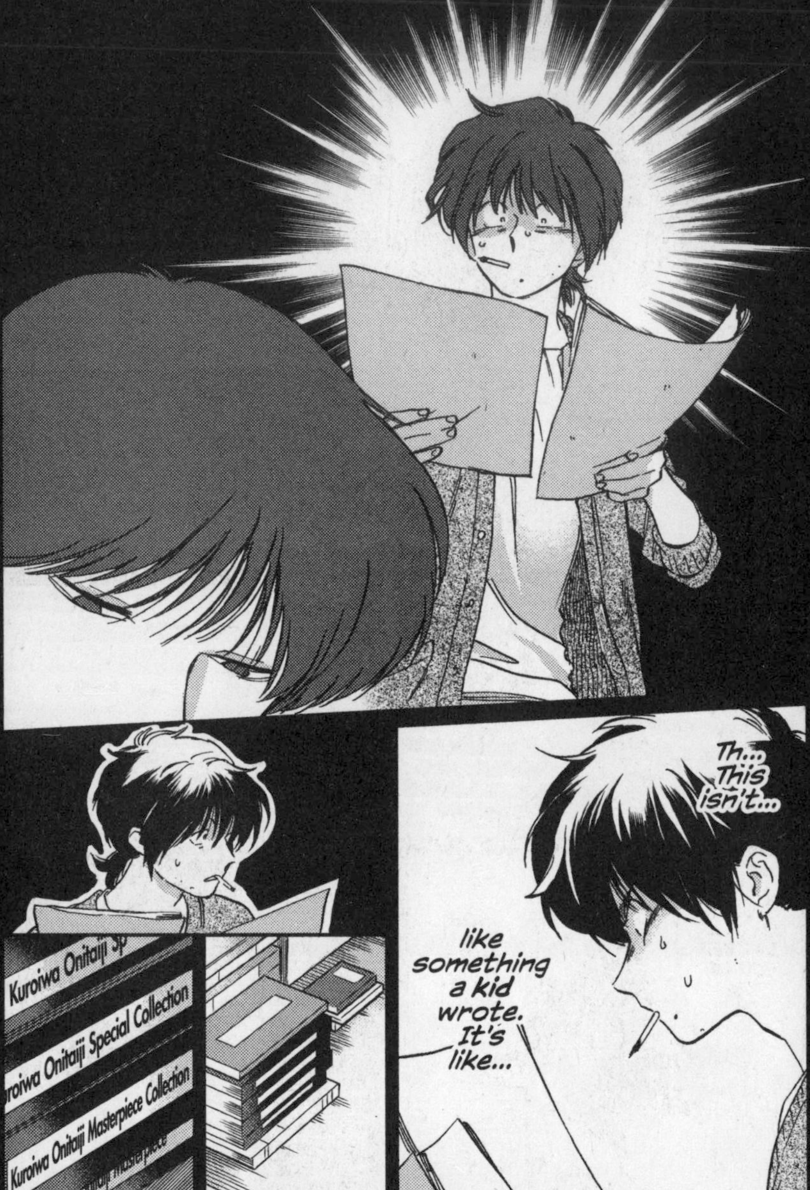
Th... This isn't...
like something a kid wrote. It's like...
Kuroiwa Onitaiji Sp
Kuroiwa Onitaiji Special Collection
roiwa Onitaiji Masterpiece Collection
Kuroiwa Onitaiji Masterpiece

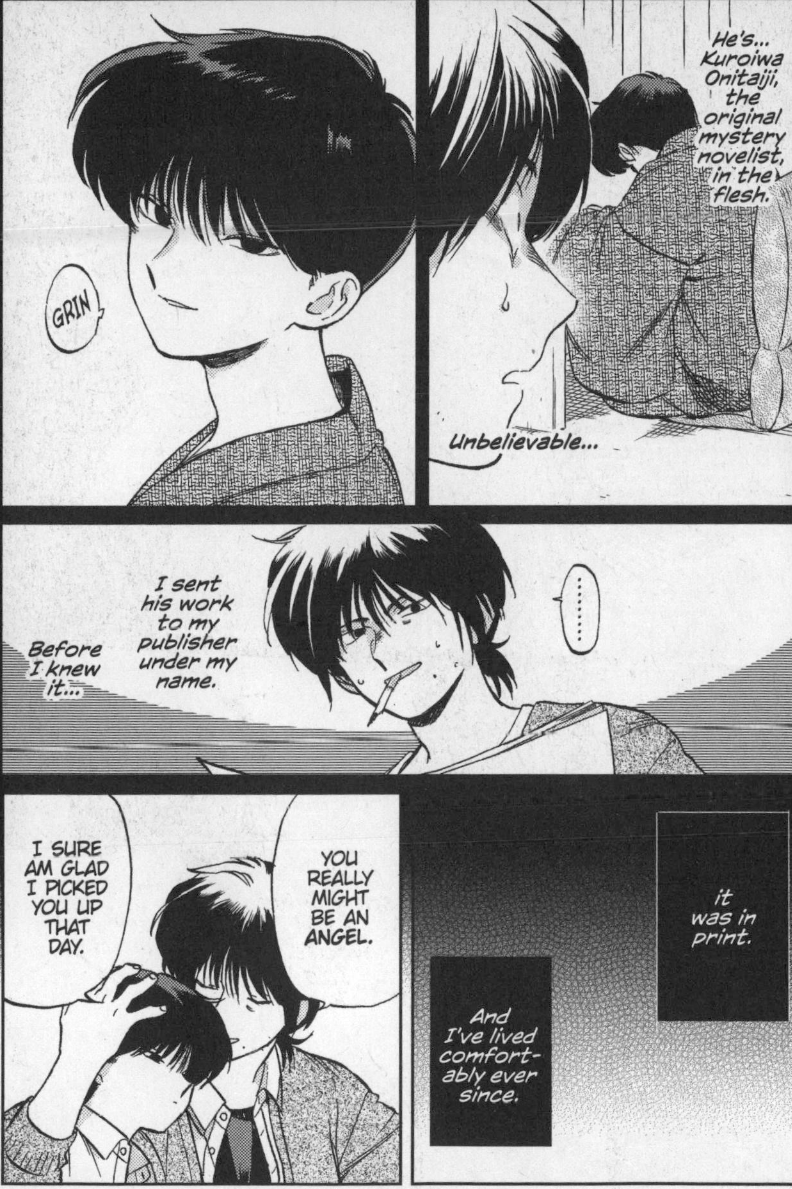
He's... Kuroiwa Onitaiji, the original mystery novelist, in the flesh.
Unbelievable...
GRIN
......
I sent his work to my publisher under my name.
Before I knew it...
it was in print.
And I've lived comfortably ever since.
YOU REALLY MIGHT BE AN ANGEL.
I SURE AM GLAD I PICKED YOU UP THAT DAY.

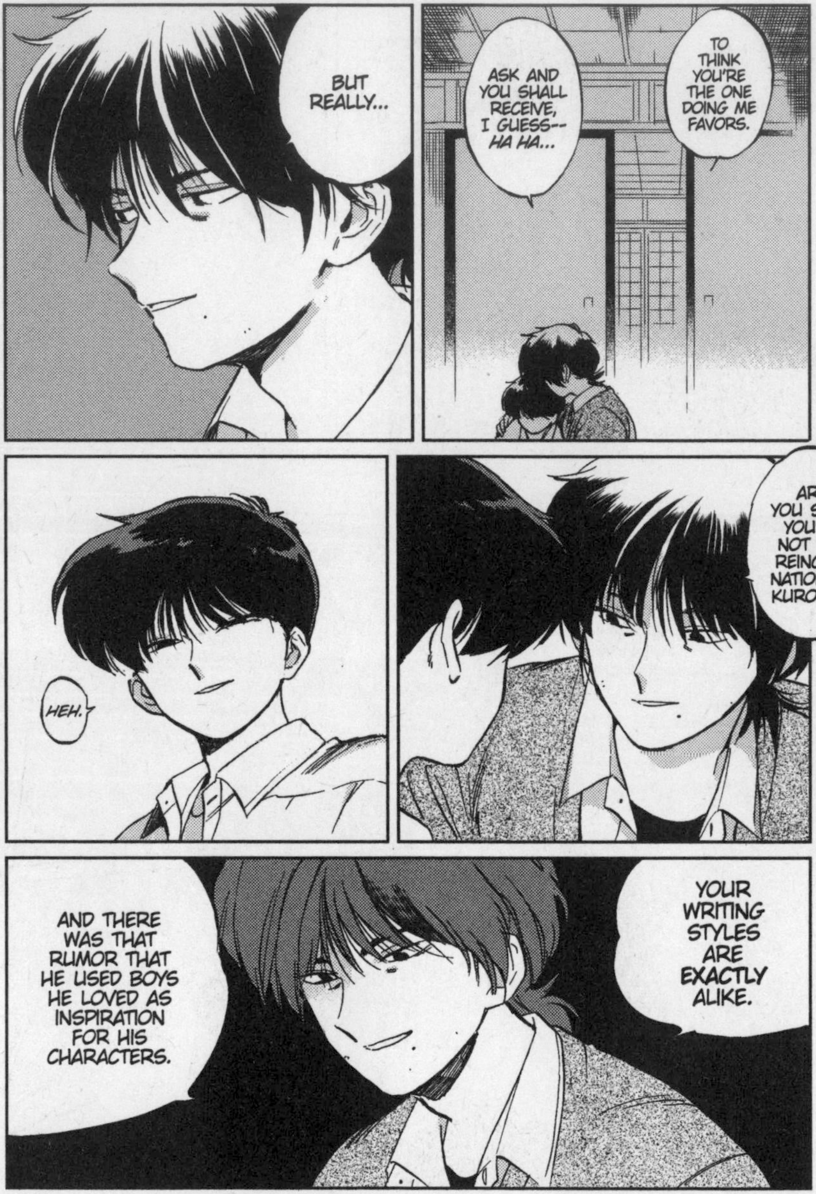
TO THINK YOU'RE THE ONE DOING ME FAVORS.
ASK AND YOU SHALL RECEIVE, I GUESS-- HA HA...
BUT REALLY...
ARE YOU SURE YOU'RE NOT THE REINCARNATION OF KUROIWA?
HEH.
YOUR WRITING STYLES ARE EXACTLY ALIKE.
AND THERE WAS THAT RUMOR THAT HE USED BOYS HE LOVED AS INSPIRATION FOR HIS CHARACTERS.

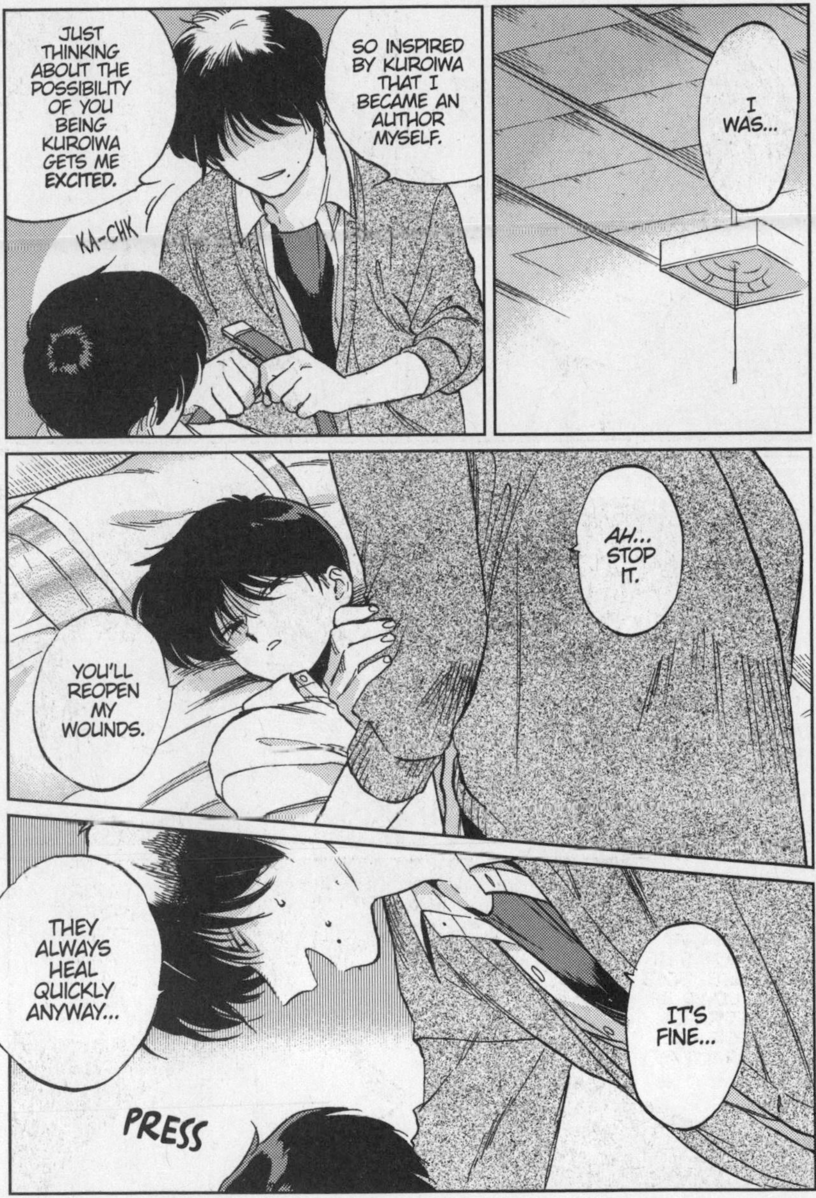
I WAS...
SO INSPIRED BY KUROIWA THAT I BECAME AN AUTHOR MYSELF.
JUST THINKING ABOUT THE POSSIBILITY OF YOU BEING KUROIWA GETS ME EXCITED.
KA-CHK
AH... STOP IT.
YOU'LL REOPEN MY WOUNDS.
IT'S FINE...
THEY ALWAYS HEAL QUICKLY ANYWAY...
PRESS

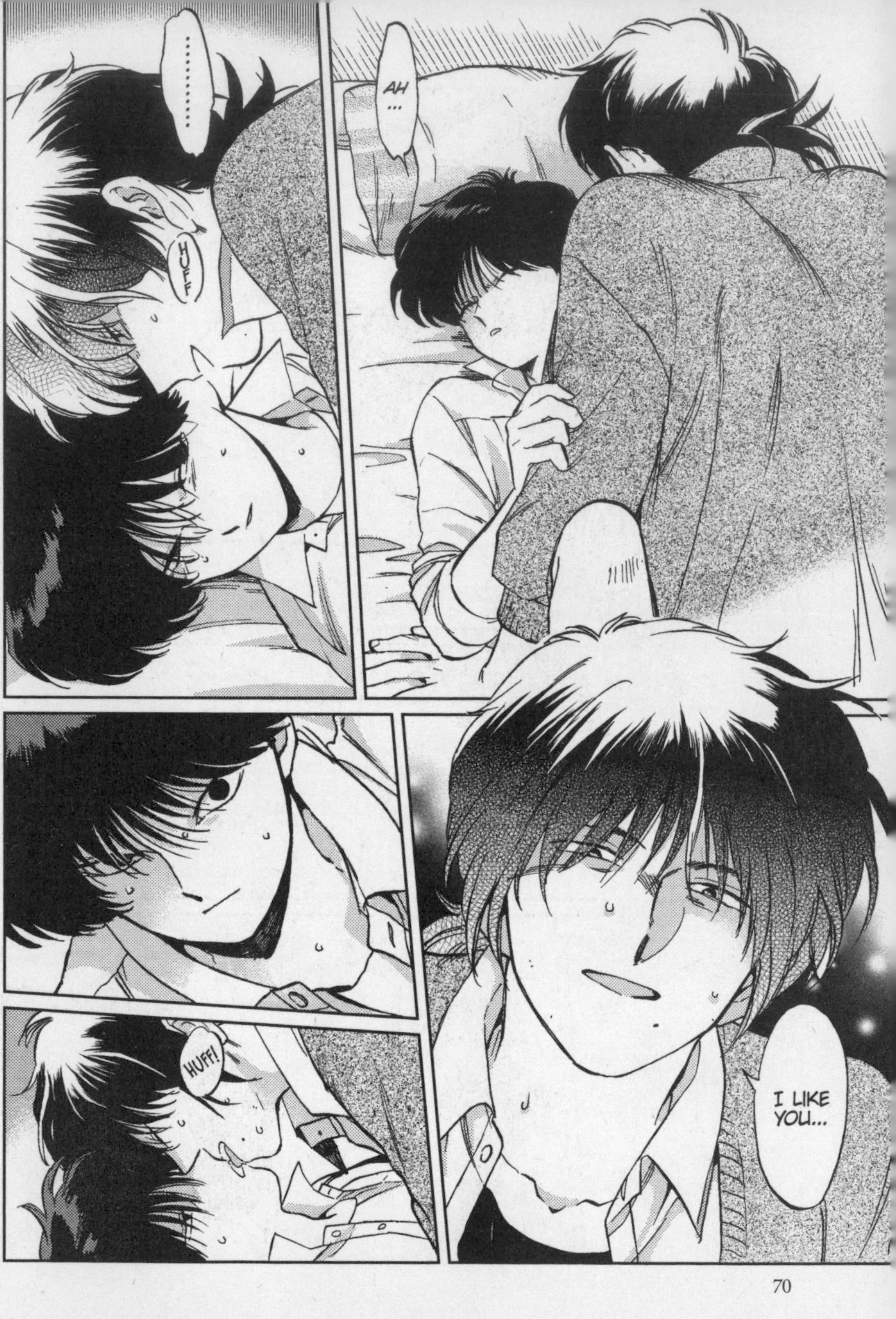
AH ...
......
HUFF
I LIKE YOU...
HUFF!

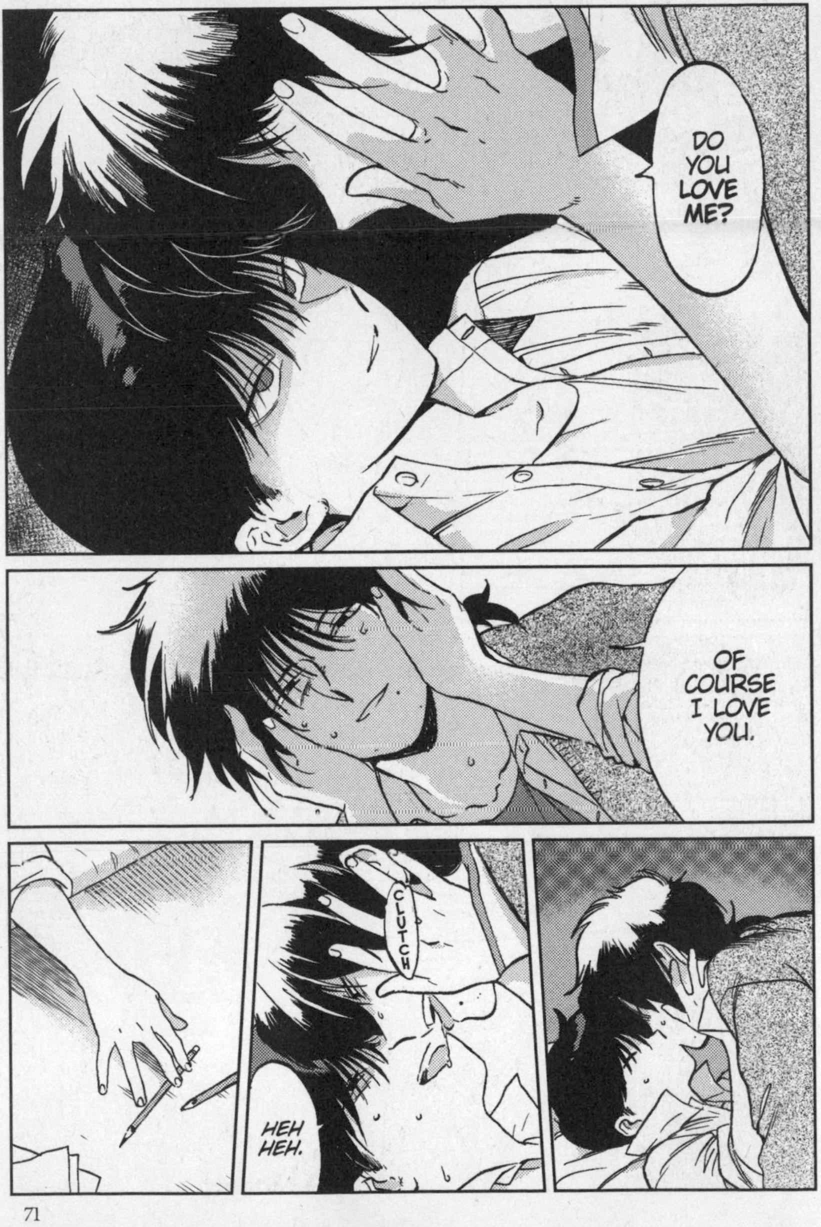
DO YOU LOVE ME?
OF COURSE I LOVE YOU.
CLUTCH
HEH HEH.

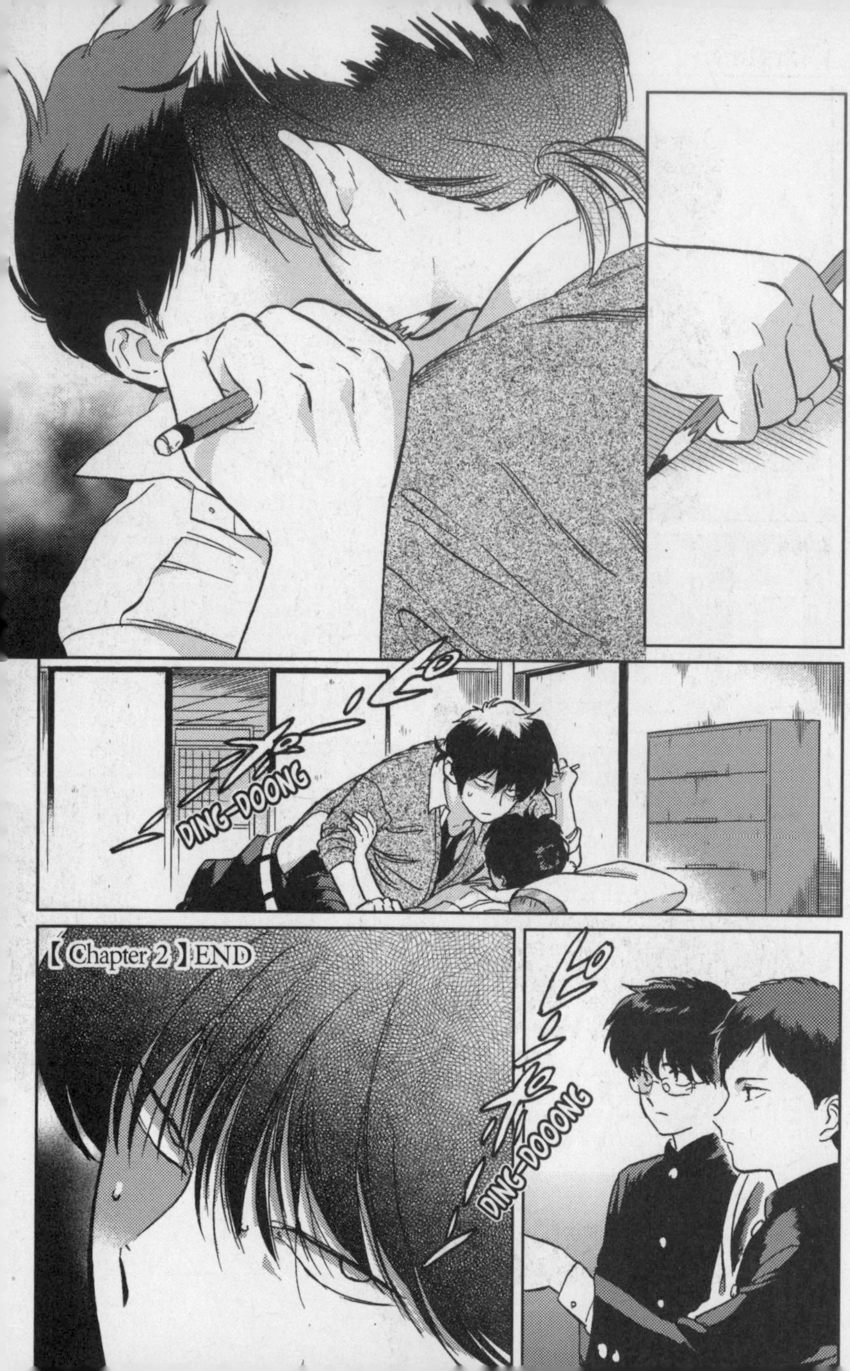
DING-DOONG
DING-DOOONG
【 Chapter 2 】END

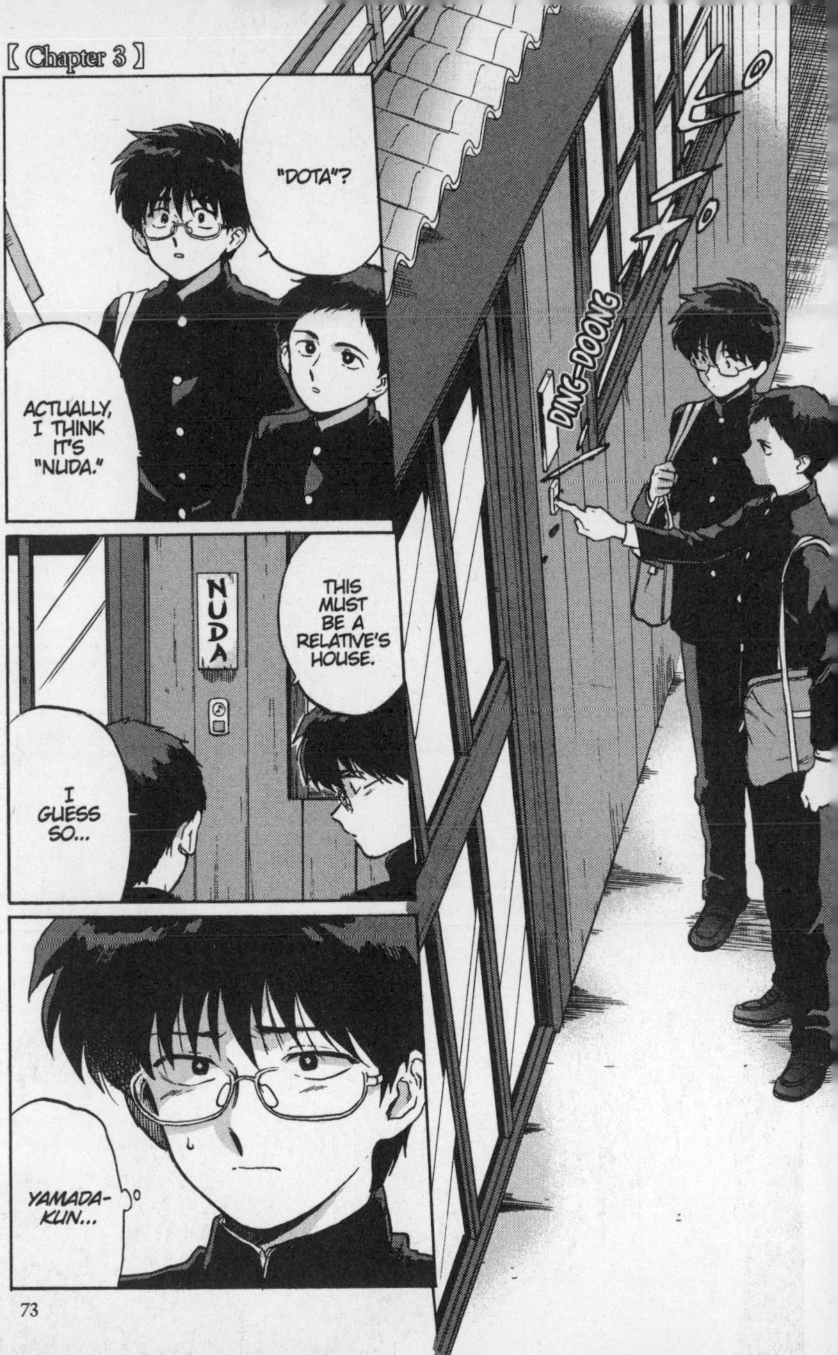
DING-DOONG
"DOTA"?
ACTUALLY, I THINK IT'S "NUDA."
NUDA
THIS MUST BE A RELATIVE'S HOUSE.
I GUESS SO...
YAMADA-KUN...

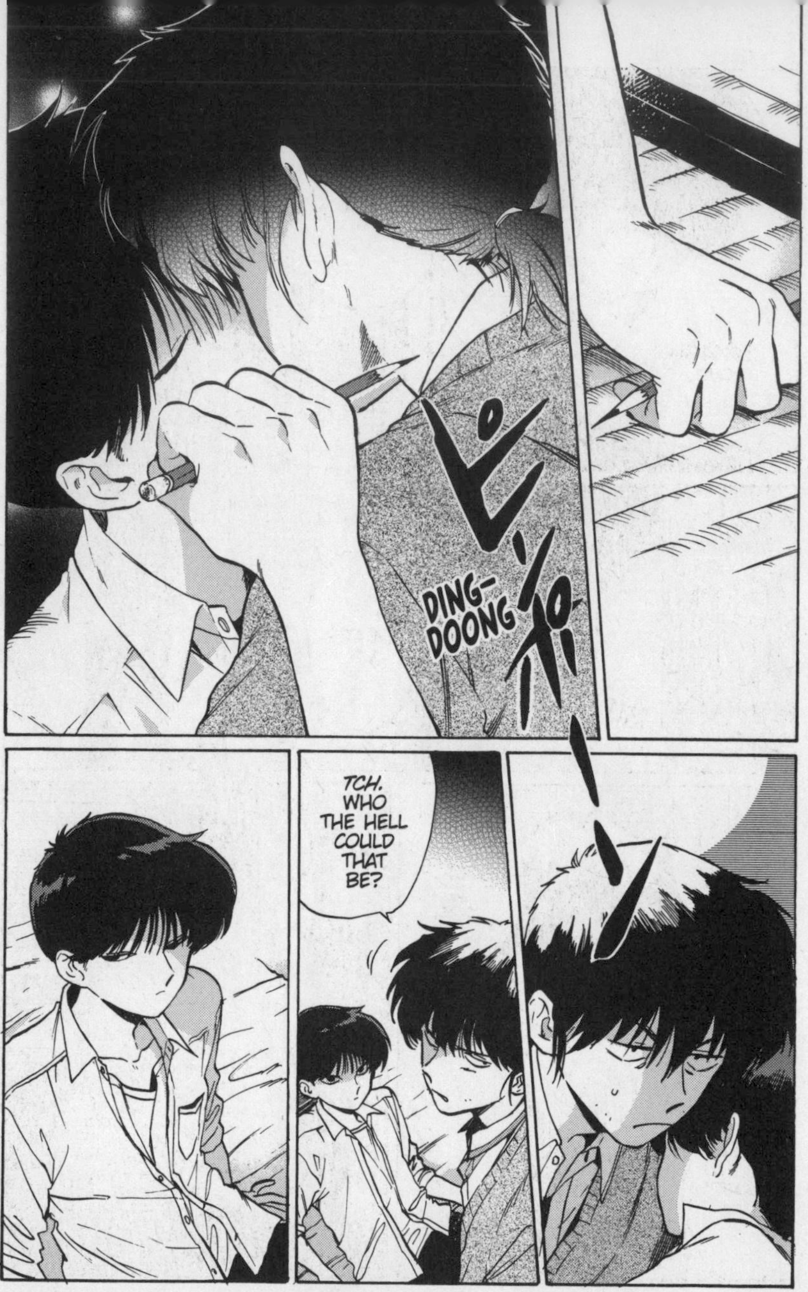
DING-DOONG
TCH. WHO THE HELL COULD THAT BE?

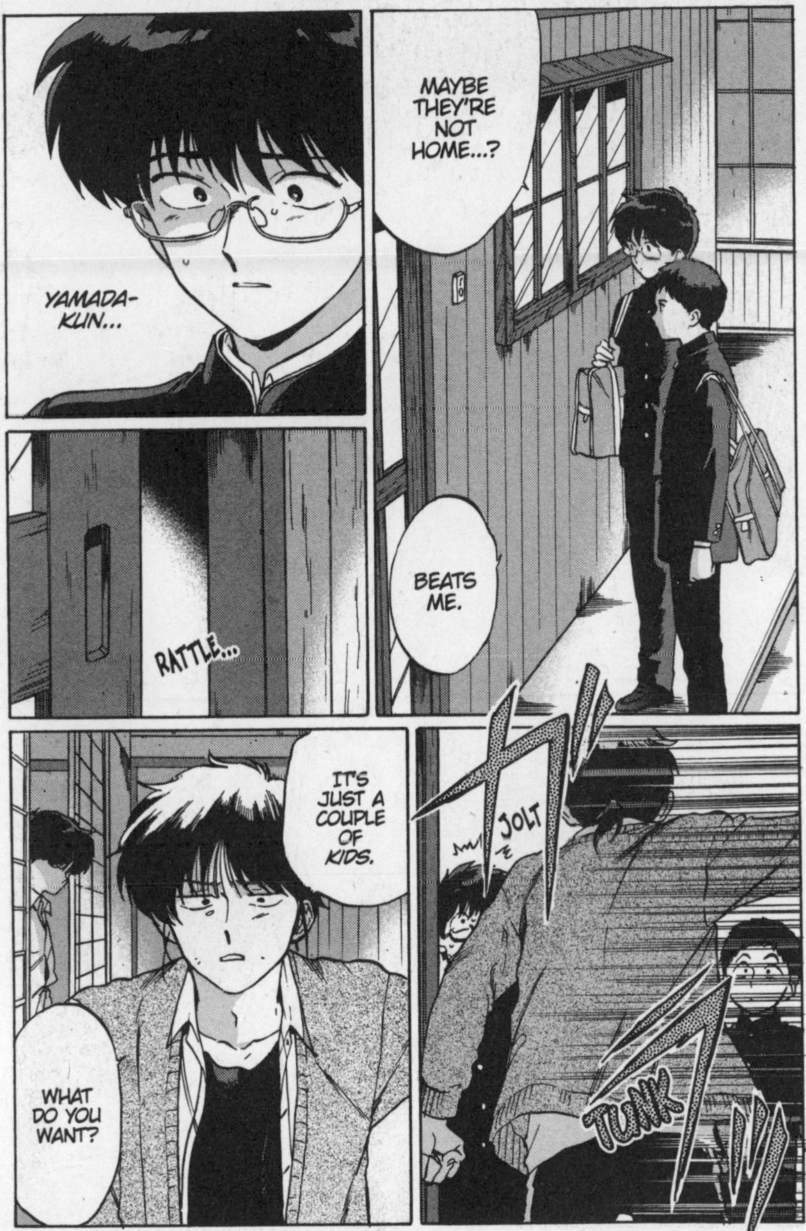
MAYBE THEY'RE NOT HOME...?
BEATS ME.
YAMADA-KUN...
RATTLE...
JOLT
TUNK
IT'S JUST A COUPLE OF KIDS.
WHAT DO YOU WANT?

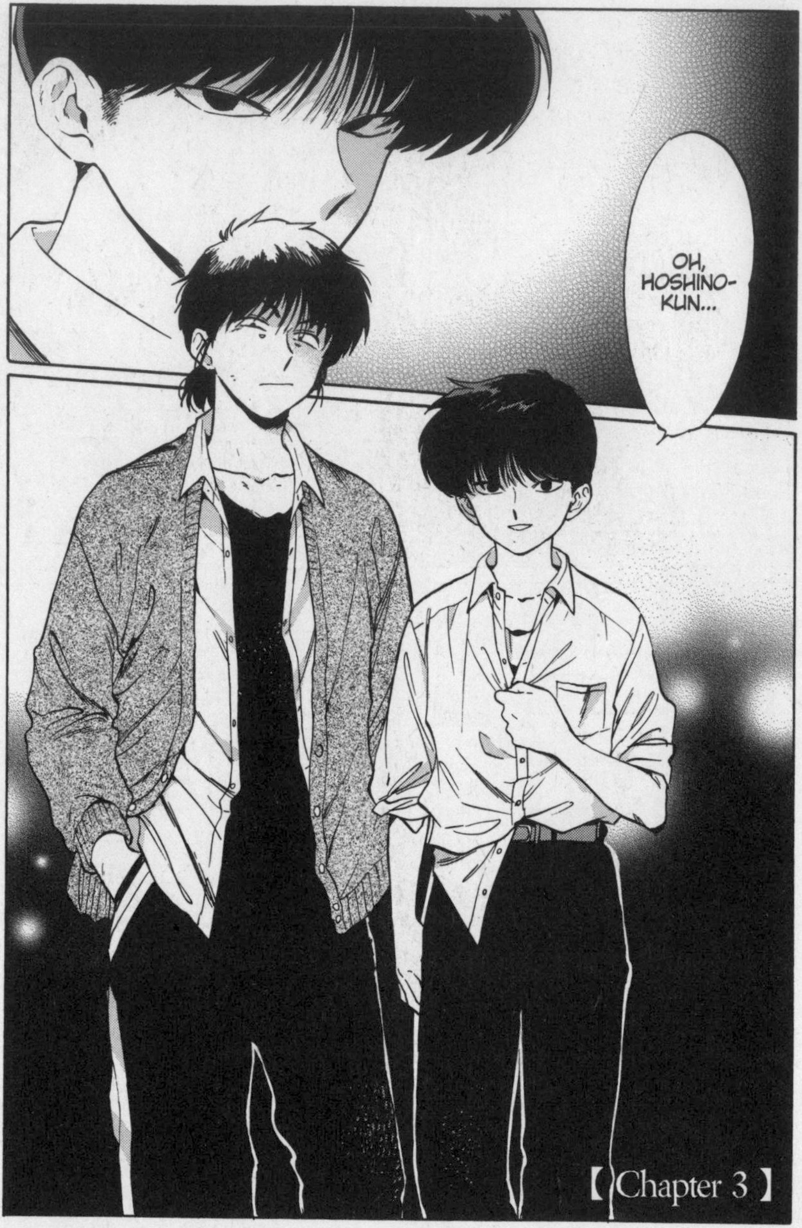
OH, HOSHINO-KUN...
【 Chapter 3 】

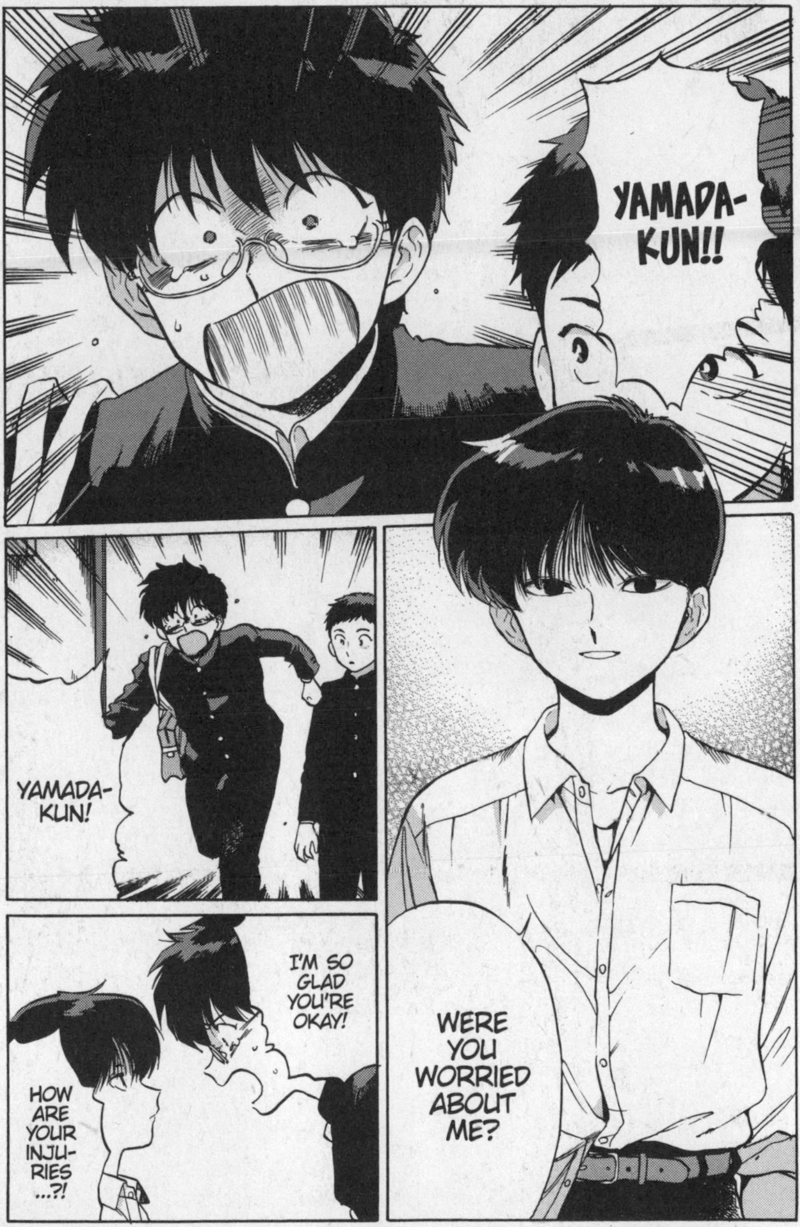
YAMADA-KUN!!
WERE YOU WORRIED ABOUT ME?
YAMADA-KUN!
I'M SO GLAD YOU'RE OKAY!
HOW ARE YOUR INJURIES ...?!

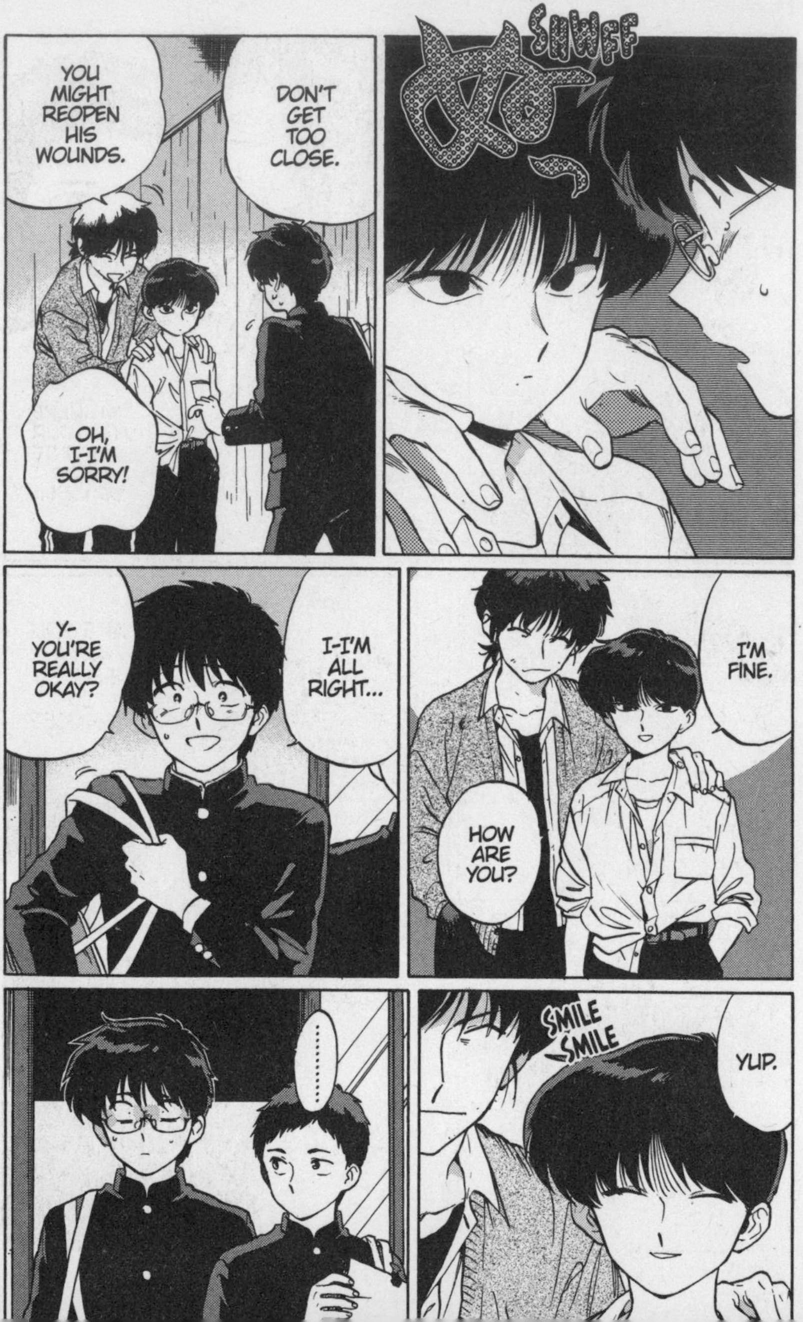
SHWFF
DON'T GET TOO CLOSE.
YOU MIGHT REOPEN HIS WOUNDS.
OH, I-I'M SORRY!
I'M FINE.
HOW ARE YOU?
I-I'M ALL RIGHT...
Y-YOU'RE REALLY OKAY?
YUP.
SMILE SMILE
....

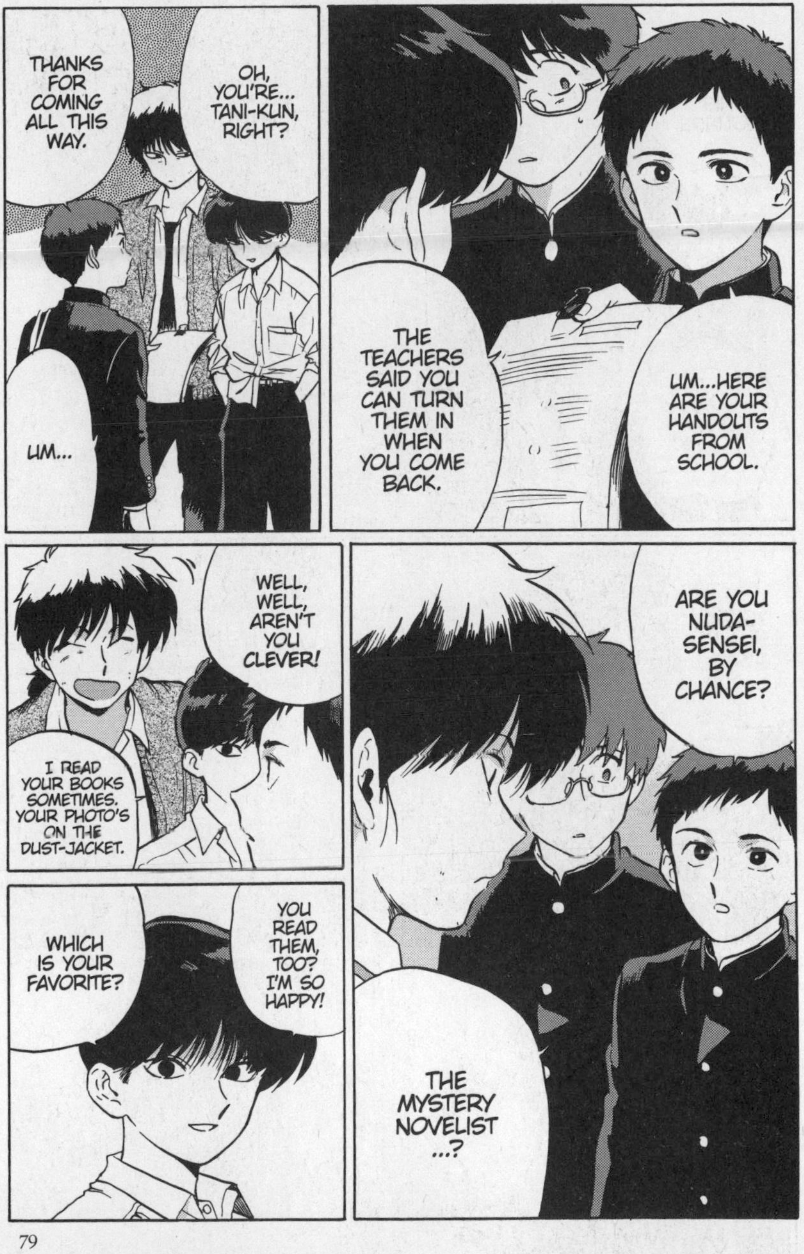
UM...HERE ARE YOUR HANDOUTS FROM SCHOOL.
THE TEACHERS SAID YOU CAN TURN THEM IN WHEN YOU COME BACK.
OH, YOU'RE... TANI-KUN, RIGHT?
THANKS FOR COMING ALL THIS WAY.
UM...
ARE YOU NUDA-SENSEI, BY CHANCE?
THE MYSTERY NOVELIST ...?
WELL, WELL, AREN'T YOU CLEVER!
I READ YOUR BOOKS SOMETIMES. YOUR PHOTO'S ON THE DUST-JACKET.
YOU READ THEM, TOO? I'M SO HAPPY!
WHICH IS YOUR FAVORITE?

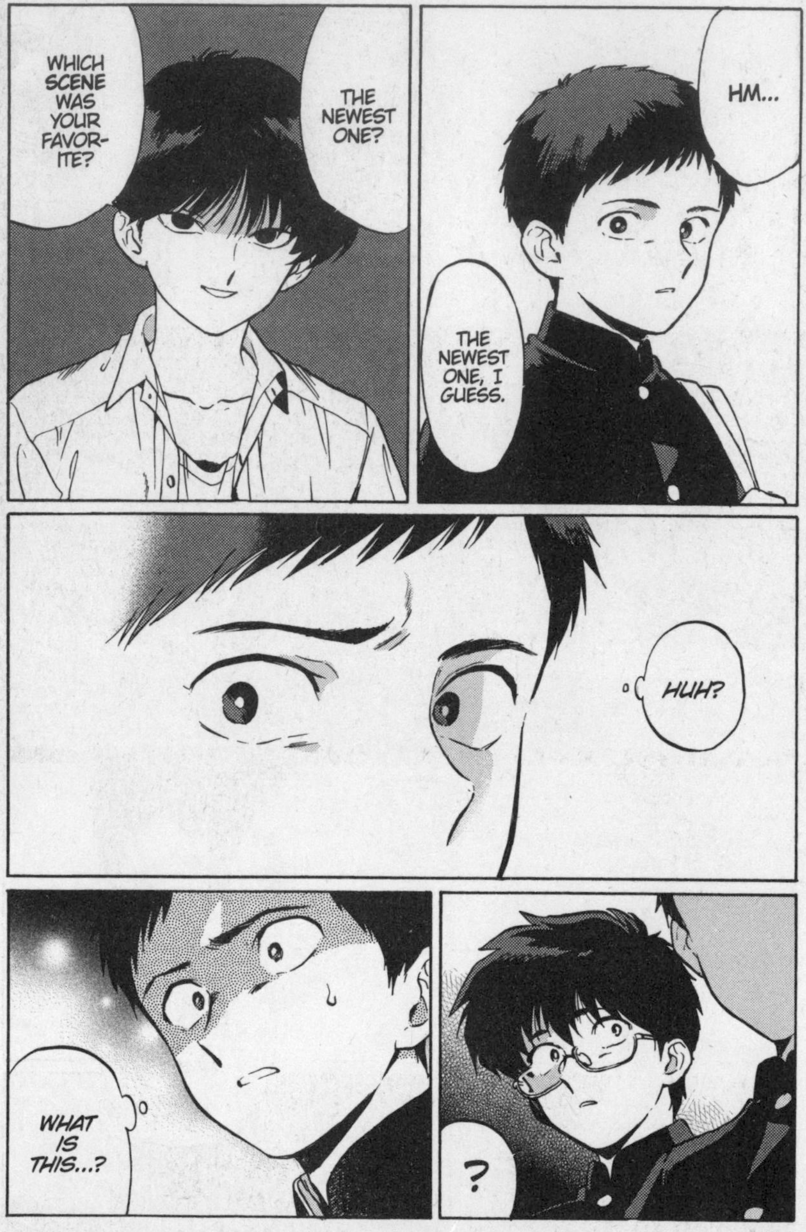
HM...
THE NEWEST ONE, I GUESS.
WHICH SCENE WAS YOUR FAVOR-ITE?
THE NEWEST ONE?
HUH?
?
WHAT IS THIS...?

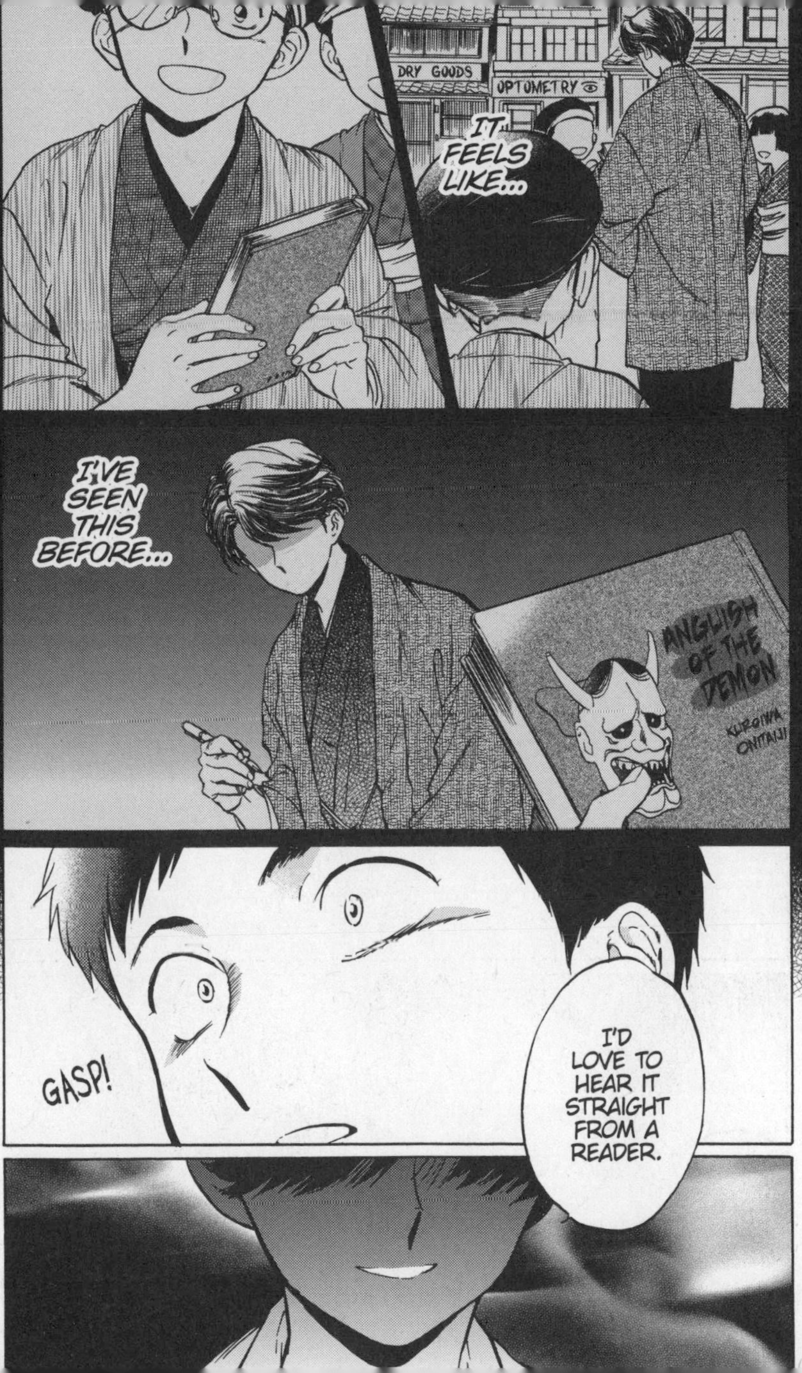
DRY GOODS
OPTOMETRY
IT FEELS LIKE...
I'VE SEEN THIS BEFORE...
ANGLISH OF THE DEMON
KUROIWA ONITAIJI
I'D LOVE TO HEAR IT STRAIGHT FROM A READER.
GASP!

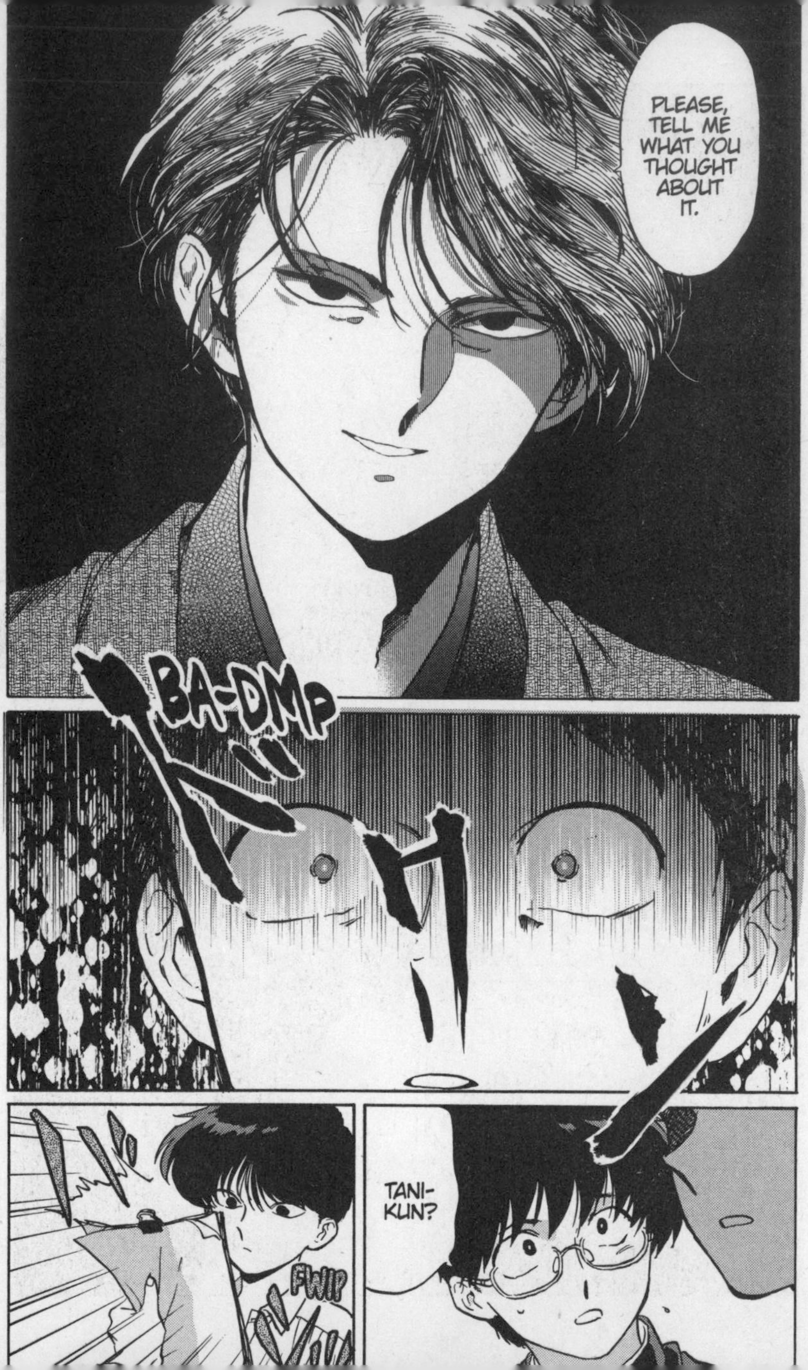
PLEASE, TELL ME WHAT YOU THOUGHT ABOUT IT.
BA-DMP
TANI-KUN?
FWIP

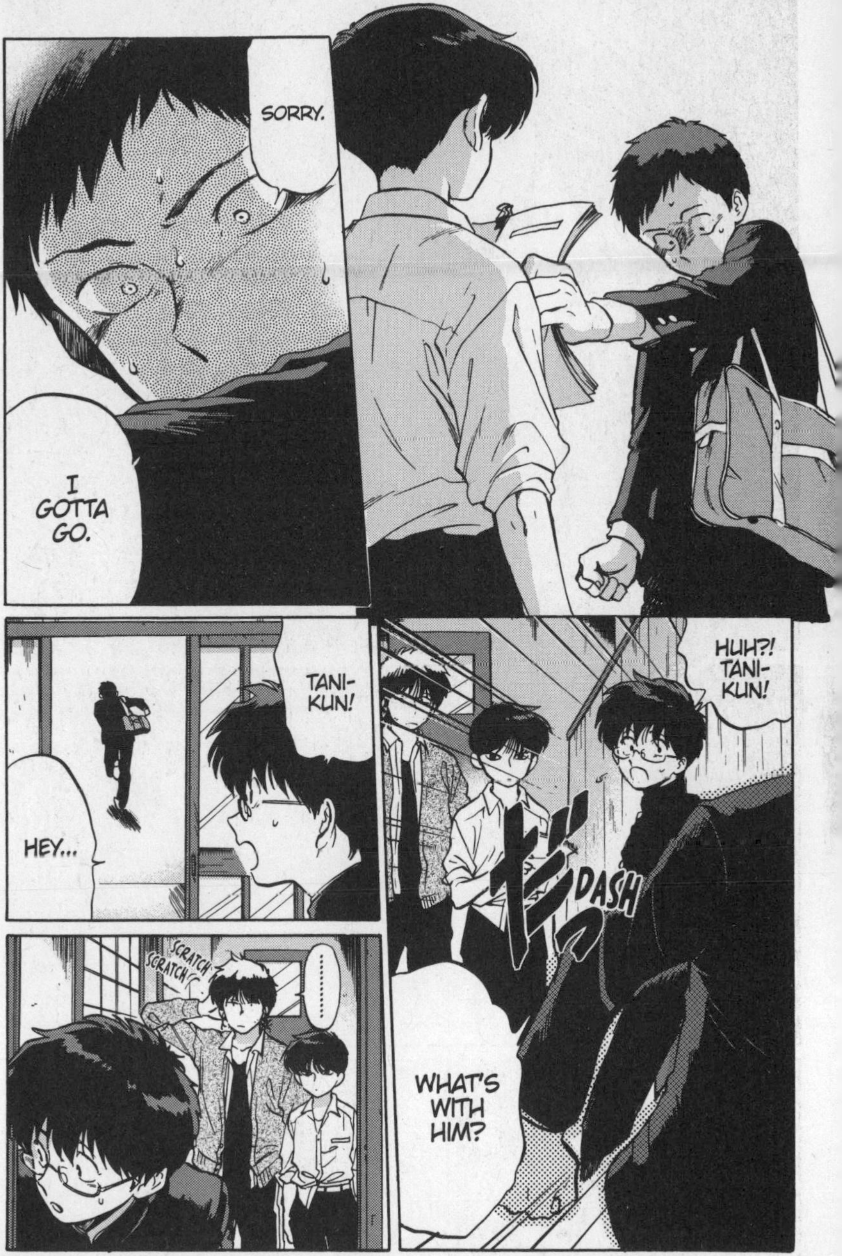
SORRY.
I GOTTA GO.
HUH?! TANI-KUN!
DASH
WHAT'S WITH HIM?
TANI-KUN!
HEY...
SCRATCH SCRATCH
......

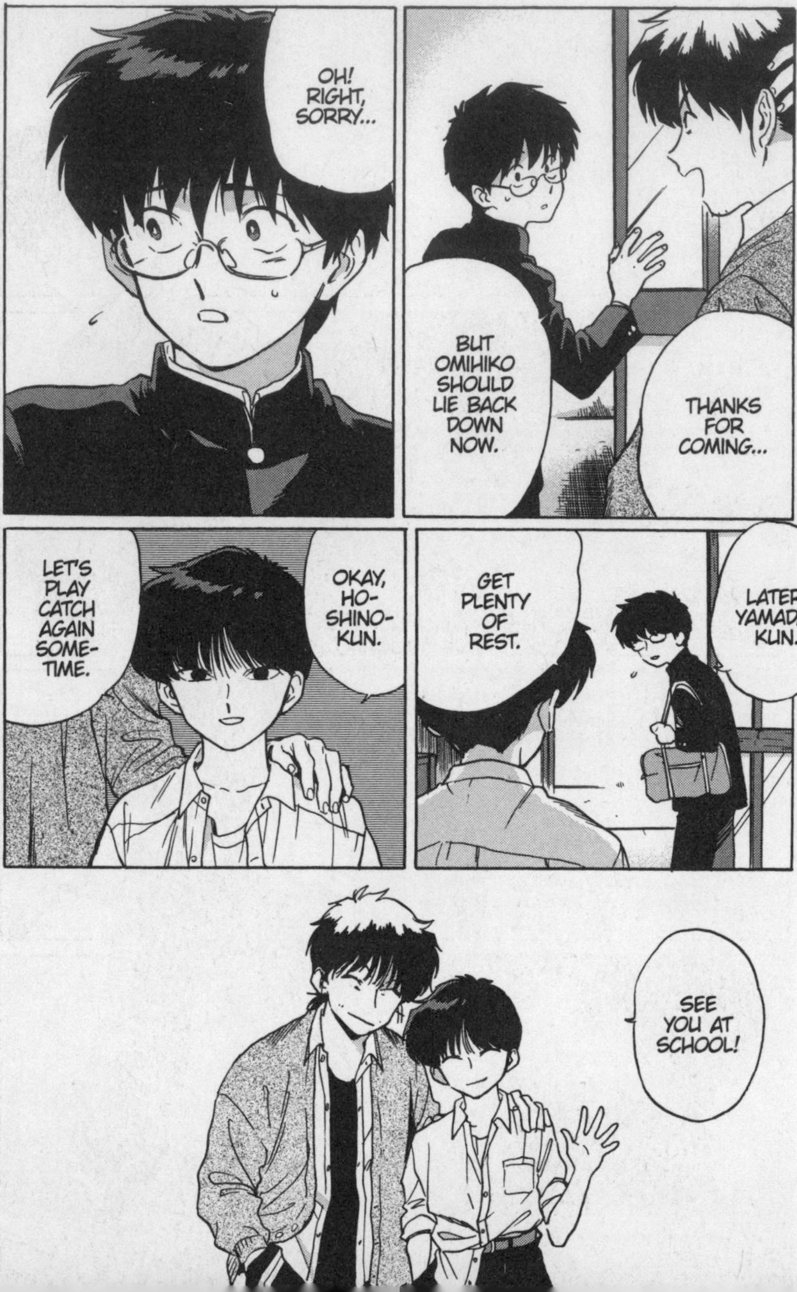
THANKS FOR COMING...
BUT OMIHIKO SHOULD LIE BACK DOWN NOW.
OH! RIGHT, SORRY...
LATER, YAMADA-KUN.
GET PLENTY OF REST.
OKAY, HO-SHINO-KUN.
LET'S PLAY CATCH AGAIN SOME-TIME.
SEE YOU AT SCHOOL!

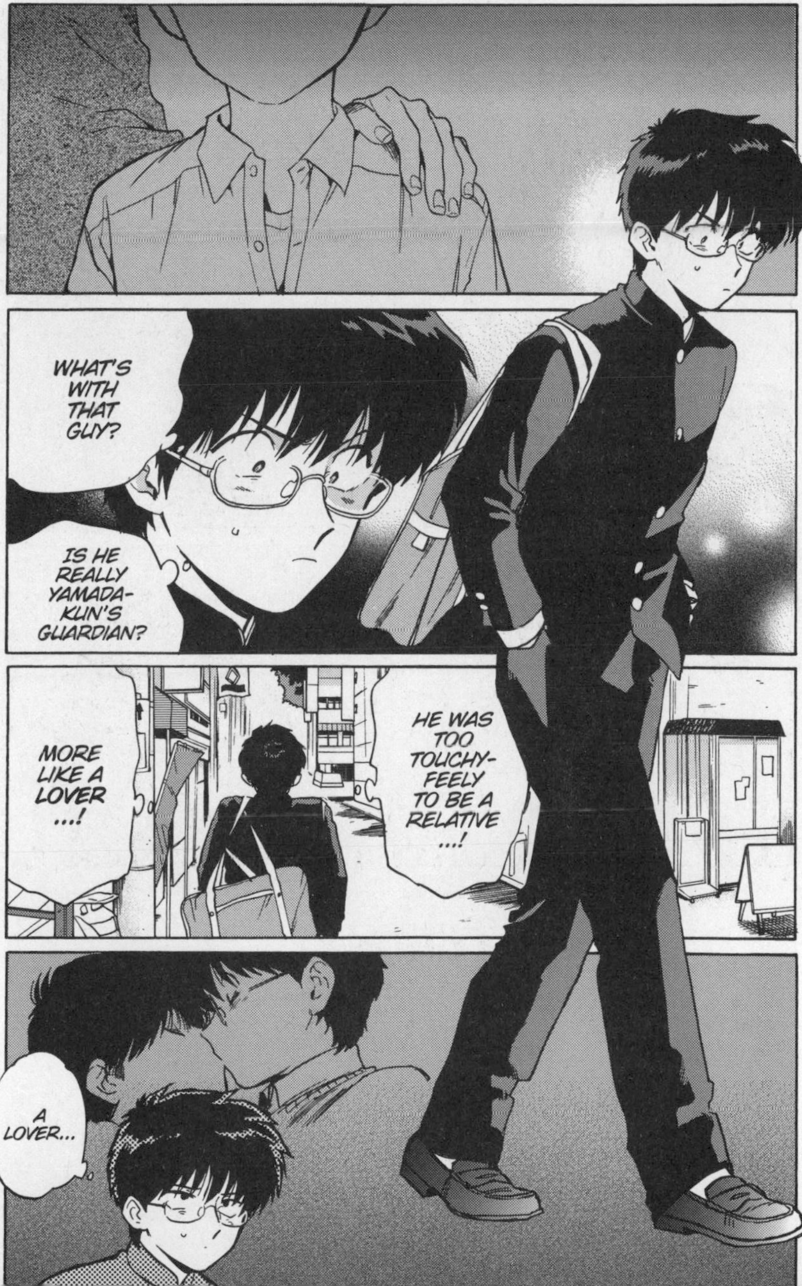
WHAT'S WITH THAT GUY?
IS HE REALLY YAMADA-KUN'S GUARDIAN?
HE WAS TOO TOUCHY-FEELY TO BE A RELATIVE ...!
MORE LIKE A LOVER ...!
A LOVER...

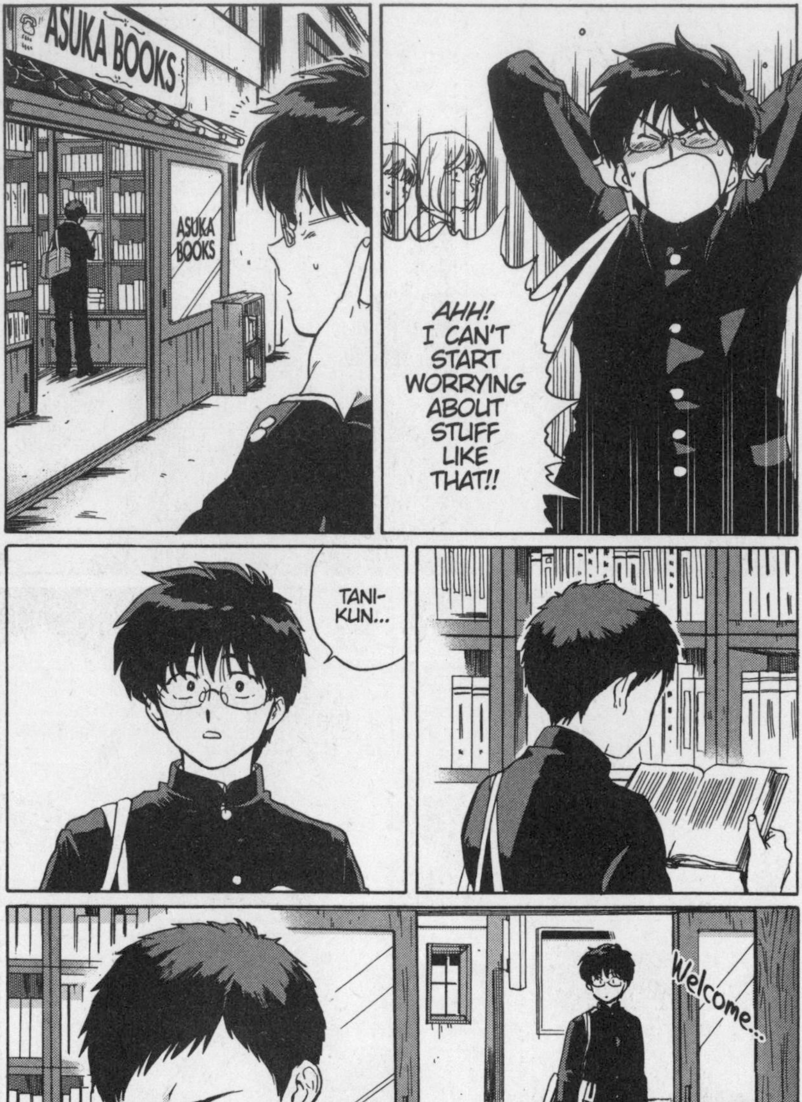
AHH! I CAN'T START WORRYING ABOUT STUFF LIKE THAT!!
ASUKA BOOKS
ASUKA BOOKS
TANI-KUN...
Welcome...

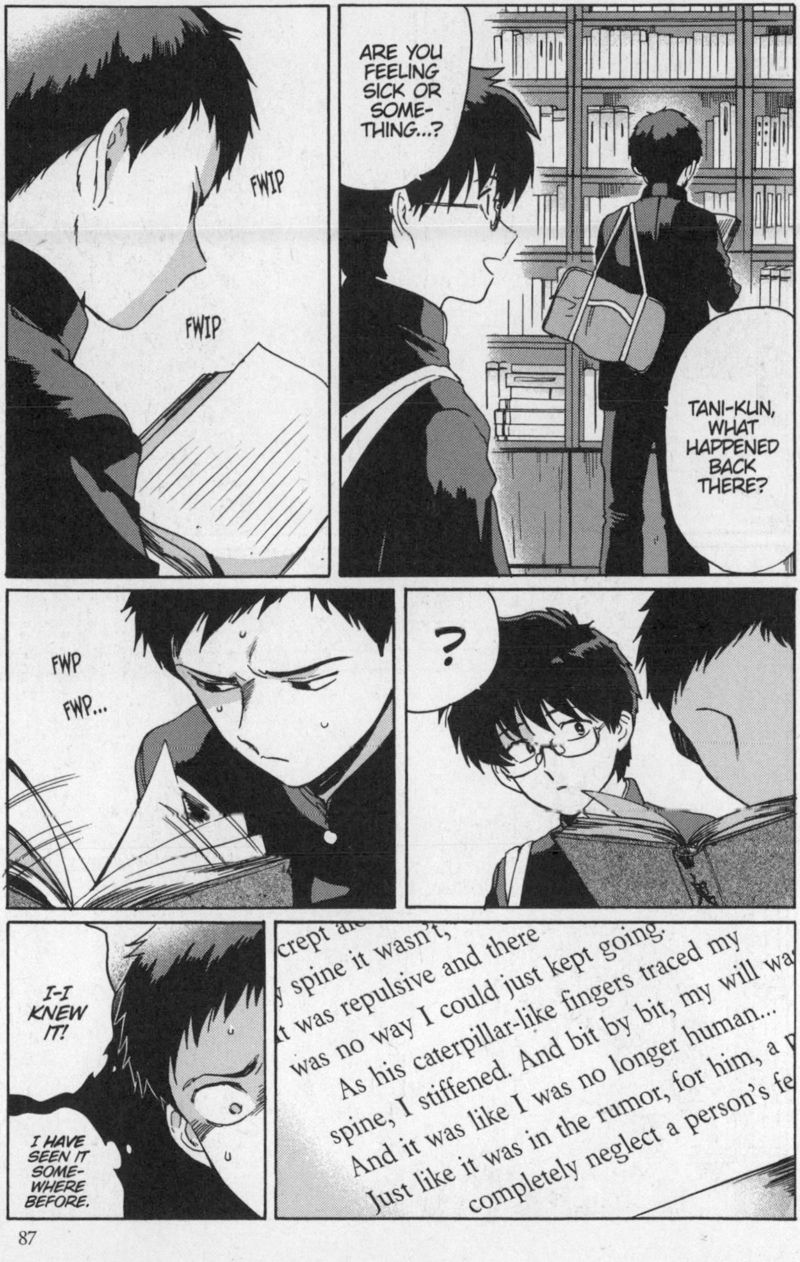
TANI-KUN, WHAT HAPPENED BACK THERE?
ARE YOU FEELING SICK OR SOME-THING...?
FWIP
FWIP
?
FWP
FWP...
crept
spine it wasn't,
was repulsive and there
was no way I could just kept going.
As his caterpillar-like fingers traced my
spine, I stiffened. And bit by bit, my will
And it was like I was no longer human...
Just like it was in the rumor, for him, a
completely neglect a person's
I-I KNEW IT!
I HAVE SEEN IT SOME-WHERE BEFORE.

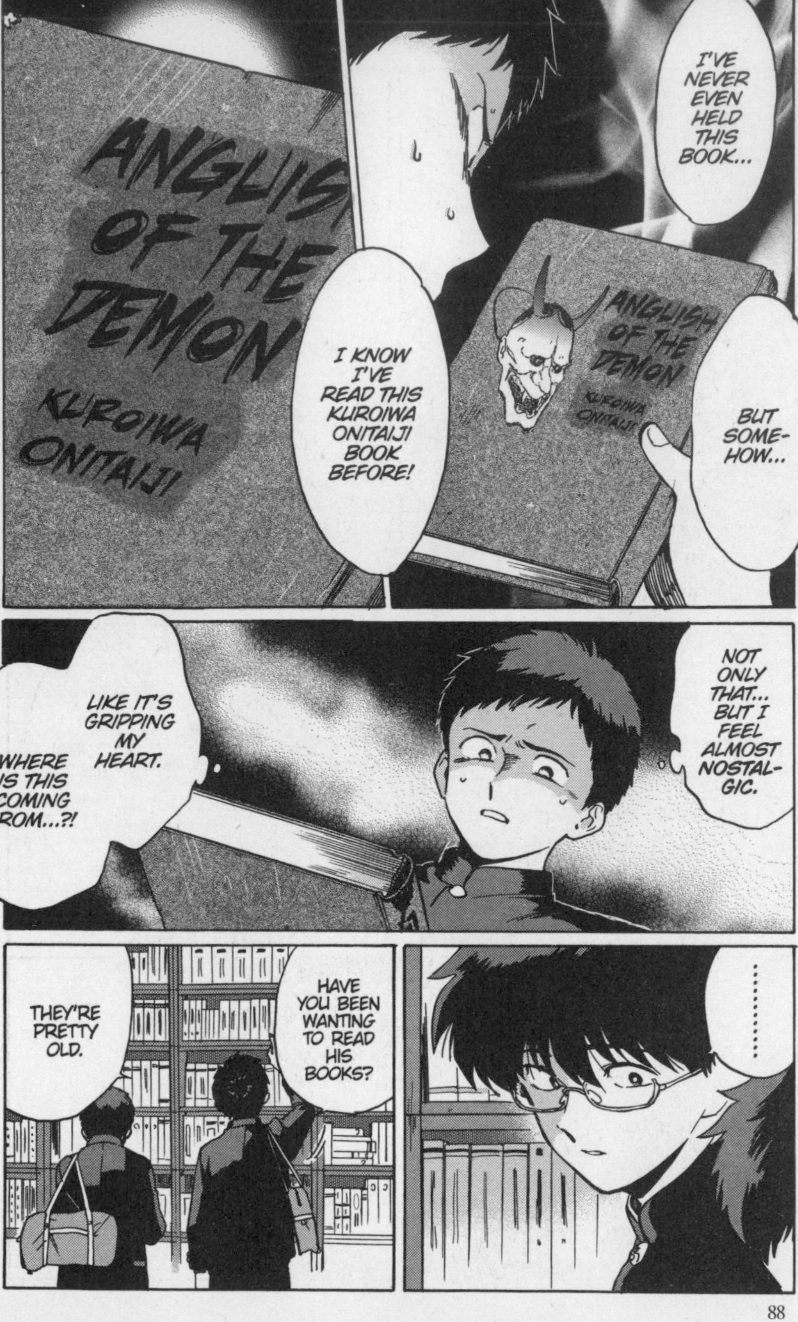
I'VE NEVER EVEN HELD THIS BOOK...
BUT SOME-HOW...
ANGUISH OF THE DEMON
KUROIWA ONITAIJI
I KNOW I'VE READ THIS KUROIWA ONITAIJI BOOK BEFORE!
ANGUISH OF THE DEMON
KUROIWA ONITAIJI
NOT ONLY THAT... BUT I FEEL ALMOST NOSTAL-GIC.
LIKE IT'S GRIPPING MY HEART.
WHERE IS THIS COMING FROM...?!
......
HAVE YOU BEEN WANTING TO READ HIS BOOKS?
THEY'RE PRETTY OLD.

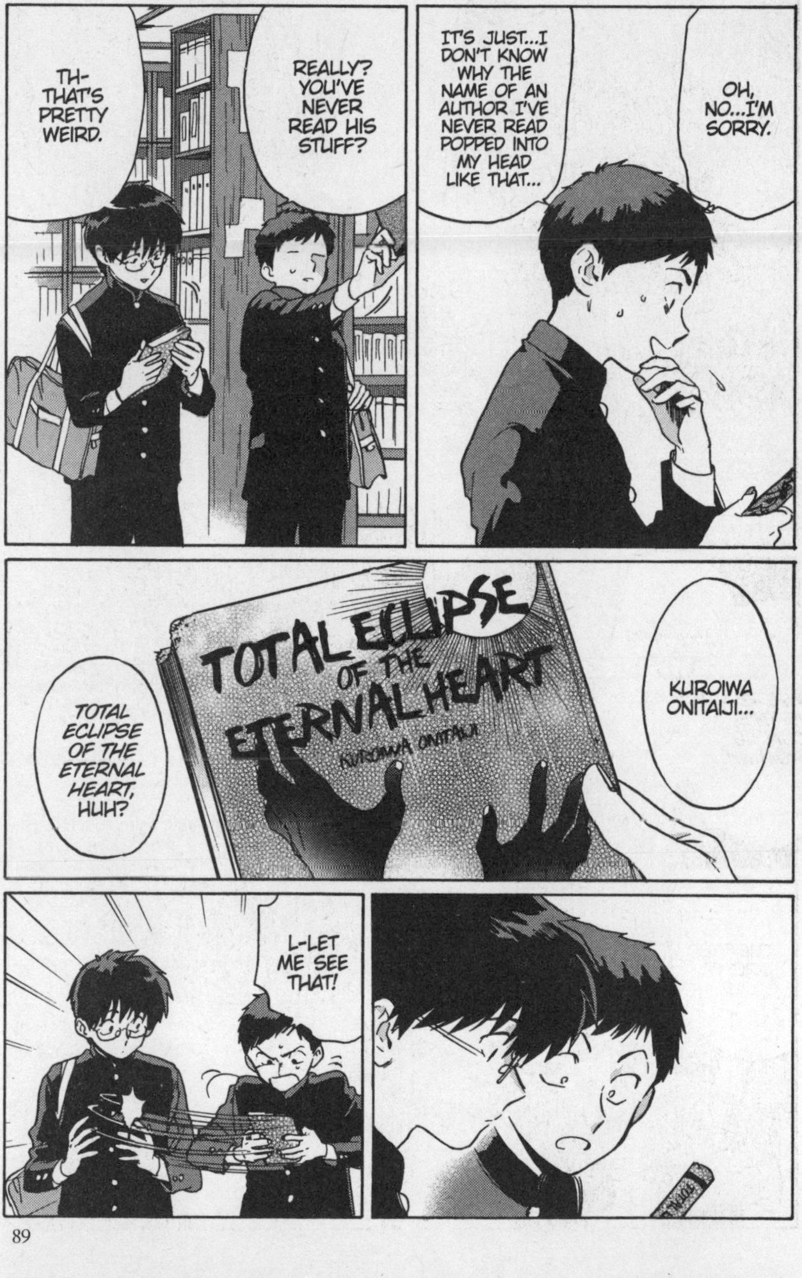
OH, NO...I'M SORRY.
IT'S JUST...I DON'T KNOW WHY THE NAME OF AN AUTHOR I'VE NEVER READ POPPED INTO MY HEAD LIKE THAT...
REALLY? YOU'VE NEVER READ HIS STUFF?
TH-THAT'S PRETTY WEIRD.
KUROIWA ONITAIJI...
TOTAL ECLIPSE OF THE ETERNAL HEART
KUROIWA ONITAIJI
TOTAL ECLIPSE OF THE ETERNAL HEART, HUH?
L-LET ME SEE THAT!

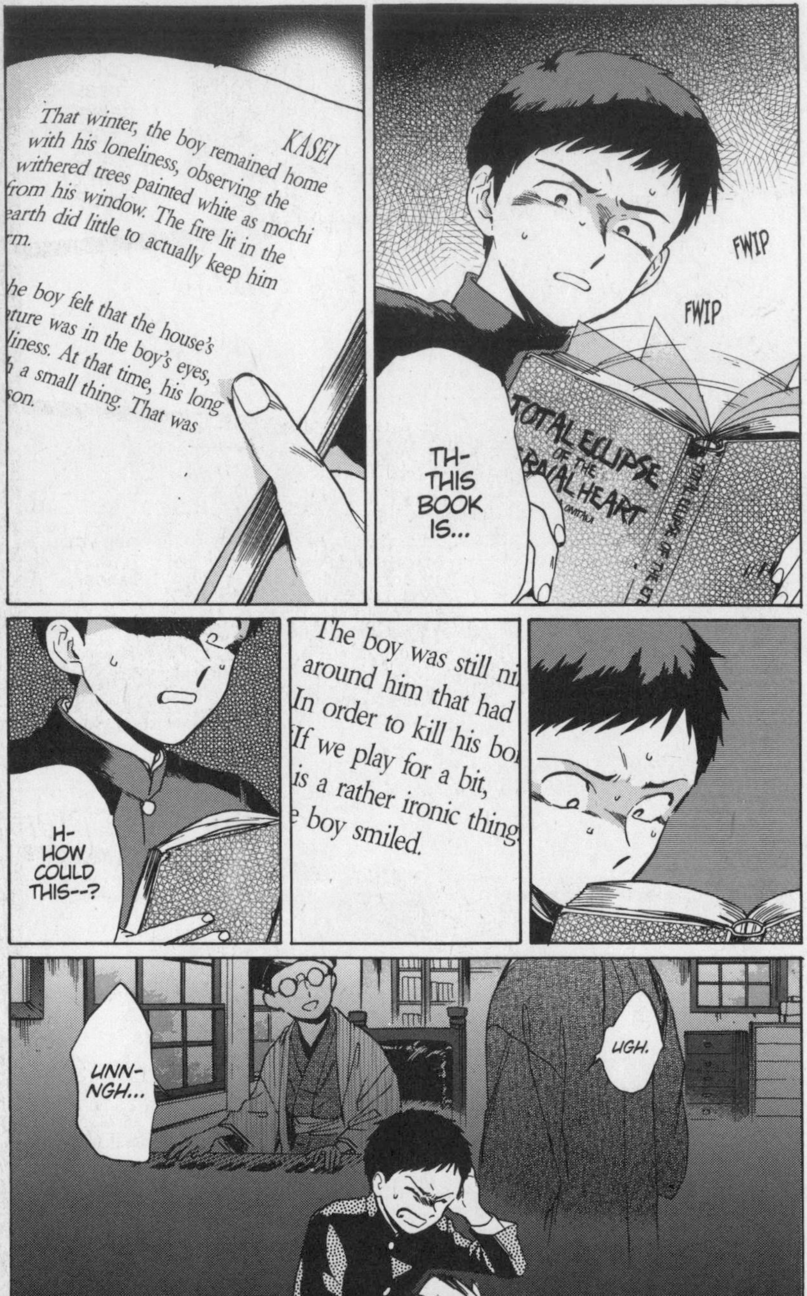
FWIP
FWIP
TH- THIS BOOK IS...
TOTAL ECLIPSE OF THE
KASEI
That winter, the boy remained home
with his loneliness, observing the
withered trees painted white as mochi
from his window. The fire lit in the
earth did little to actually keep him
rm.
he boy felt that the house's
ature was in the boy's eyes,
liness. At that time, his long
h a small thing. That was
son.
The boy was still ni
around him that had
In order to kill his bo
If we play for a bit,
is a rather ironic thing
e boy smiled.
H- HOW COULD THIS--?
UGH.
UNN- NGH...

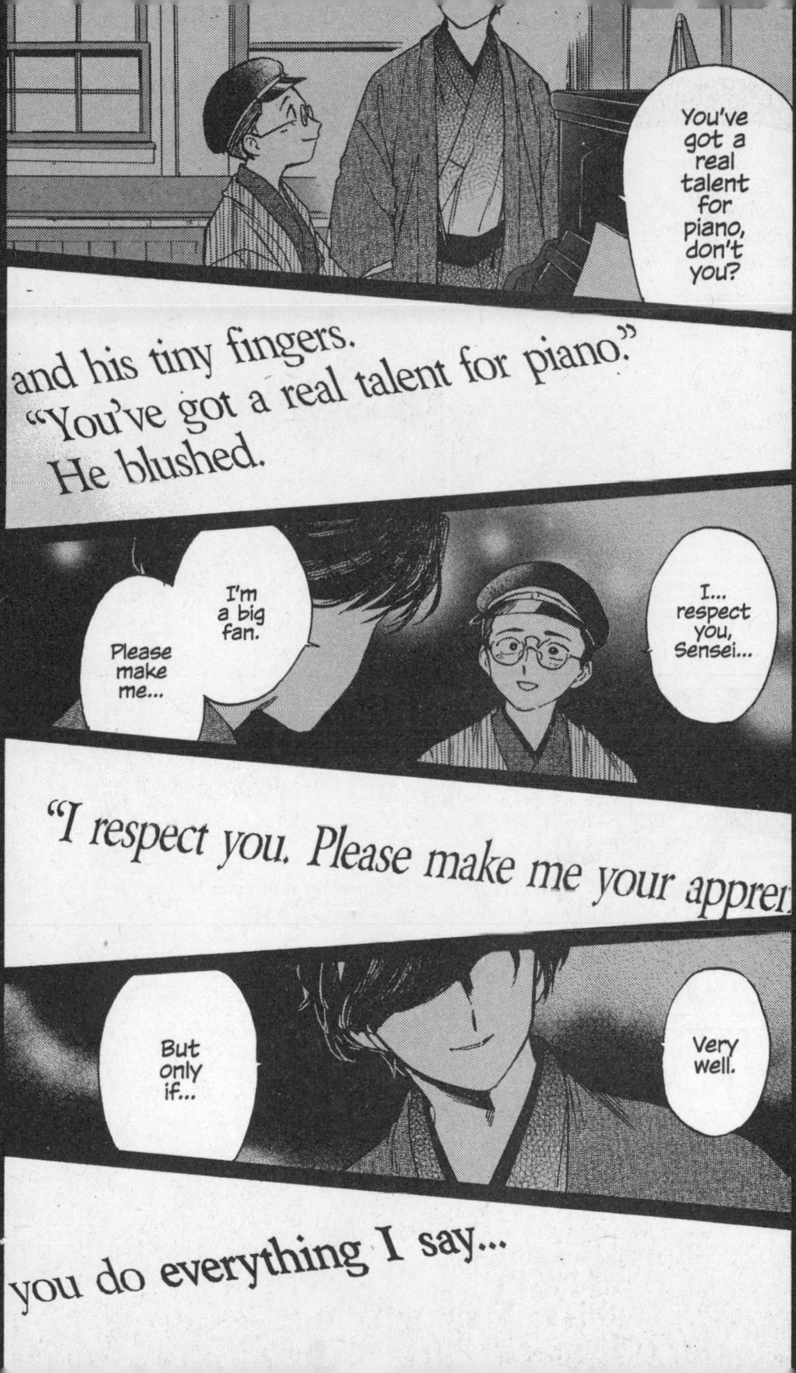

You've got a real talent for piano, don't you?
and his tiny fingers.
“You've got a real talent for piano.”
He blushed.
I... respect you, Sensei...
I'm a big fan.
Please make me...
“I respect you. Please make me your appre
Very well.
But only if...
you do everything I say...

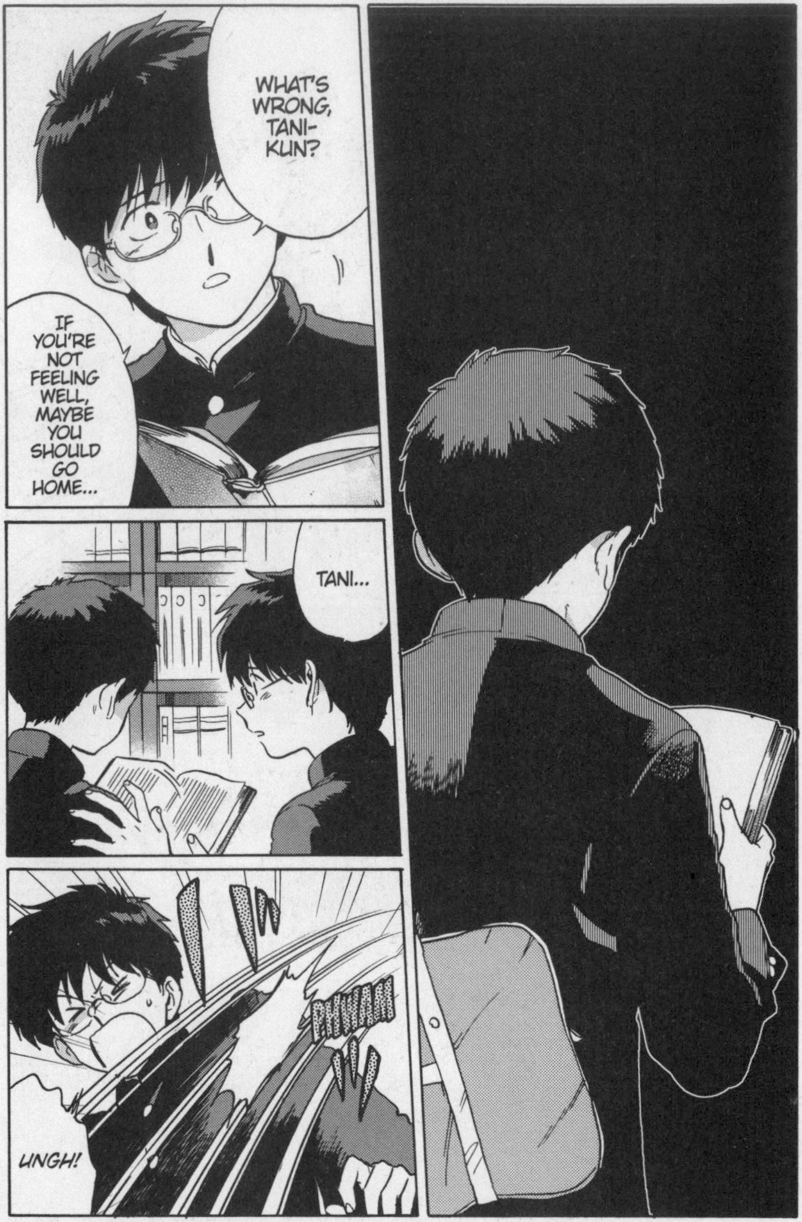
WHAT'S WRONG, TANI-KUN?
IF YOU'RE NOT FEELING WELL, MAYBE YOU SHOULD GO HOME...
TANI...
PHWAM
UNGH!

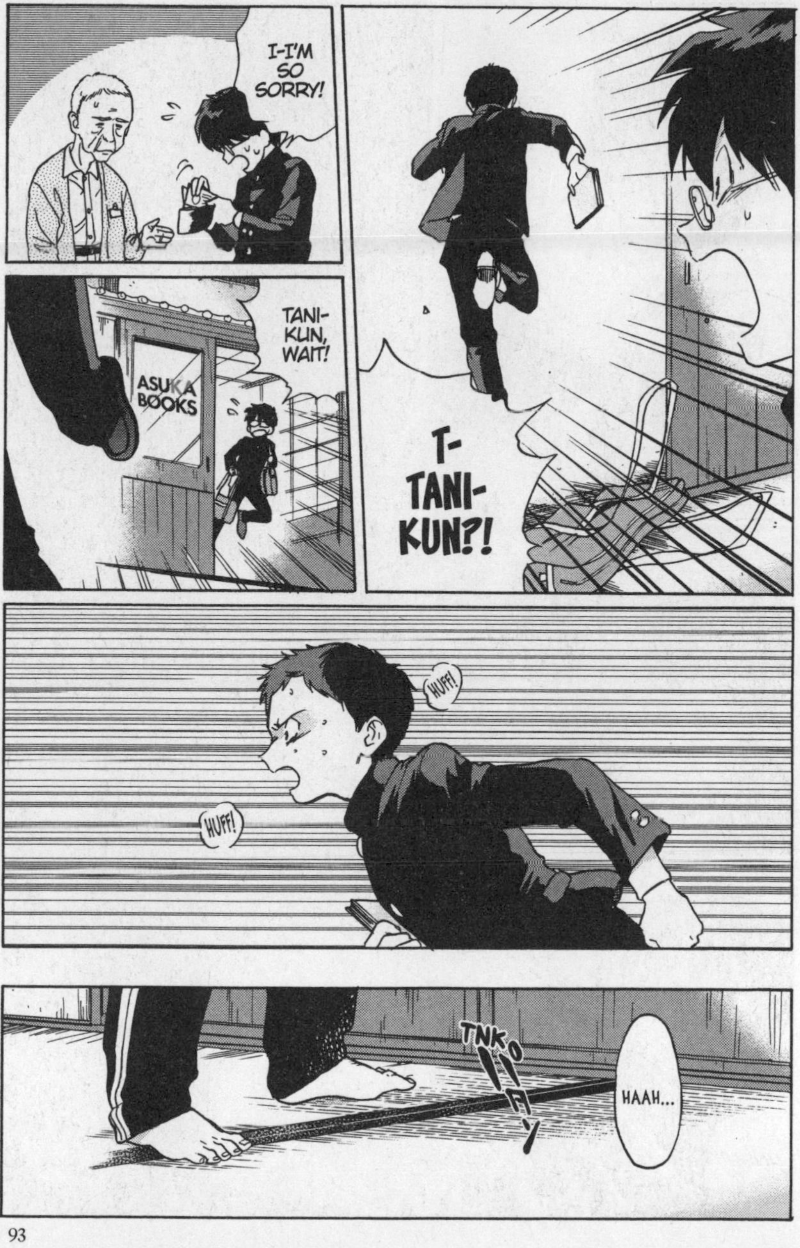
T-TANI-KUN?!
I-I'M SO SORRY!
TANI-KUN, WAIT!
ASUKA BOOKS
HUFF!
HUFF!
HAAH...
TNKO

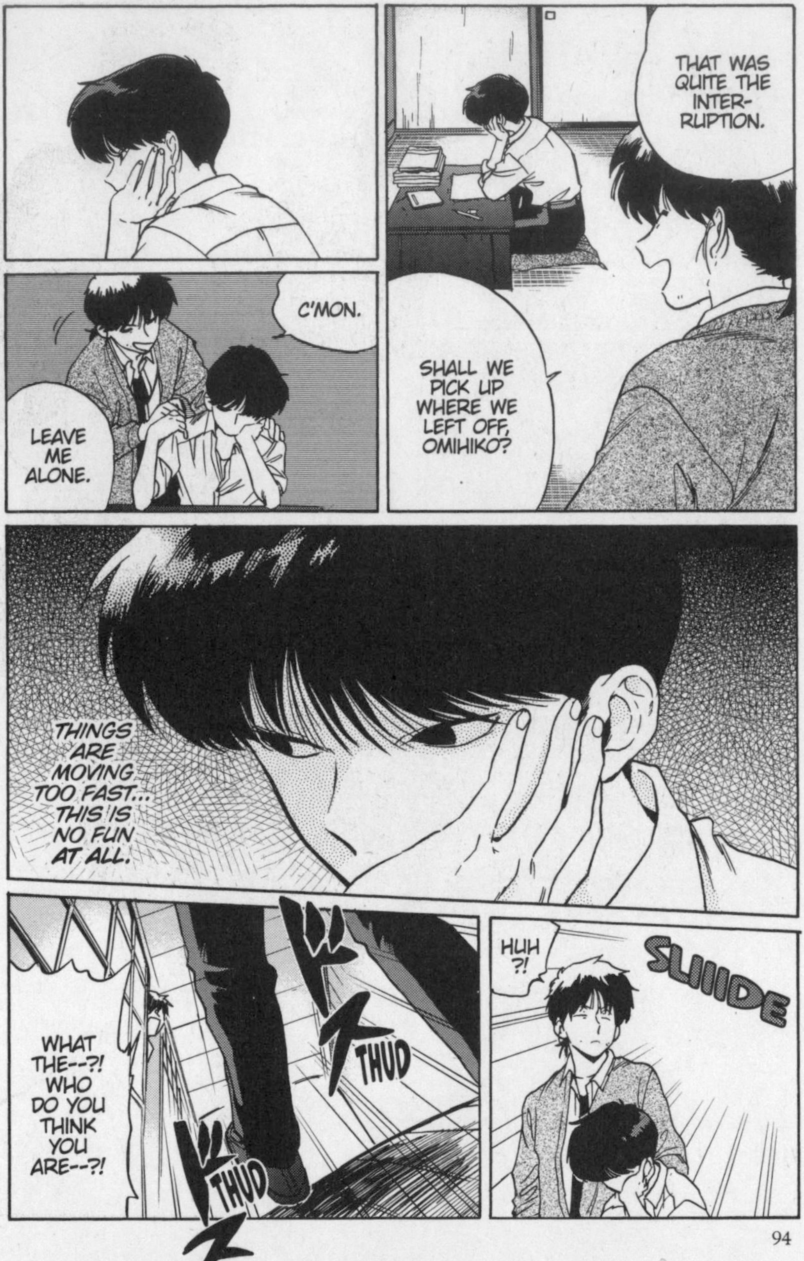
THAT WAS QUITE THE INTER-RUPTION.
SHALL WE PICK UP WHERE WE LEFT OFF, OMIHIKO?
C'MON.
LEAVE ME ALONE.
THINGS ARE MOVING TOO FAST... THIS IS NO FUN AT ALL.
SLIIDE
HUH ?!
THUD
WHAT THE--?! WHO DO YOU THINK YOU ARE--?!
THUD

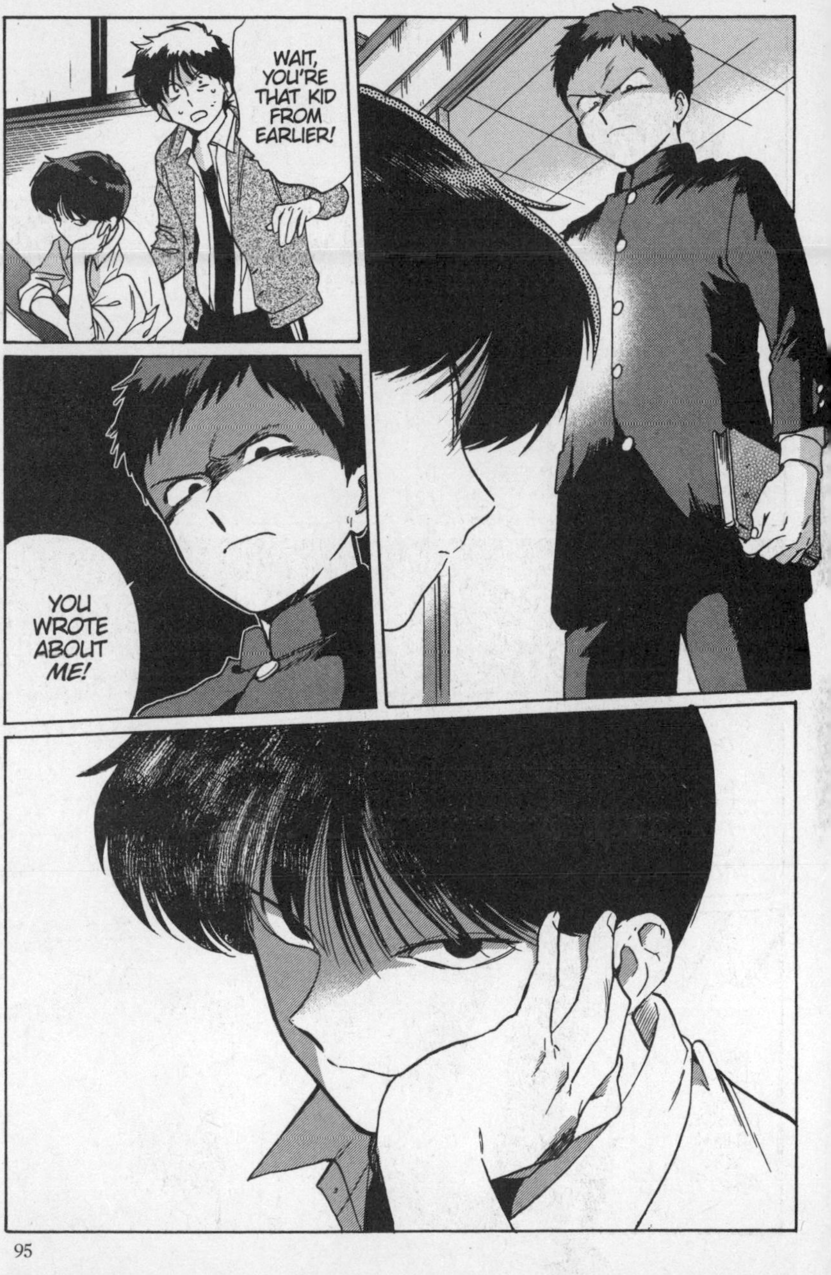
WAIT, YOU'RE THAT KID FROM EARLIER!
YOU WROTE ABOUT ME!

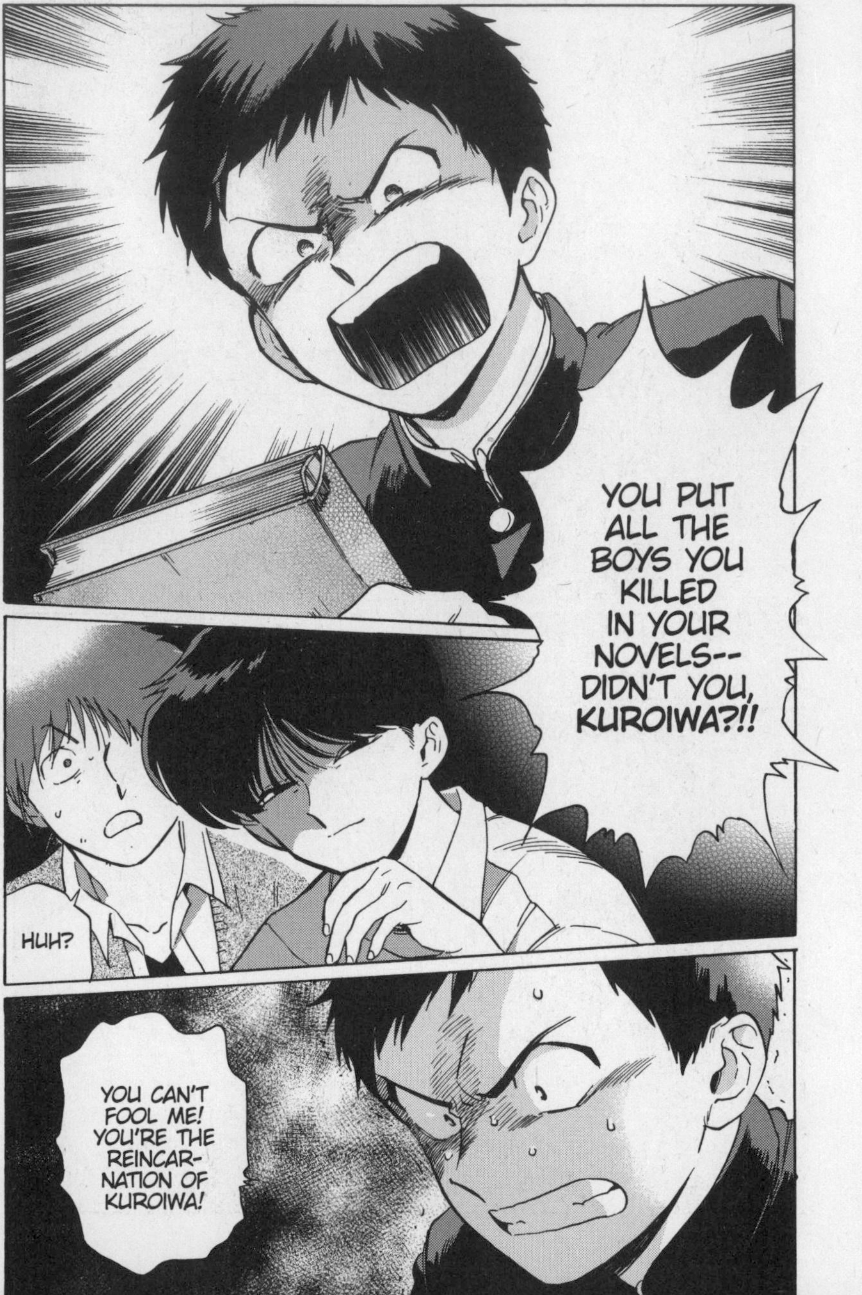
YOU PUT ALL THE BOYS YOU KILLED IN YOUR NOVELS-- DIDN'T YOU, KUROIWA?!!
HUH?
YOU CAN'T FOOL ME! YOU'RE THE REINCAR-NATION OF KUROIWA!

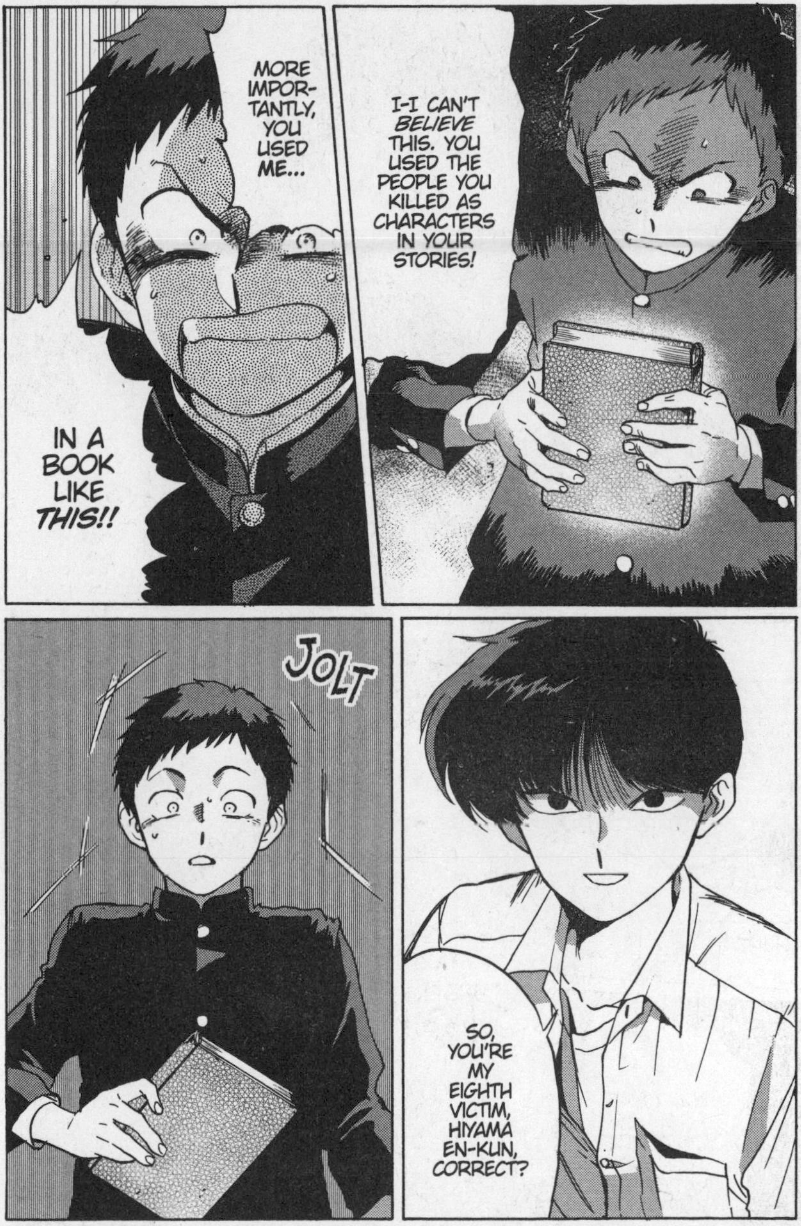
I-I CAN'T BELIEVE THIS. YOU USED THE PEOPLE YOU KILLED AS CHARACTERS IN YOUR STORIES!
MORE IMPORTANTLY, YOU USED ME...
IN A BOOK LIKE THIS!!
SO, YOU'RE MY EIGHTH VICTIM, HIYAMA EN-KUN, CORRECT?
JOLT

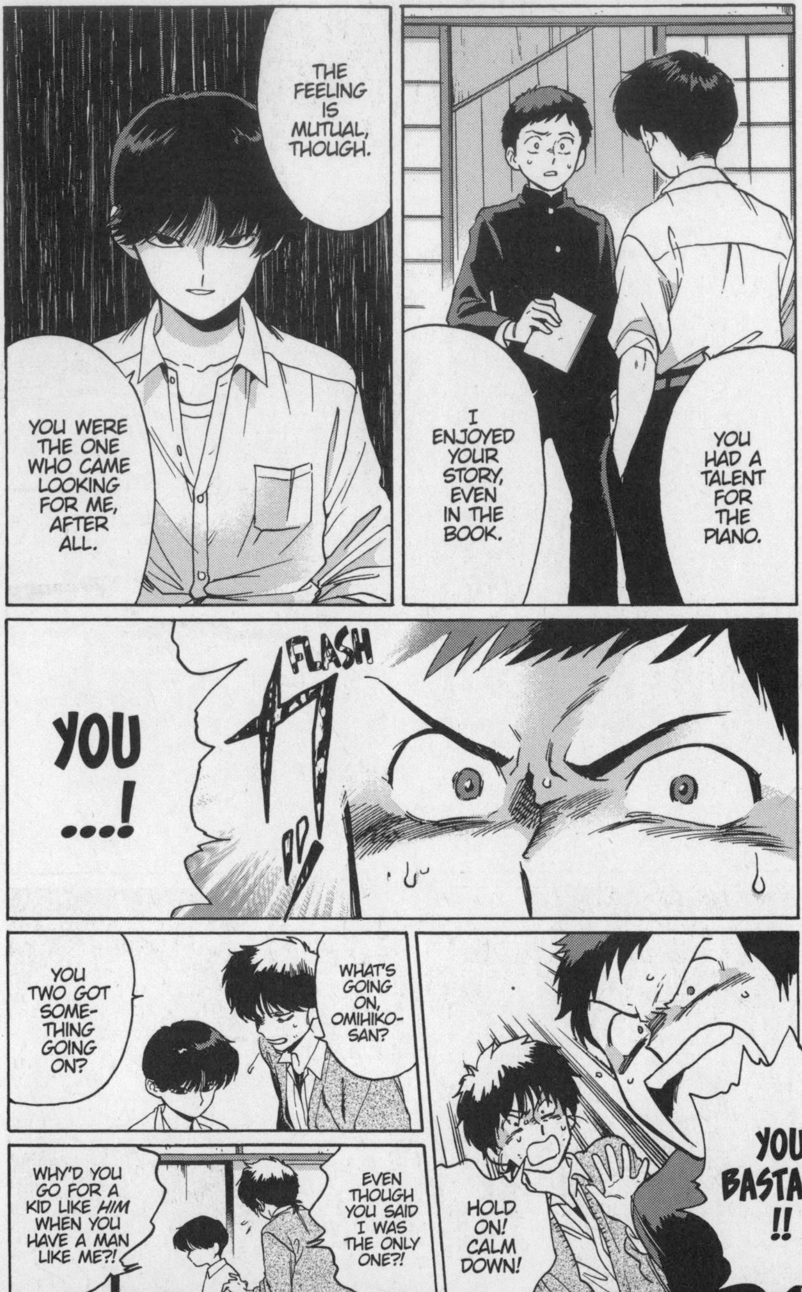
YOU HAD A TALENT FOR THE PIANO.
I ENJOYED YOUR STORY, EVEN IN THE BOOK.
THE FEELING IS MUTUAL, THOUGH.
YOU WERE THE ONE WHO CAME LOOKING FOR ME, AFTER ALL.
FLASH
YOU ....!
YOU BASTARD !!
HOLD ON! CALM DOWN!
WHAT'S GOING ON, OMIHIKO-SAN?
YOU TWO GOT SOME-THING GOING ON?
EVEN THOUGH YOU SAID I WAS THE ONLY ONE?!
WHY'D YOU GO FOR A KID LIKE *HIM* WHEN YOU HAVE A MAN LIKE ME?!

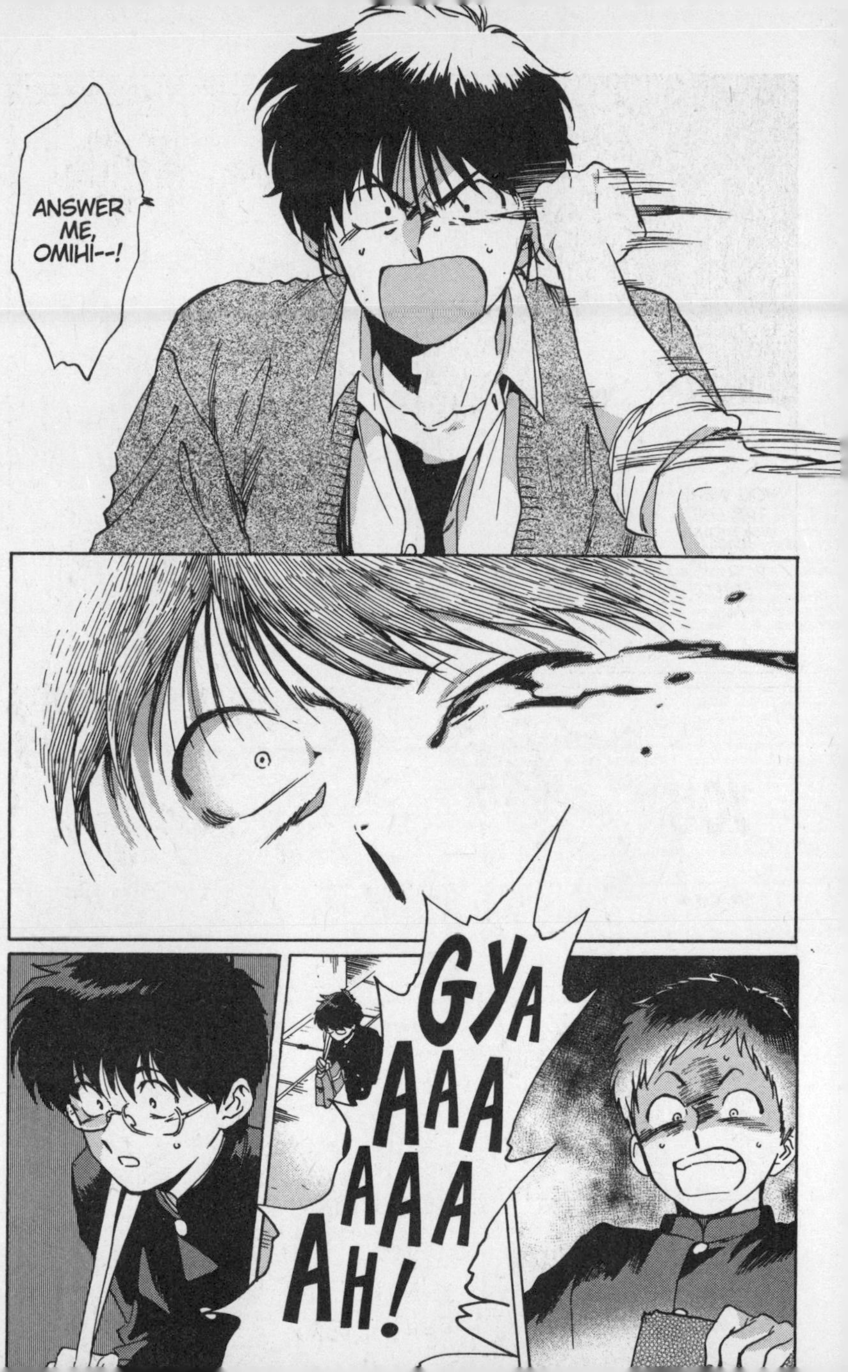
ANSWER ME, OMIHI--!
GYAAAAAAAAAH!

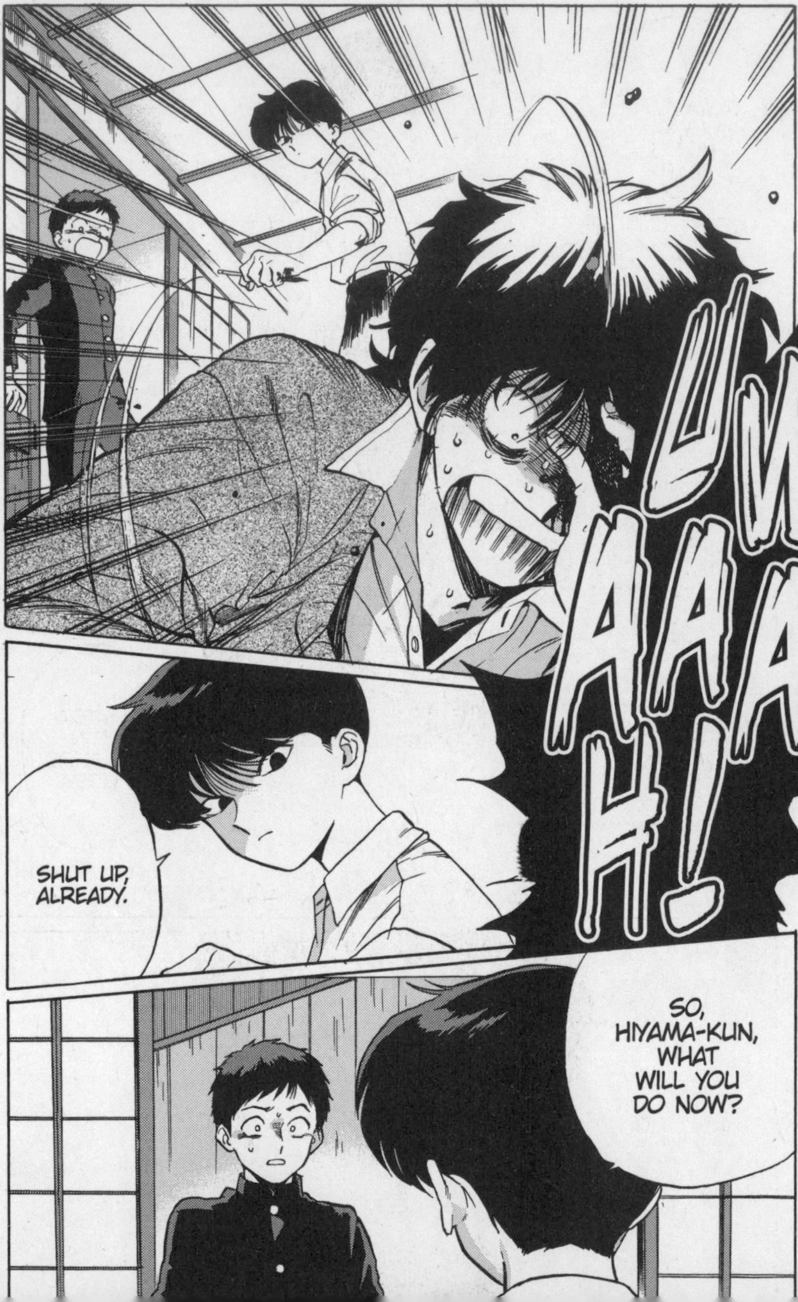
UWAAAH!
SHUT UP, ALREADY.
SO, HIYAMA-KUN, WHAT WILL YOU DO NOW?

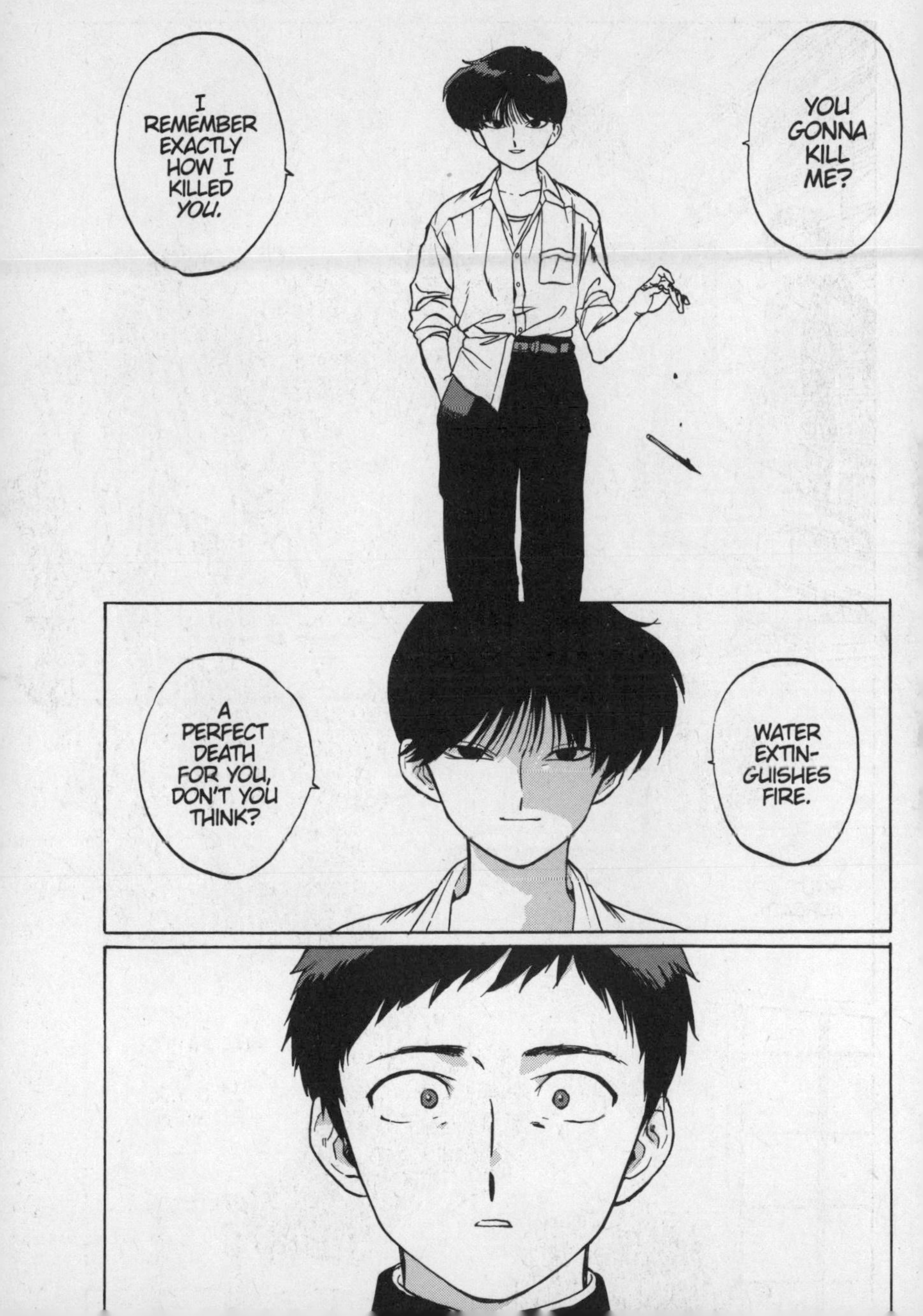
YOU GONNA KILL ME?
I REMEMBER EXACTLY HOW I KILLED YOU.
WATER EXTIN-GUISHES FIRE.
A PERFECT DEATH FOR YOU, DON'T YOU THINK?

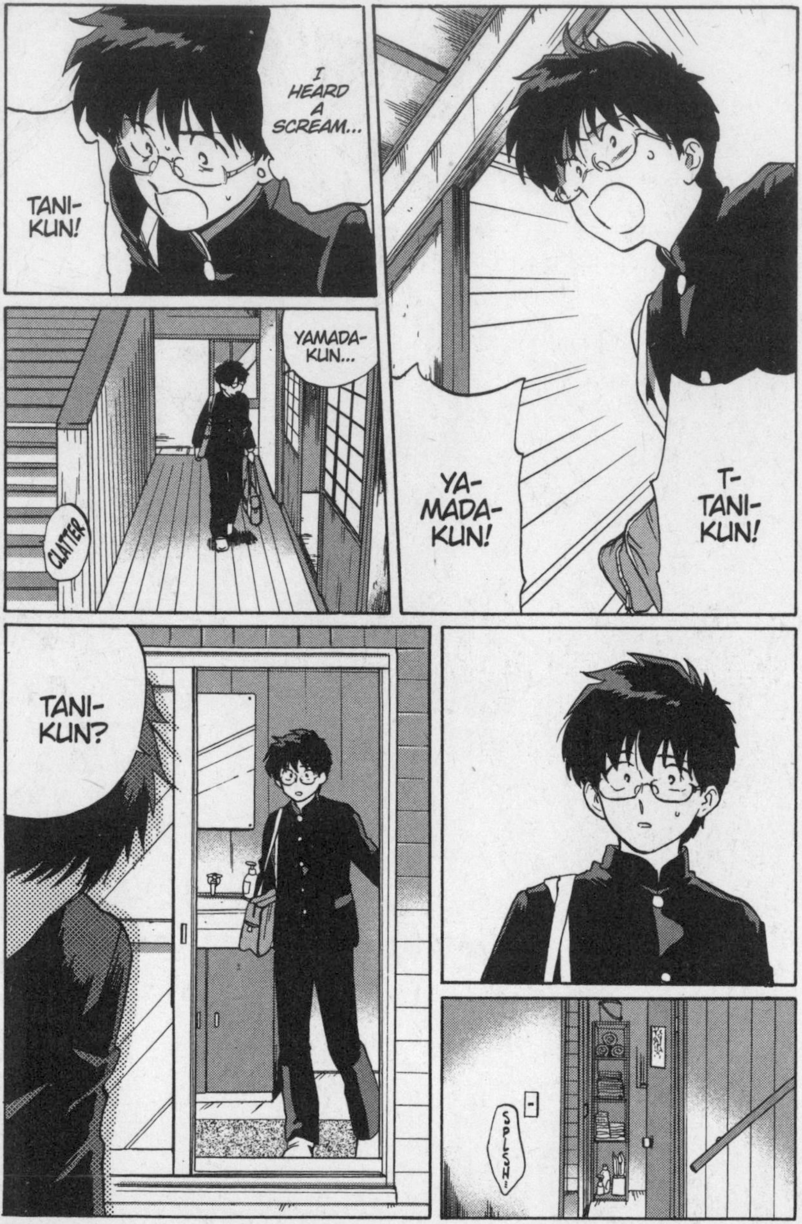
T-TANI-KUN!
YA-MADA-KUN!
I HEARD A SCREAM...
TANI-KUN!
YAMADA-KUN...
CLATTER
SPLSH...
TANI-KUN?

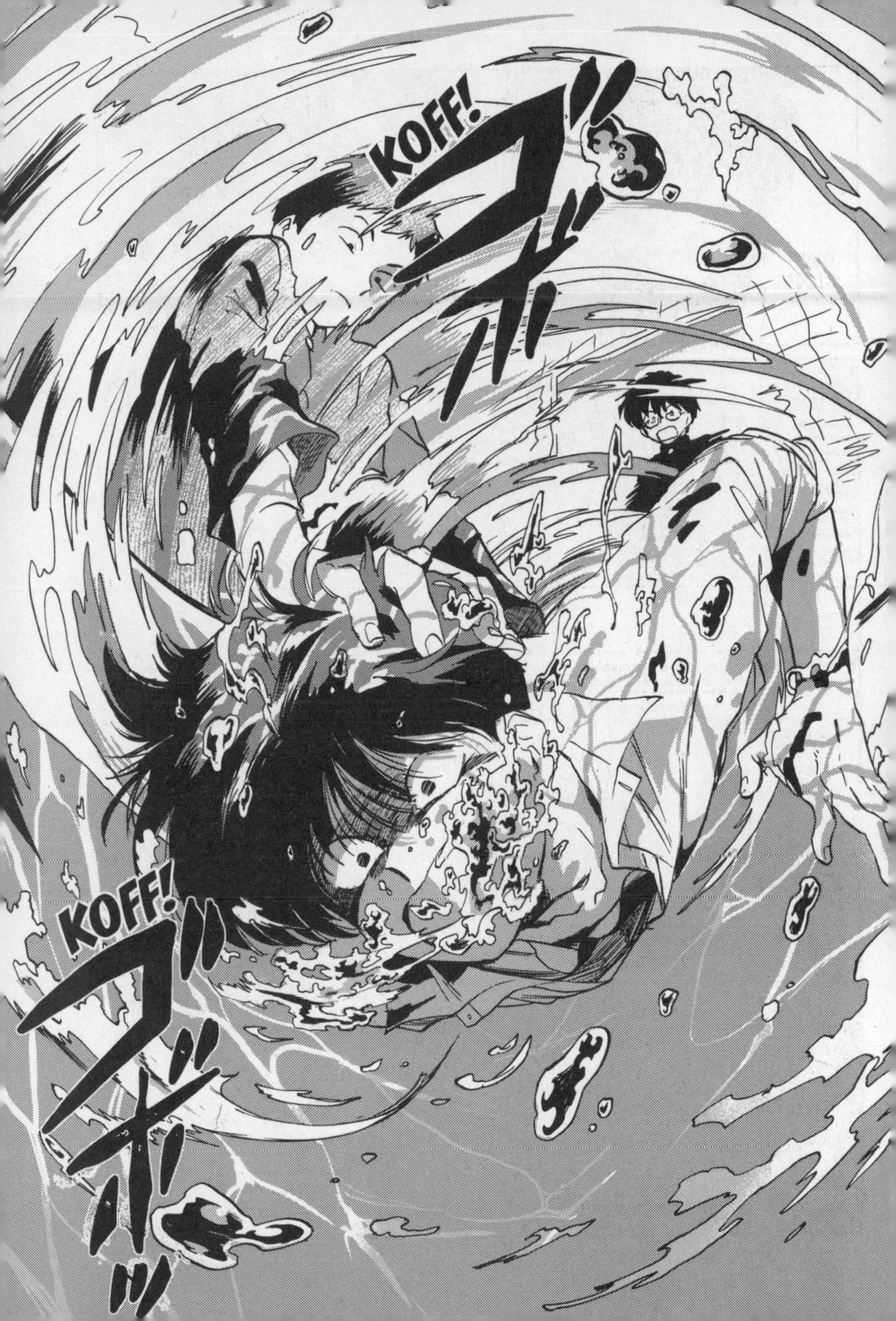
KOFF!
KOFF!

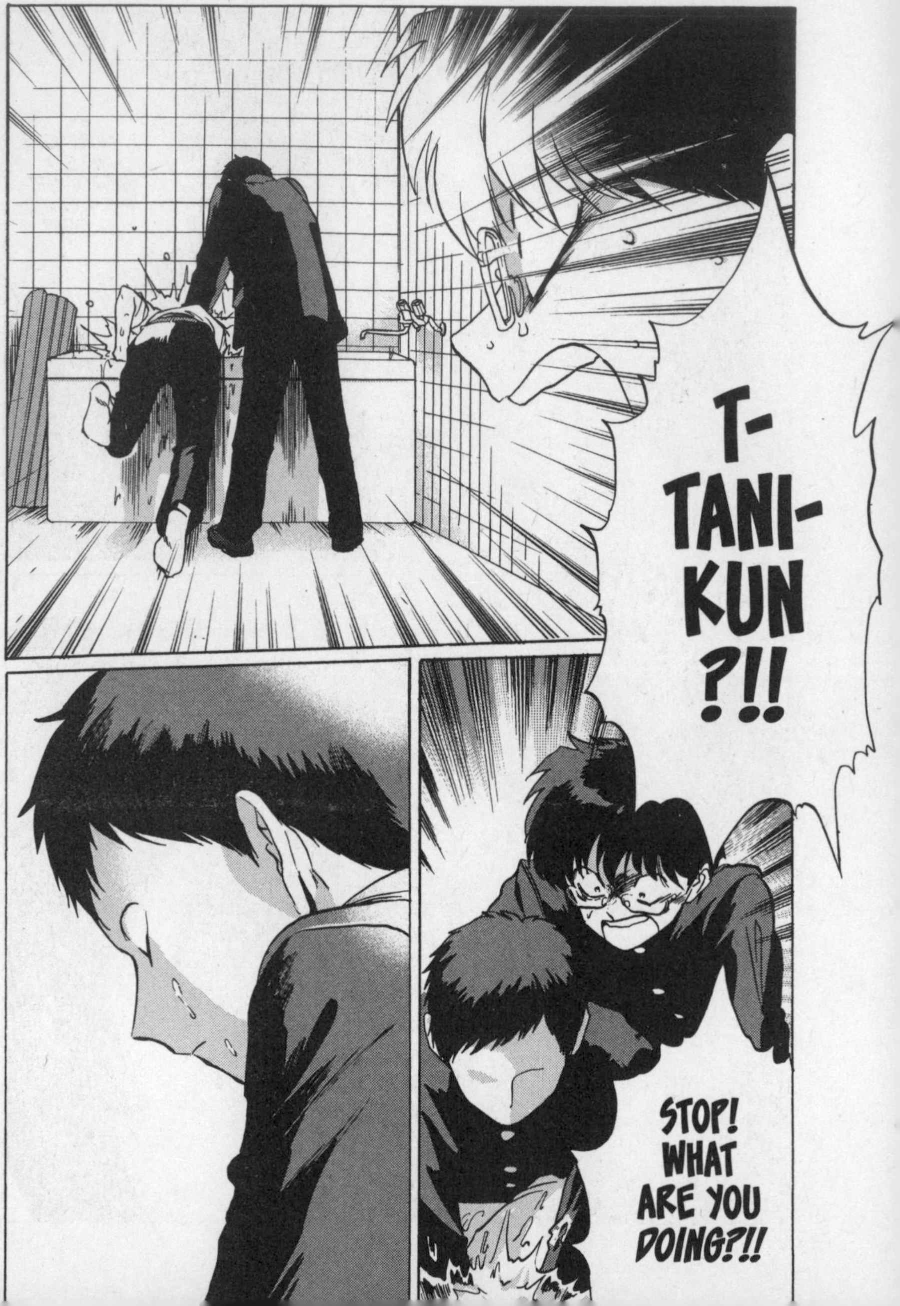
T-TANI-KUN?!!
STOP! WHAT ARE YOU DOING?!!

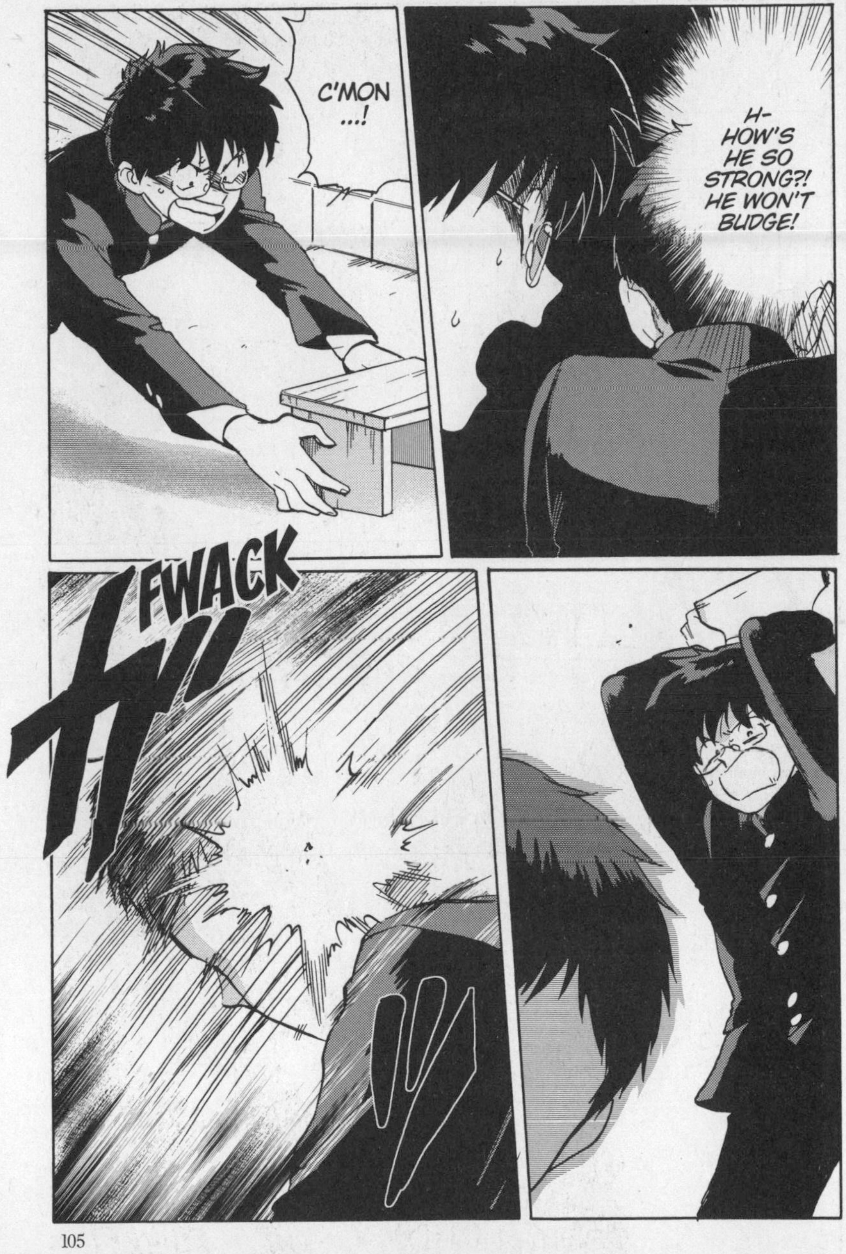
H- HOW'S HE SO STRONG?! HE WON'T BUDGE!
C'MON ...!
FWACK

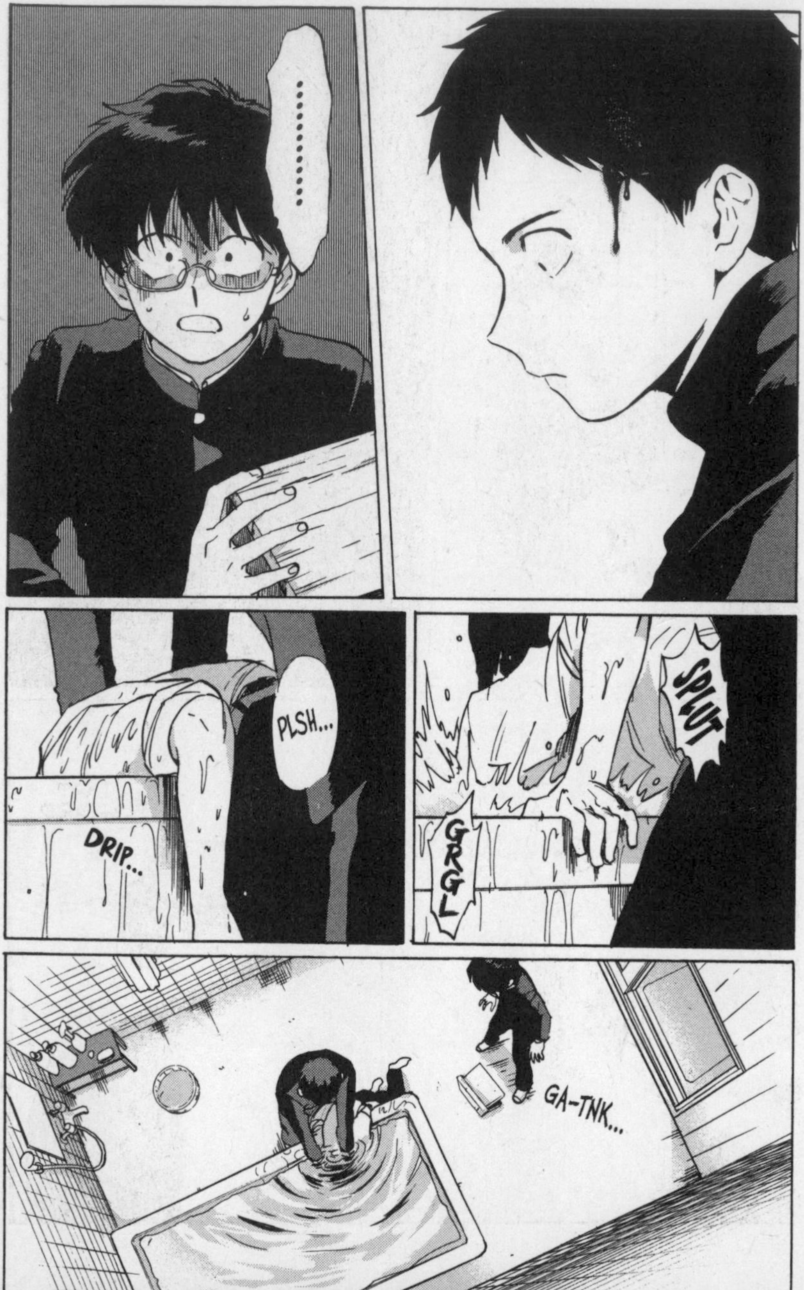
....
SPLUT
GRGL
PLSH...
DRIP...
GA-TNK...

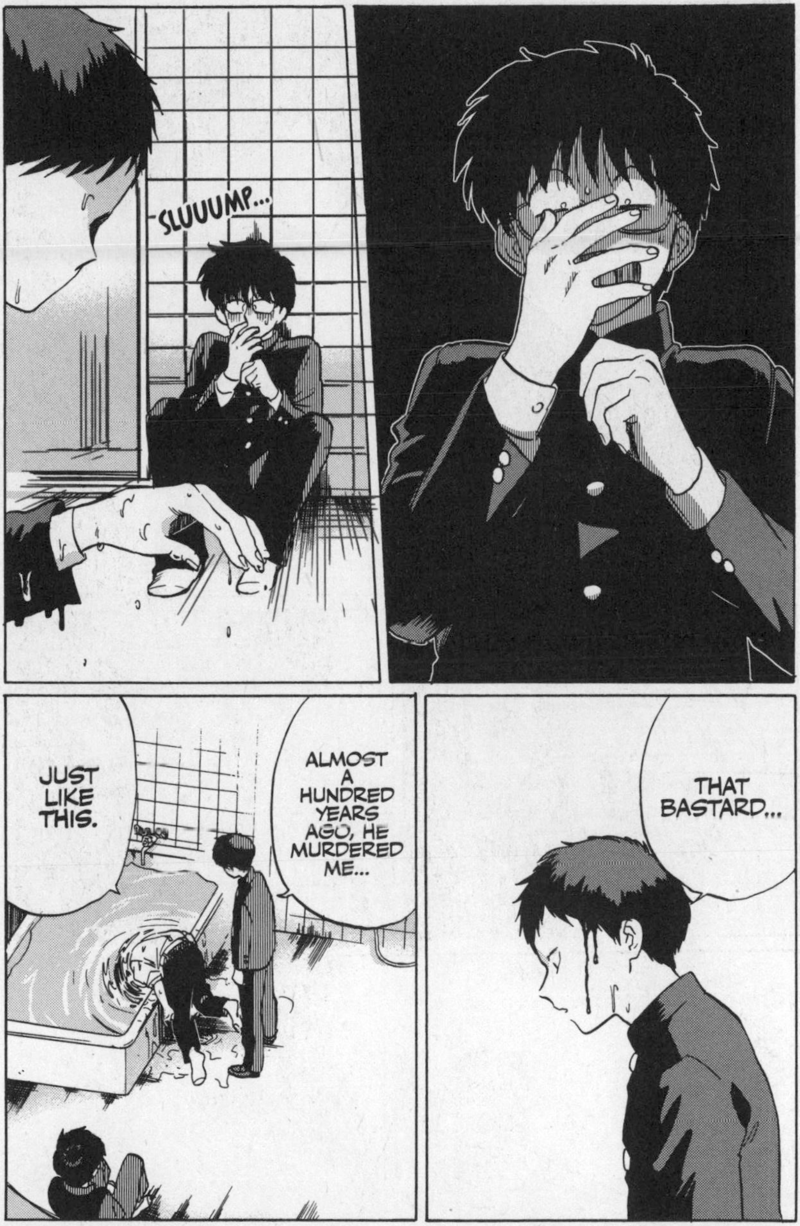
SLUUUMP...
THAT BASTARD...
ALMOST A HUNDRED YEARS AGO, HE MURDERED ME...
JUST LIKE THIS.

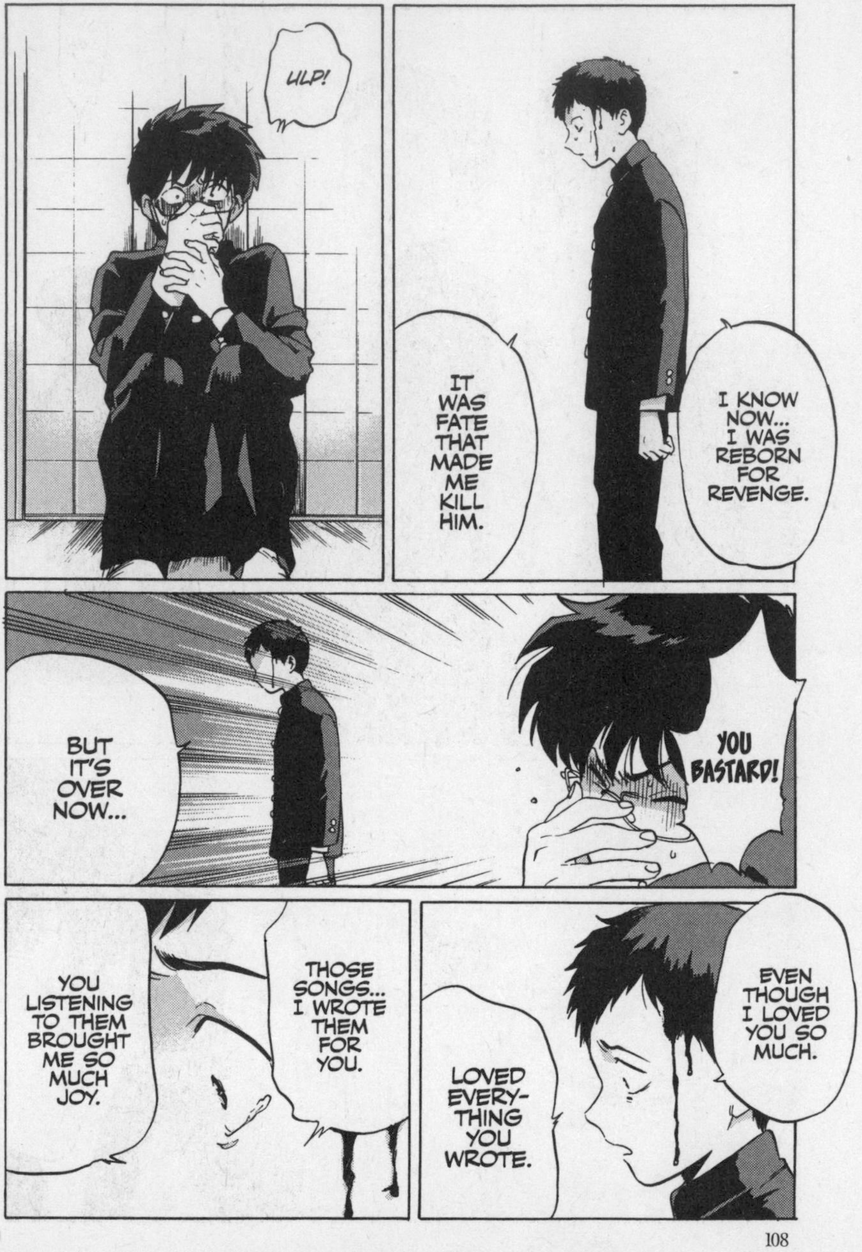
I KNOW NOW... I WAS REBORN FOR REVENGE.
IT WAS FATE THAT MADE ME KILL HIM.
ULP!
YOU BASTARD!
BUT IT'S OVER NOW...
EVEN THOUGH I LOVED YOU SO MUCH.
LOVED EVERY-THING YOU WROTE.
THOSE SONGS... I WROTE THEM FOR YOU.
YOU LISTENING TO THEM BROUGHT ME SO MUCH JOY.

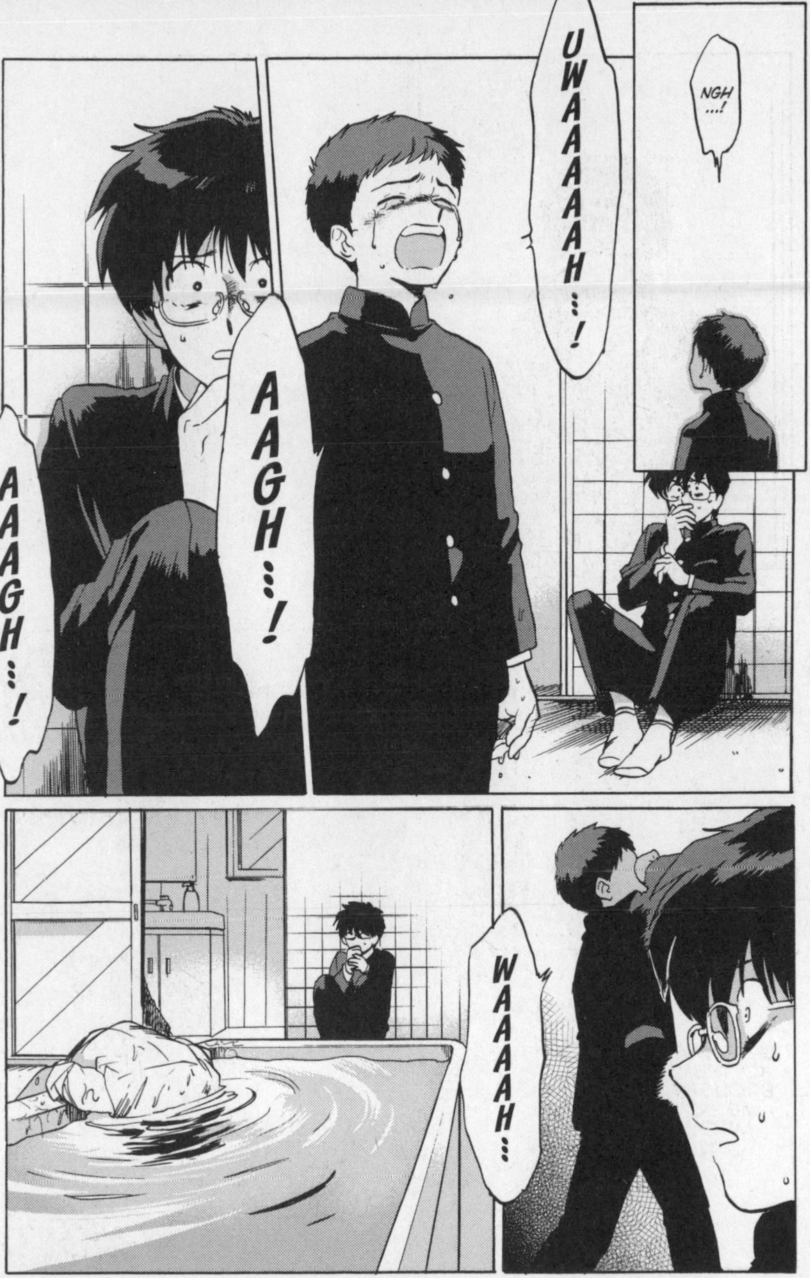
NGH ...!
UWAAAAAAAH...!
AAGH...!
AAAAGH...!
WAAAAAH...

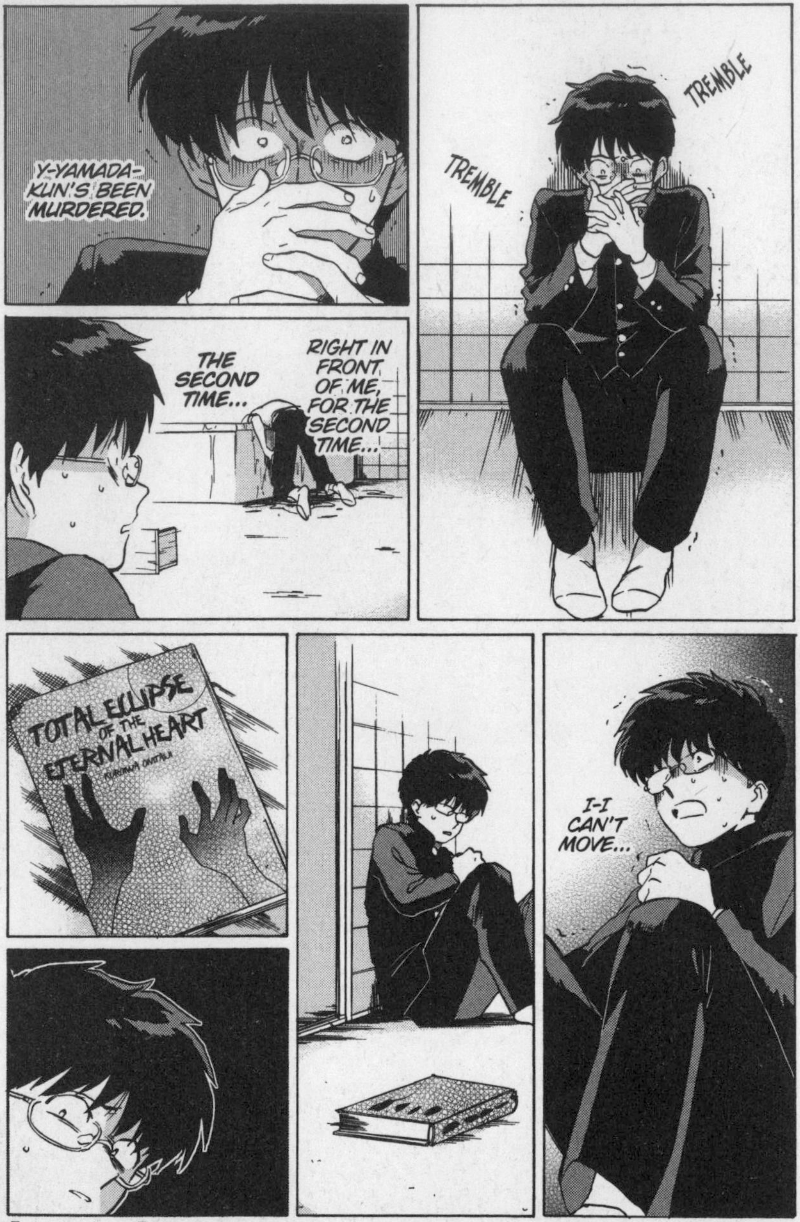
TREMBLE
TREMBLE
Y-YAMADA-KUN'S BEEN MURDERED.
RIGHT IN FRONT OF ME, FOR THE SECOND TIME...
THE SECOND TIME...
I-I CAN'T MOVE...
TOTAL ECLIPSE OF THE ETERNAL HEART

【 Chapter 3 】END

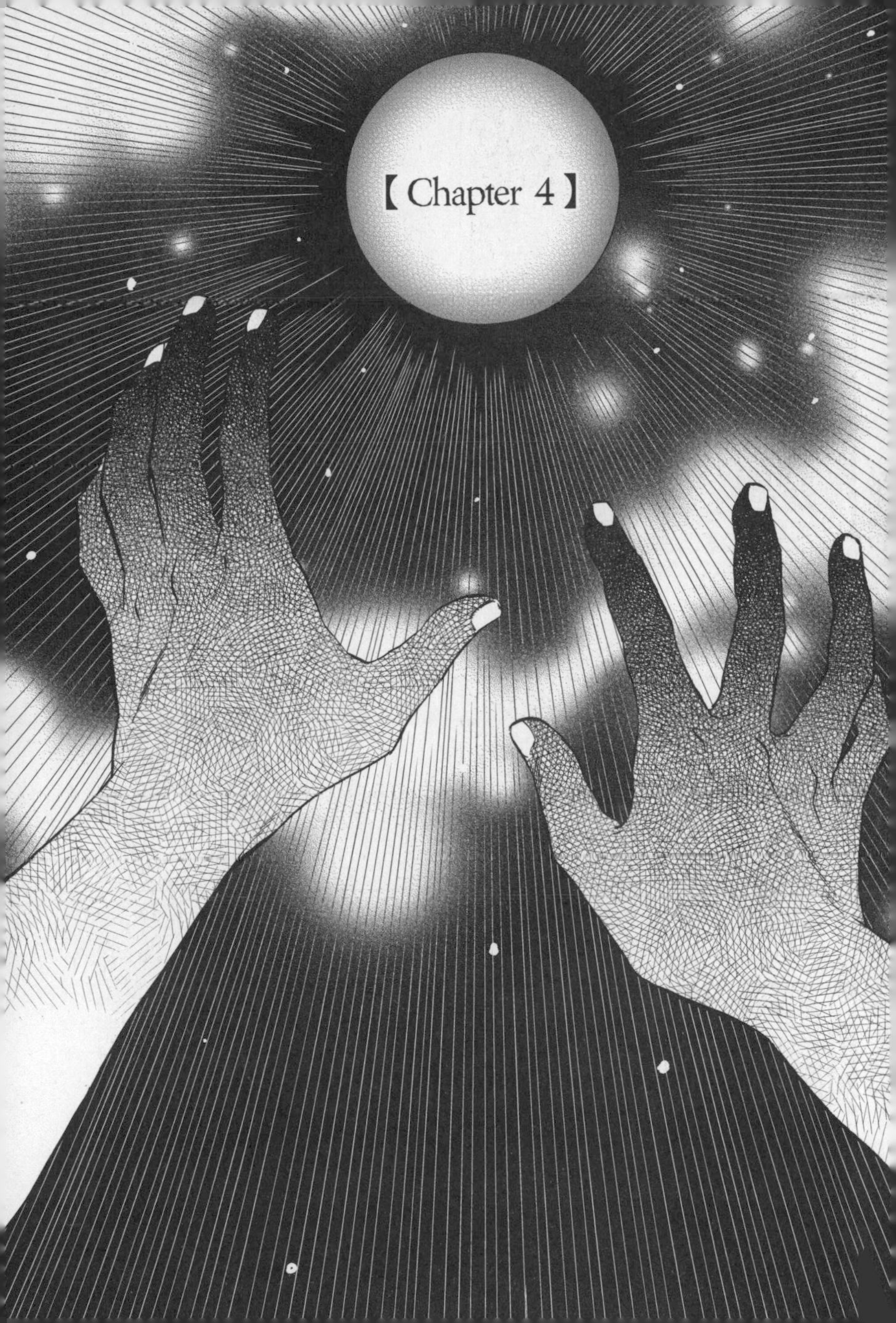
【Chapter 4】

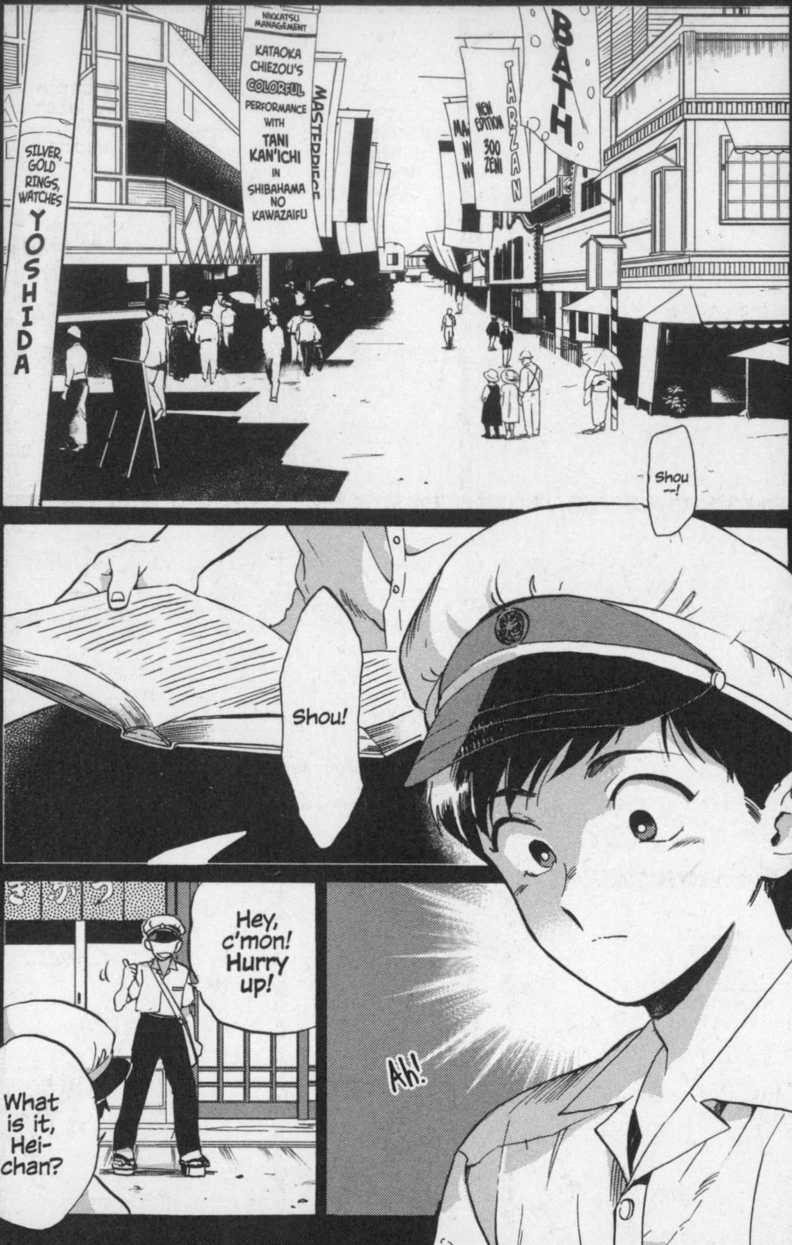
BATH
TARZAN
NEW EDITION 300 ZENI
MASTERPIECE
NIKKATSU MANAGEMENT
KATAOKA CHIEZOU'S COLORFUL PERFORMANCE WITH TANI KAN'ICHI IN SHIBAHAMA NO KAWAZAIFU
SILVER, GOLD RINGS, WATCHES
YOSHIDA
Shou --!
Shou!
Ah!
Hey, c'mon! Hurry up!
What is it, Hei-chan?

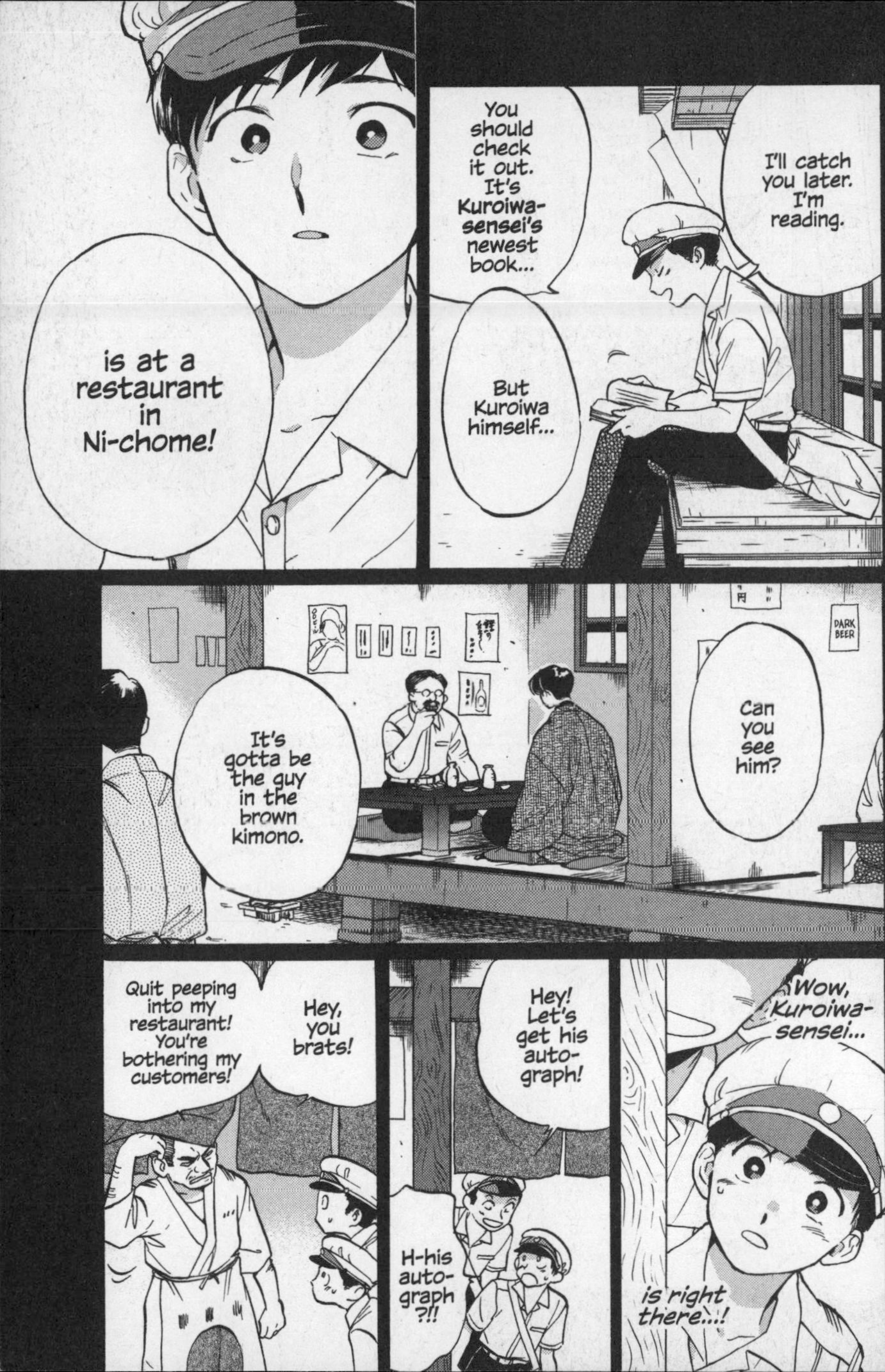
I'll catch you later. I'm reading.
You should check it out. It's Kuroiwa-sensei's newest book...
But Kuroiwa himself...
is at a restaurant in Ni-chome!
DARK BEER
Can you see him?
It's gotta be the guy in the brown kimono.
Wow, Kuroiwa-sensei...
is right there...!
Hey! Let's get his auto-graph!
H-his auto-graph?!!
Hey, you brats!
Quit peeping into my restaurant! You're bothering my customers!

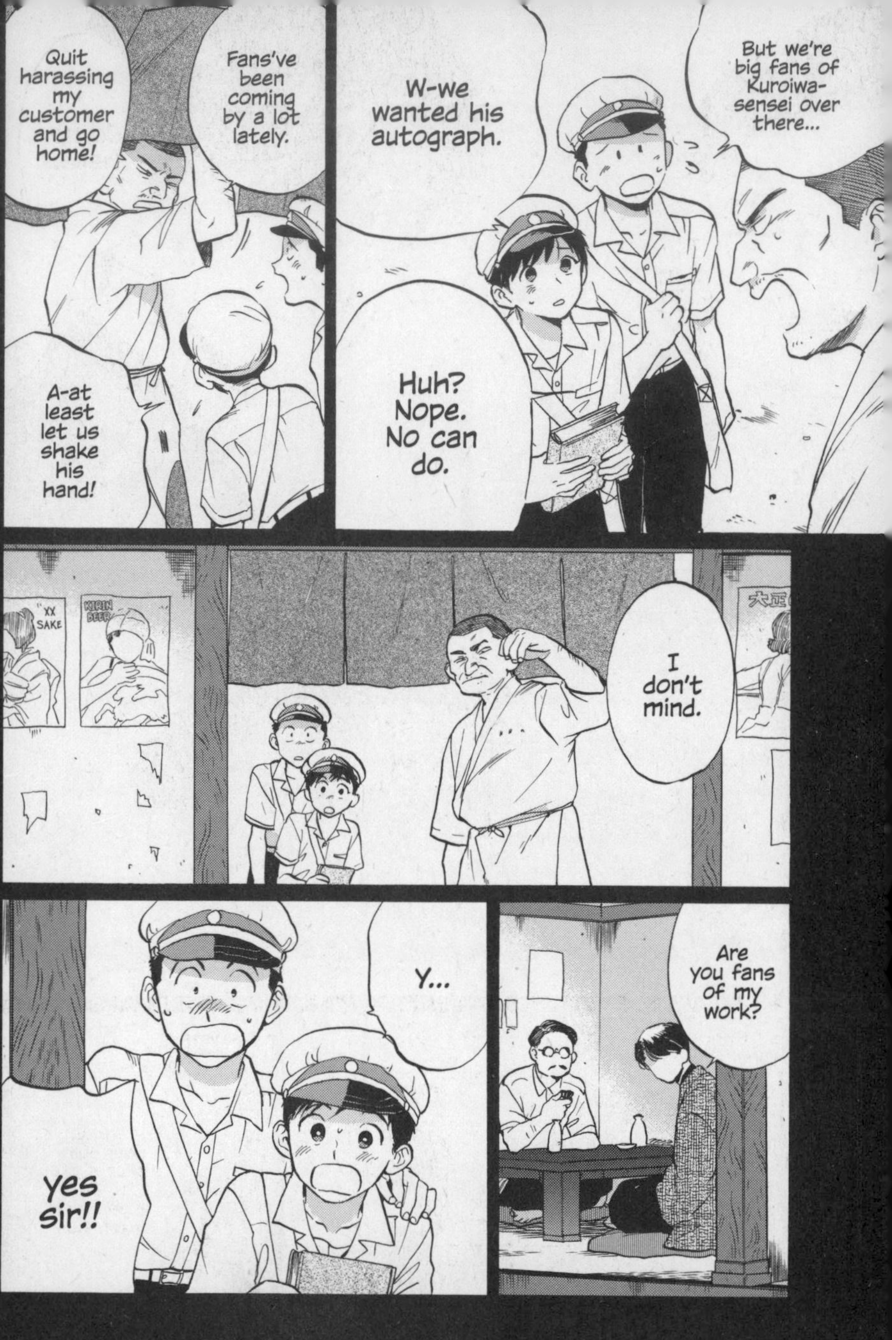
But we're big fans of Kuroiwa-sensei over there...
W-we wanted his autograph.
Huh? Nope. No can do.
Fans've been coming by a lot lately.
Quit harassing my customer and go home!
A-at least let us shake his hand!
I don't mind.
KIRIN BEER
XX SAKE
Are you fans of my work?
Y...
yes sir!!

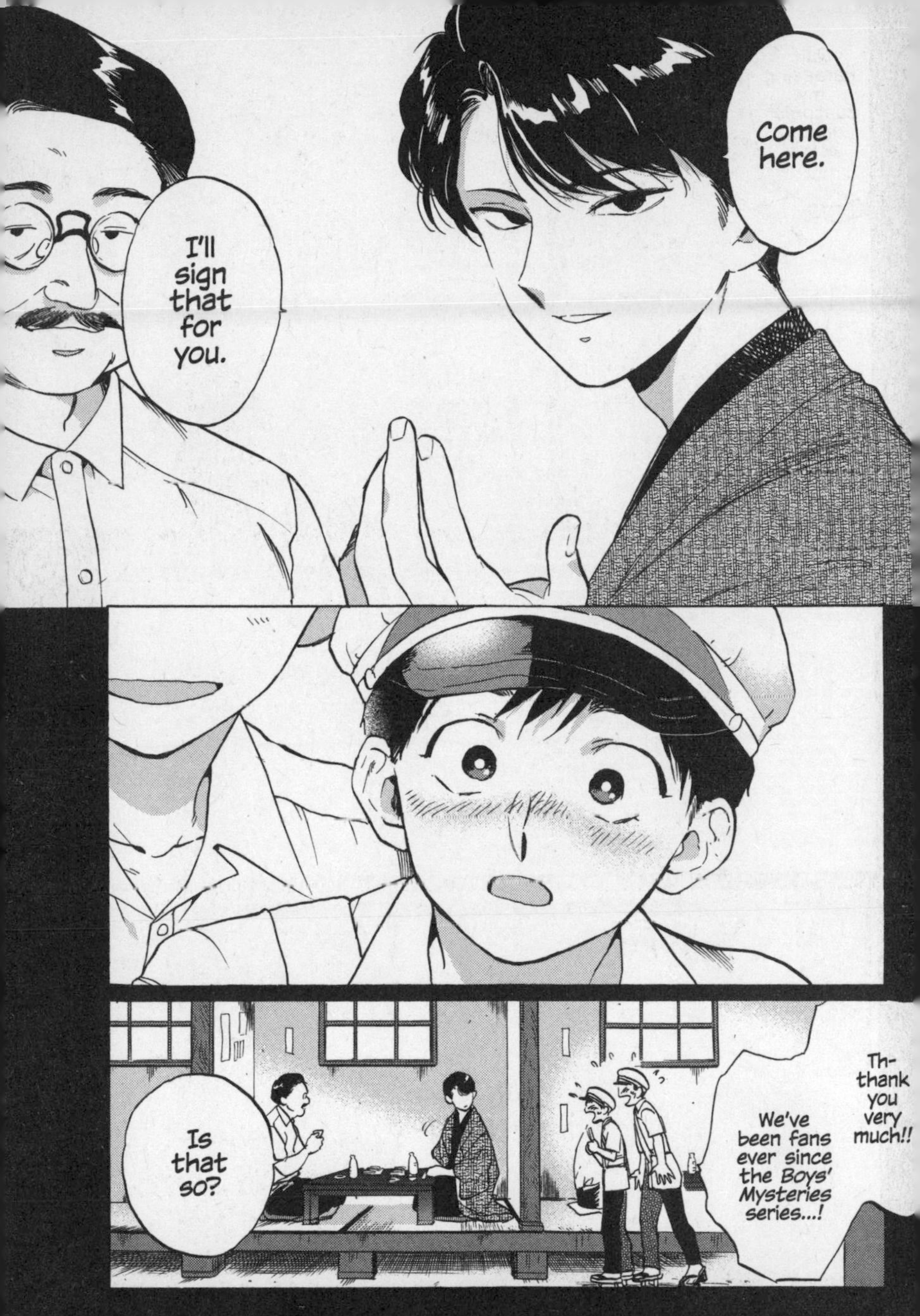
Come here.
I'll sign that for you.
Th-thank you very much!!
We've been fans ever since the Boys' Mysteries series...!
Is that so?

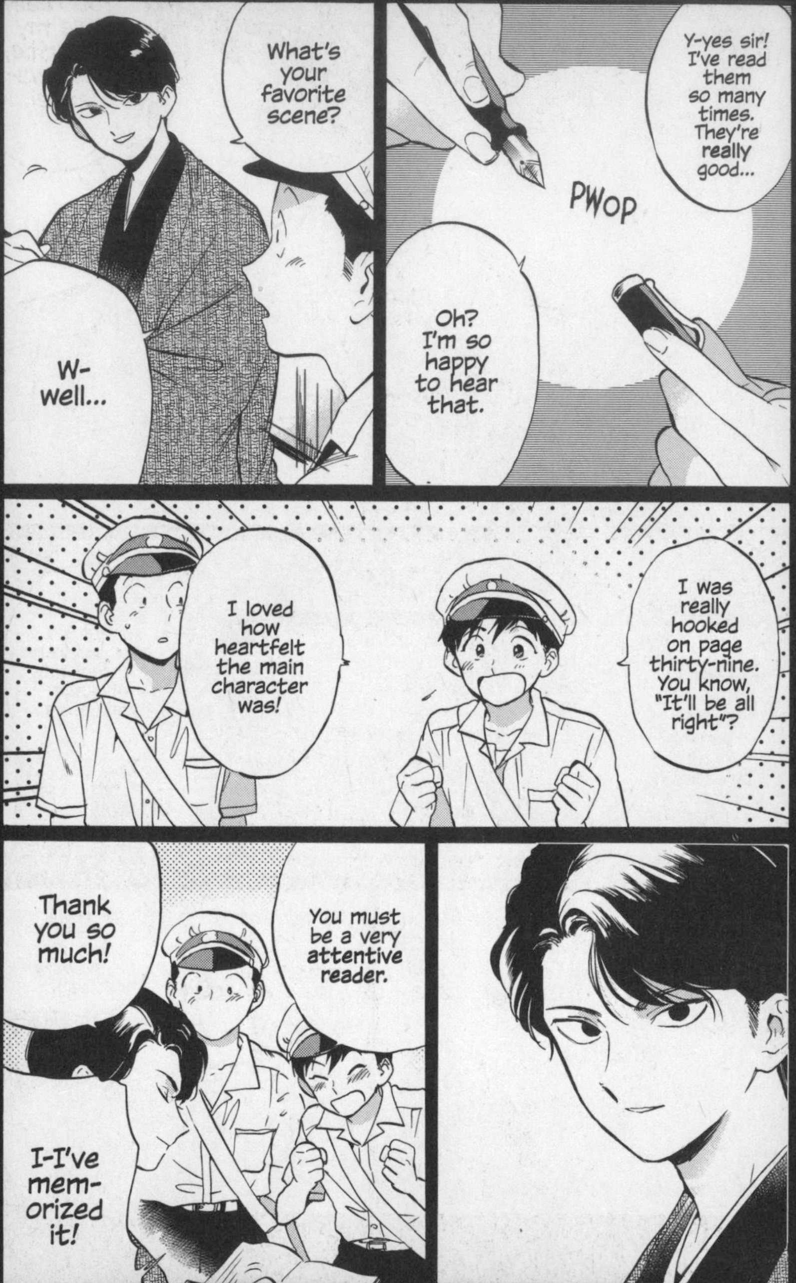
Y-yes sir! I've read them so many times. They're really good...
PWOP
Oh? I'm so happy to hear that.
What's your favorite scene?
W- well...
I was really hooked on page thirty-nine. You know, "It'll be all right"?
I loved how heartfelt the main character was!
You must be a very attentive reader.
Thank you so much!
I-I've mem-orized it!

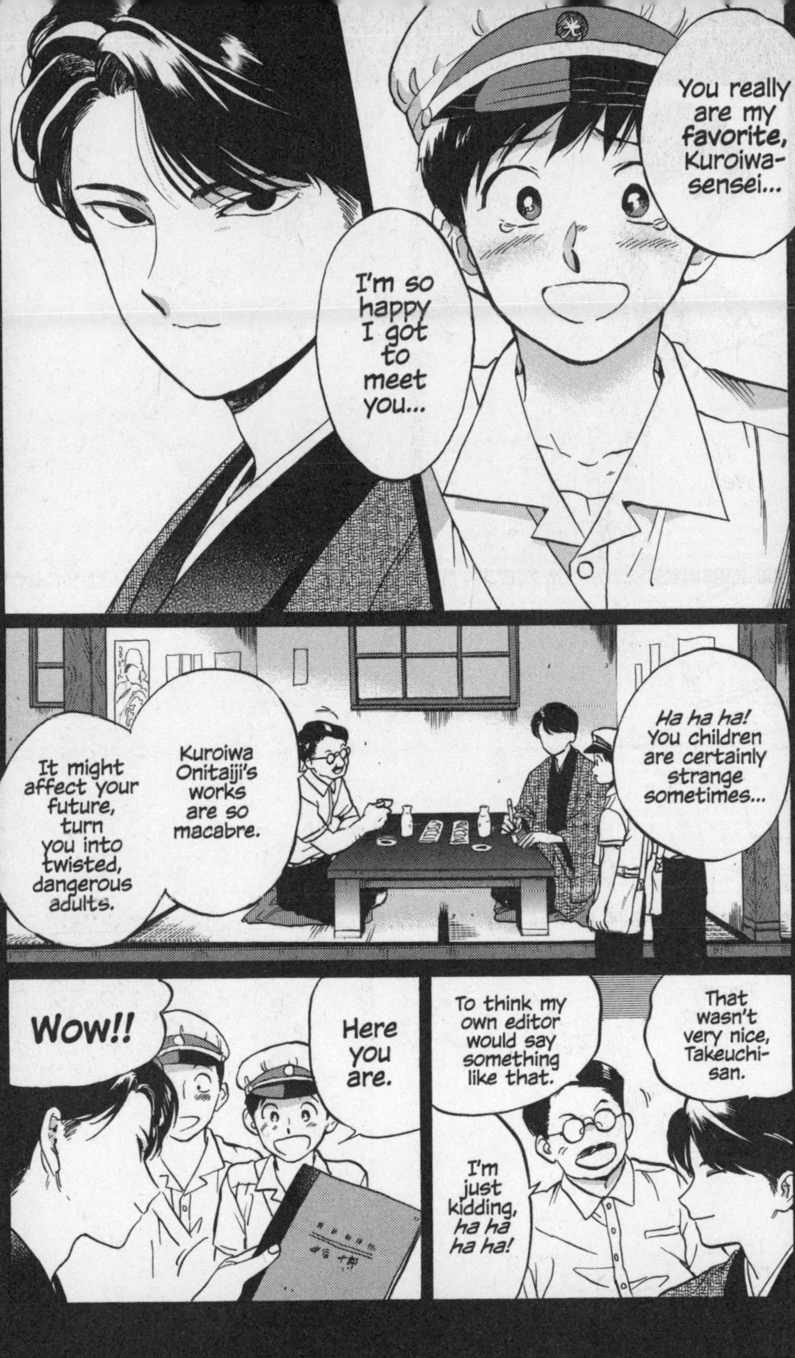
You really are my favorite, Kuroiwa-sensei...
I'm so happy I got to meet you...
Ha ha ha! You children are certainly strange sometimes...
Kuroiwa Onitaiji's works are so macabre.
It might affect your future, turn you into twisted, dangerous adults.
That wasn't very nice, Takeuchi-san.
To think my own editor would say something like that.
I'm just kidding, *ha ha ha ha!*
Here you are.
WOW!!

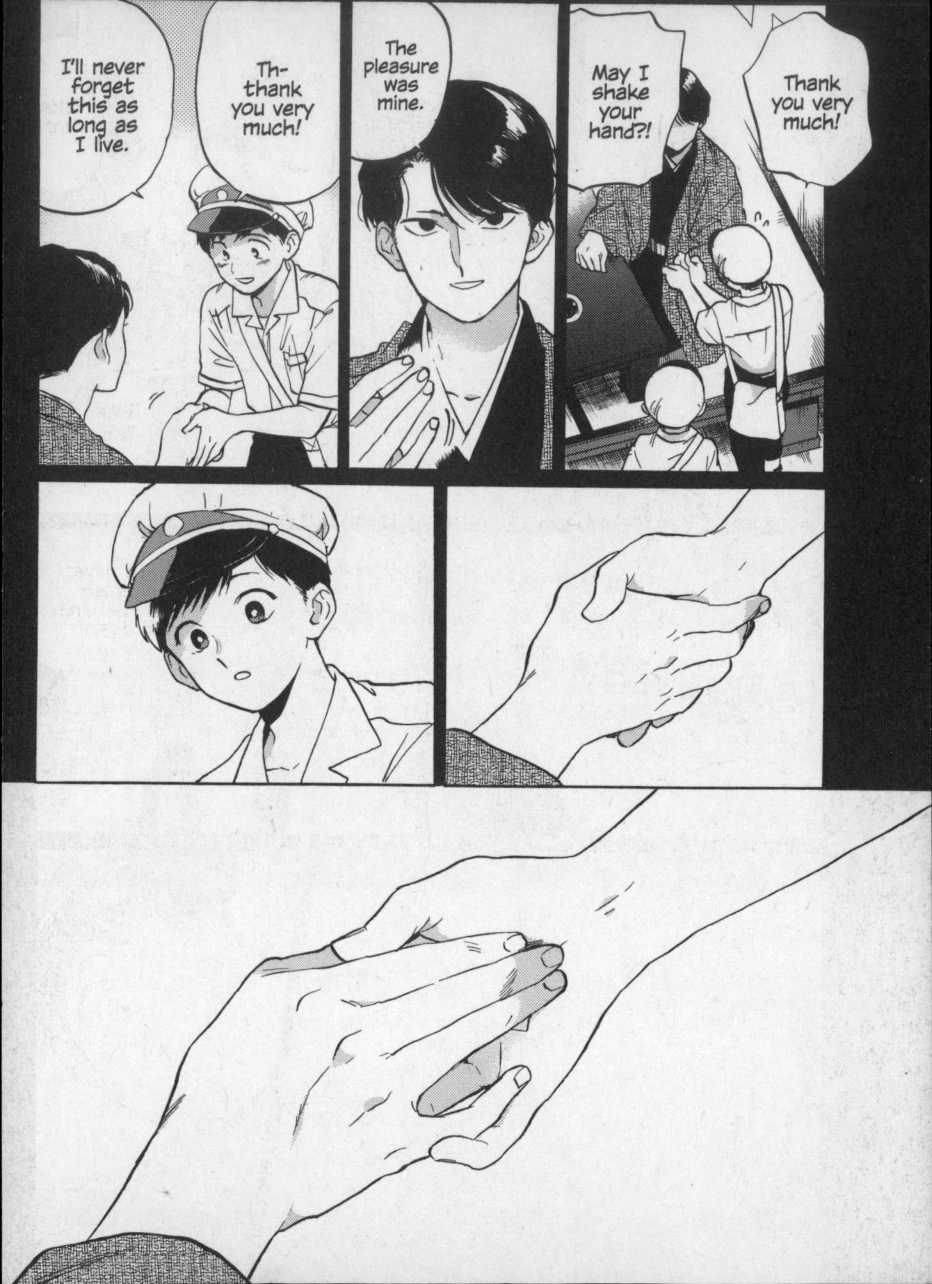
Thank you very much!
May I shake your hand?!
The pleasure was mine.
Th- thank you very much!
I'll never forget this as long as I live.

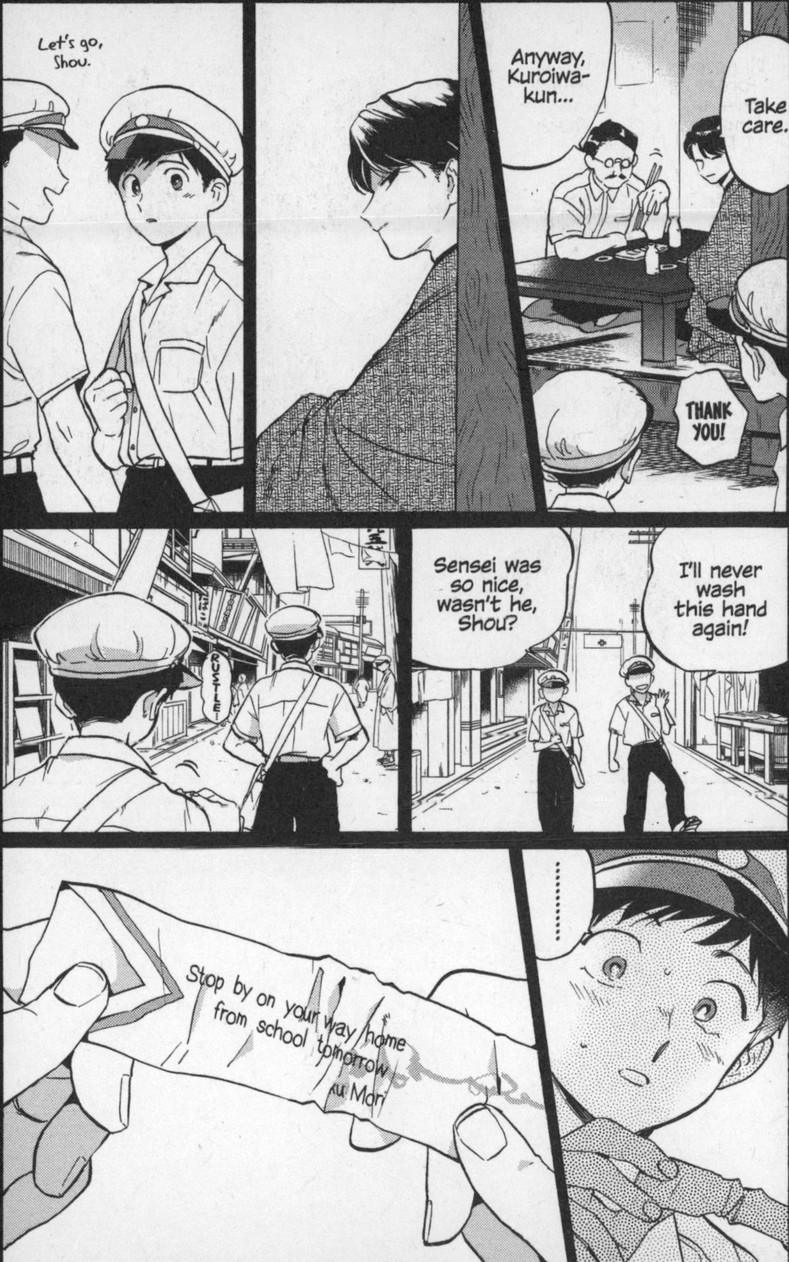

Take care.
Anyway, Kuroiwa-kun...
THANK YOU!
Let's go, Shou.
I'll never wash this hand again!
Sensei was so nice, wasn't he, Shou?
RUSTLE...
......
Stop by on your way home from school tomorrow
u Mori

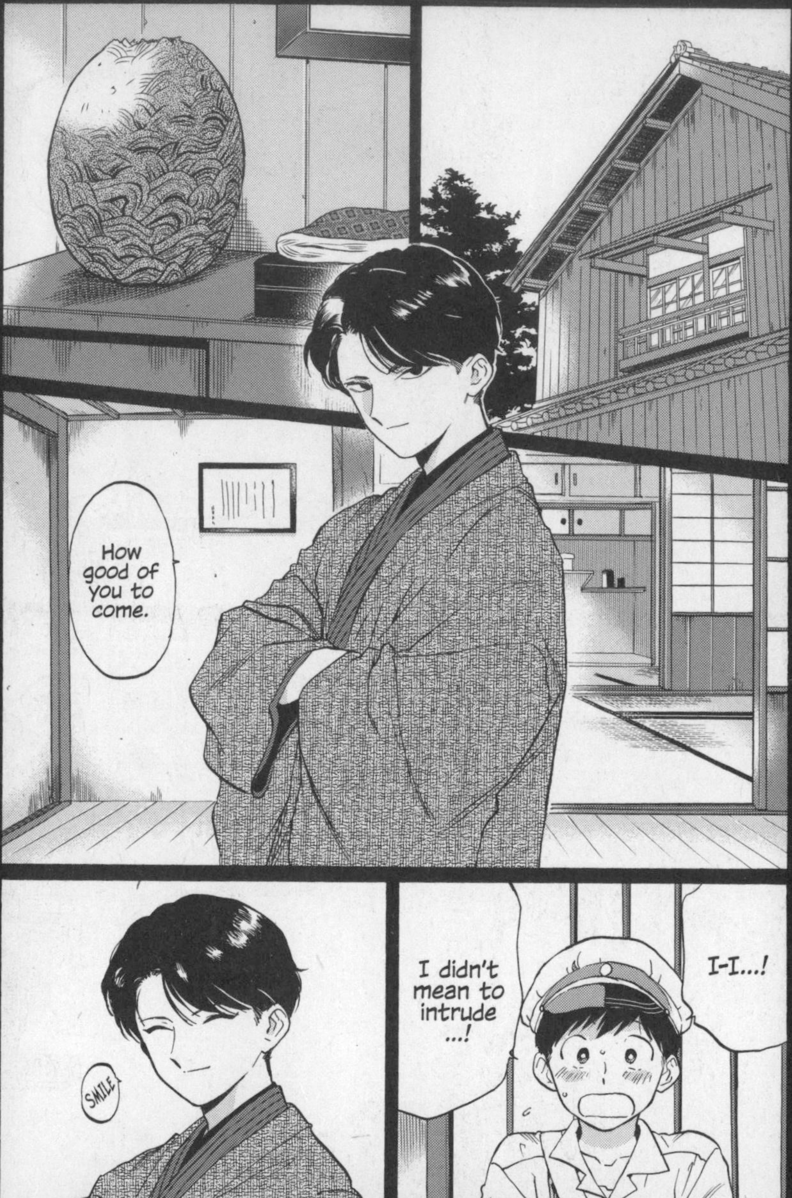
How good of you to come.
I-I...!
I didn't mean to intrude ...!
SMILE

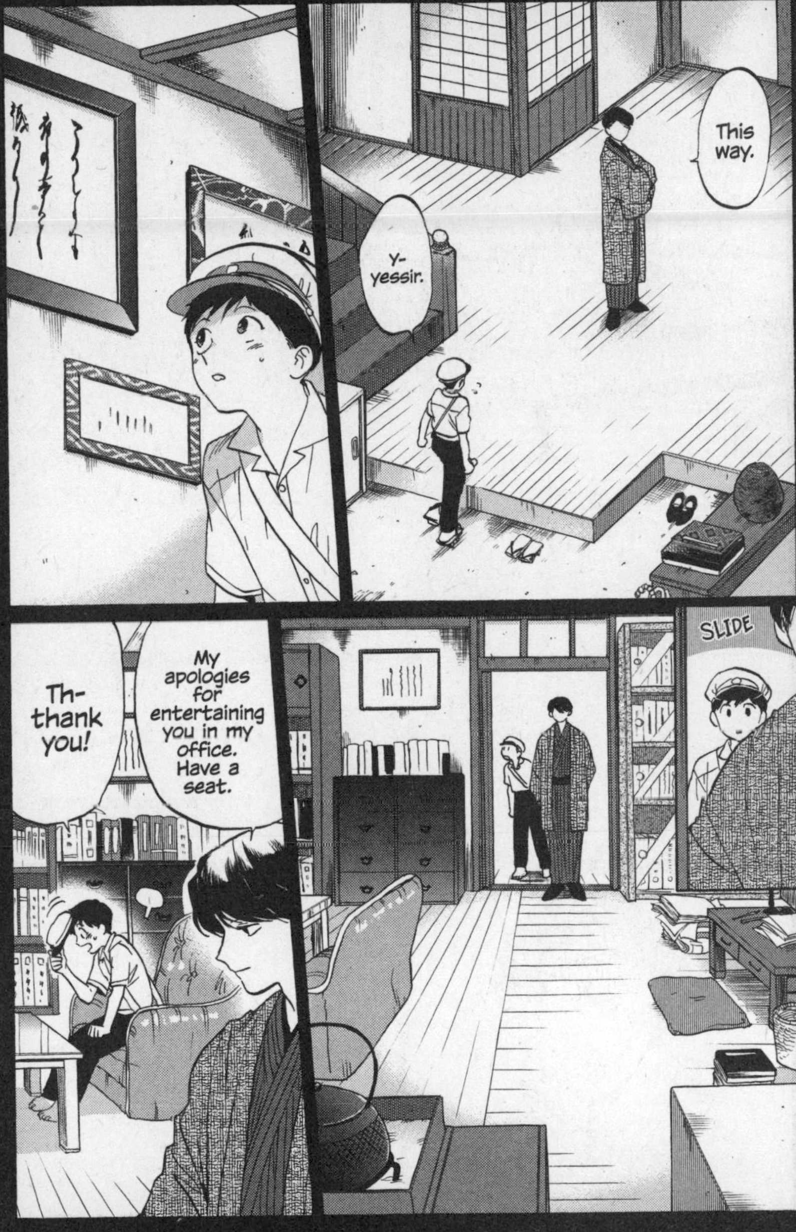
This way.
Y-yessir.
SLIDE
My apologies for entertaining you in my office. Have a seat.
Th-thank you!

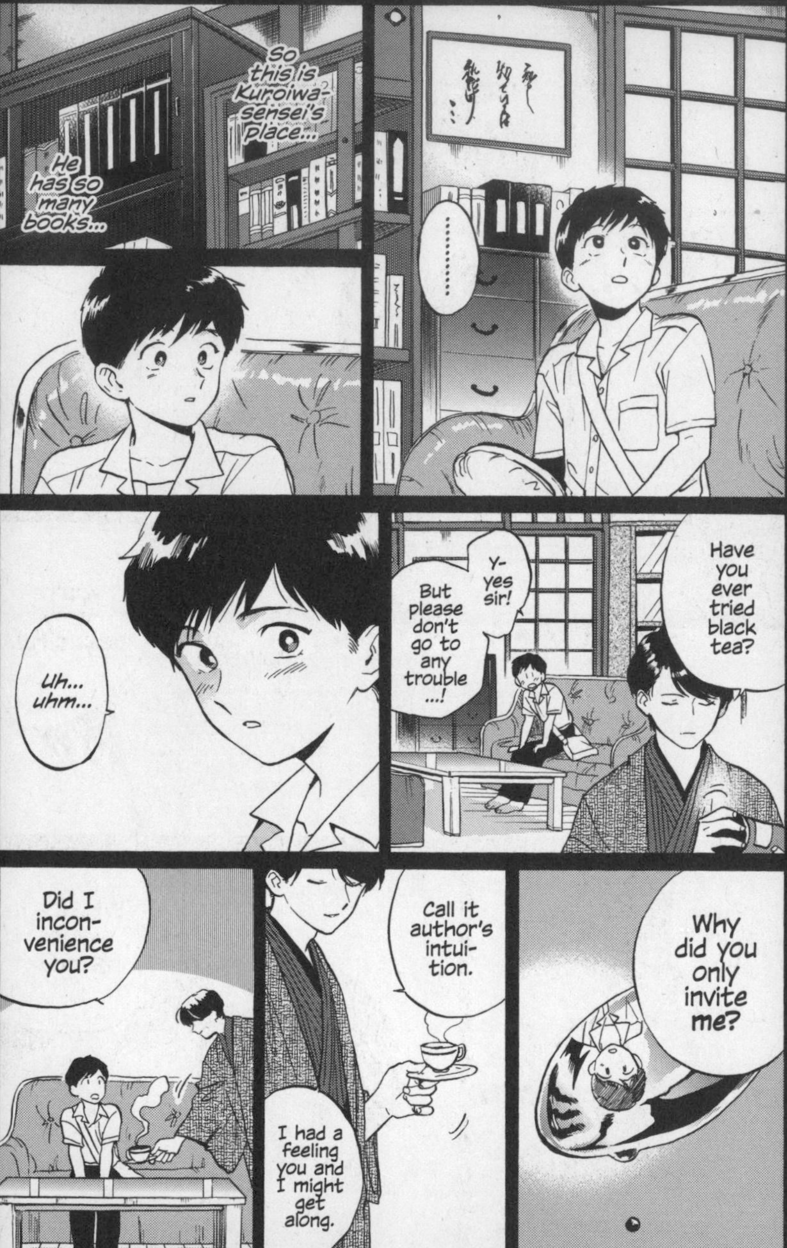
......
So this is Kuroiwa-sensei's place...
He has so many books...
Have you ever tried black tea?
Y-yes sir!
But please don't go to any trouble ...!
Uh... uhm...
Why did you only invite me?
Call it author's intuition.
I had a feeling you and I might get along.
Did I inconvenience you?

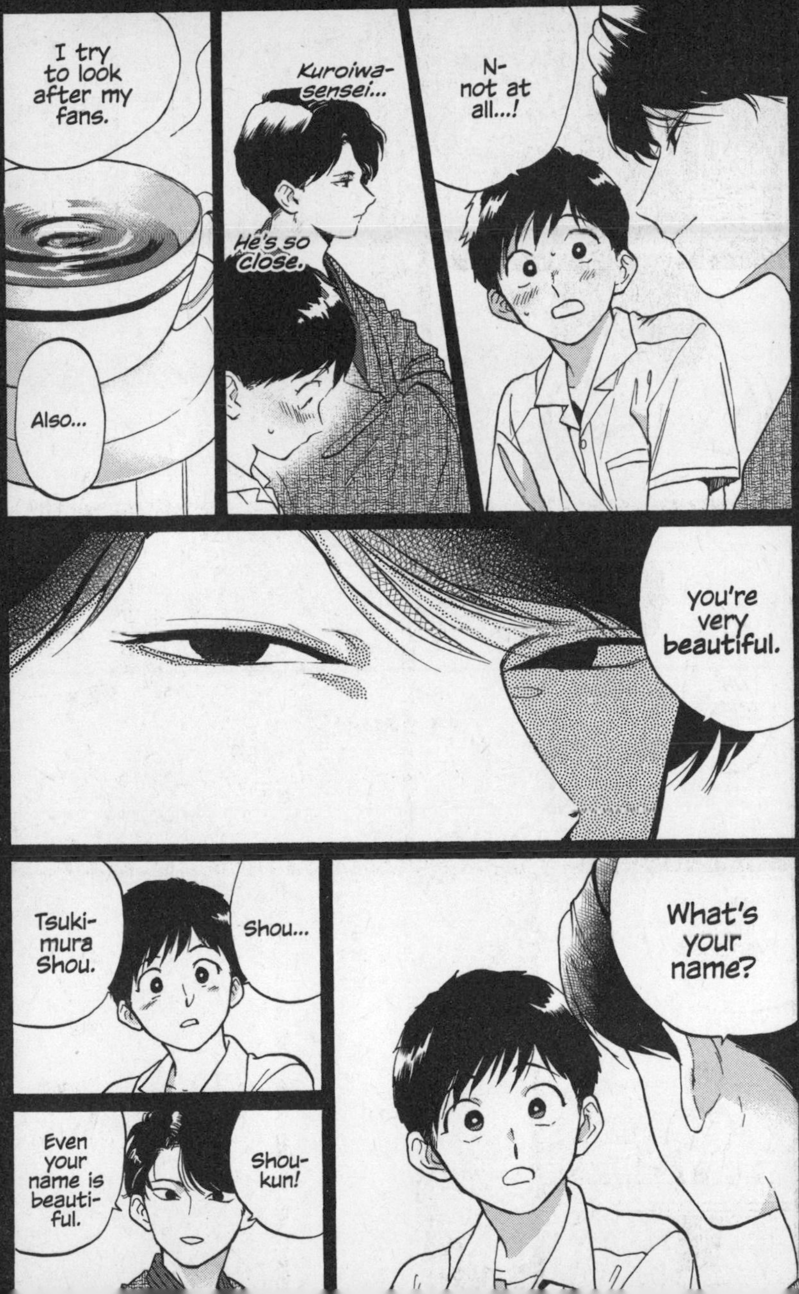
N-not at all...!
Kuroiwa-sensei...
He's so close.
I try to look after my fans.
Also...
you're very beautiful.
What's your name?
Tsuki-mura Shou.
Shou...
Shou-kun!
Even your name is beauti-ful.

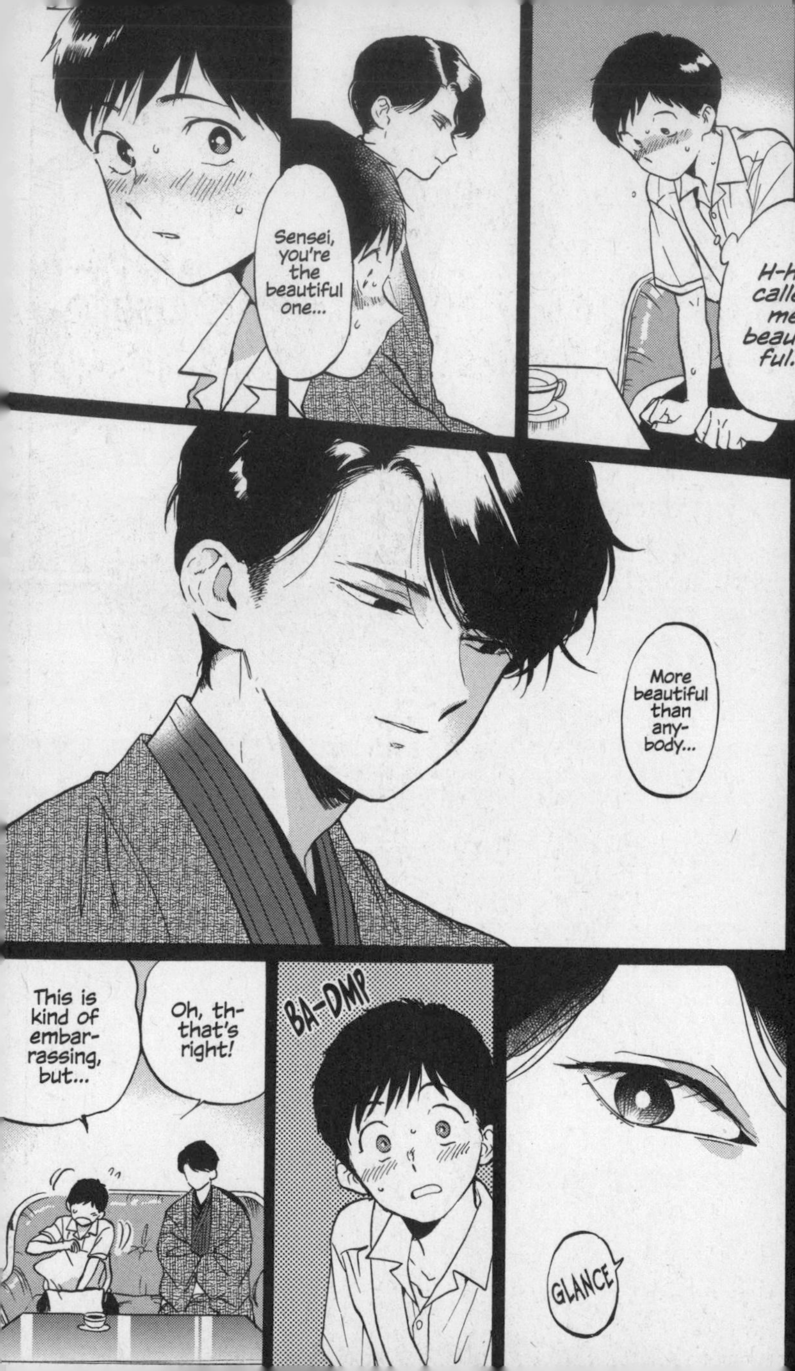
H-he called me beauti-ful...
Sensei, you're the beautiful one...
More beautiful than any-body...
GLANCE
BA-DMP
Oh, th-that's right!
This is kind of embar-rassing, but...

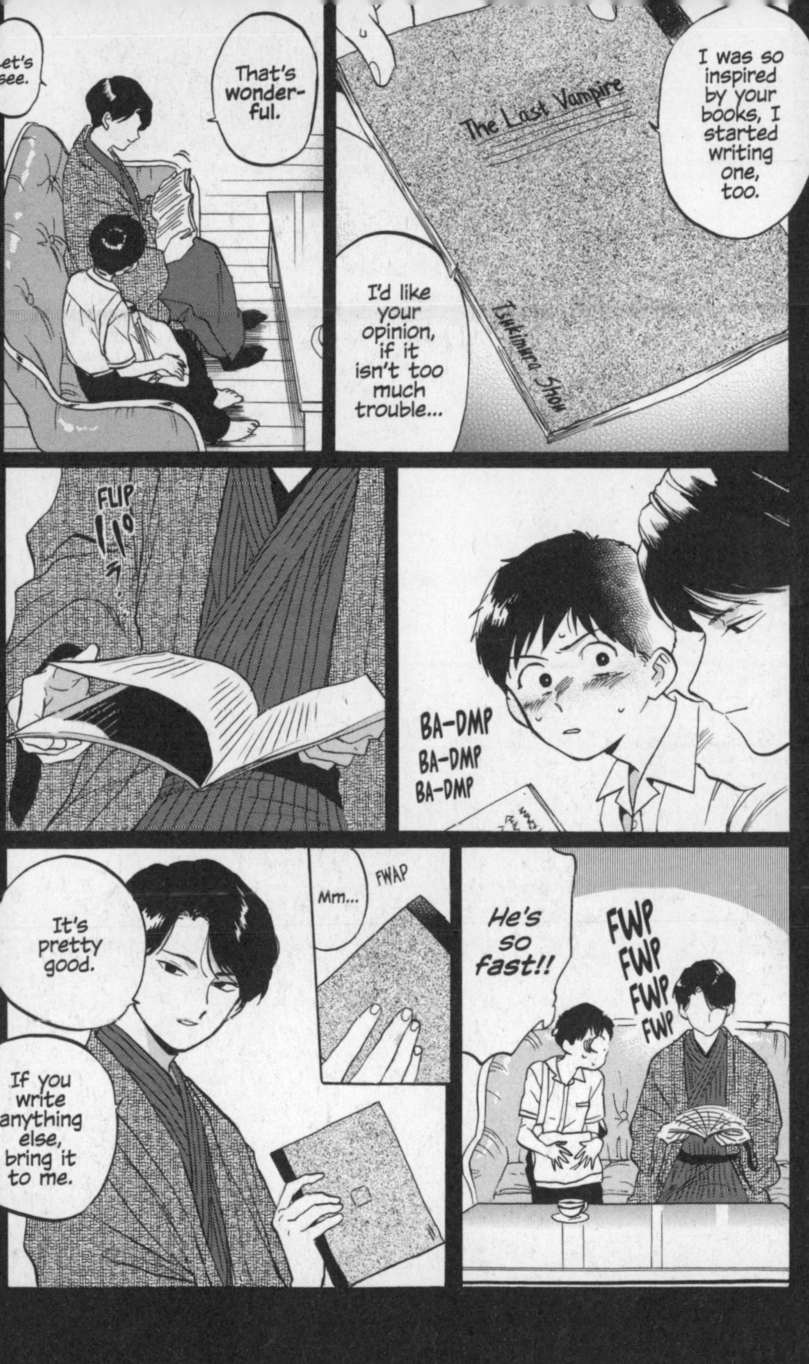
I was so inspired by your books, I started writing one, too.
The Last Vampire
Tsukimura Shou
I'd like your opinion, if it isn't too much trouble...
That's wonderful.
Let's see.
BA-DMP
BA-DMP
BA-DMP
FLIP
He's so fast!!
FWP
FWP
FWP
FWP
FWAP
Mm...
It's pretty good.
If you write anything else, bring it to me.

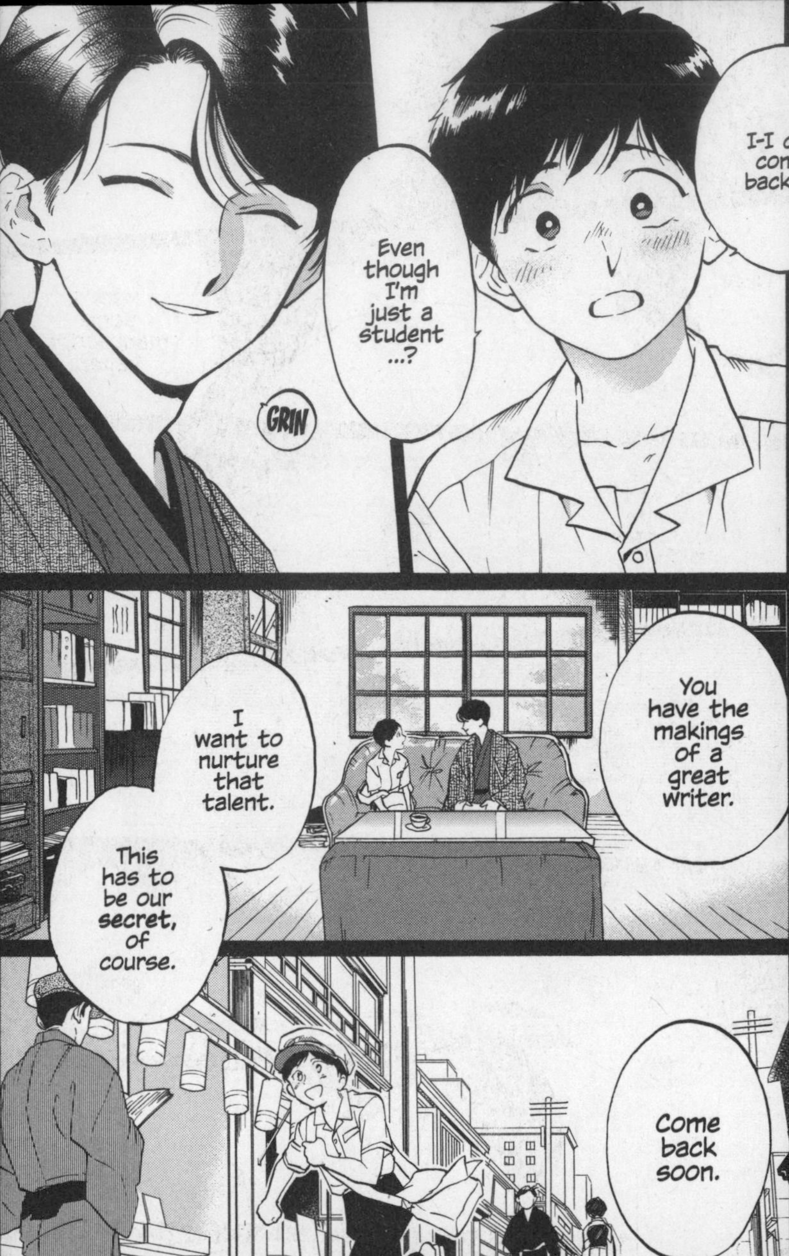
I-I can come back...?
Even though I'm just a student ...?
GRIN
You have the makings of a great writer.
I want to nurture that talent.
This has to be our secret, of course.
Come back soon.

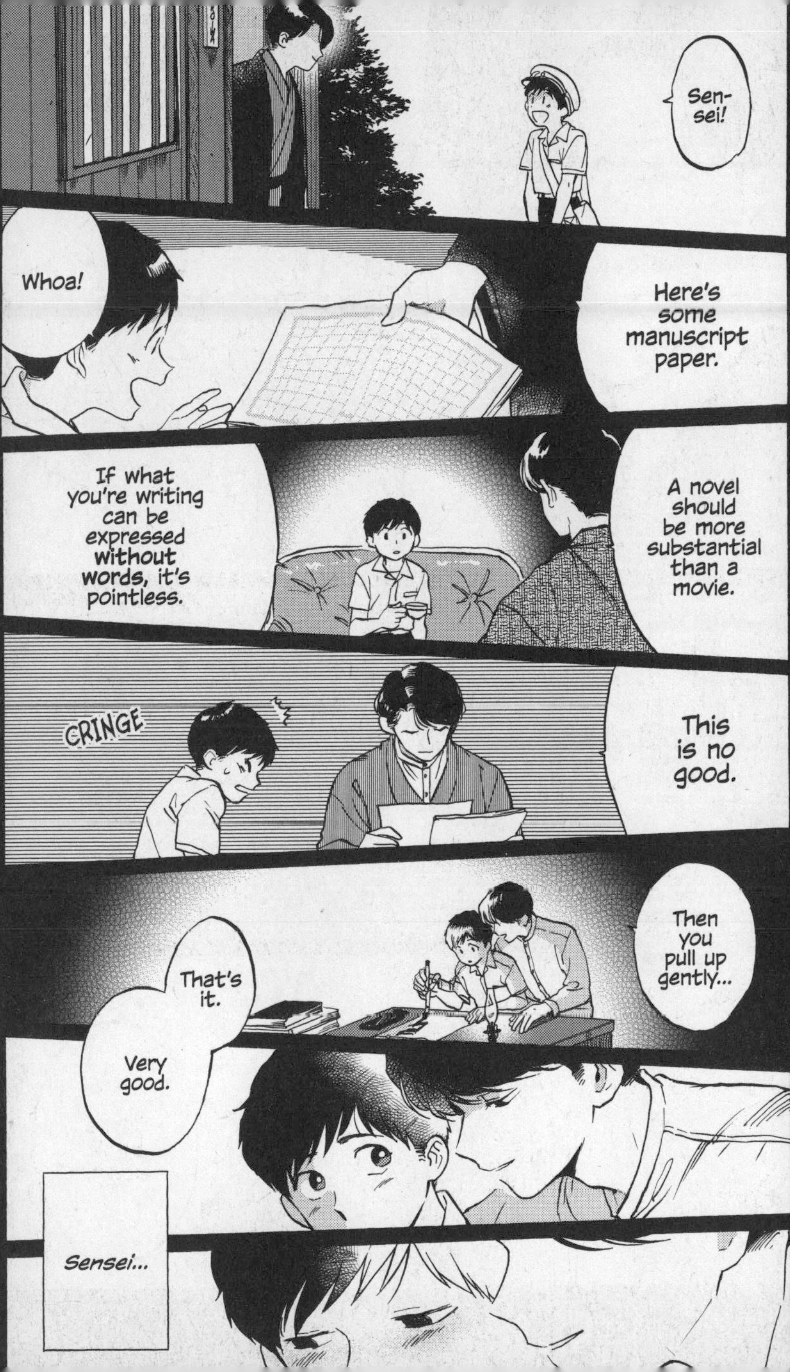
Sen-sei!
Here's some manuscript paper.
Whoa!
A novel should be more substantial than a movie.
If what you're writing can be expressed without words, it's pointless.
This is no good.
CRINGE
Then you pull up gently...
That's it.
Very good.
Sensei...

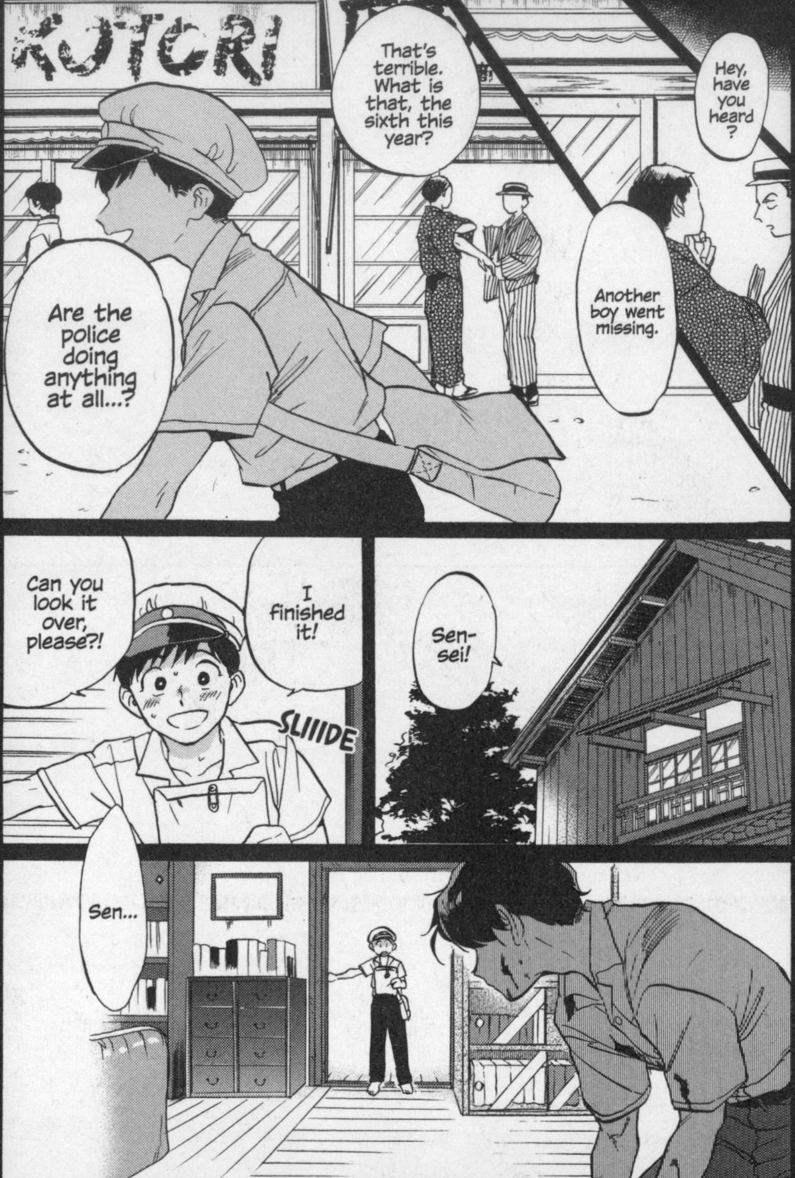
Hey, have you heard?
Another boy went missing.
That's terrible. What is that, the sixth this year?
Are the police doing anything at all...?
Sen-sei!
I finished it!
Can you look it over, please?!
SLIIIDE
Sen...

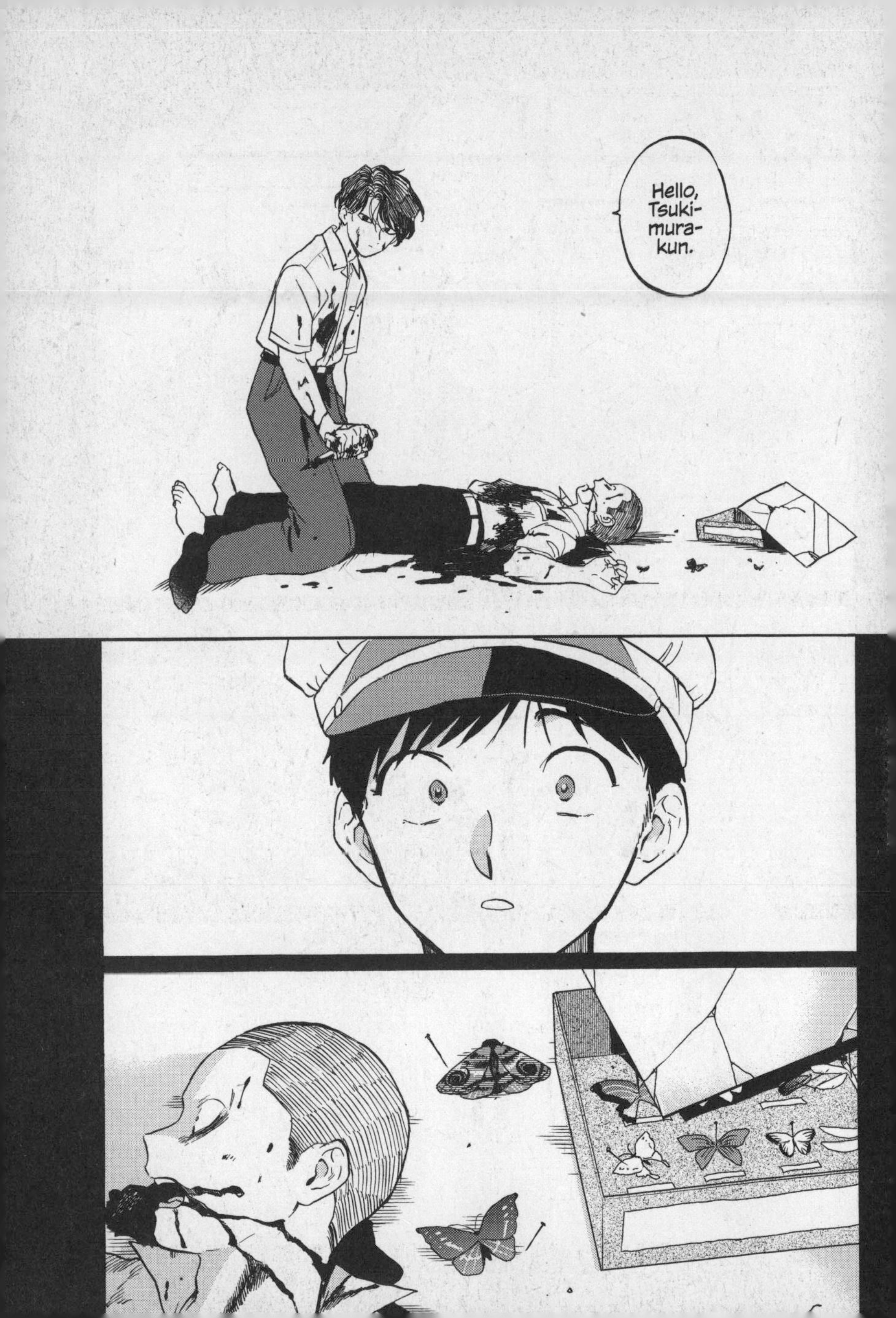
Hello, Tsuki-mura-kun.

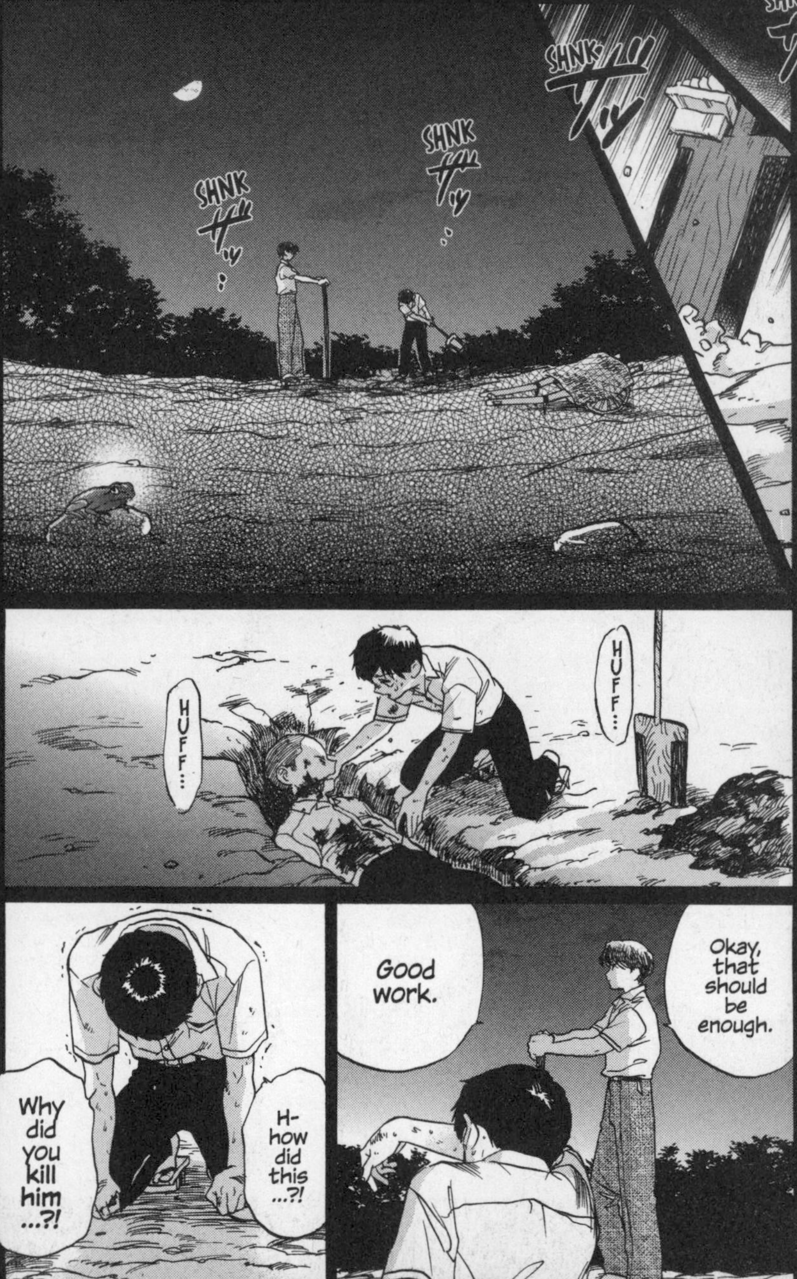
SHNK
SHNK
SHNK
SHNK
HUFF...
HUFF...
Okay, that should be enough.
Good work.
H-how did this ...?!
Why did you kill him ...?!

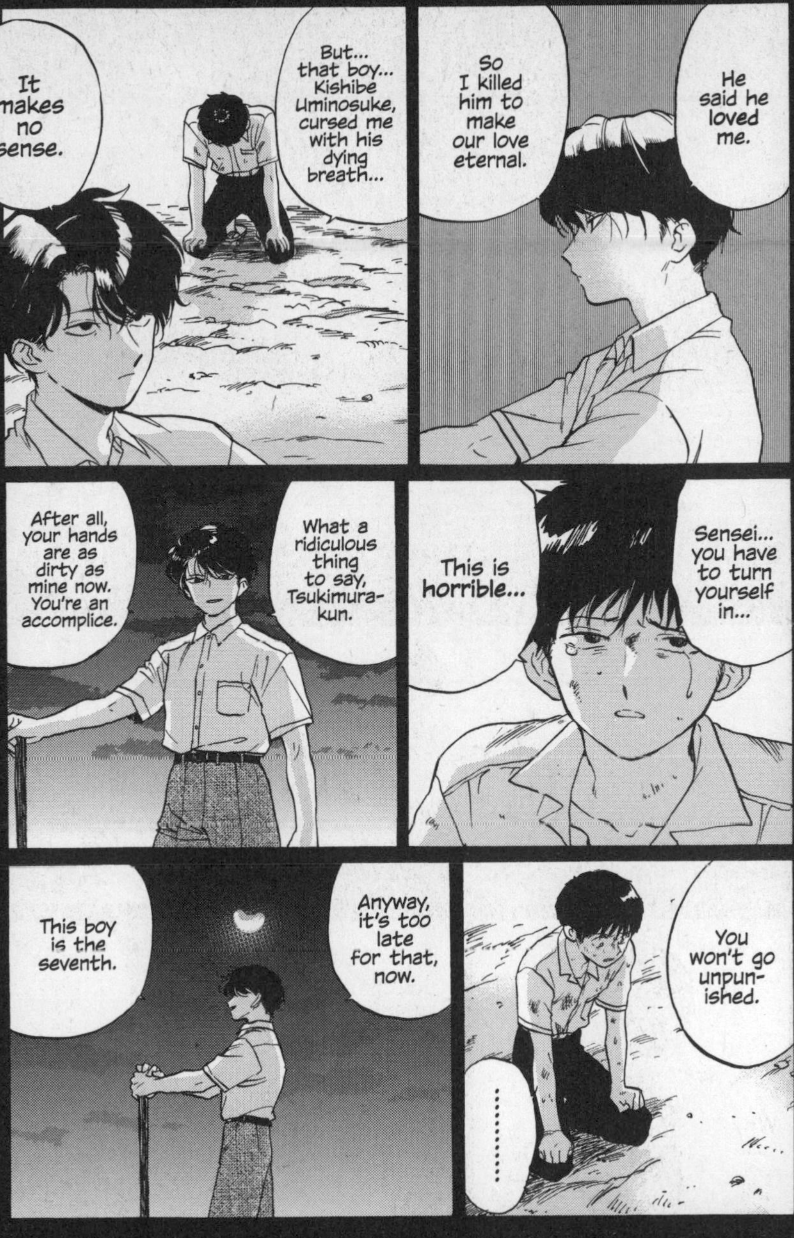
He said he loved me.
So I killed him to make our love eternal.
But... that boy... Kishibe Uminosuke, cursed me with his dying breath...
It makes no sense.
Sensei... you have to turn yourself in...
This is horrible...
What a ridiculous thing to say, Tsukimura-kun.
After all, your hands are as dirty as mine now. You're an accomplice.
You won't go unpunished.
......
Anyway, it's too late for that, now.
This boy is the seventh.

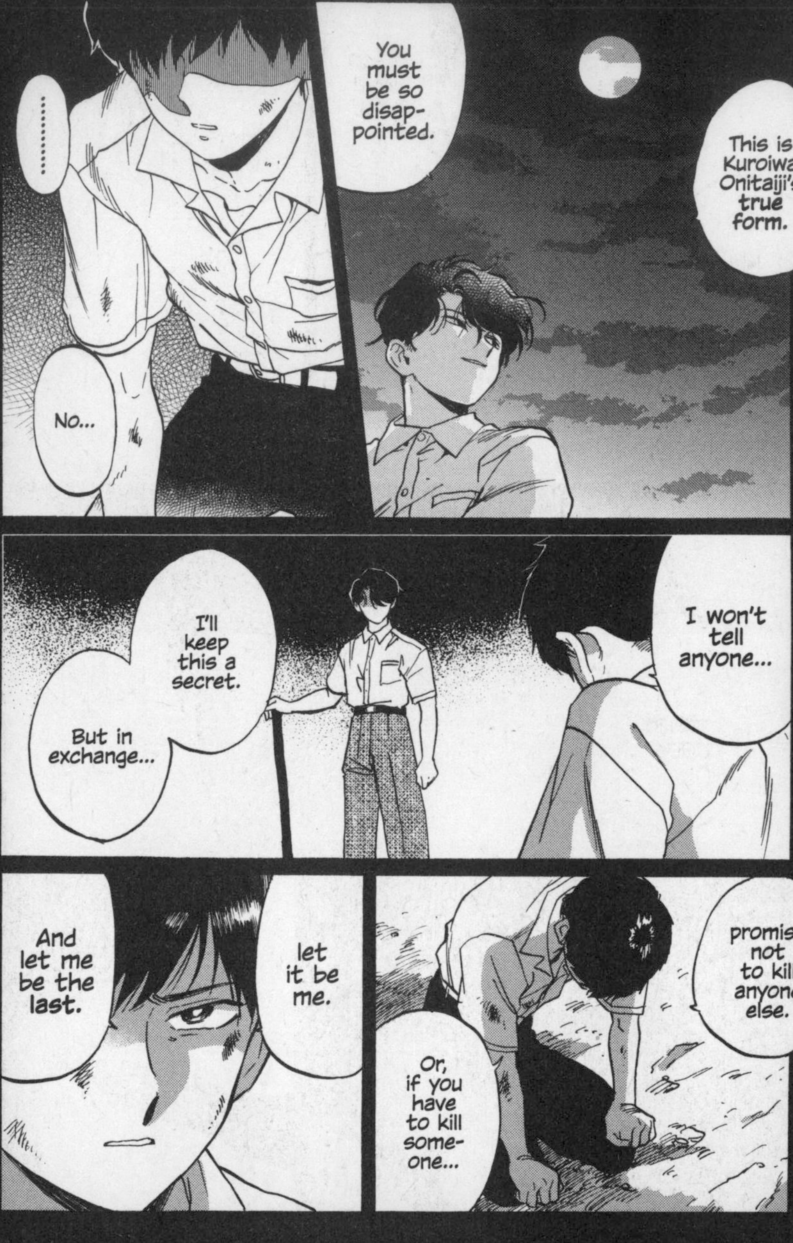
This is Kuroiwa Onitaiji's true form.
You must be so disap-pointed.
......
No...
I won't tell anyone...
I'll keep this a secret.
But in exchange...
promise not to kill anyone else.
Or, if you have to kill some-one...
let it be me.
And let me be the last.

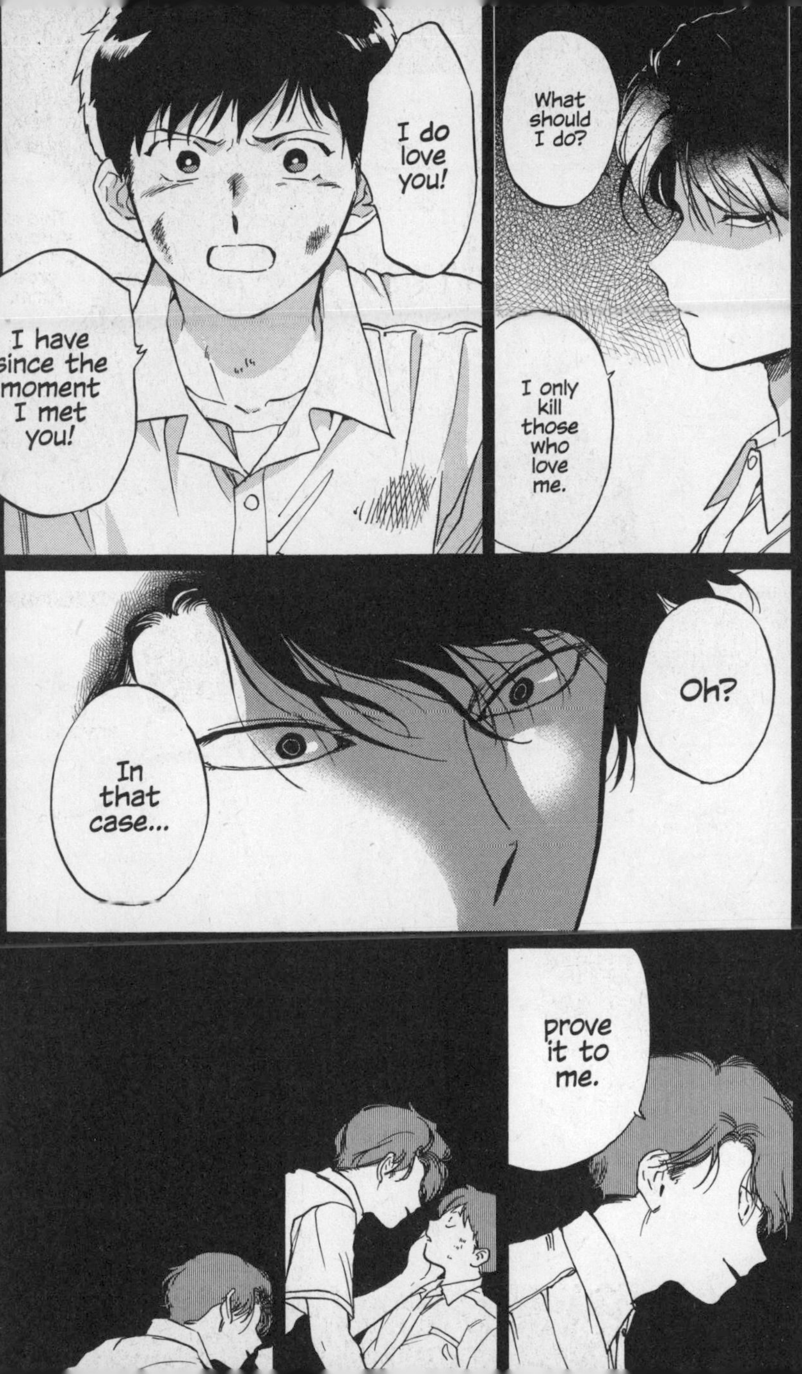
What should I do?
I only kill those who love me.
I do love you!
I have since the moment I met you!
Oh?
In that case...
prove it to me.

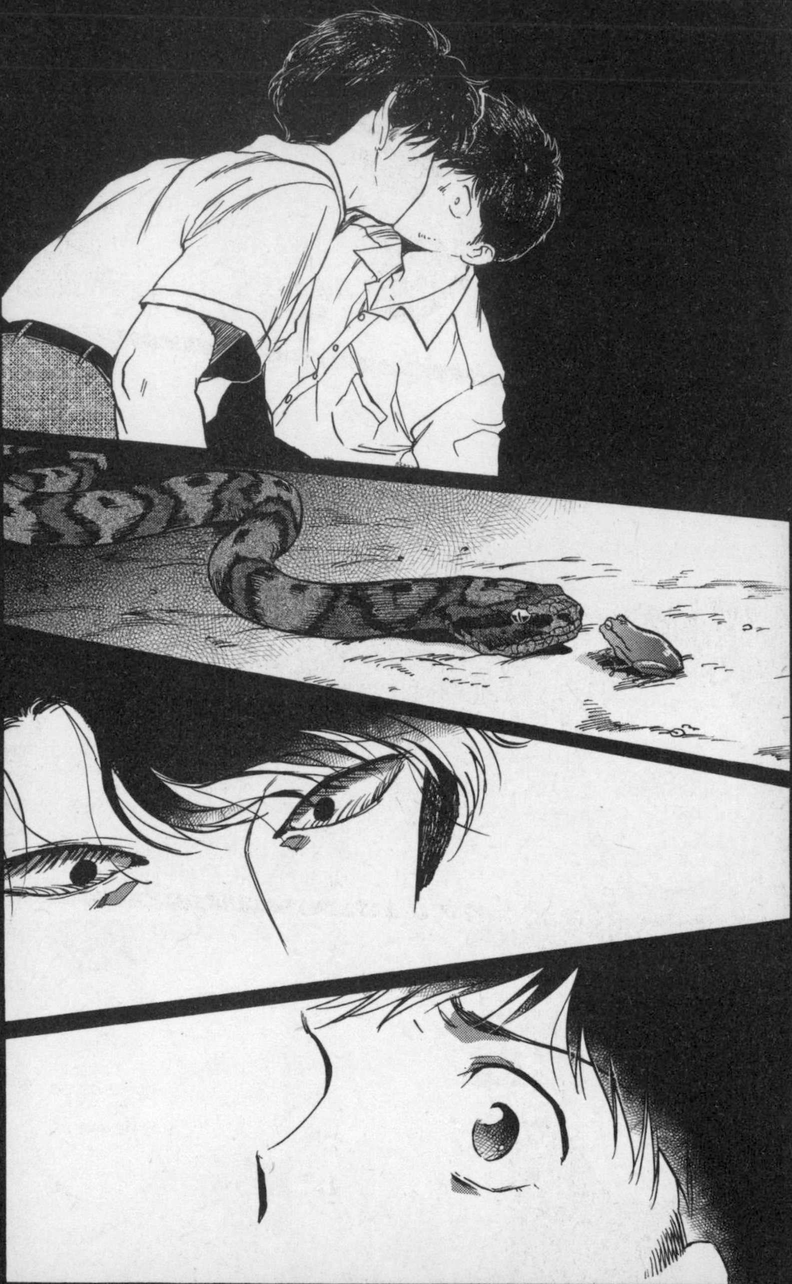

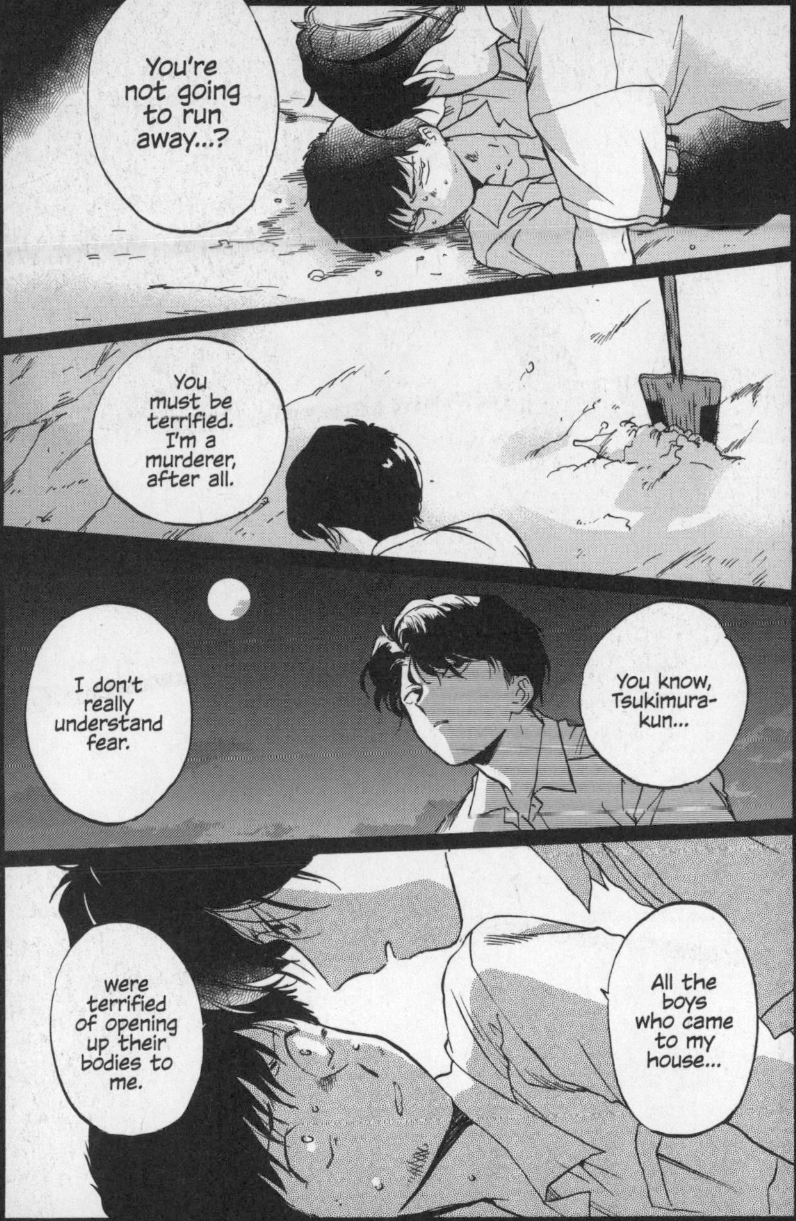
You're not going to run away...?
You must be terrified. I'm a murderer, after all.
You know, Tsukimura-kun...
I don't really understand fear.
All the boys who came to my house...
were terrified of opening up their bodies to me.

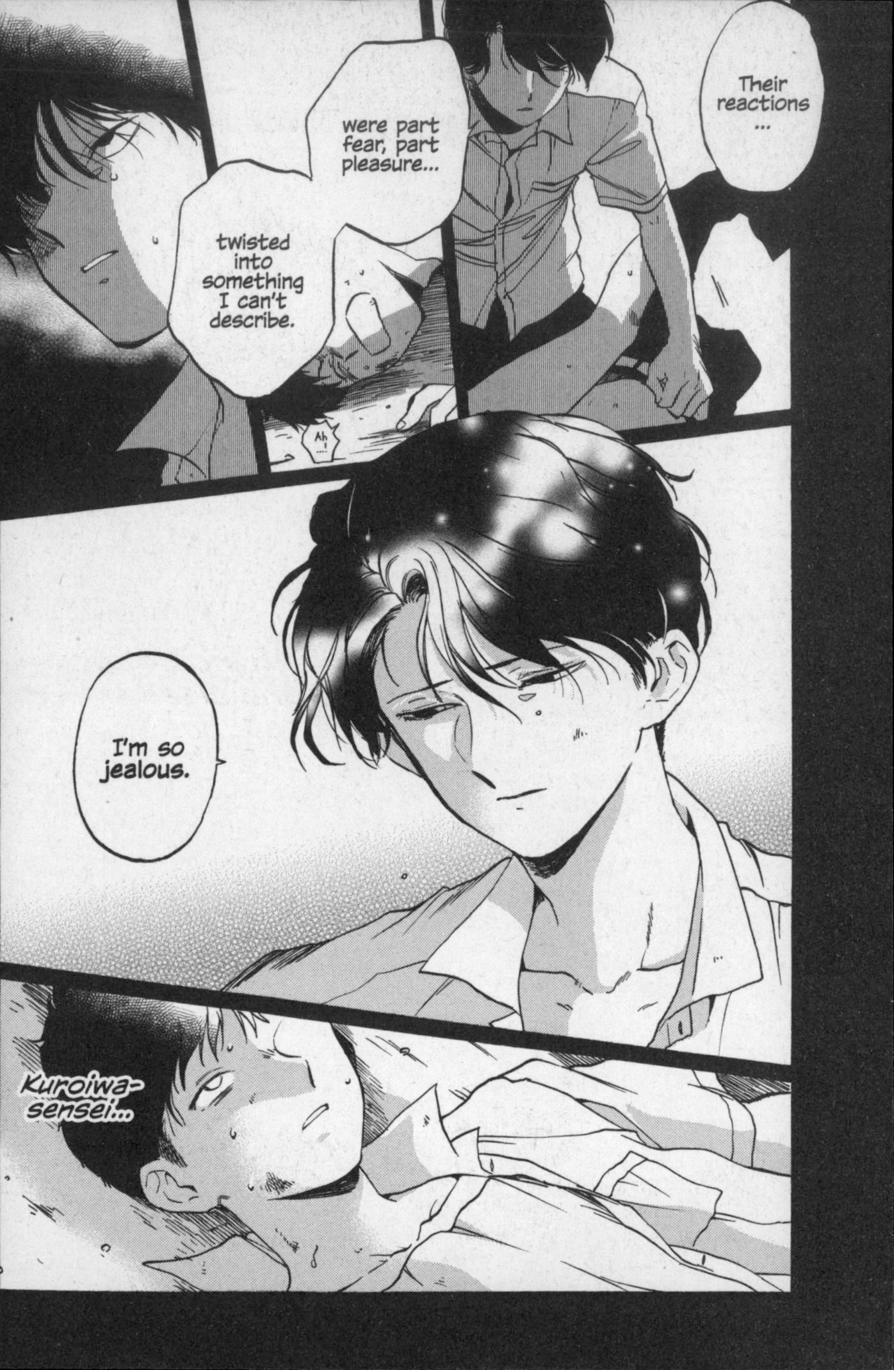
Their reactions ...
were part fear, part pleasure...
twisted into something I can't describe.
Ah ...!
I'm so jealous.
Kuroiwa-sensei...

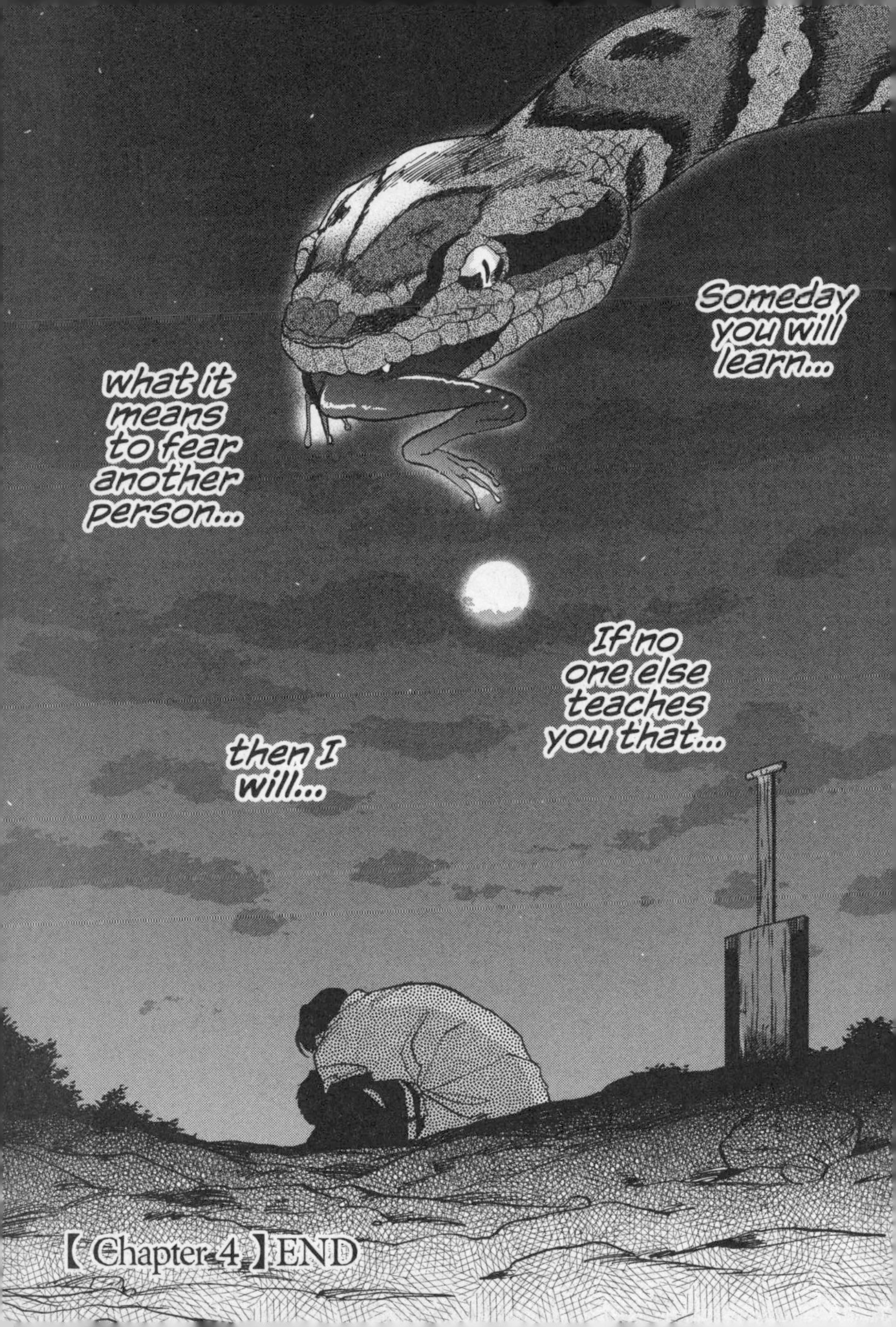
Someday you will learn...
what it means to fear another person...
If no one else teaches you that...
then I will...
【 Chapter 4 】END

【 Chapter 5 】

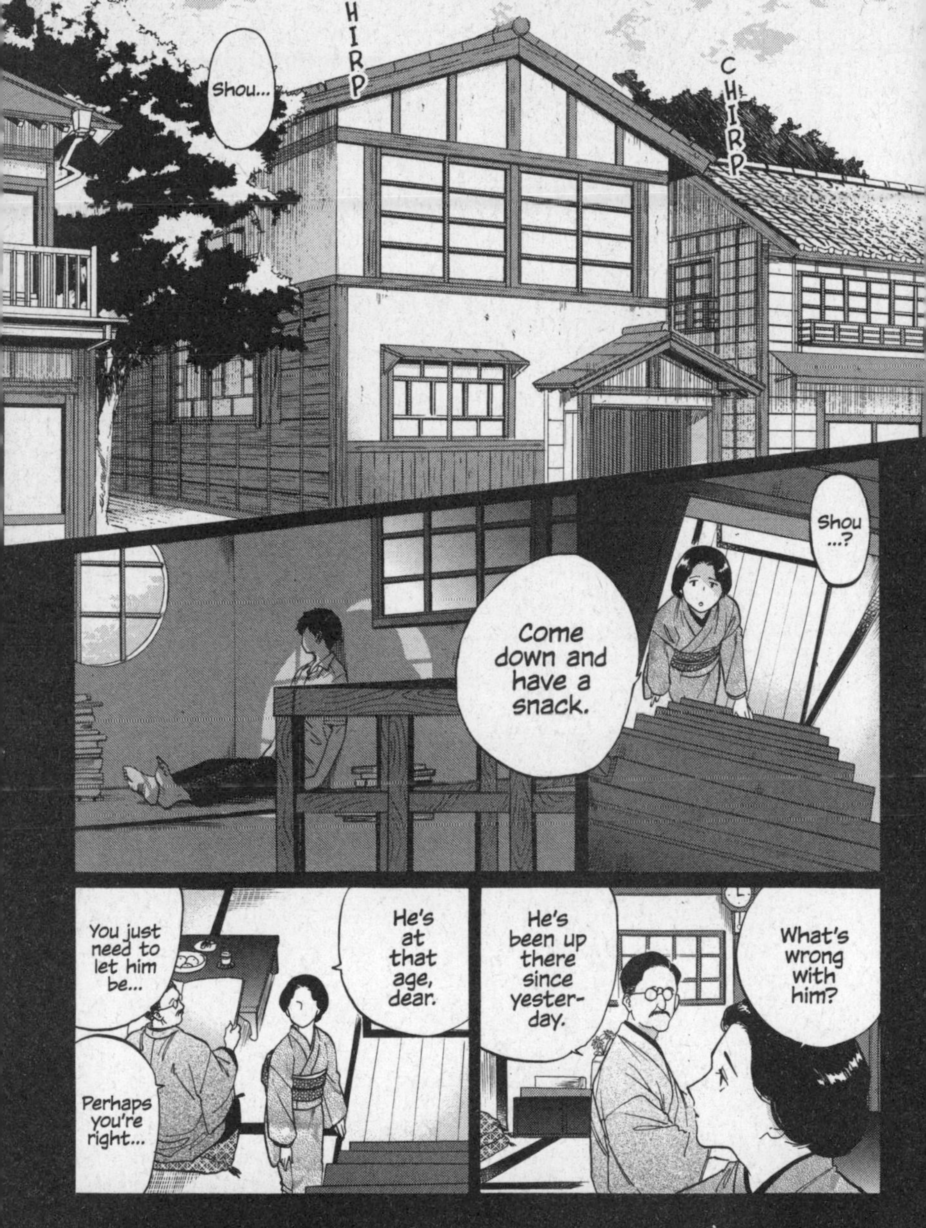

CHIRP
CHIRP
Shou...
Shou ...?
Come down and have a snack.
What's wrong with him?
He's been up there since yester-day.
He's at that age, dear.
You just need to let him be...
Perhaps you're right...

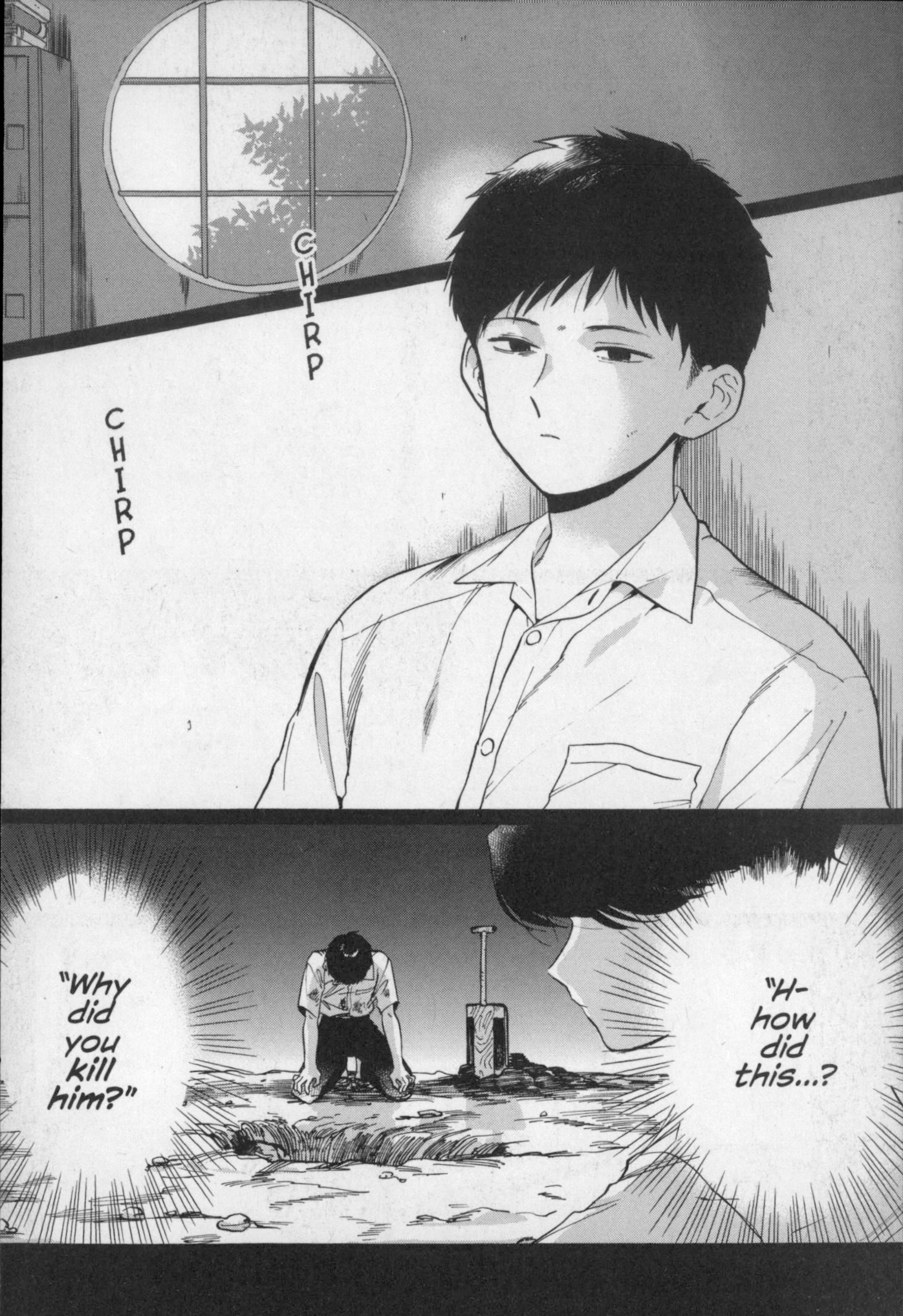
CHIRP
CHIRP
"H-how did this...?
"Why did you kill him?"

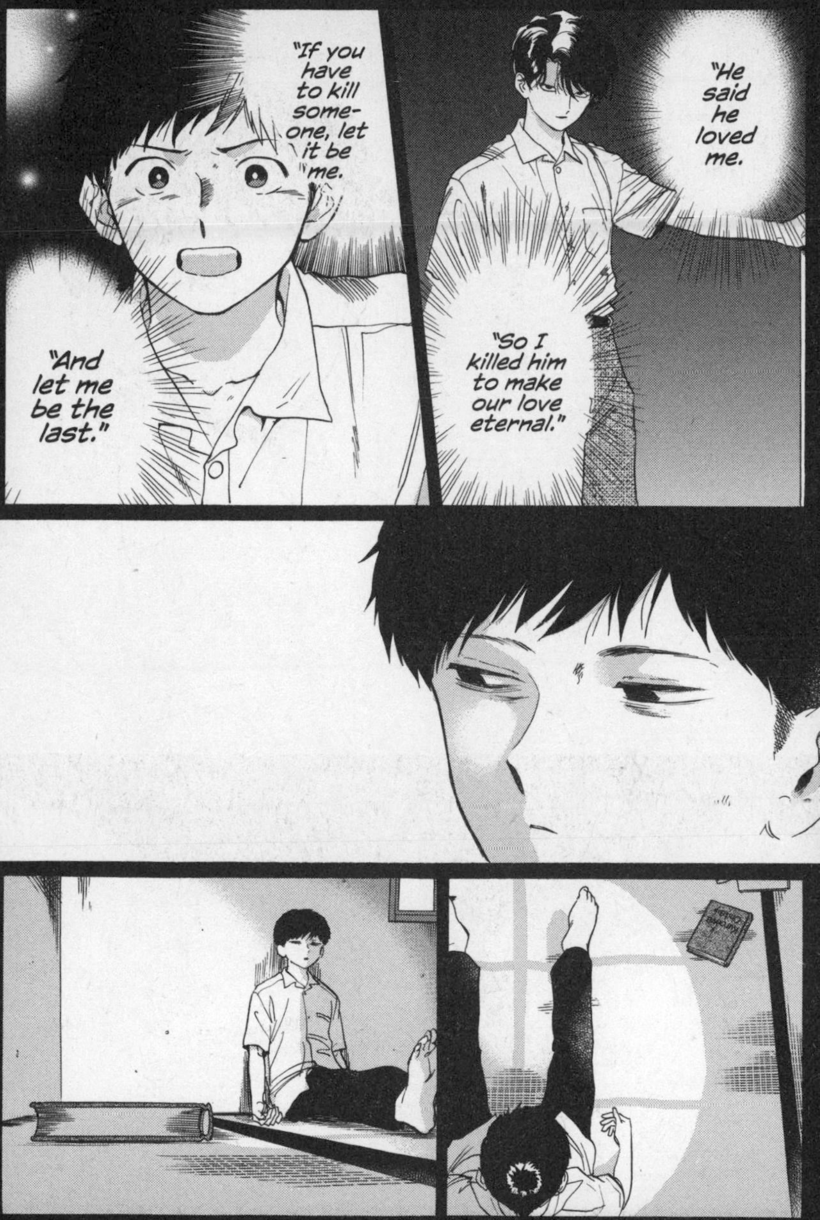
"He said he loved me.
"So I killed him to make our love eternal."
"If you have to kill some-one, let it be me.
"And let me be the last."

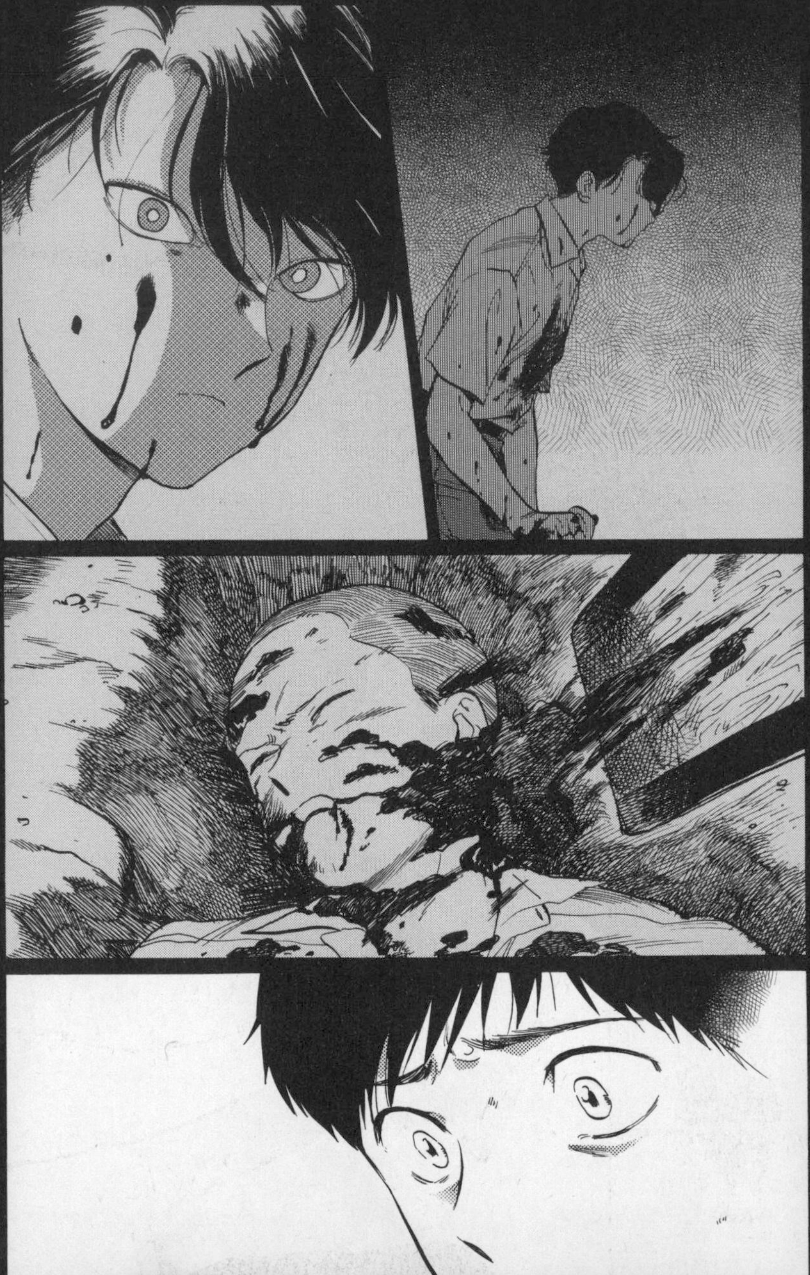

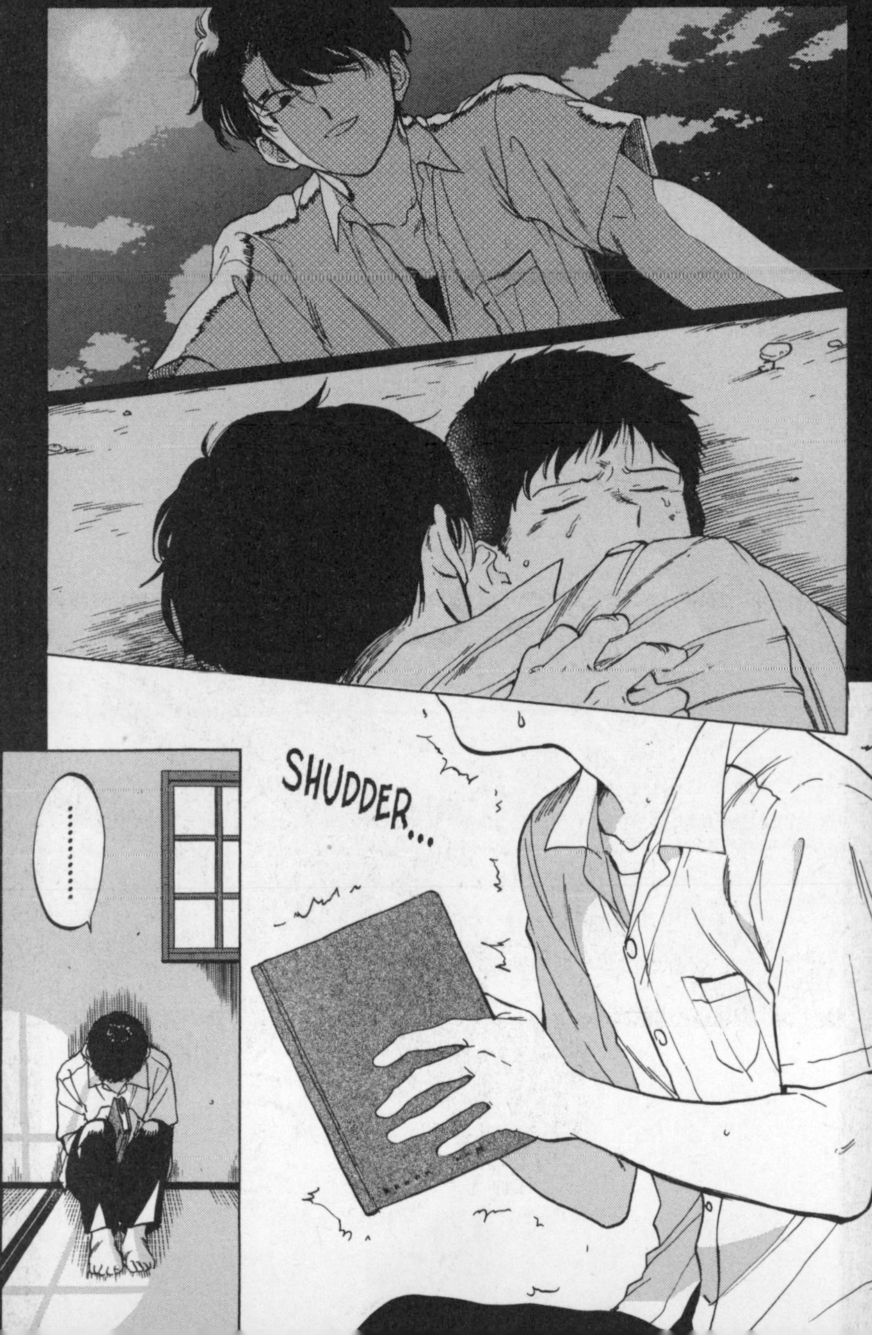
SHUDDER...
......

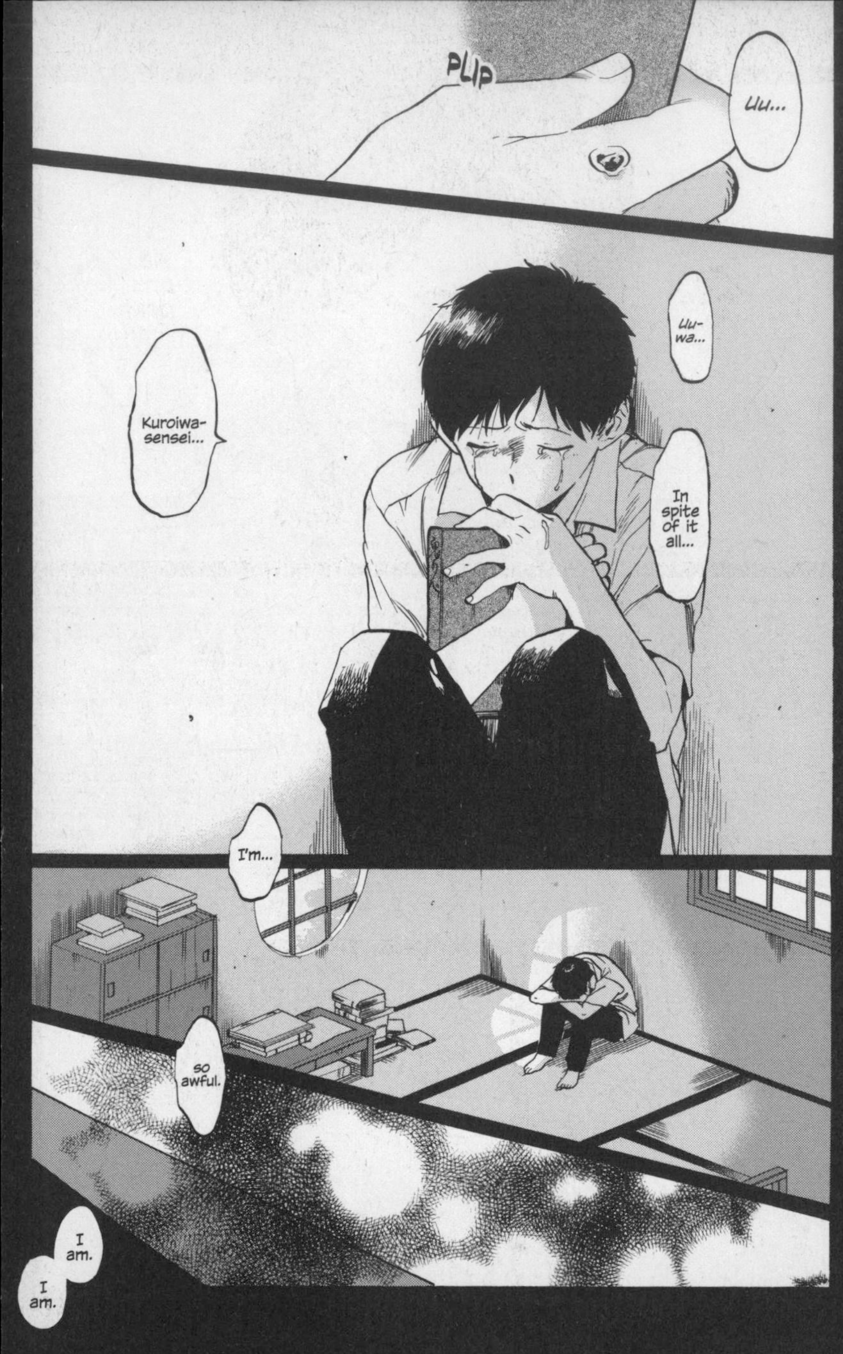
Uu...
PLIP
Uu-wa...
In spite of it all...
Kuroiwa-sensei...
I'm...
so awful.
I am.
I am.

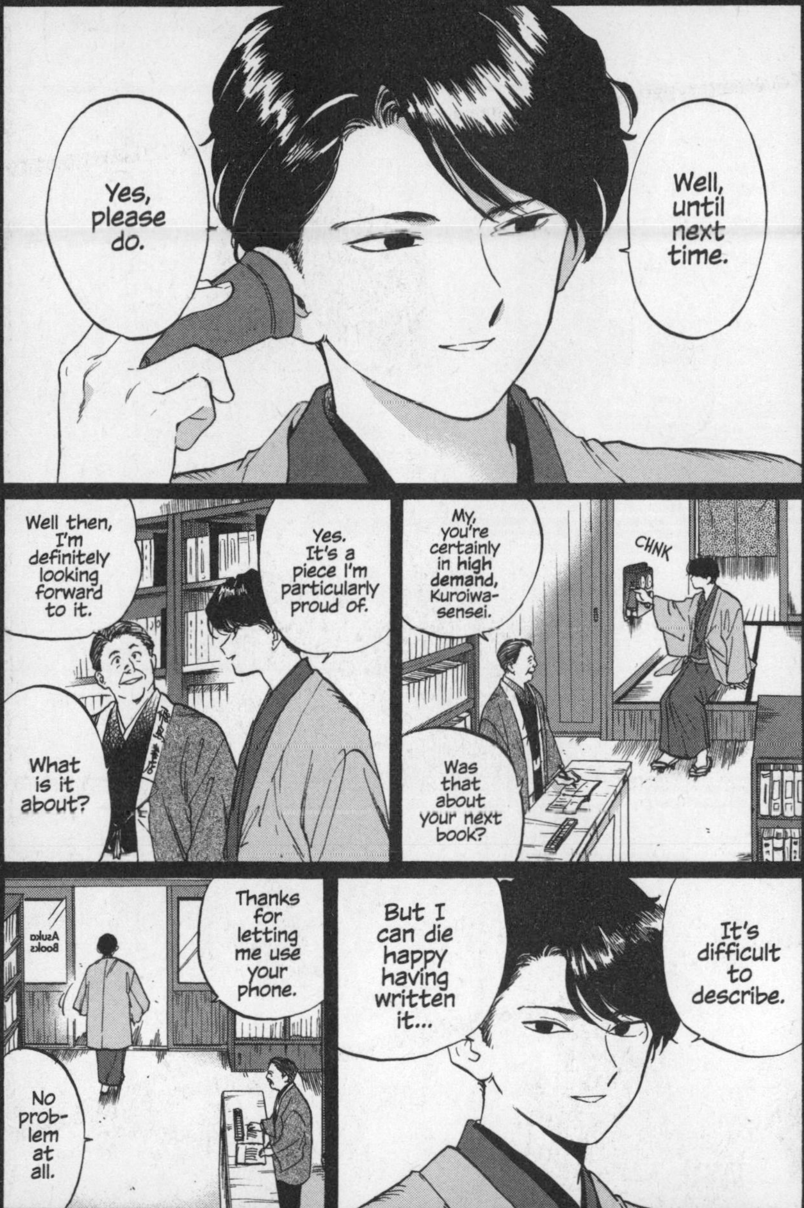
Well, until next time.
Yes, please do.
CHNK
My, you're certainly in high demand, Kuroiwa-sensei.
Was that about your next book?
Yes. It's a piece I'm particularly proud of.
Well then, I'm definitely looking forward to it.
What is it about?
It's difficult to describe.
But I can die happy having written it...
Thanks for letting me use your phone.
Asuka Books
No problem at all.

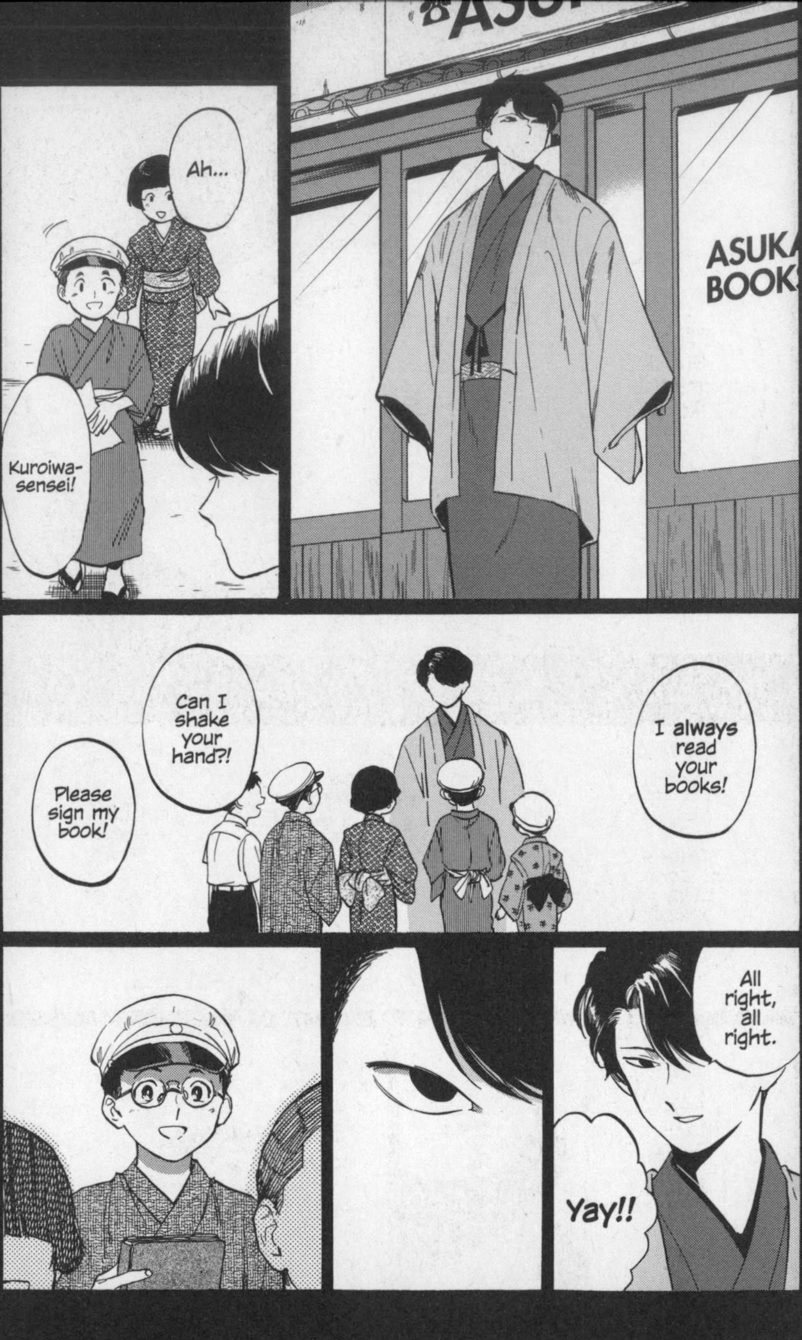
ASUKA
BOOKS
Ah...
Kuroiwa-sensei!
I always read your books!
Can I shake your hand?!
Please sign my book!
All right, all right.
Yay!!

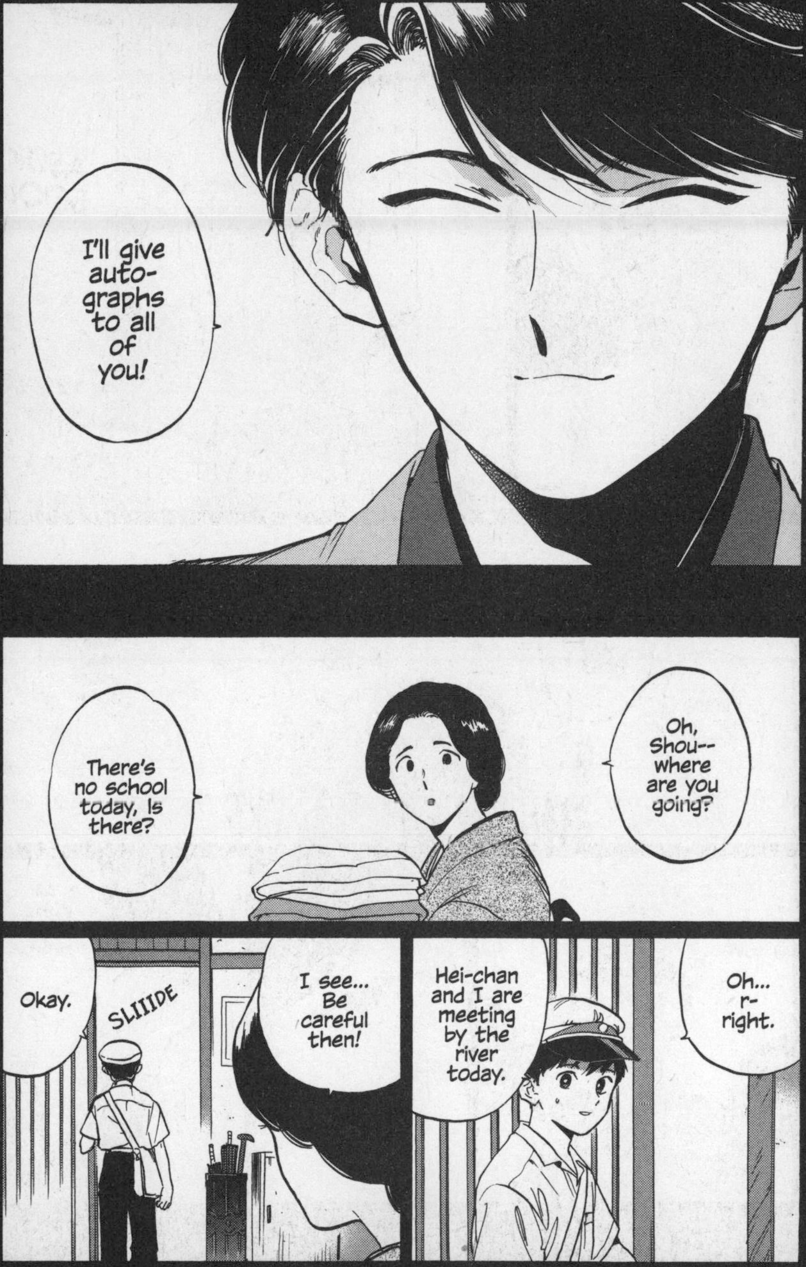
I'll give auto-graphs to all of you!
Oh, Shou-- where are you going?
There's no school today, Is there?
Oh... r- right.
Hei-chan and I are meeting by the river today.
I see... Be careful then!
SLIIIDE
Okay.

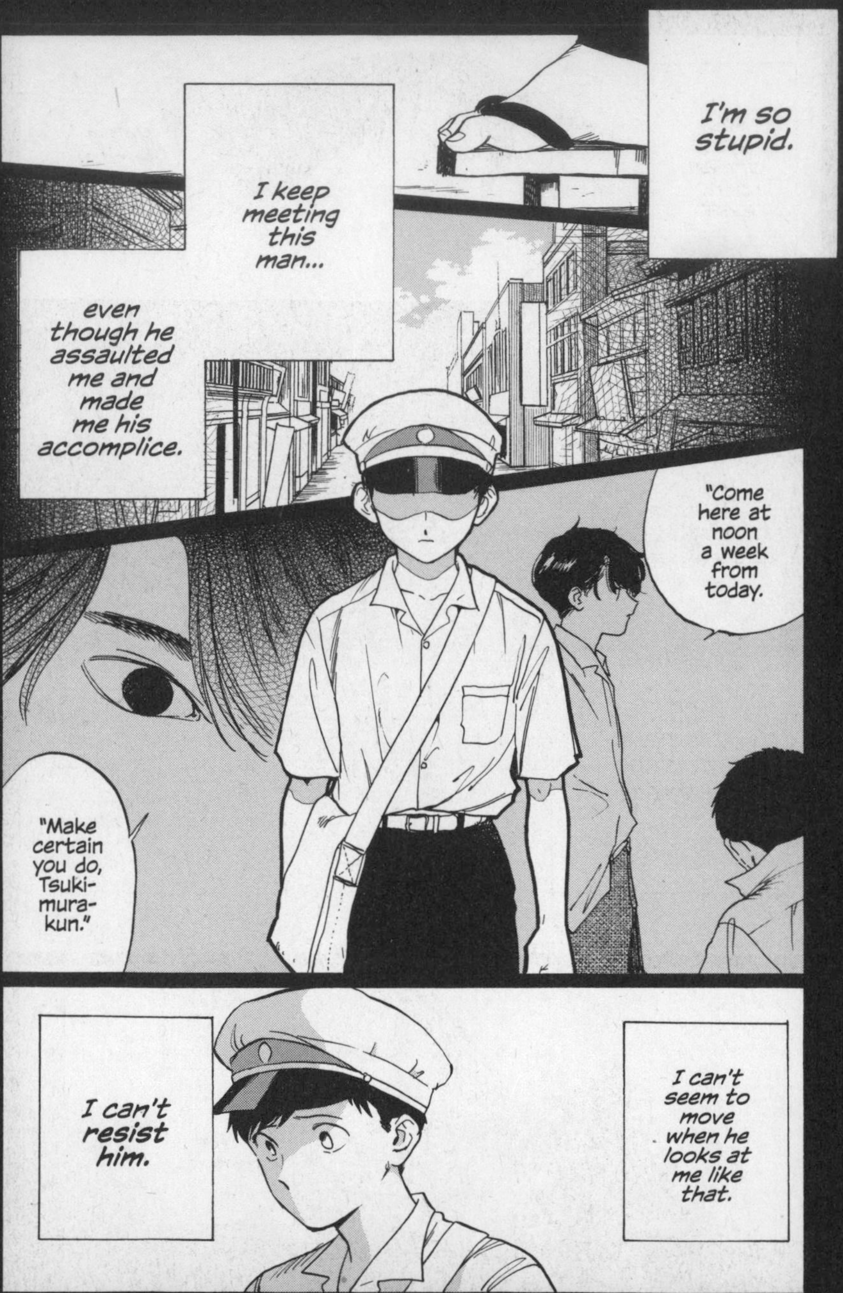
I'm so stupid.
I keep meeting this man...
even though he assaulted me and made me his accomplice.
"Come here at noon a week from today.
"Make certain you do, Tsukimura-kun."
I can't seem to move when he looks at me like that.
I can't resist him.

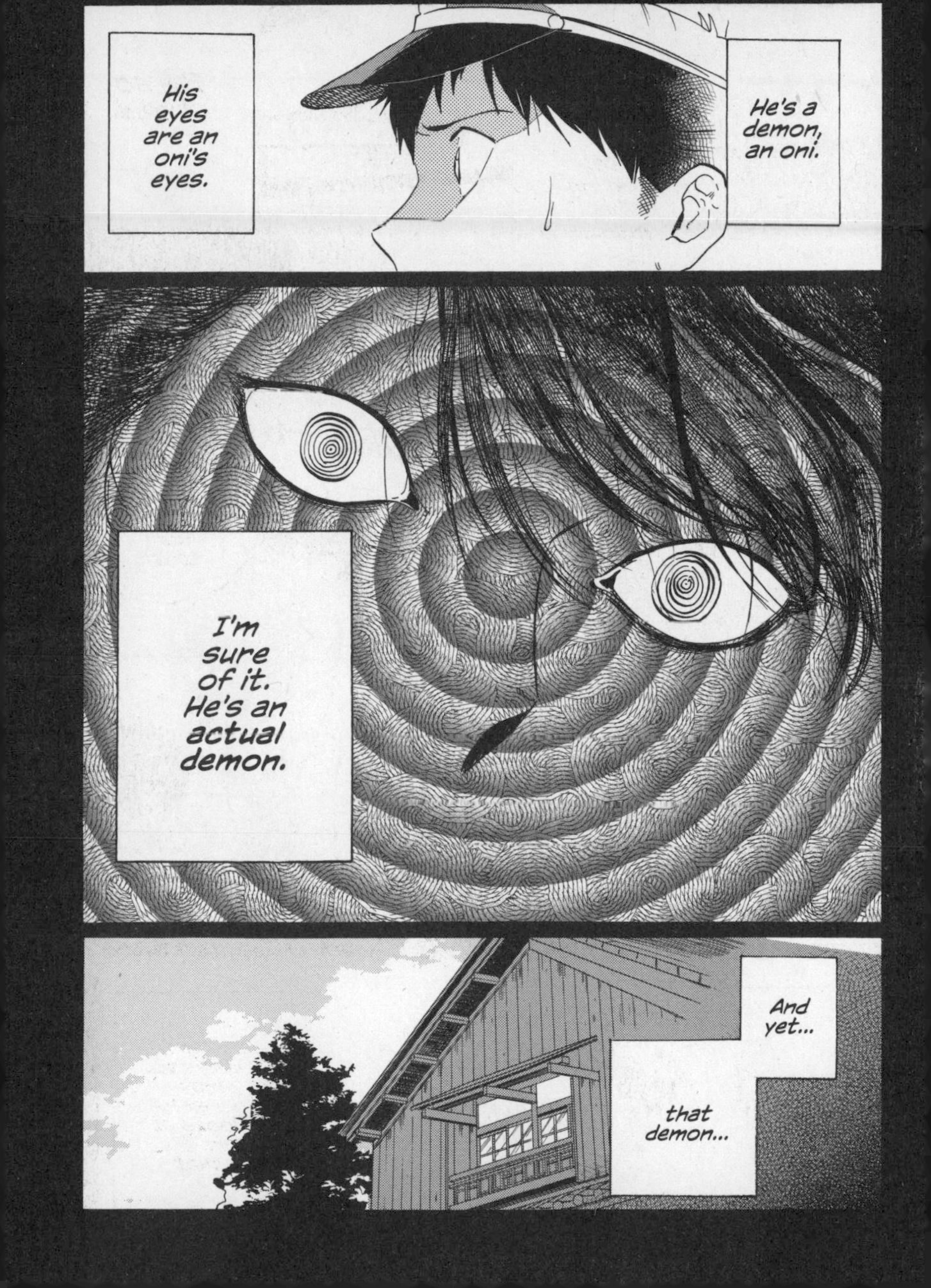
He's a demon, an oni.
His eyes are an oni's eyes.
I'm sure of it. He's an actual demon.
And yet...
that demon...

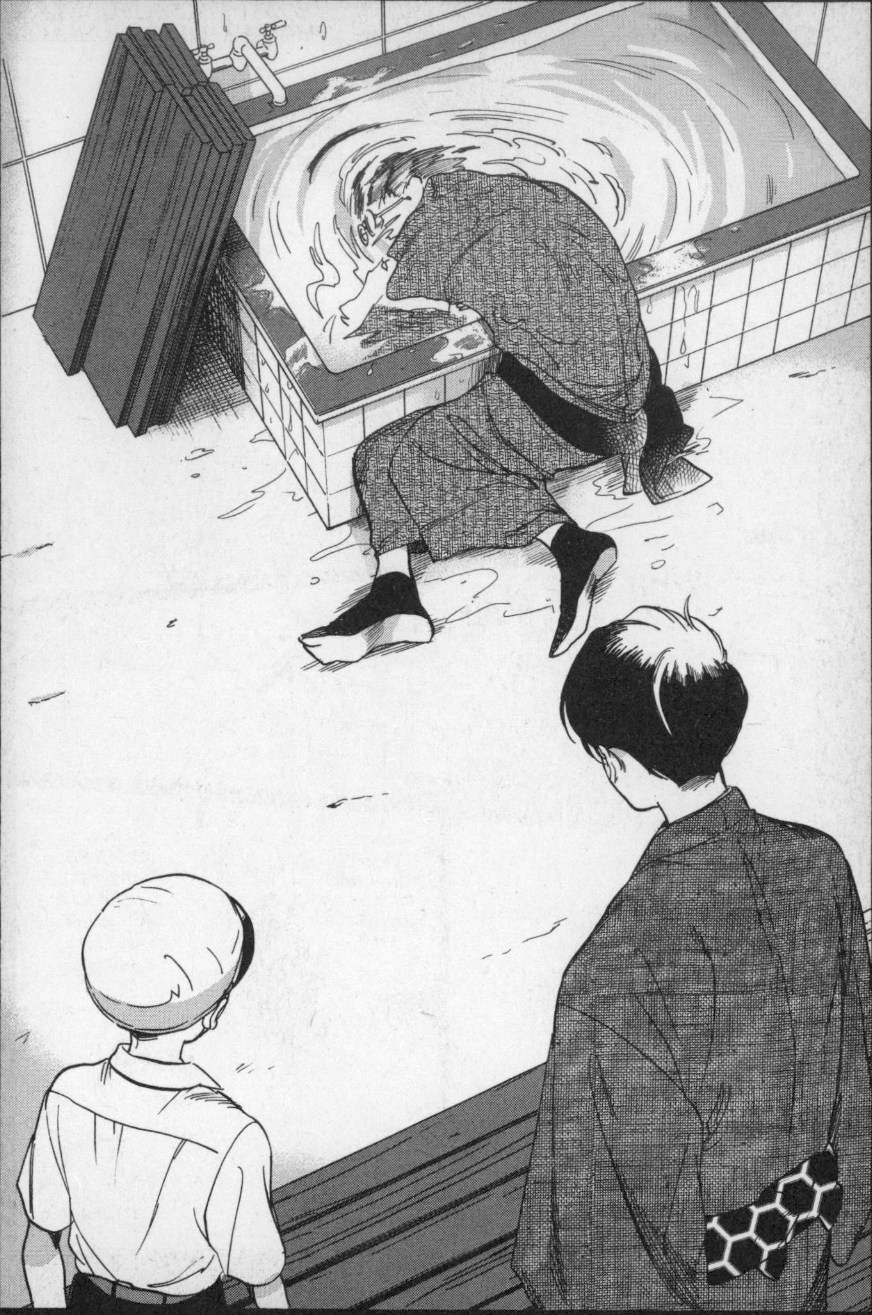

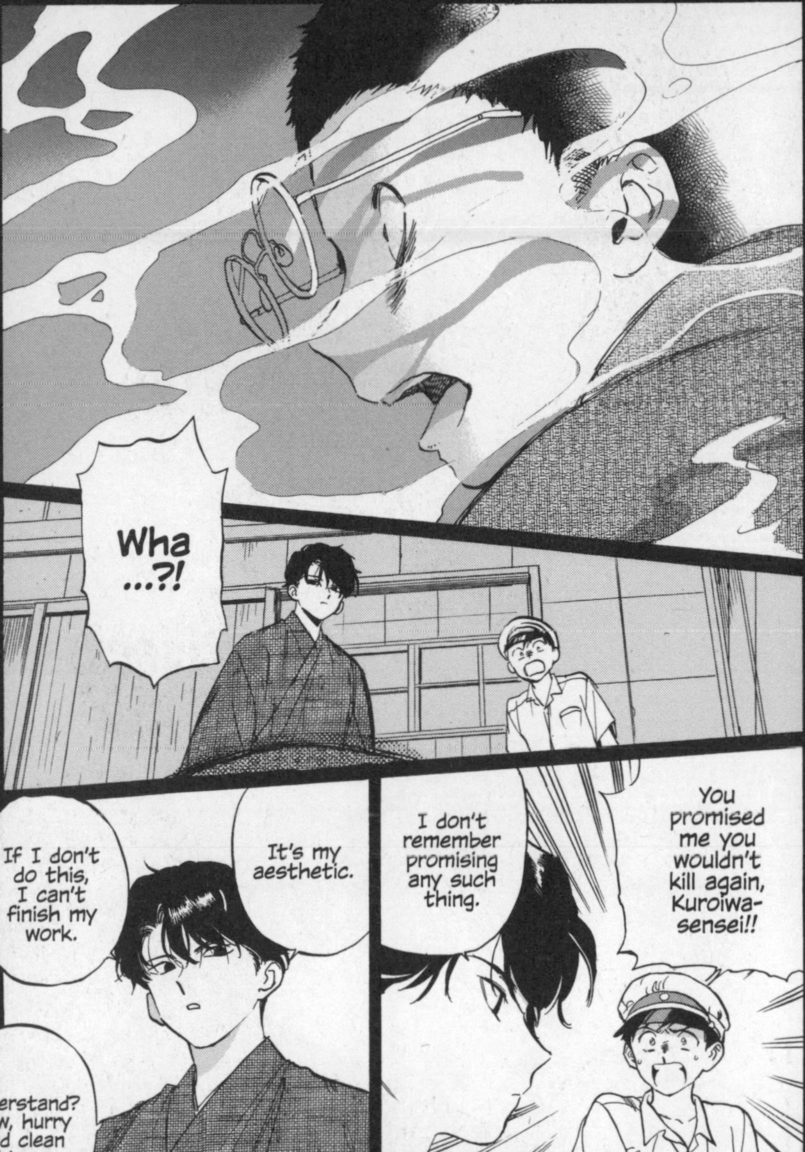
Wha...?!
You promised me you wouldn't kill again, Kuroiwa-sensei!!
I don't remember promising any such thing.
It's my aesthetic.
If I don't do this, I can't finish my work.
Understand? Now, hurry and clean this up.

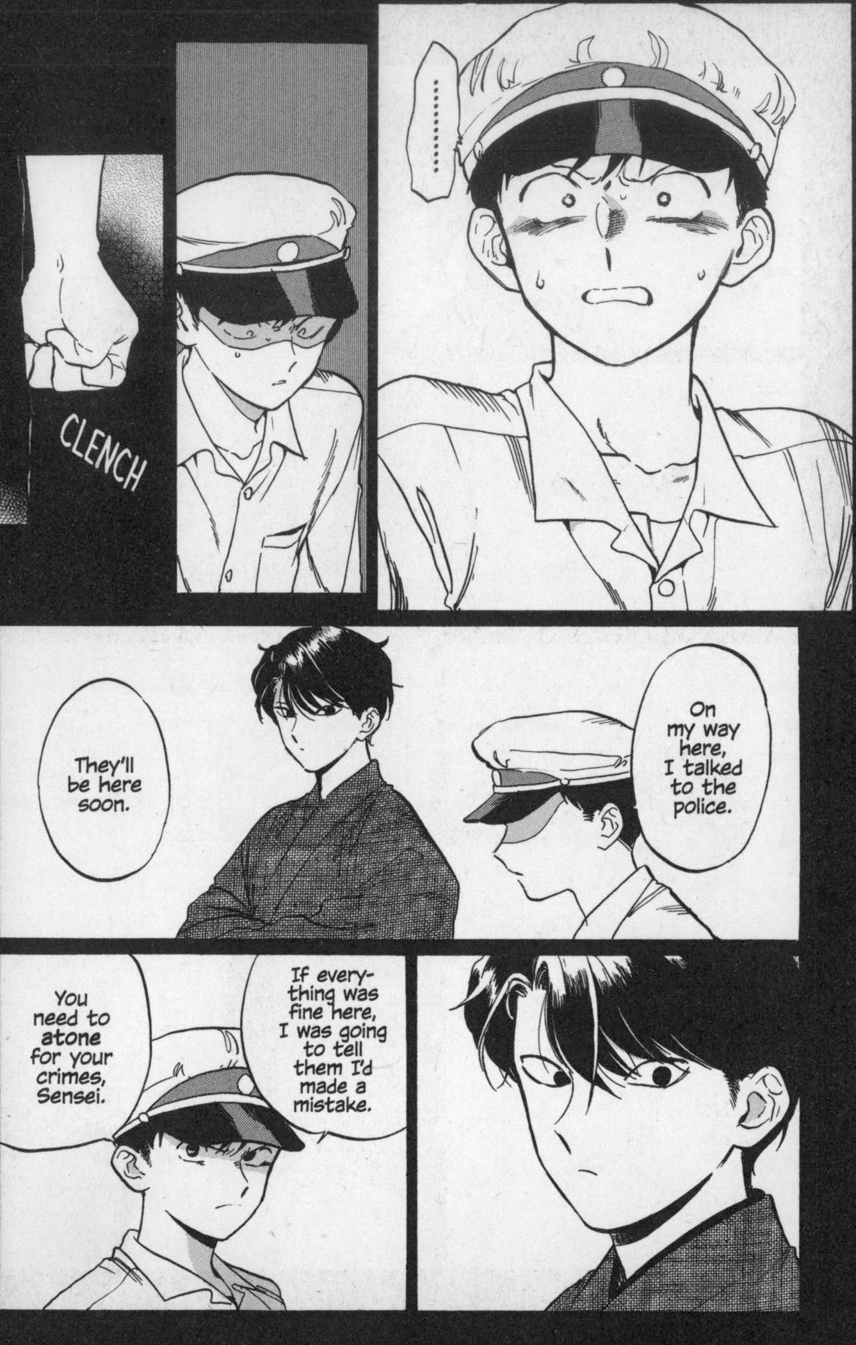
......
CLENCH
On my way here, I talked to the police.
They'll be here soon.
If every-thing was fine here, I was going to tell them I'd made a mistake.
You need to atone for your crimes, Sensei.

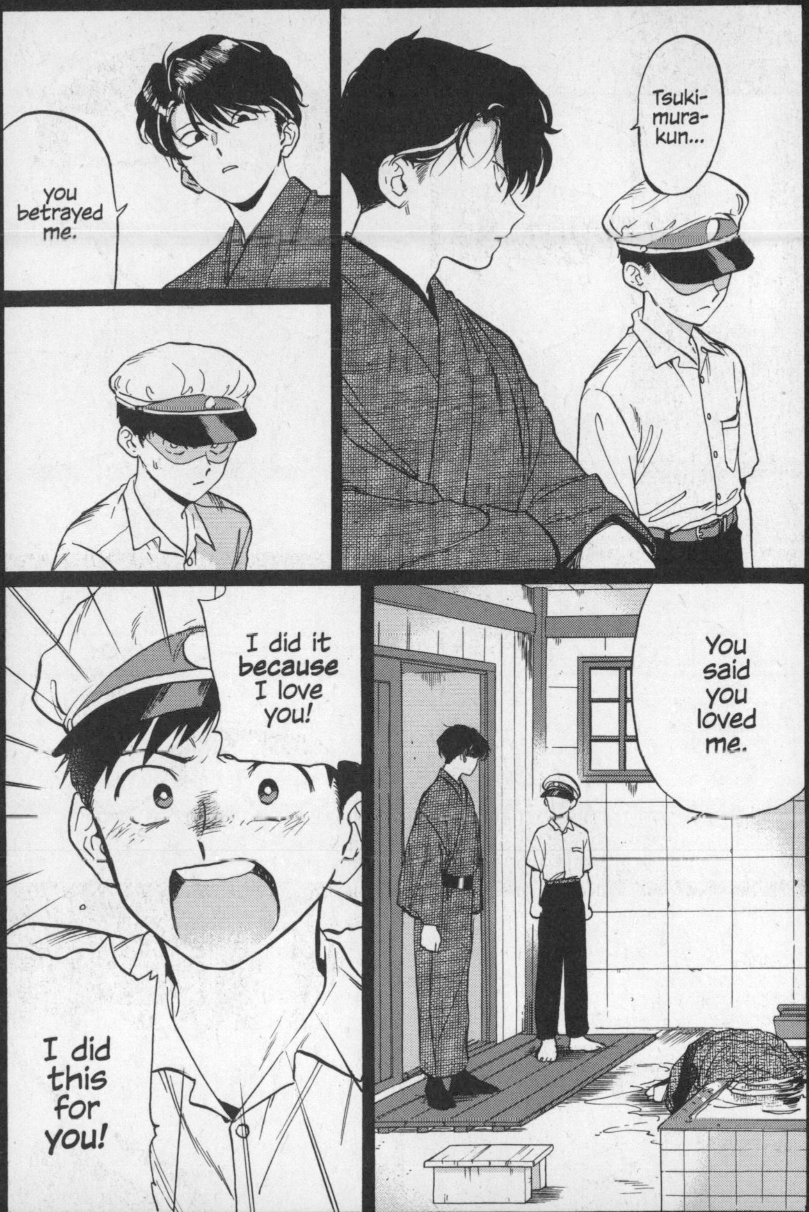
Tsuki-mura-kun...
you betrayed me.
You said you loved me.
I did it because I love you!
I did this for you!

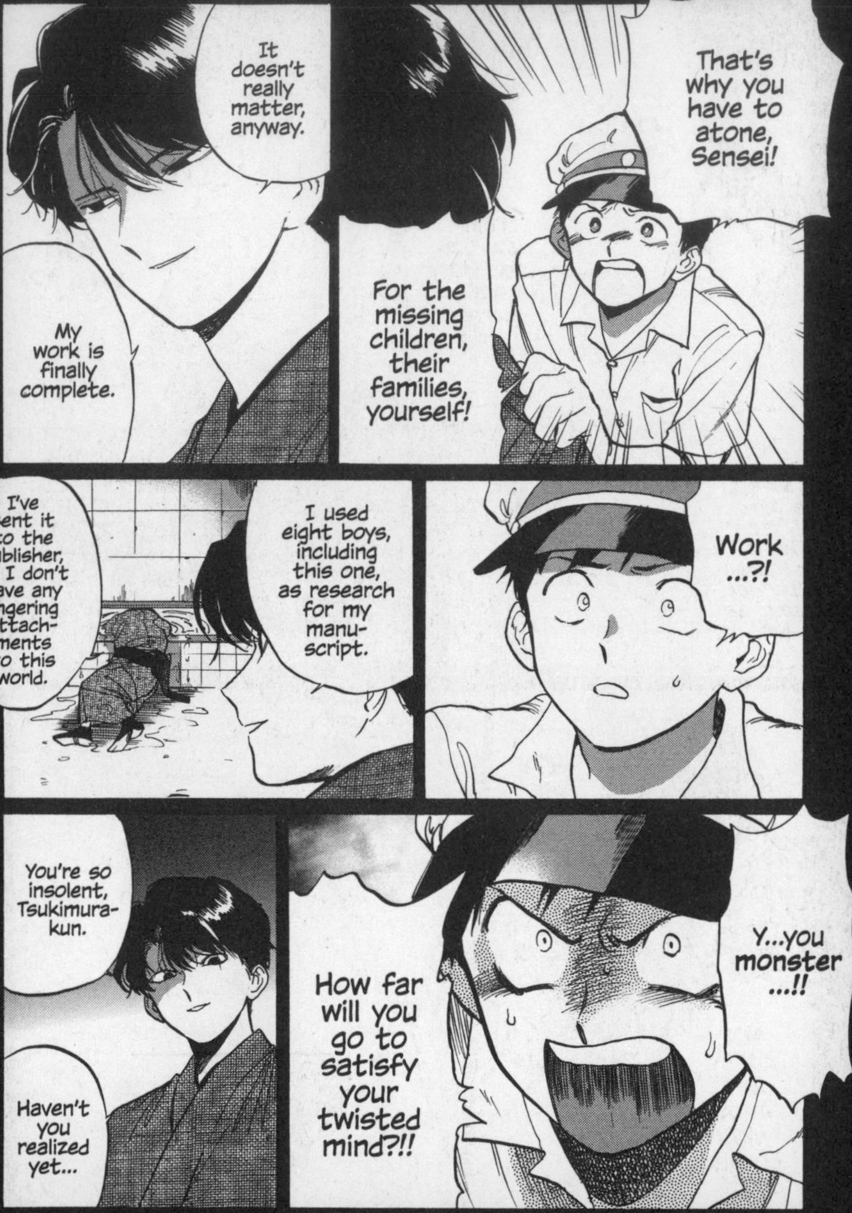
That's why you have to atone, Sensei!
For the missing children, their families, yourself!
It doesn't really matter, anyway.
My work is finally complete.
Work ...?!
I used eight boys, including this one, as research for my manuscript.
I've sent it to the publisher, so I don't have any lingering attachments to this world.
Y...you monster ...!!
How far will you go to satisfy your twisted mind?!!
You're so insolent, Tsukimura-kun.
Haven't you realized yet...

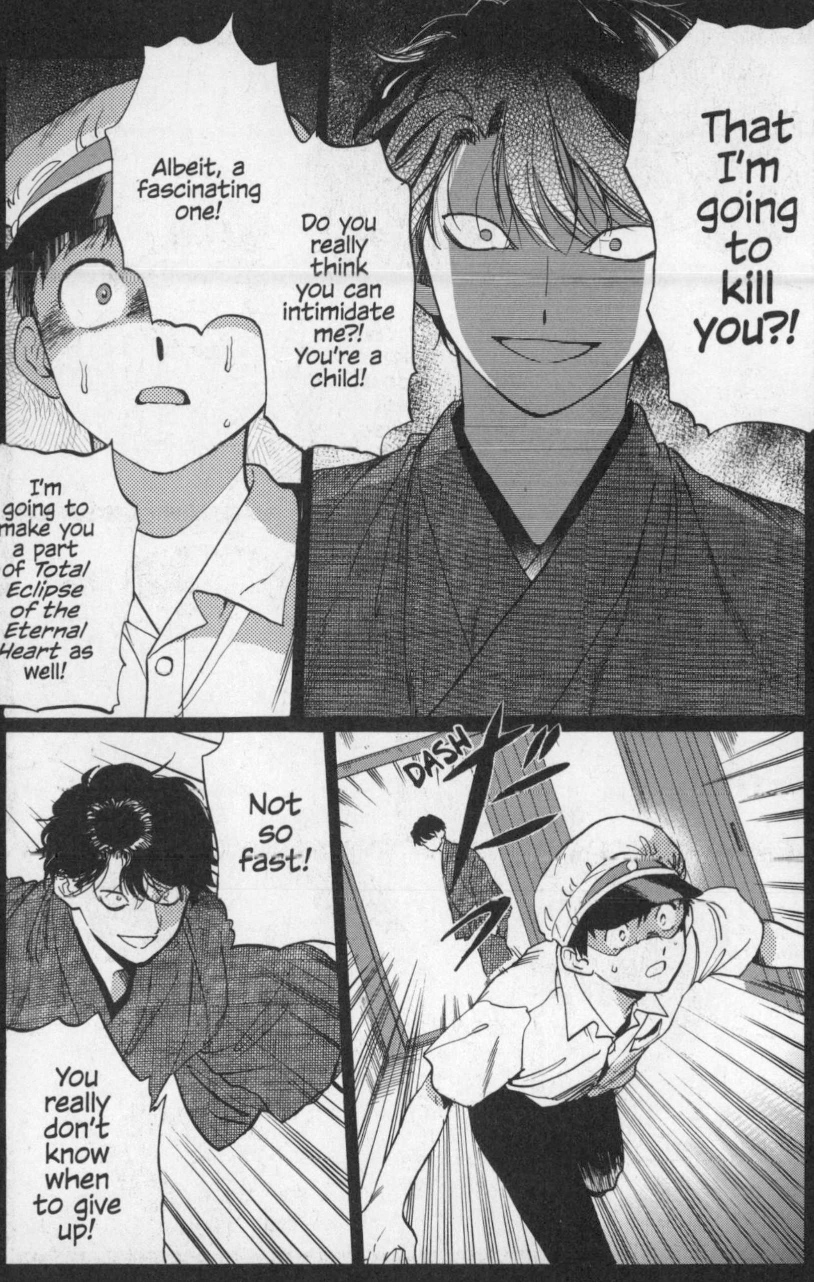
That I'm going to kill you?!
Do you really think you can intimidate me?! You're a child!
Albeit, a fascinating one!
I'm going to make you a part of *Total Eclipse of the Eternal Heart* as well!
DASH
Not so fast!
You really don't know when to give up!

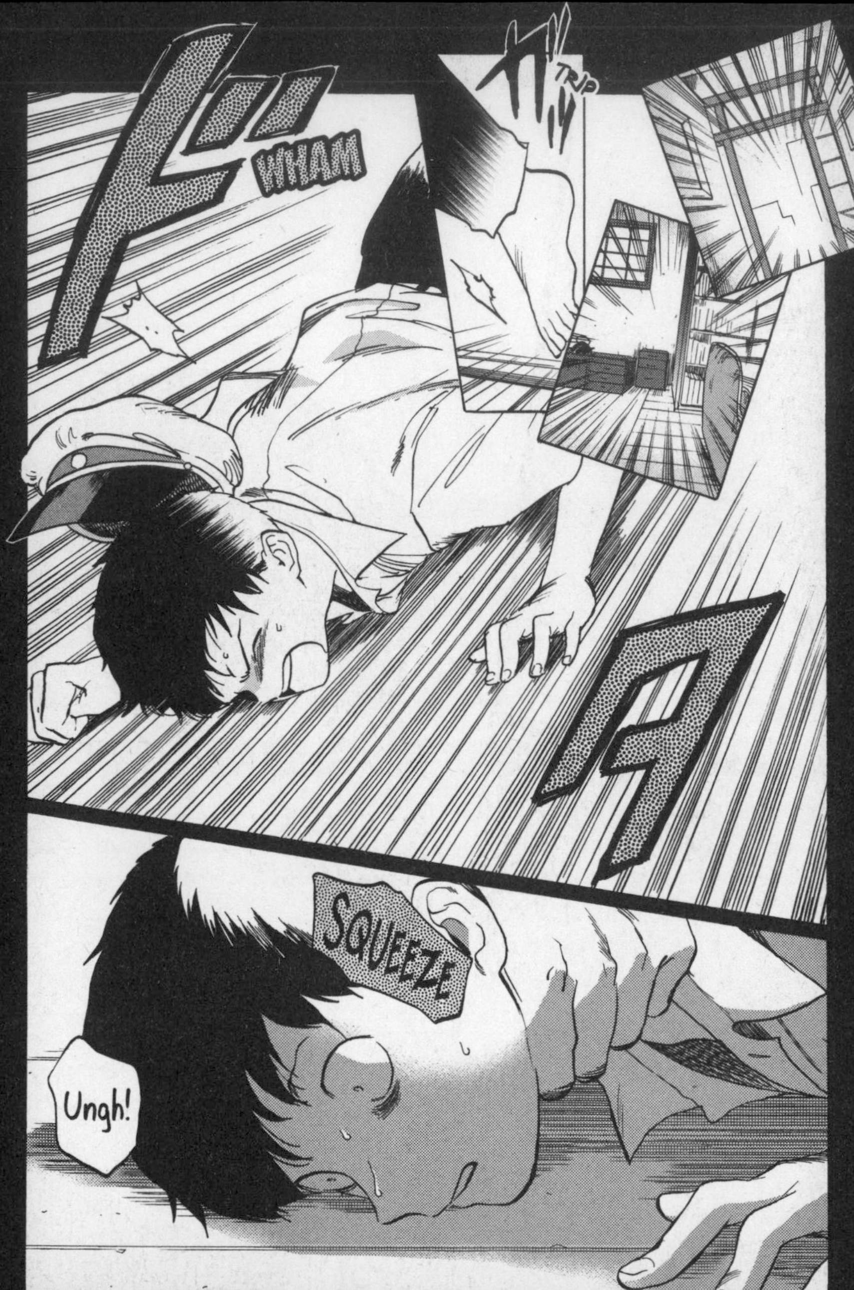
TRIP
WHAM
SQUEEZE
Ungh!

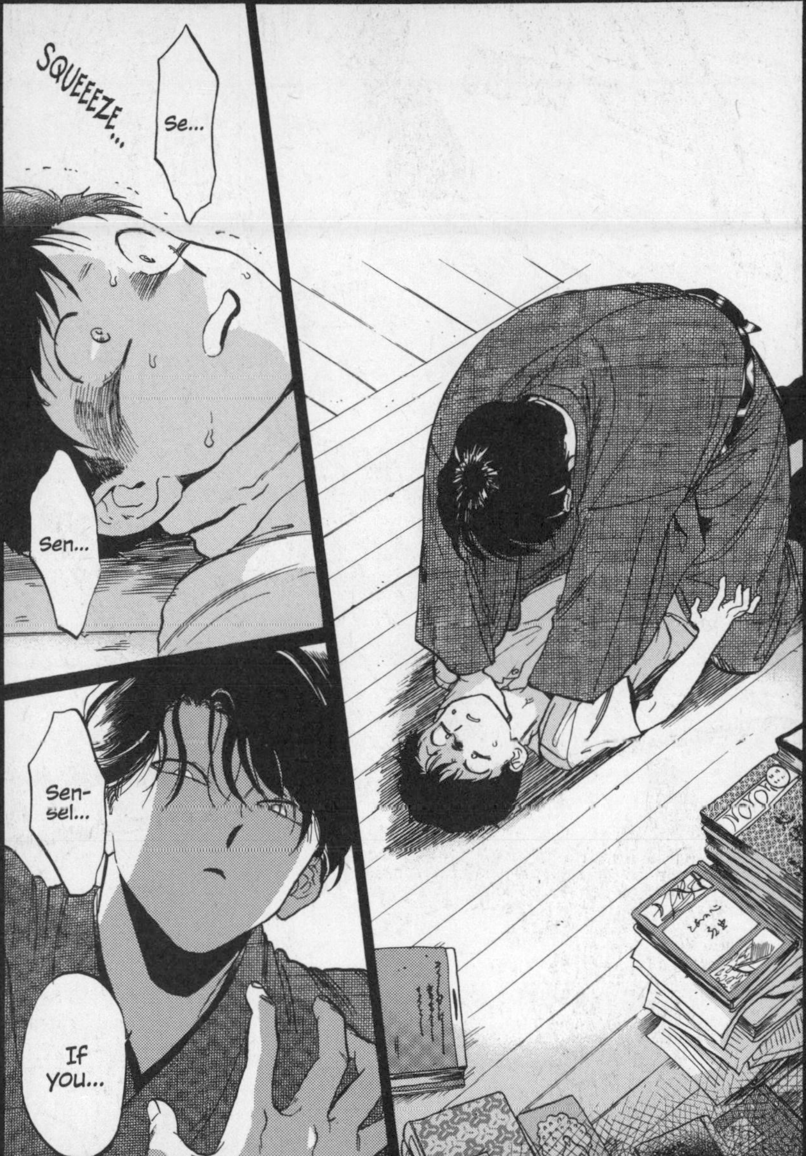
SQUEEEZE...
Se...
Sen...
Sen-sei...
If you...

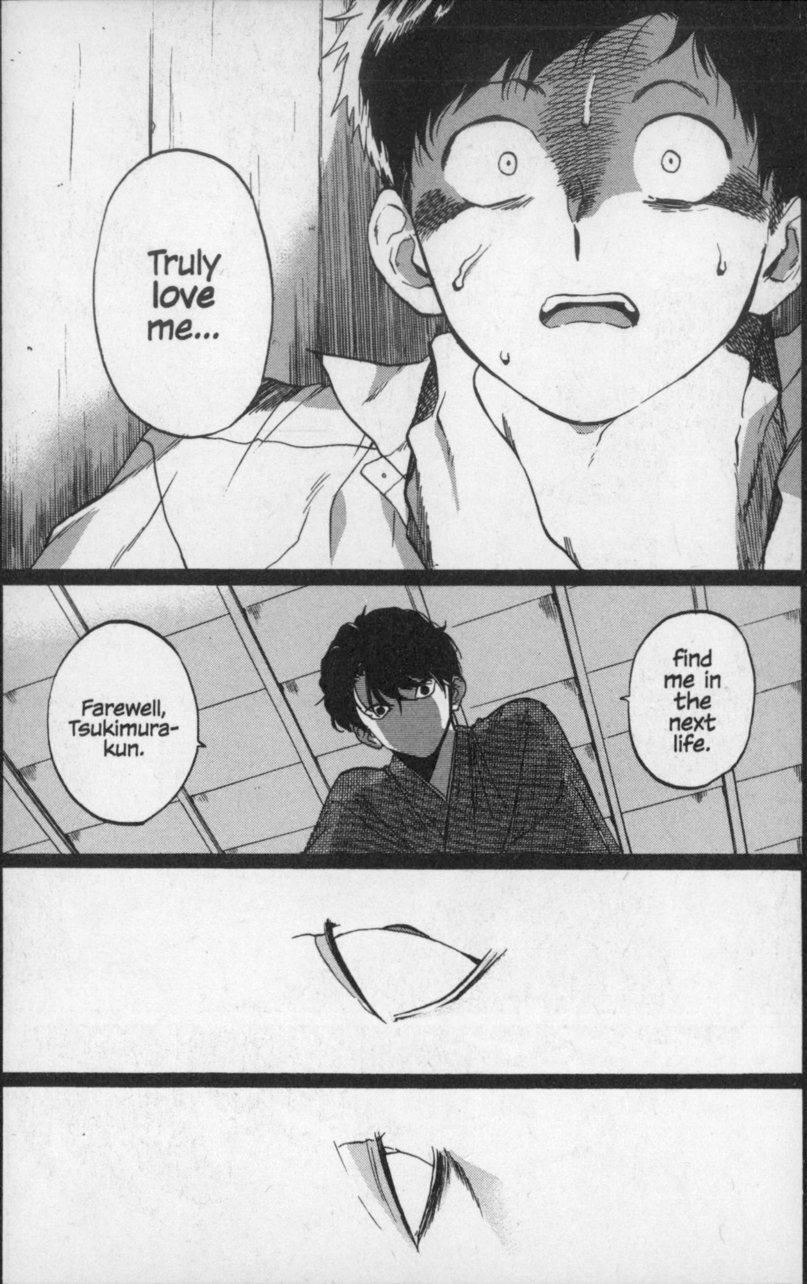
Truly love me...
find me in the next life.
Farewell, Tsukimura-kun.

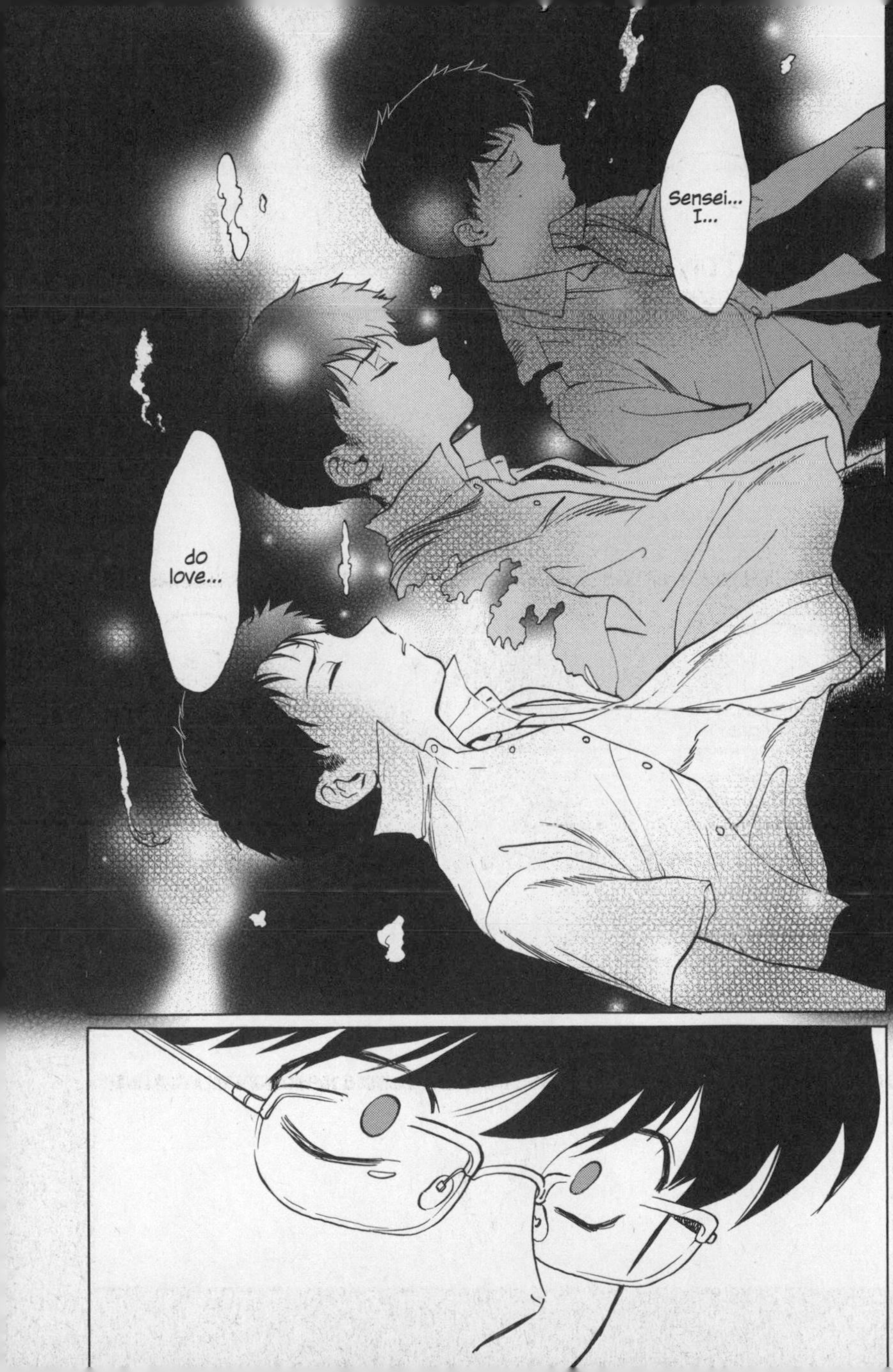
Sensei... I...
do love...

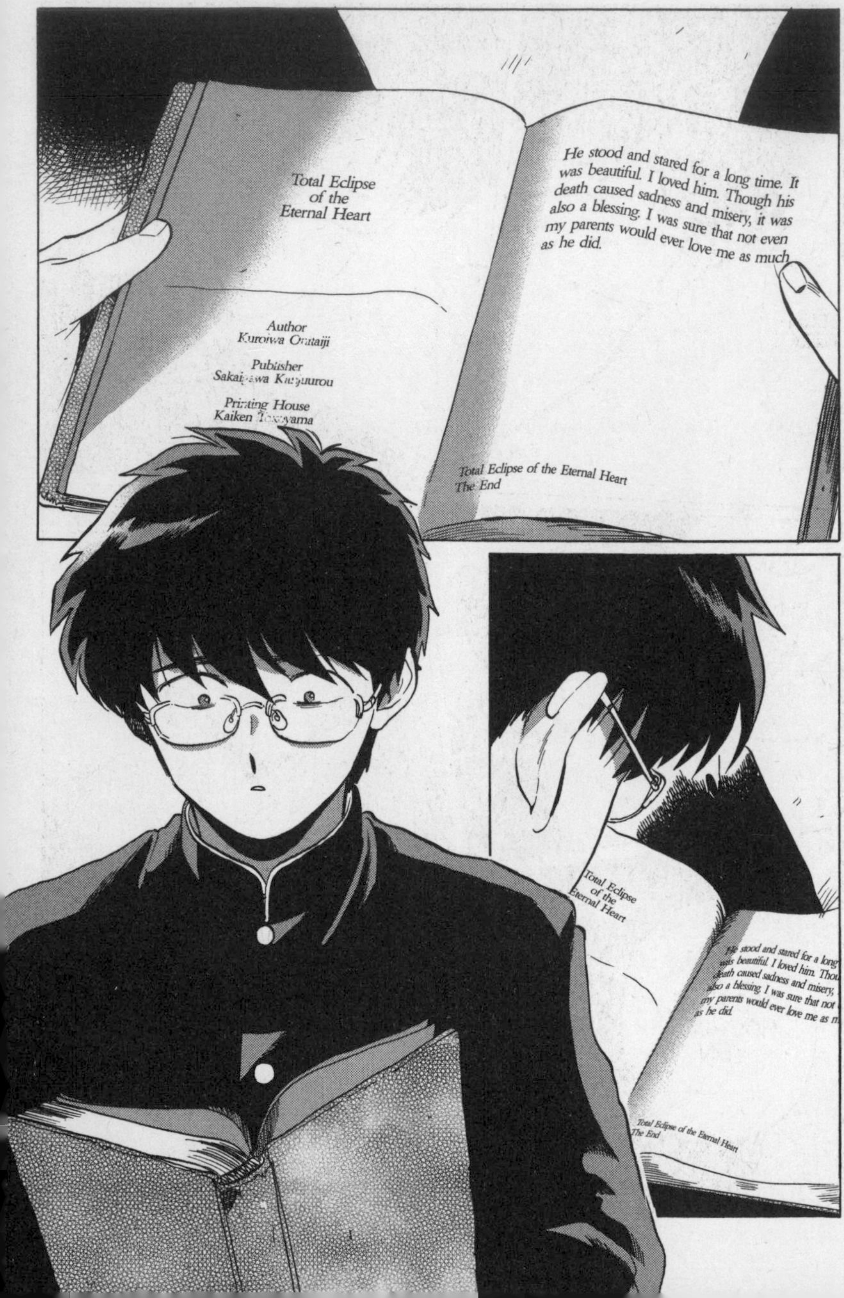
Total Eclipse of the Eternal Heart
Author
Kuroiwa
Publisher
Printing House
Kaiken
He stood and stared for a long time. It was beautiful. I loved him. Though his death caused sadness and misery, it was also a blessing. I was sure that not even my parents would ever love me as much as he did.
Total Eclipse of the Eternal Heart
The End

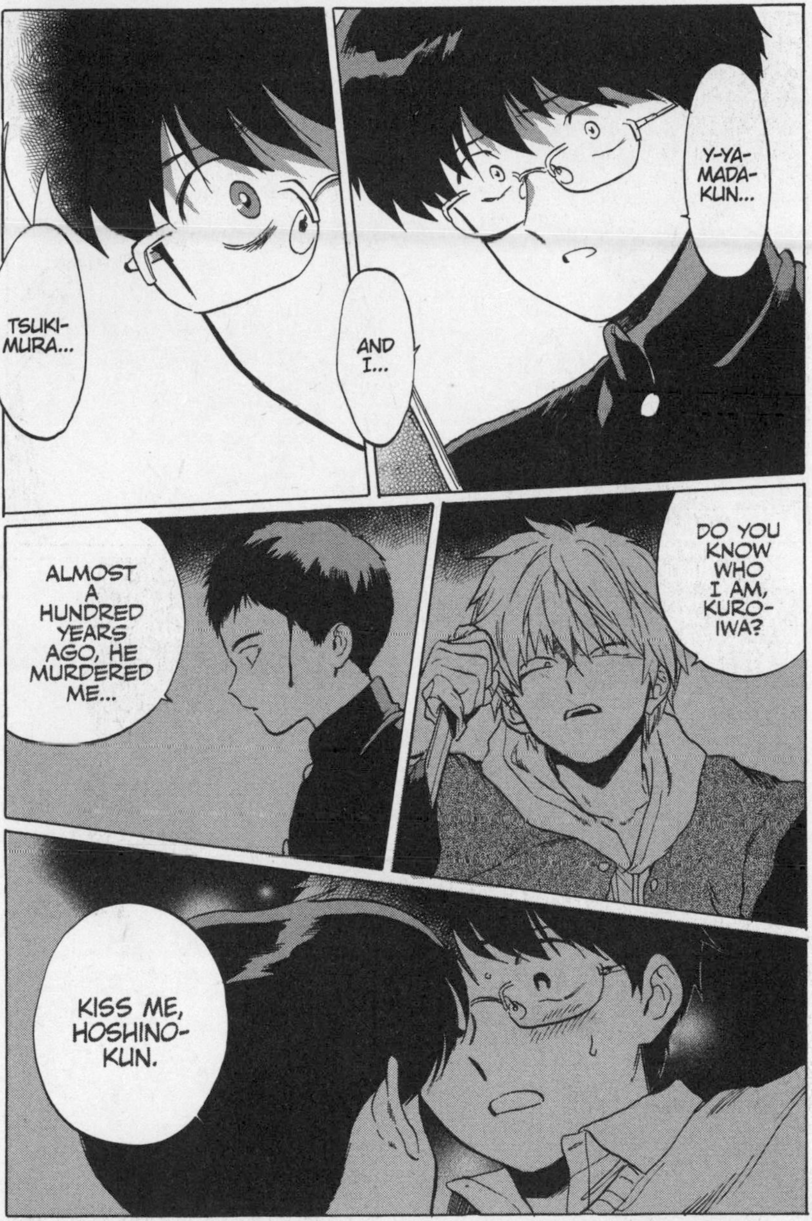
Y-YAMADA-KUN...
AND I...
TSUKI-MURA...
DO YOU KNOW WHO I AM, KURO-IWA?
ALMOST A HUNDRED YEARS AGO, HE MURDERED ME...
KISS ME, HOSHINO-KUN.

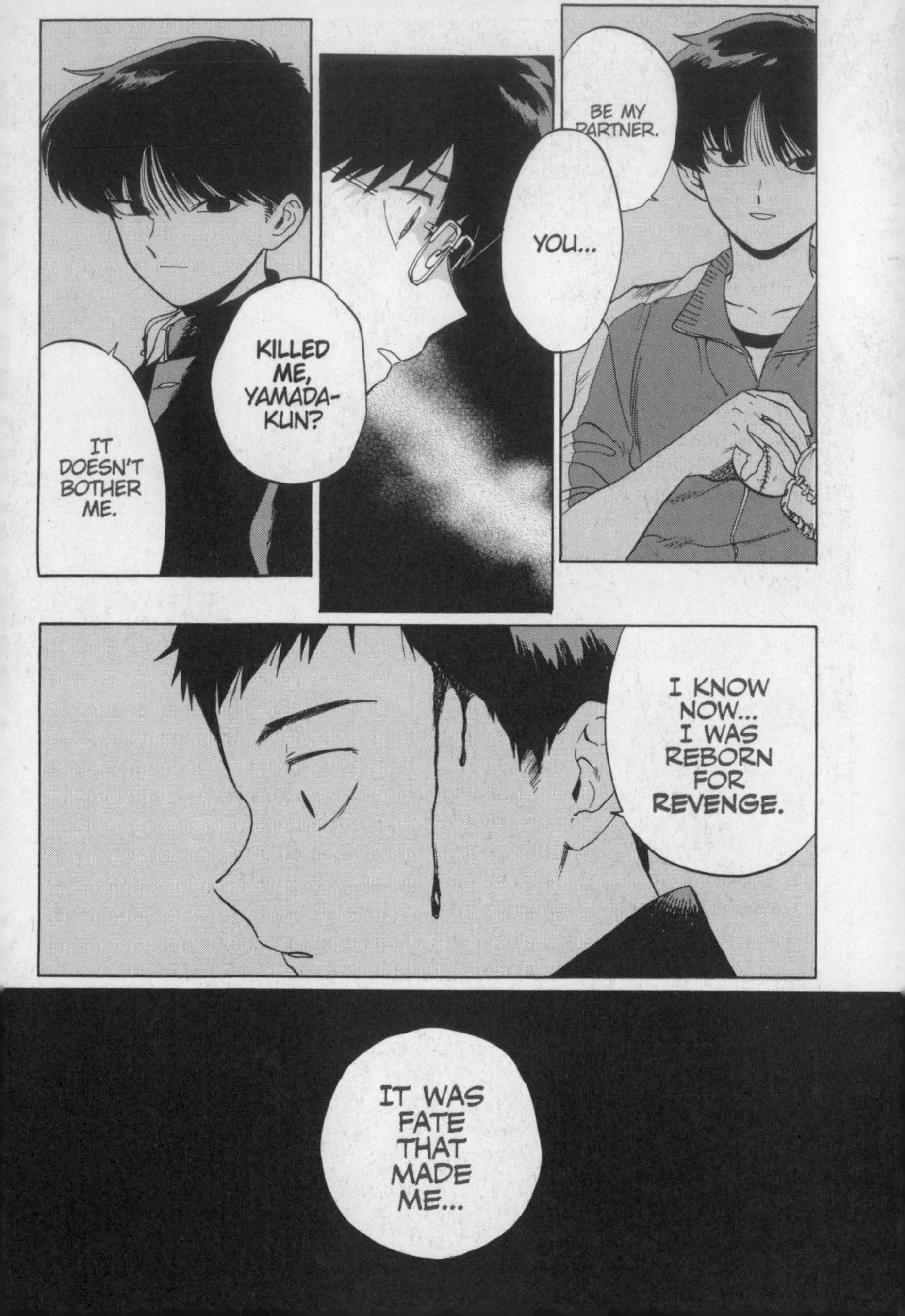
BE MY PARTNER.
YOU...
KILLED ME, YAMADA-KUN?
IT DOESN'T BOTHER ME.
I KNOW NOW... I WAS REBORN FOR REVENGE.
IT WAS FATE THAT MADE ME...

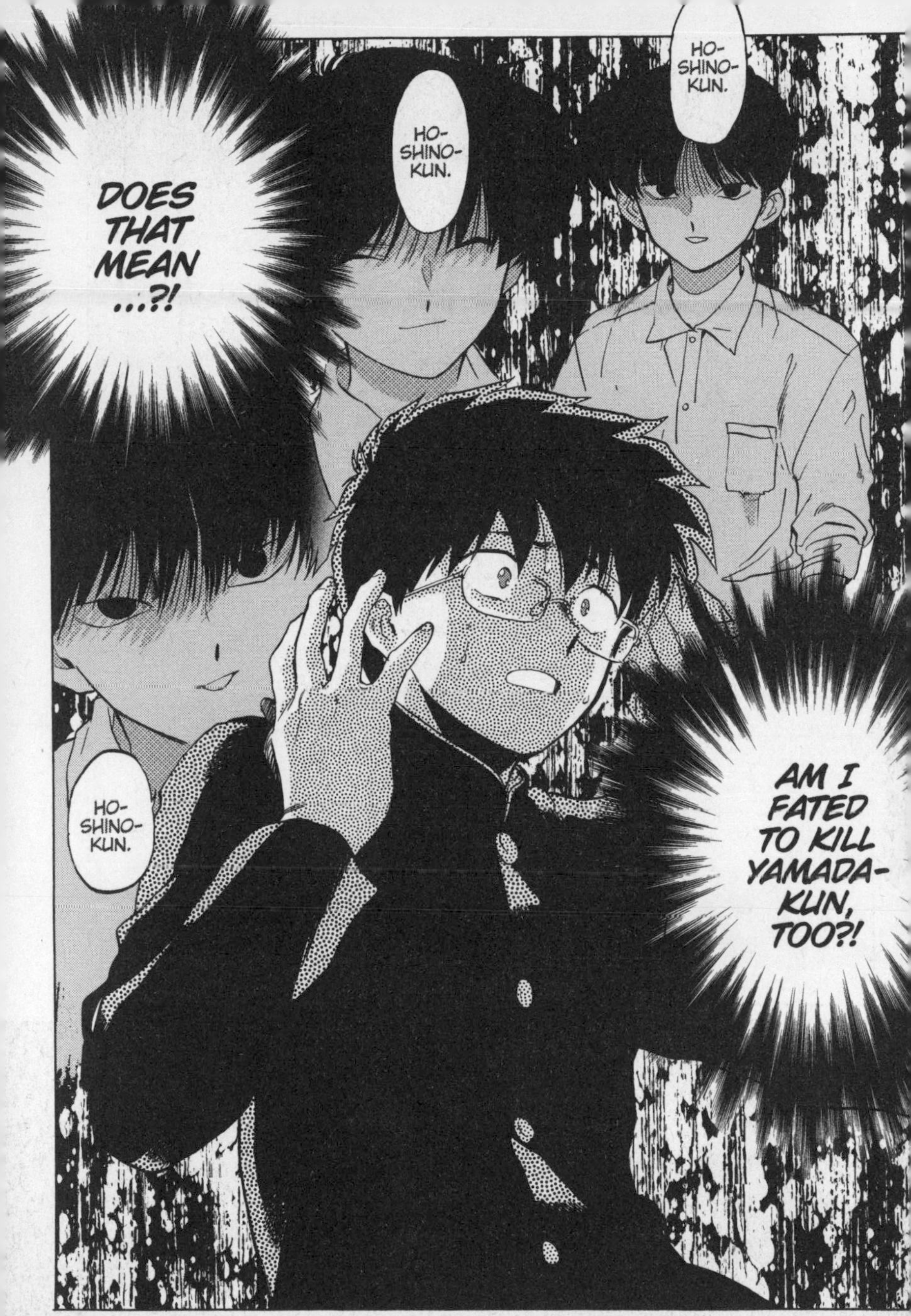
HO-SHINO-KUN.
HO-SHINO-KUN.
DOES THAT MEAN ...?!
AM I FATED TO KILL YAMADA-KUN, TOO?!
HO-SHINO-KUN.

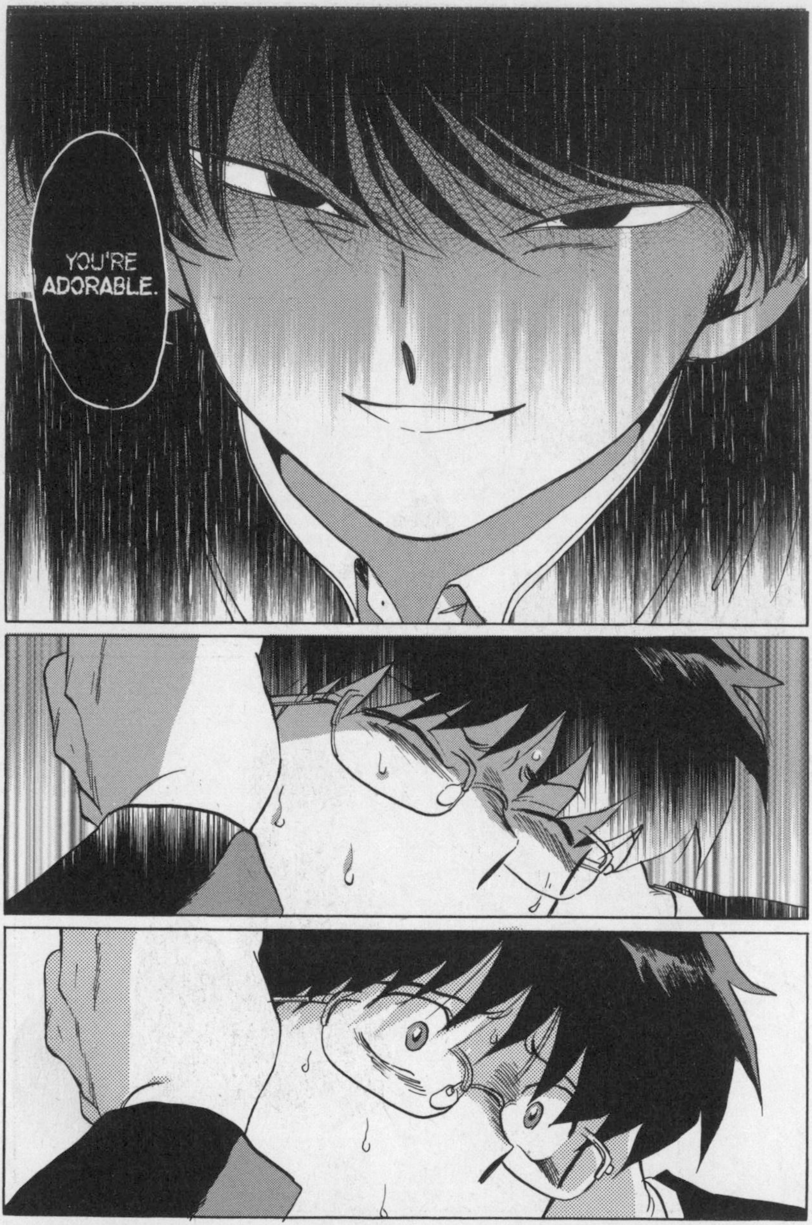
YOU'RE ADORABLE.

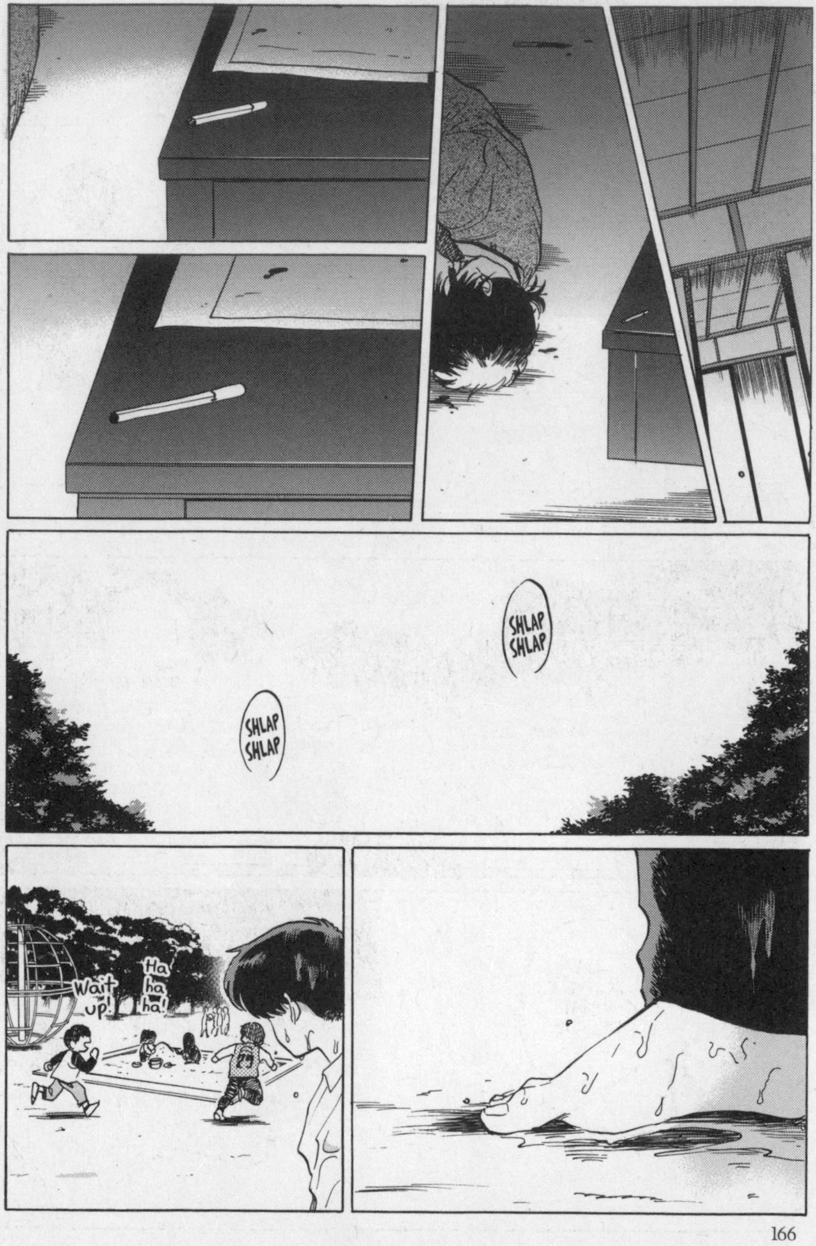
SHLAP SHLAP
SHLAP SHLAP
Ha ha ha!
Wait up!

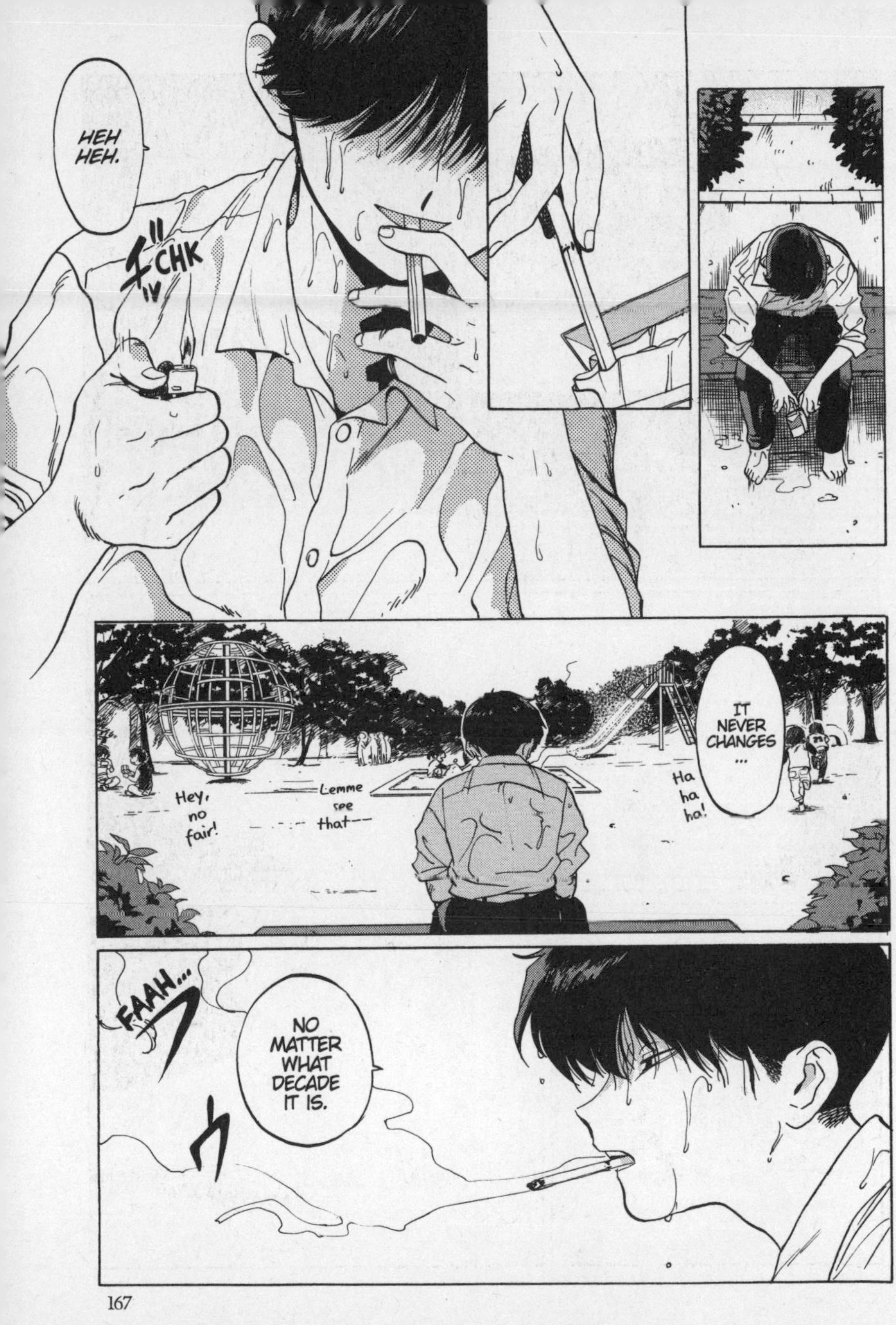
HEH HEH.
CHK
IT NEVER CHANGES...
Ha ha ha!
Lemme see that—
Hey, no fair!
NO MATTER WHAT DECADE IT IS.
FAAH...

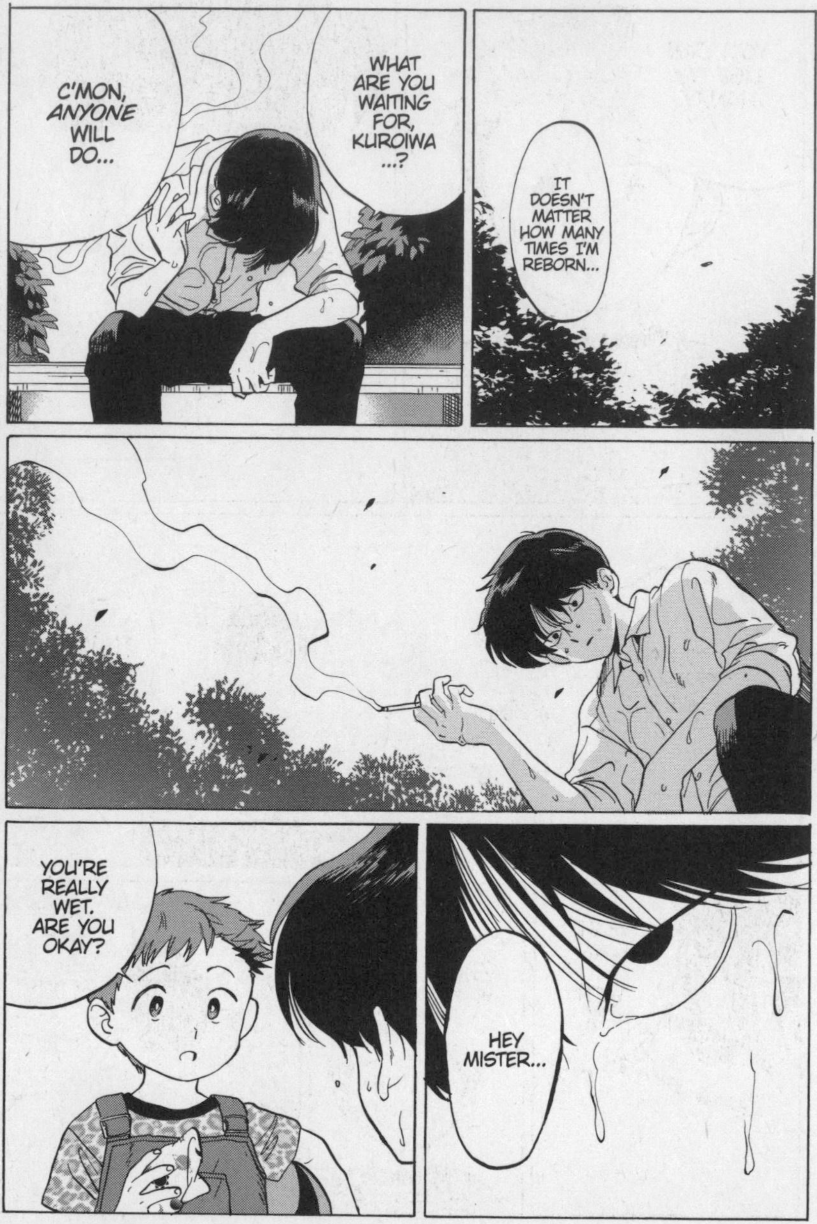
IT DOESN'T MATTER HOW MANY TIMES I'M REBORN...
WHAT ARE YOU WAITING FOR, KUROIWA ...?
C'MON, ANYONE WILL DO...
HEY MISTER...
YOU'RE REALLY WET. ARE YOU OKAY?

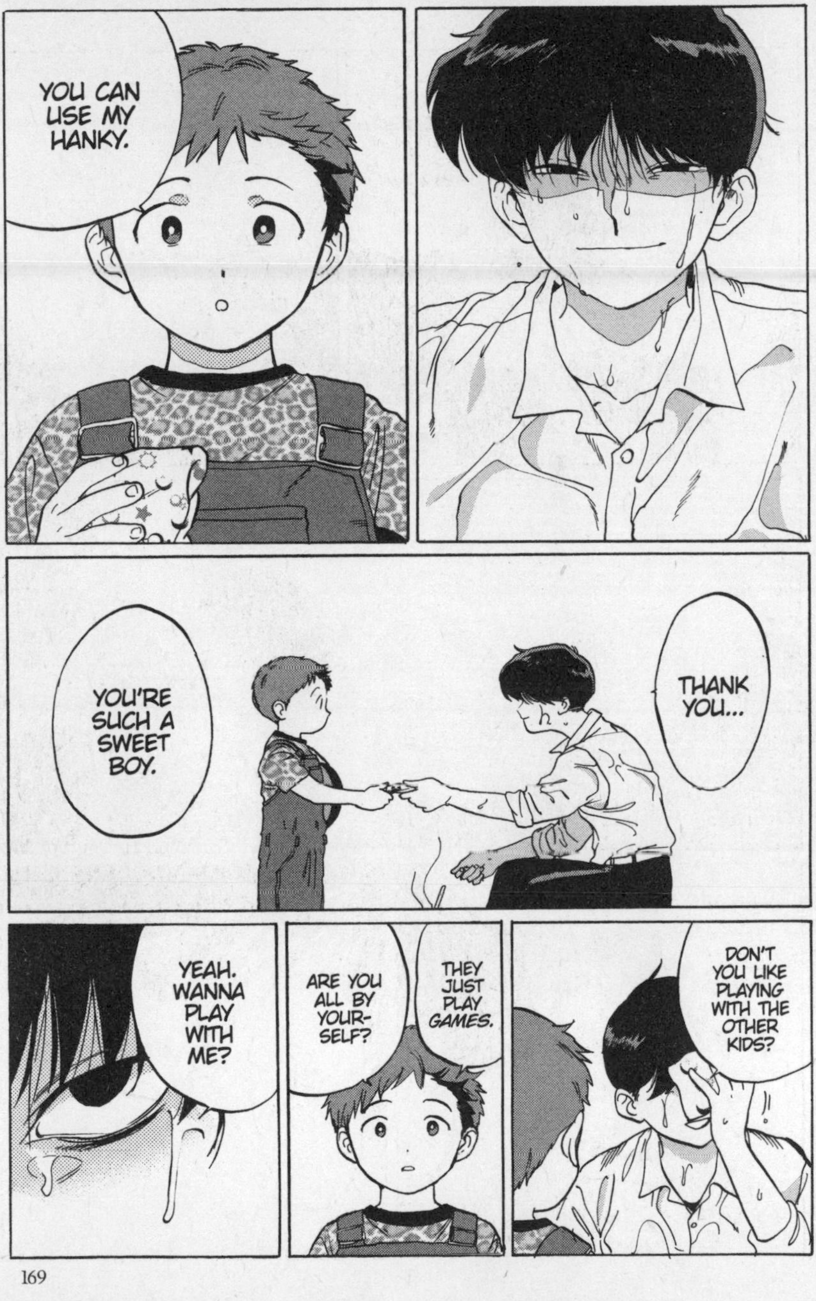
YOU CAN USE MY HANKY.
THANK YOU...
YOU'RE SUCH A SWEET BOY.
DON'T YOU LIKE PLAYING WITH THE OTHER KIDS?
THEY JUST PLAY GAMES.
ARE YOU ALL BY YOUR-SELF?
YEAH. WANNA PLAY WITH ME?

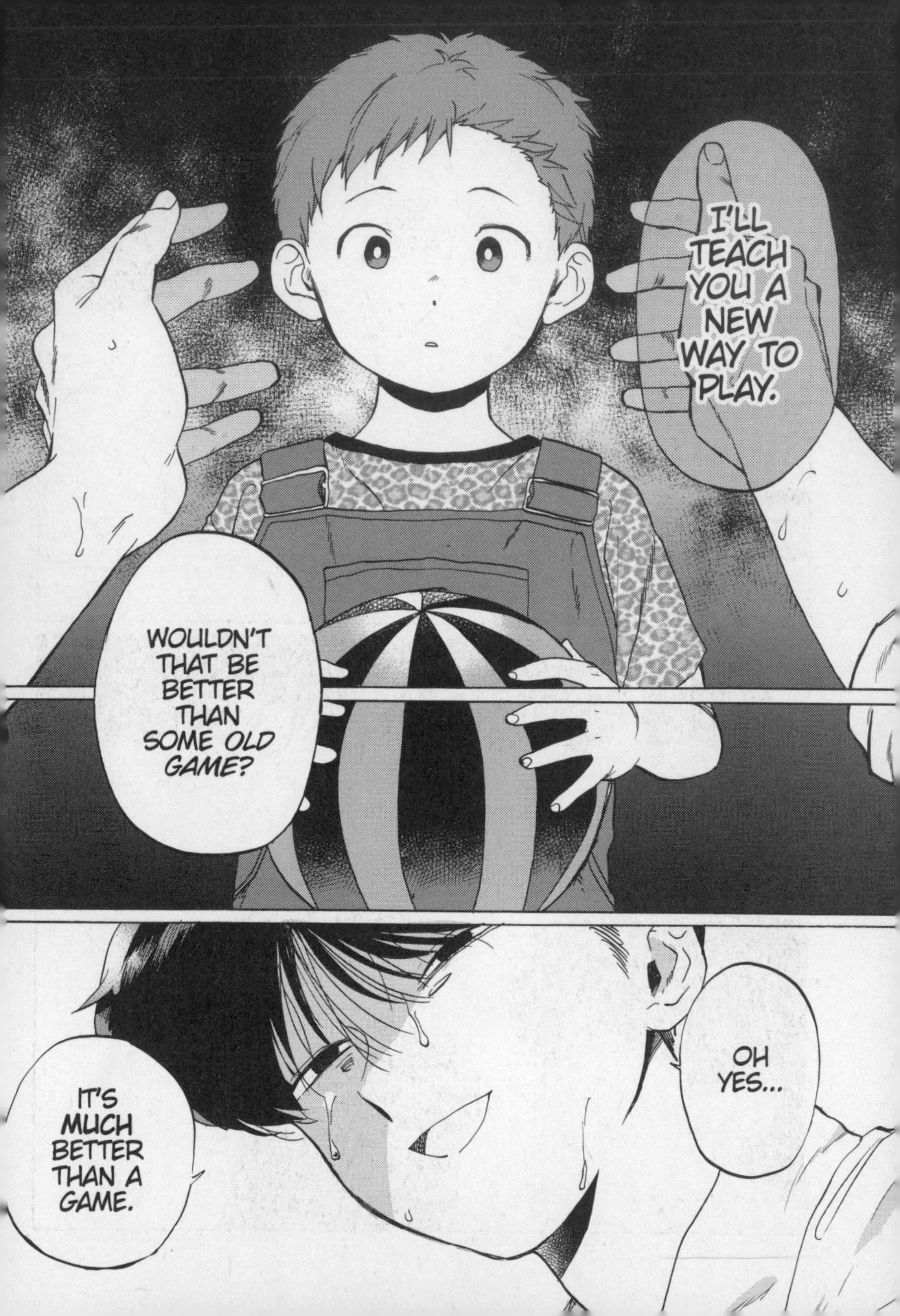
I'LL TEACH YOU A NEW WAY TO PLAY.
WOULDN'T THAT BE BETTER THAN SOME OLD GAME?
OH YES...
IT'S MUCH BETTER THAN A GAME.

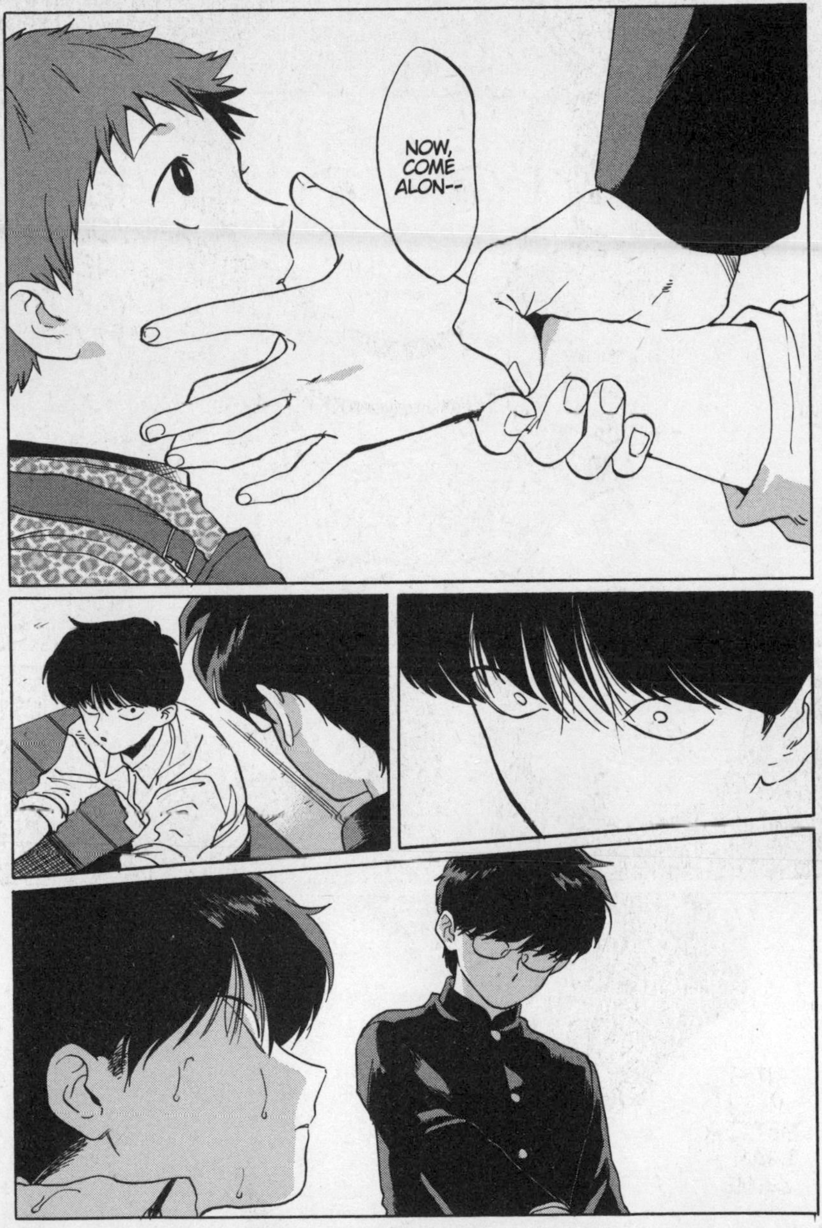
NOW, COME ALON--

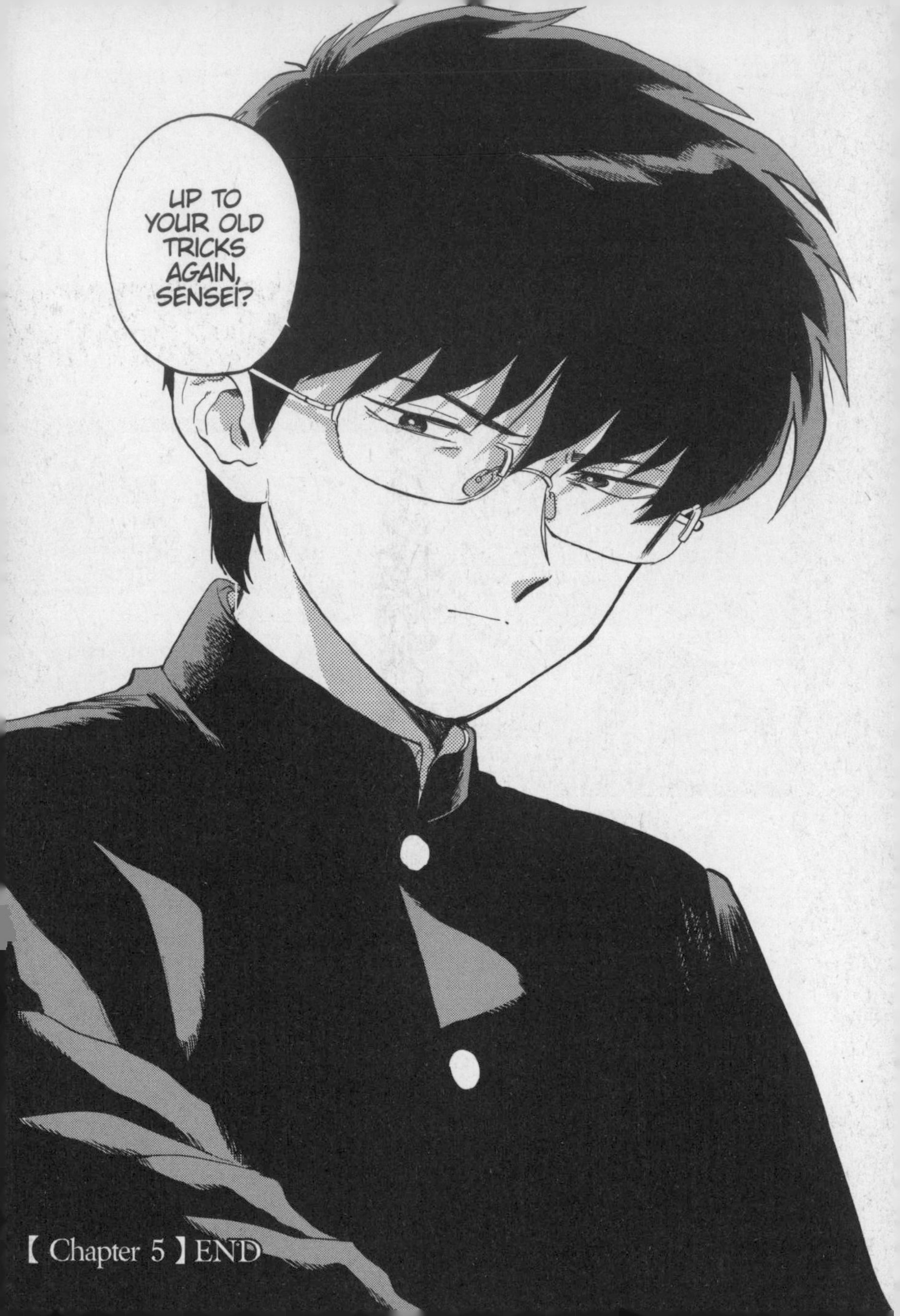
UP TO YOUR OLD TRICKS AGAIN, SENSEI?
【 Chapter 5 】END

【 Final Chapter 】

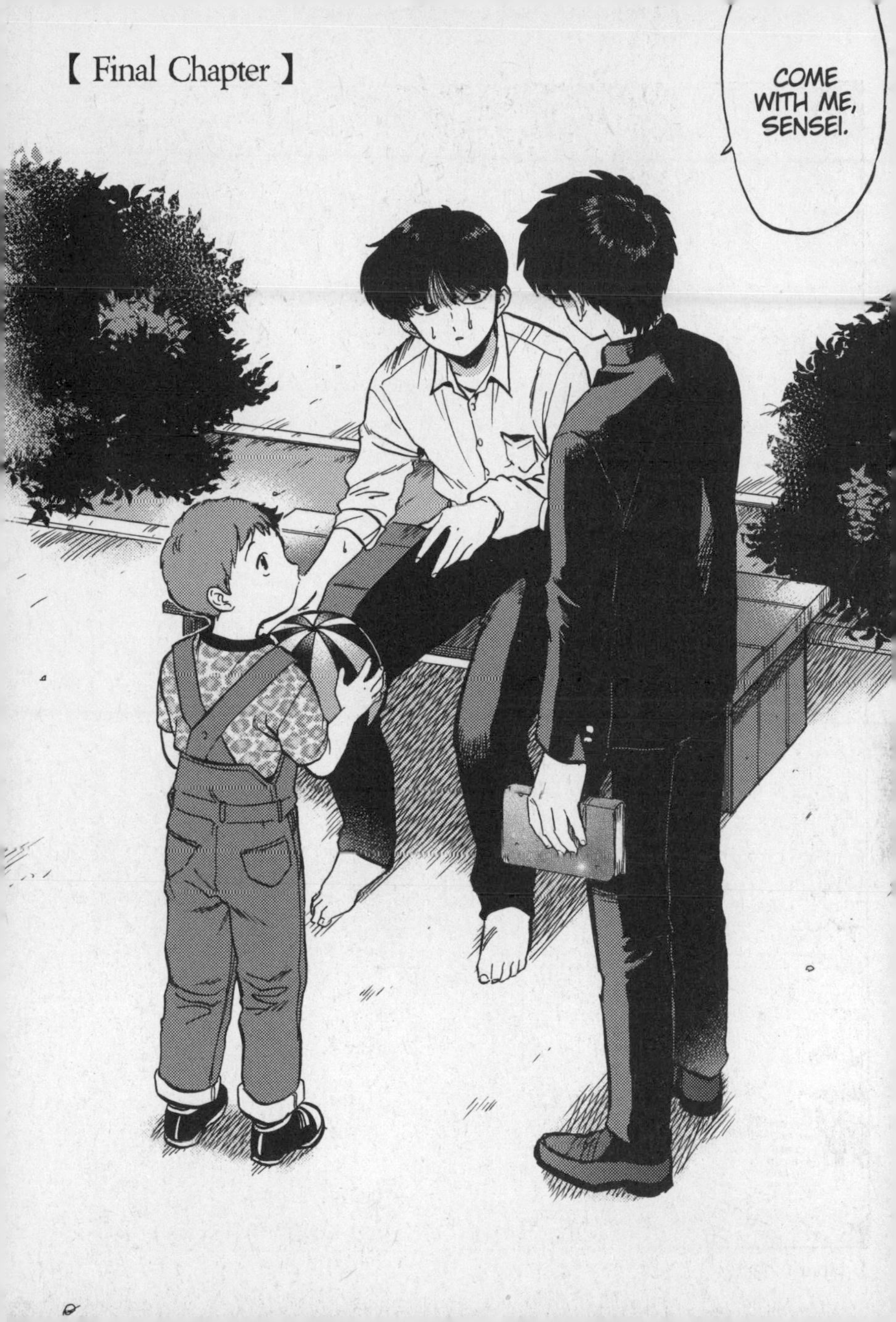
COME WITH ME, SENSEI.

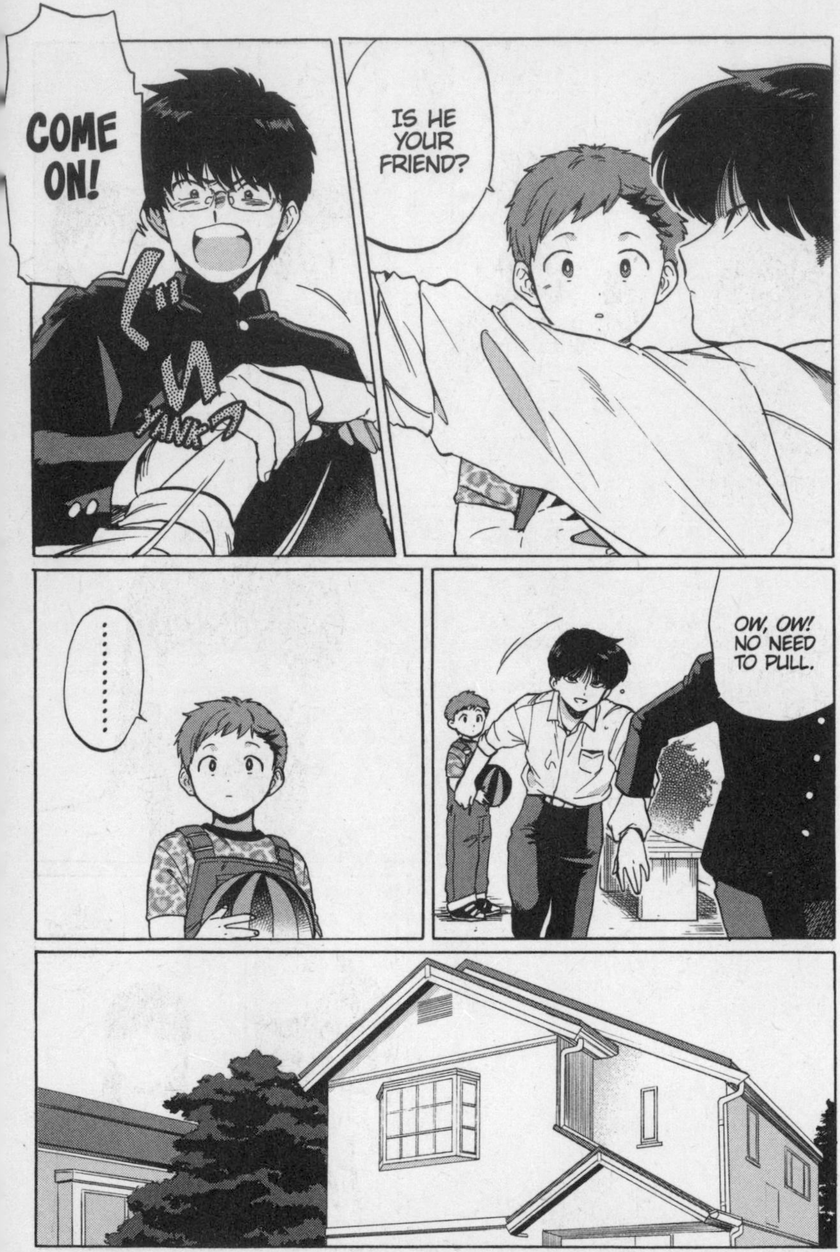
IS HE YOUR FRIEND?
COME ON!
YANK
OW, OW! NO NEED TO PULL.
......

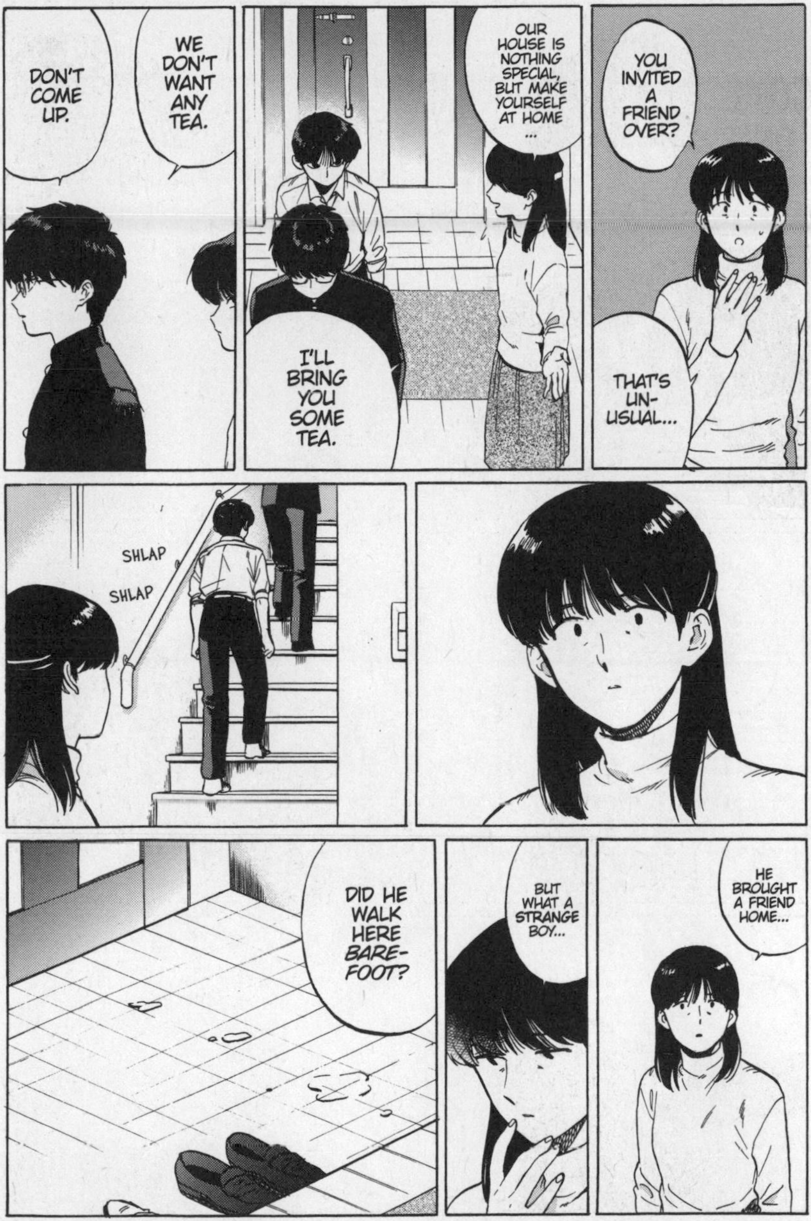
YOU INVITED A FRIEND OVER?
THAT'S UN-USUAL...
OUR HOUSE IS NOTHING SPECIAL, BUT MAKE YOURSELF AT HOME ...
I'LL BRING YOU SOME TEA.
WE DON'T WANT ANY TEA.
DON'T COME UP.
SHLAP
SHLAP
HE BROUGHT A FRIEND HOME...
BUT WHAT A STRANGE BOY...
DID HE WALK HERE BARE-FOOT?

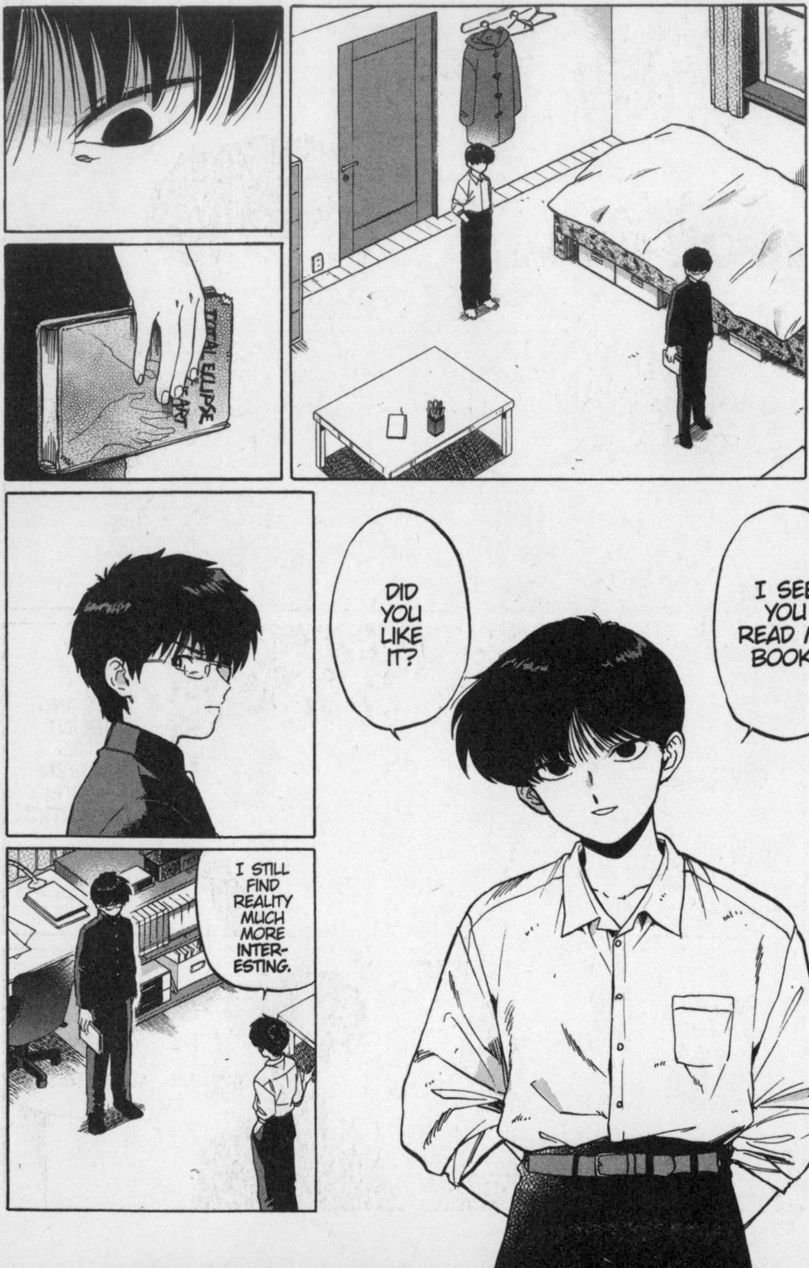
TOTAL ELLIPSE
I SEE YOU READ MY BOOK.
DID YOU LIKE IT?
I STILL FIND REALITY MUCH MORE INTER-ESTING.

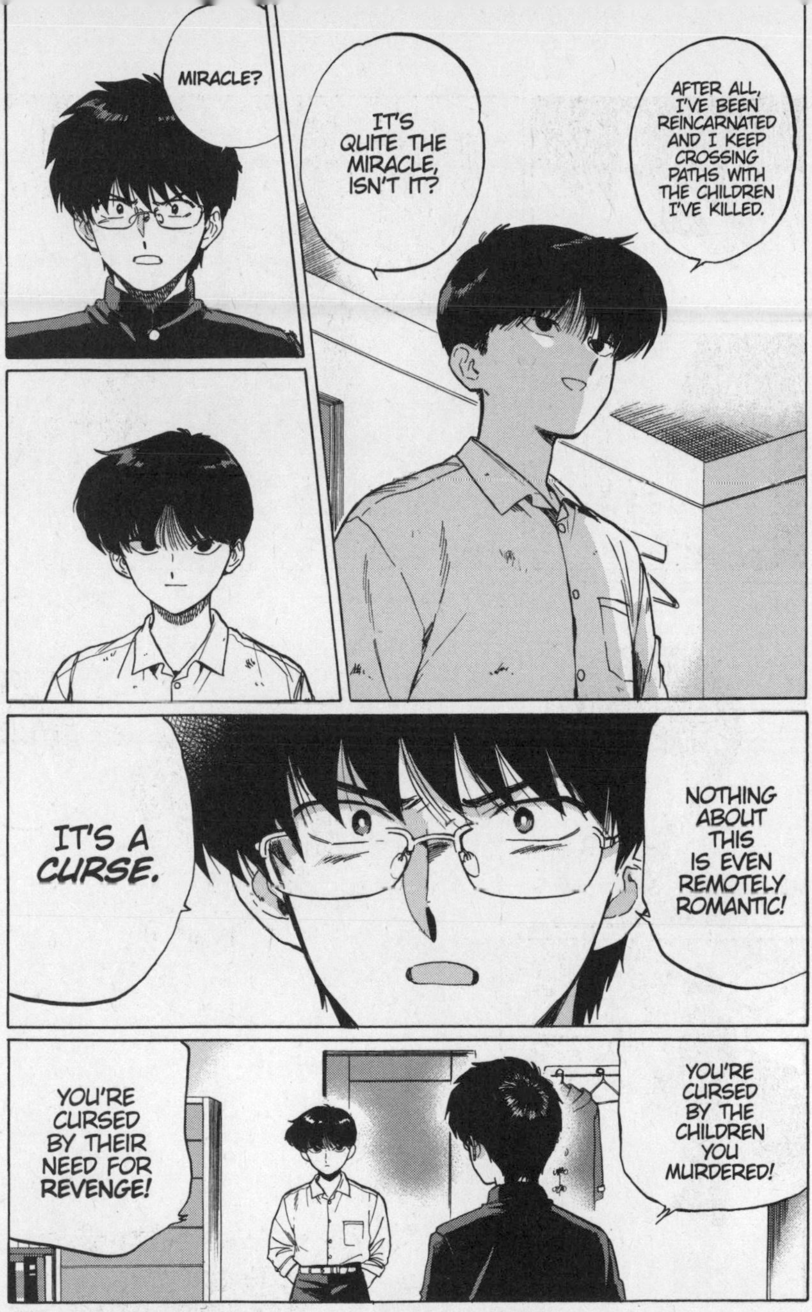
AFTER ALL, I'VE BEEN REINCARNATED AND I KEEP CROSSING PATHS WITH THE CHILDREN I'VE KILLED.
IT'S QUITE THE MIRACLE, ISN'T IT?
MIRACLE?
NOTHING ABOUT THIS IS EVEN REMOTELY ROMANTIC!
IT'S A *CURSE.*
YOU'RE CURSED BY THE CHILDREN YOU MURDERED!
YOU'RE CURSED BY THEIR NEED FOR REVENGE!

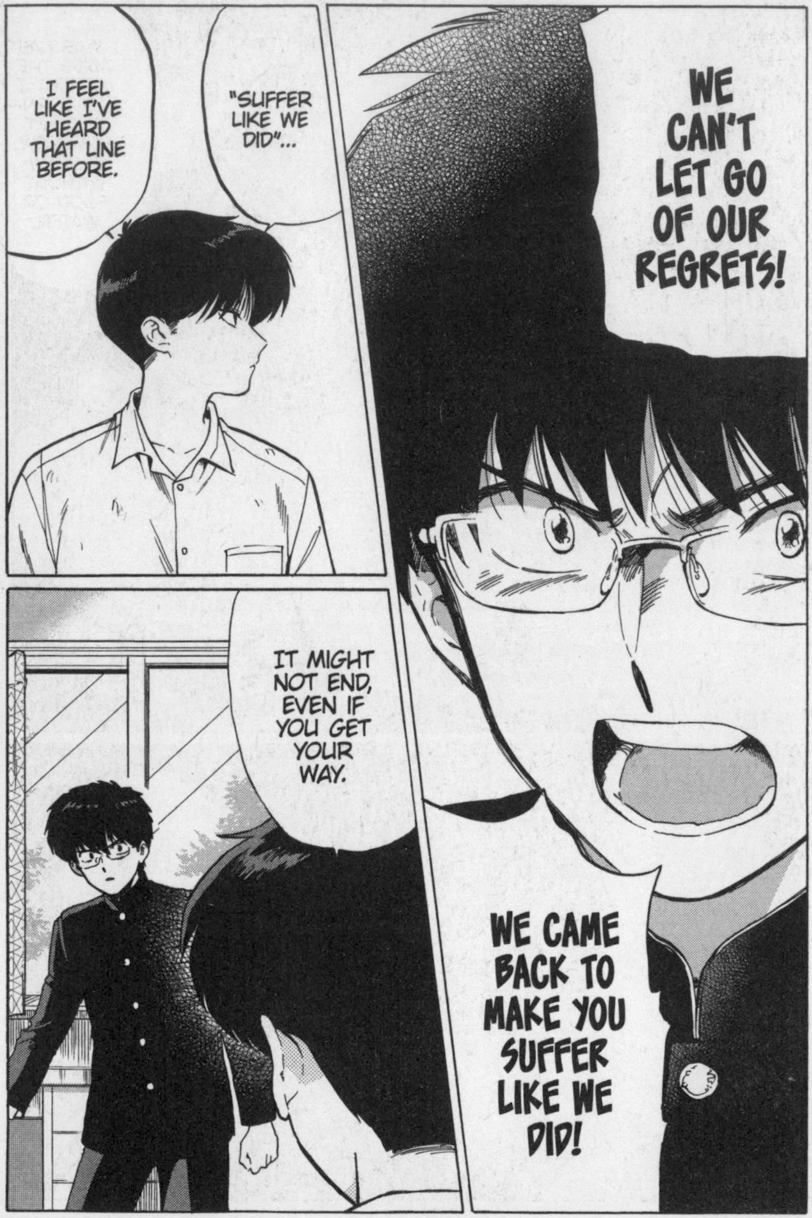
WE CAN'T LET GO OF OUR REGRETS!
WE CAME BACK TO MAKE YOU SUFFER LIKE WE DID!
"SUFFER LIKE WE DID"...
I FEEL LIKE I'VE HEARD THAT LINE BEFORE.
IT MIGHT NOT END, EVEN IF YOU GET YOUR WAY.

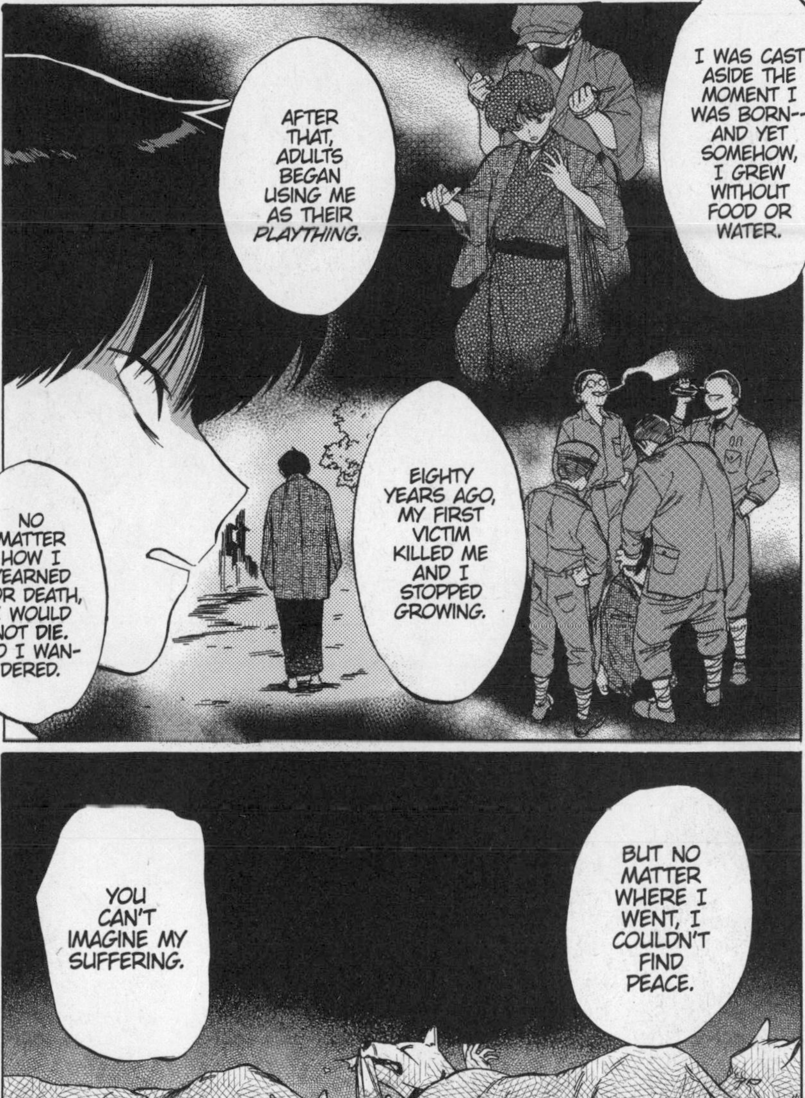
I WAS CAST ASIDE THE MOMENT I WAS BORN-- AND YET SOMEHOW, I GREW WITHOUT FOOD OR WATER.
AFTER THAT, ADULTS BEGAN USING ME AS THEIR *PLAYTHING*.
EIGHTY YEARS AGO, MY FIRST VICTIM KILLED ME AND I STOPPED GROWING.
NO MATTER HOW I YEARNED FOR DEATH, I WOULD NOT DIE. SO I WANDERED.
BUT NO MATTER WHERE I WENT, I COULDN'T FIND PEACE.
YOU CAN'T IMAGINE MY SUFFERING.

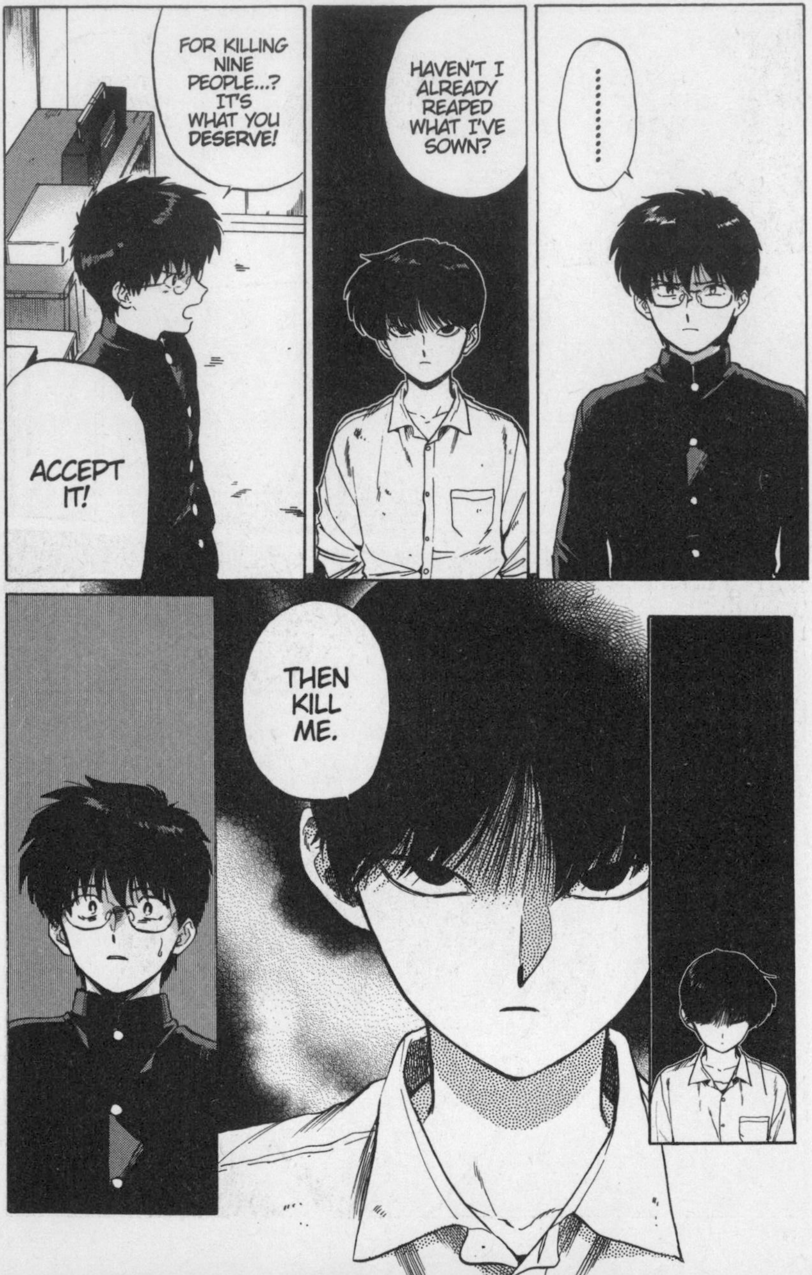
......
HAVEN'T I ALREADY REAPED WHAT I'VE SOWN?
FOR KILLING NINE PEOPLE...? IT'S WHAT YOU DESERVE!
ACCEPT IT!
THEN KILL ME.

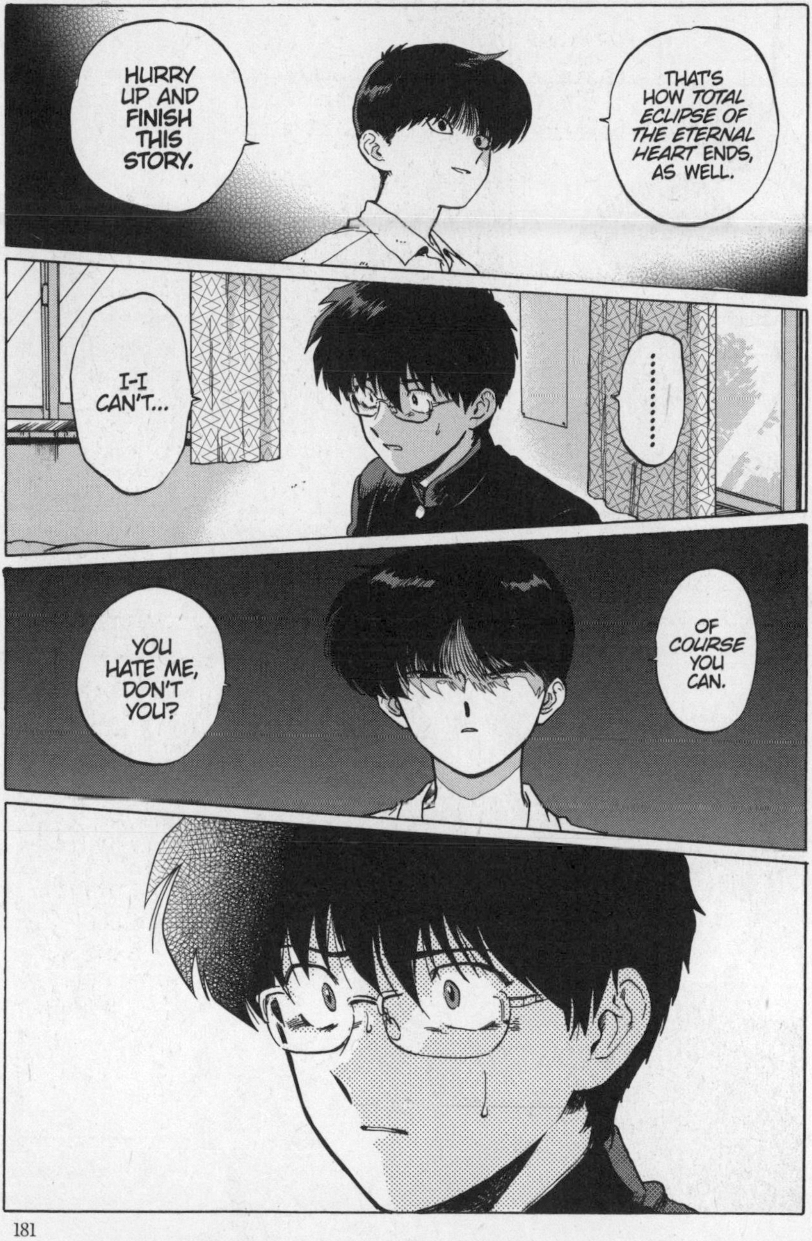
THAT'S HOW *TOTAL ECLIPSE OF THE ETERNAL HEART* ENDS, AS WELL.
HURRY UP AND FINISH THIS STORY.
......
I-I CAN'T...
OF COURSE YOU CAN.
YOU HATE ME, DON'T YOU?

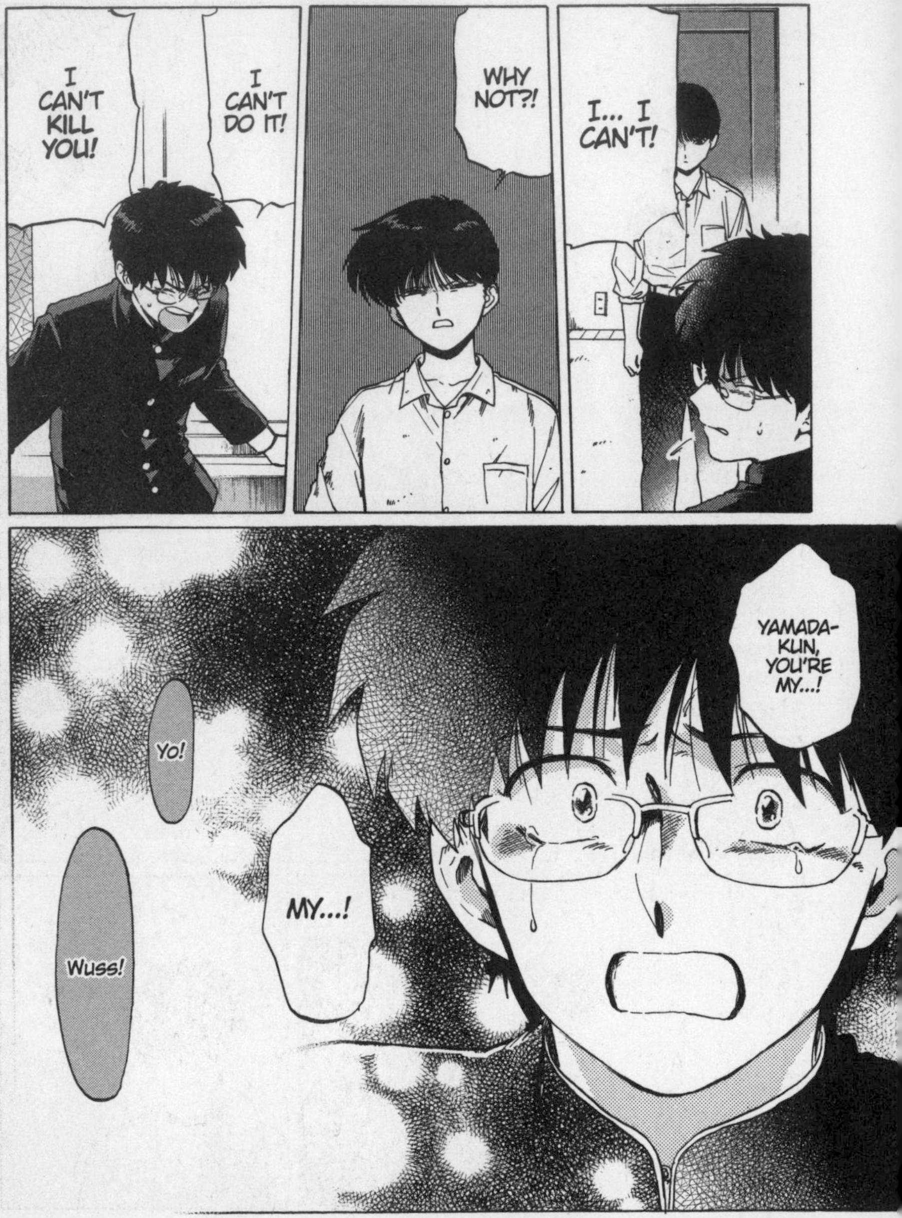
I... I CAN'T!
WHY NOT?!
I CAN'T DO IT!
I CAN'T KILL YOU!
YAMADA-KUN, YOU'RE MY...!
MY...!
Yo!
Wuss!

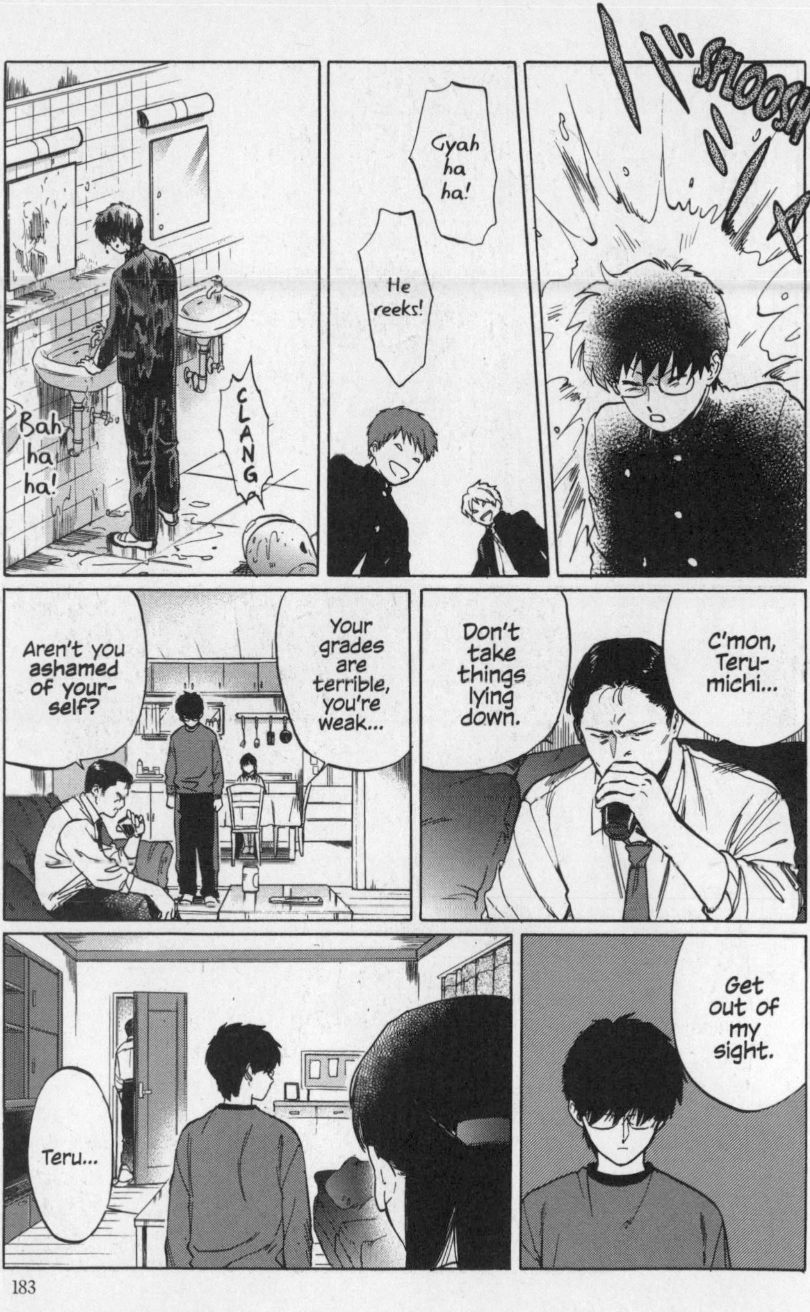
SPLOOSH
Gyah ha ha!
He reeks!
CLANG
Bah ha ha!
C'mon, Teru-michi...
Don't take things lying down.
Your grades are terrible, you're weak...
Aren't you ashamed of your-self?
Get out of my sight.
Teru...

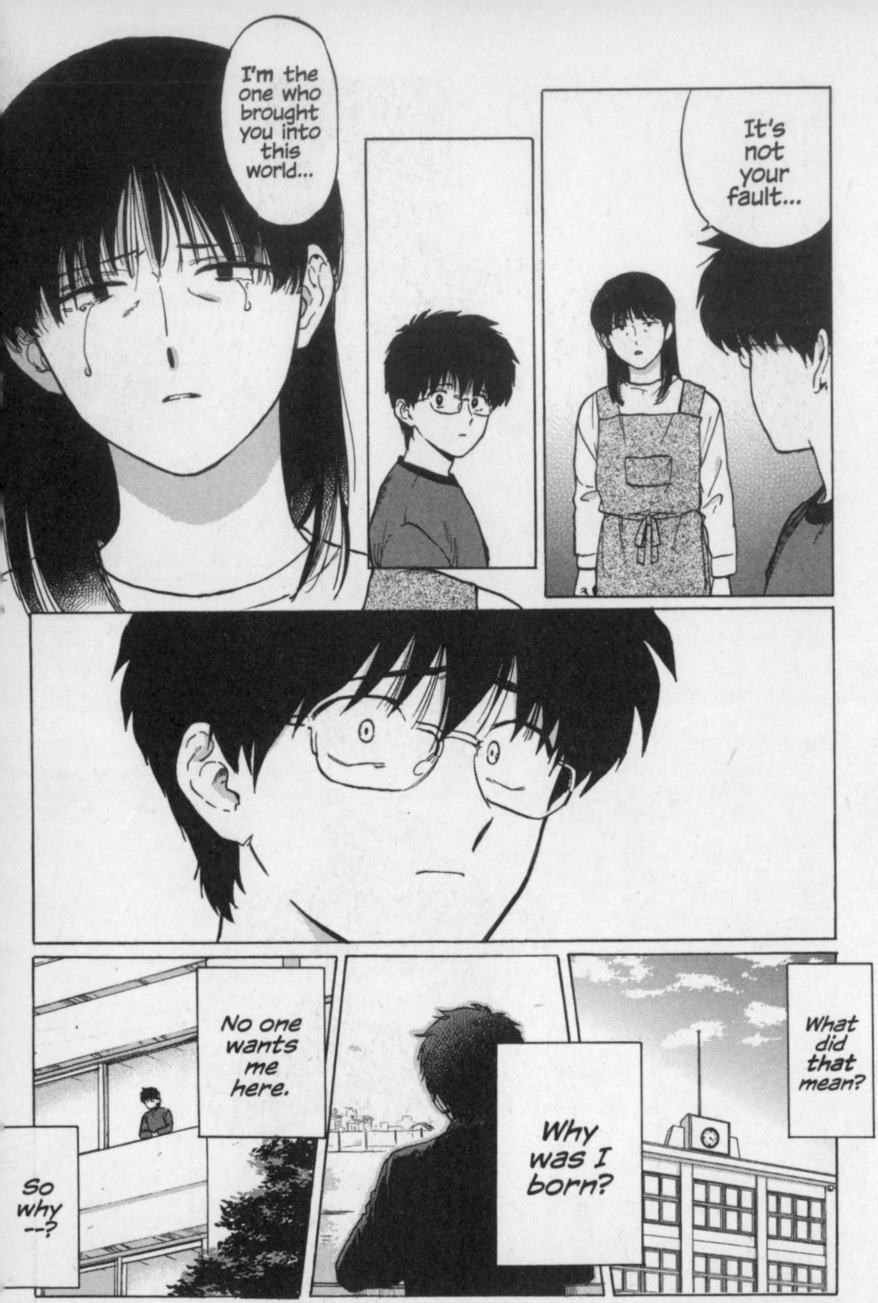
It's not your fault...
I'm the one who brought you into this world...
What did that mean?
Why was I born?
No one wants me here.
So why --?

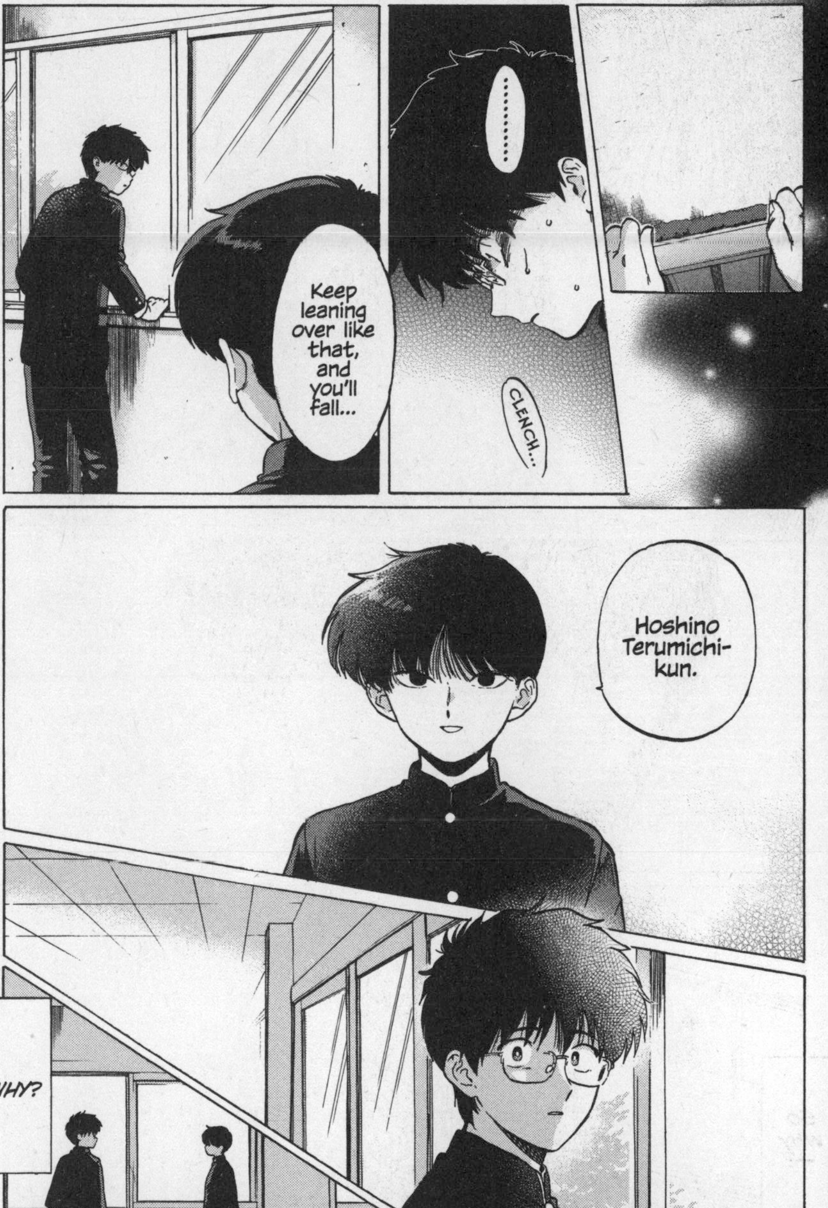
......
CLENCH...
Keep leaning over like that, and you'll fall...
Hoshino Terumichi-kun.
WHY?

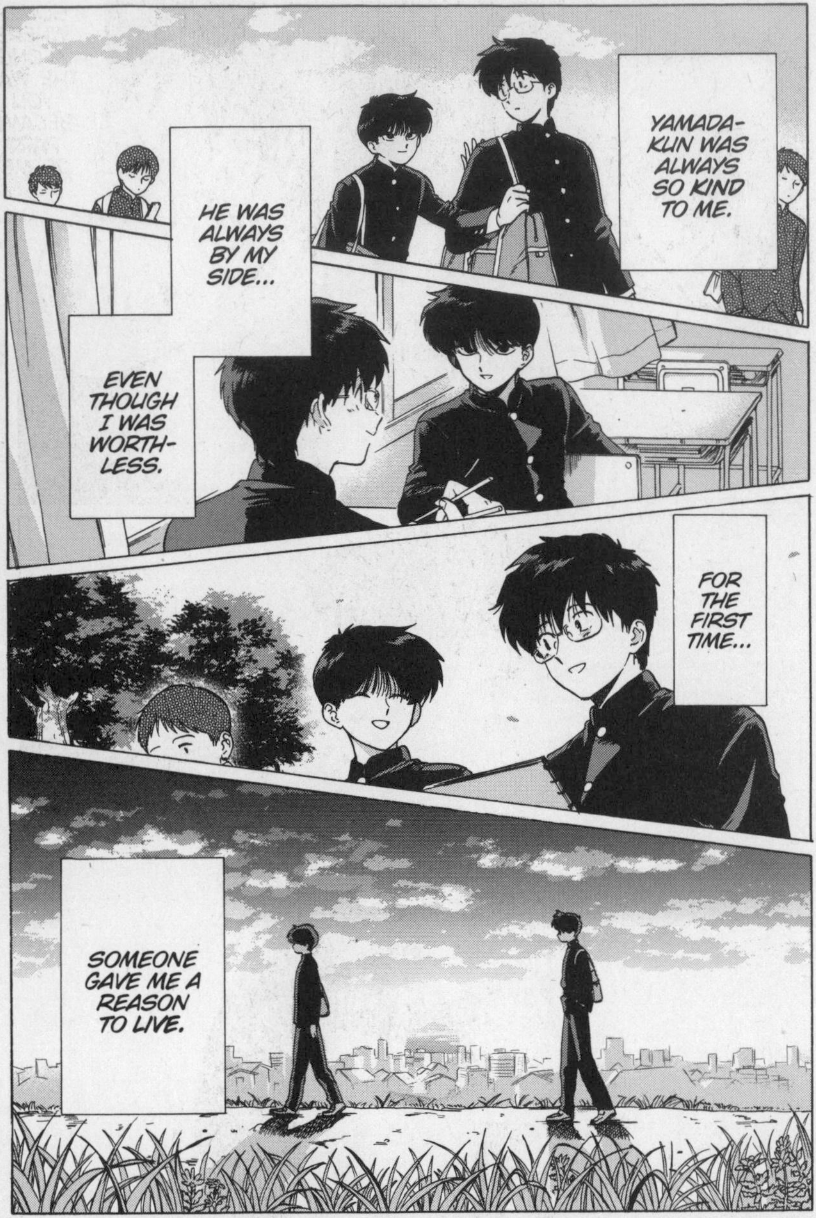
YAMADA-KUN WAS ALWAYS SO KIND TO ME.
HE WAS ALWAYS BY MY SIDE...
EVEN THOUGH I WAS WORTH-LESS.
FOR THE FIRST TIME...
SOMEONE GAVE ME A REASON TO LIVE.

SOME-WHERE ALONG THE WAY, YOU BECAME PART OF ME!

YOU'RE A TERRIBLE PERSON, BUT...!

BUT ...!

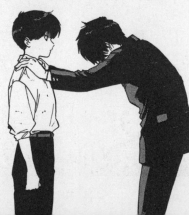

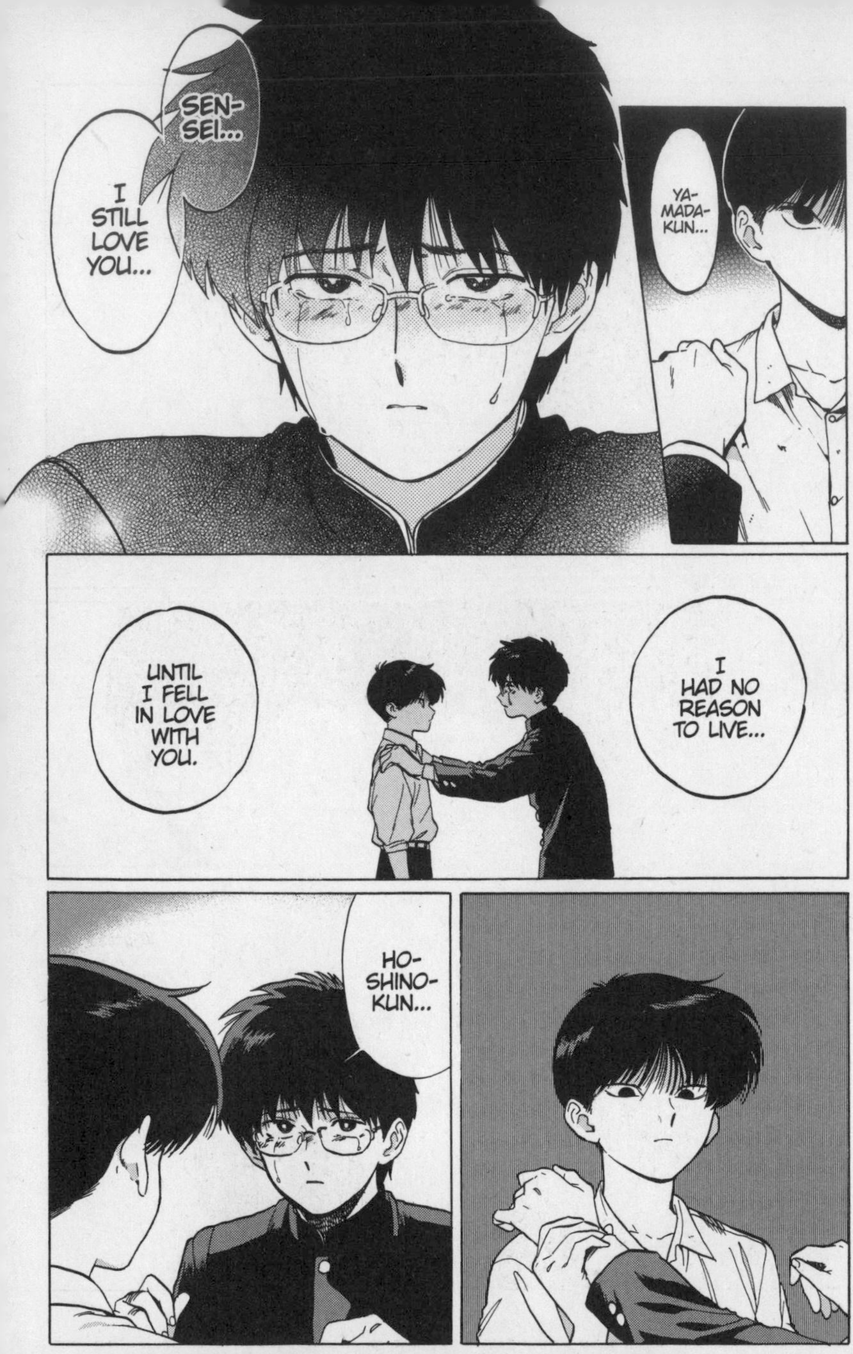
YA-MADA-KUN...
SEN-SEI...
I STILL LOVE YOU...
I HAD NO REASON TO LIVE...
UNTIL I FELL IN LOVE WITH YOU.
HO-SHINO-KUN...

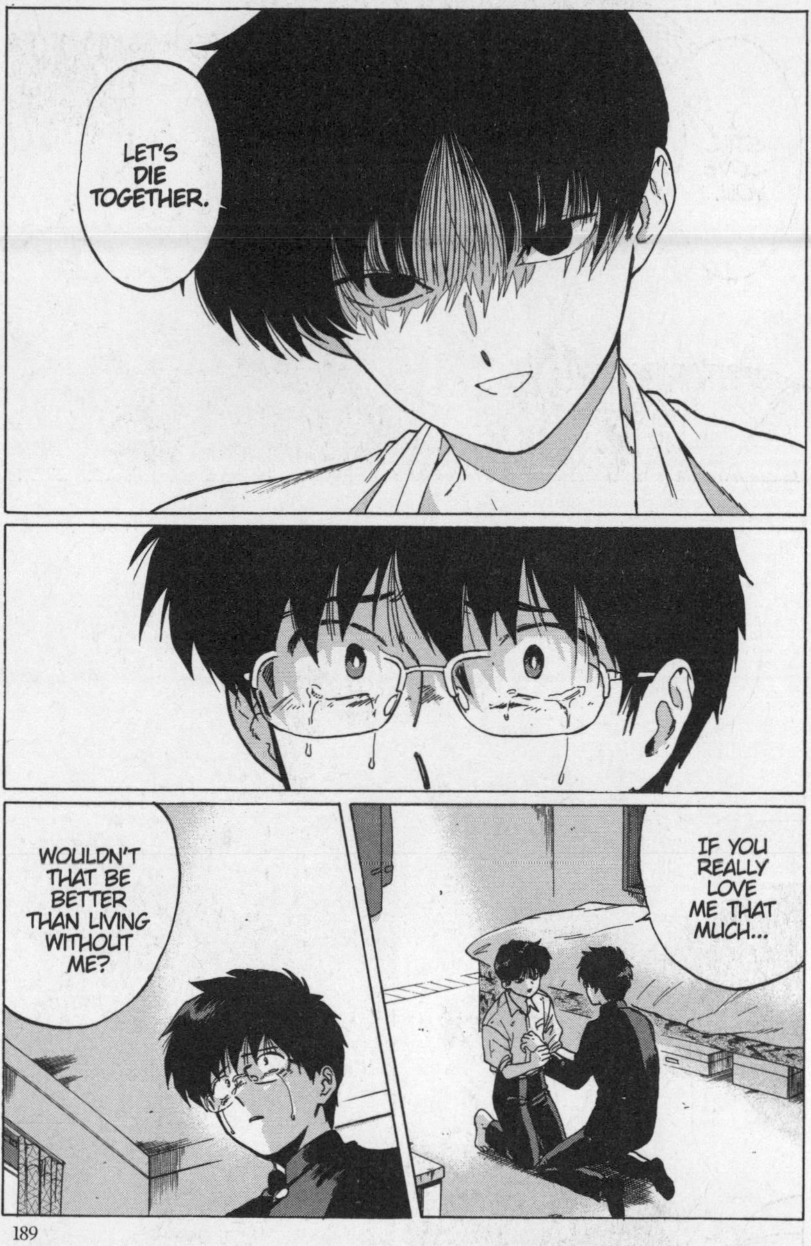
LET'S DIE TOGETHER.
IF YOU REALLY LOVE ME THAT MUCH...
WOULDN'T THAT BE BETTER THAN LIVING WITHOUT ME?

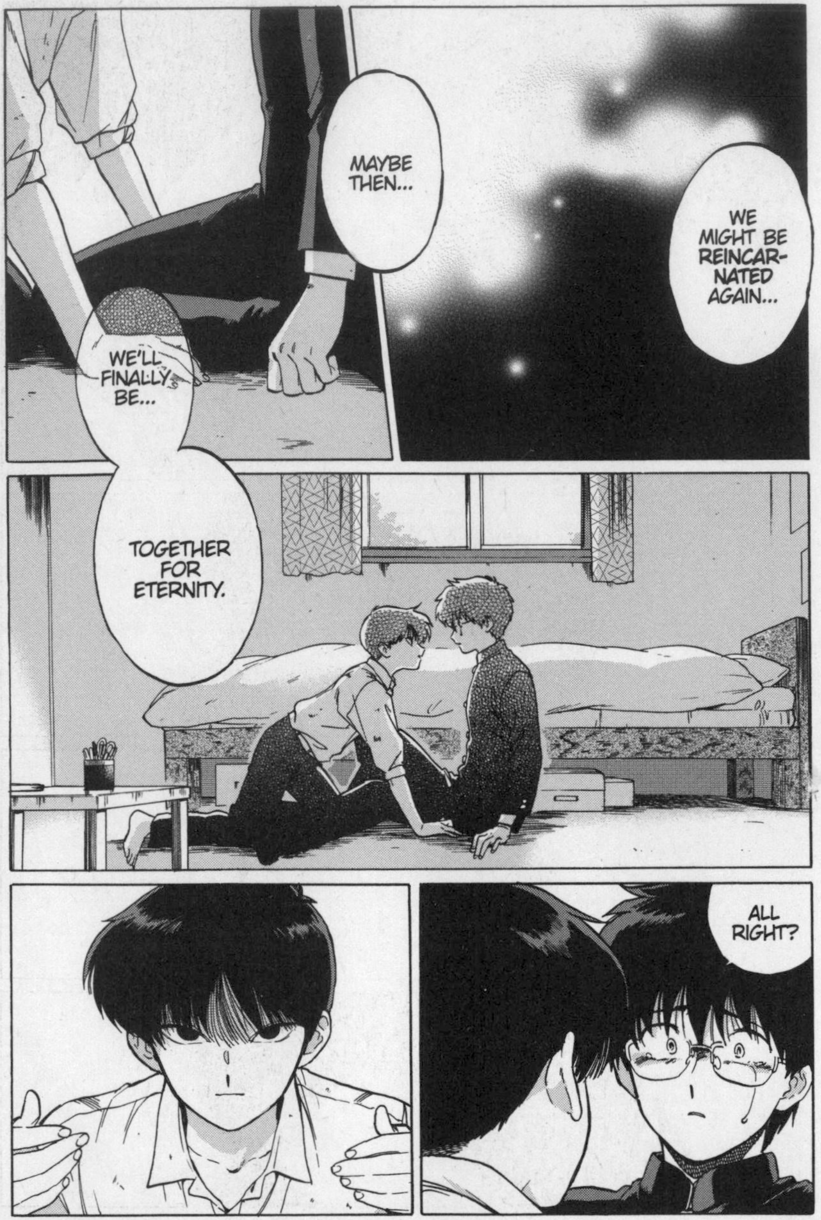
WE MIGHT BE REINCAR-NATED AGAIN...
MAYBE THEN...
WE'LL FINALLY BE...
TOGETHER FOR ETERNITY.
ALL RIGHT?

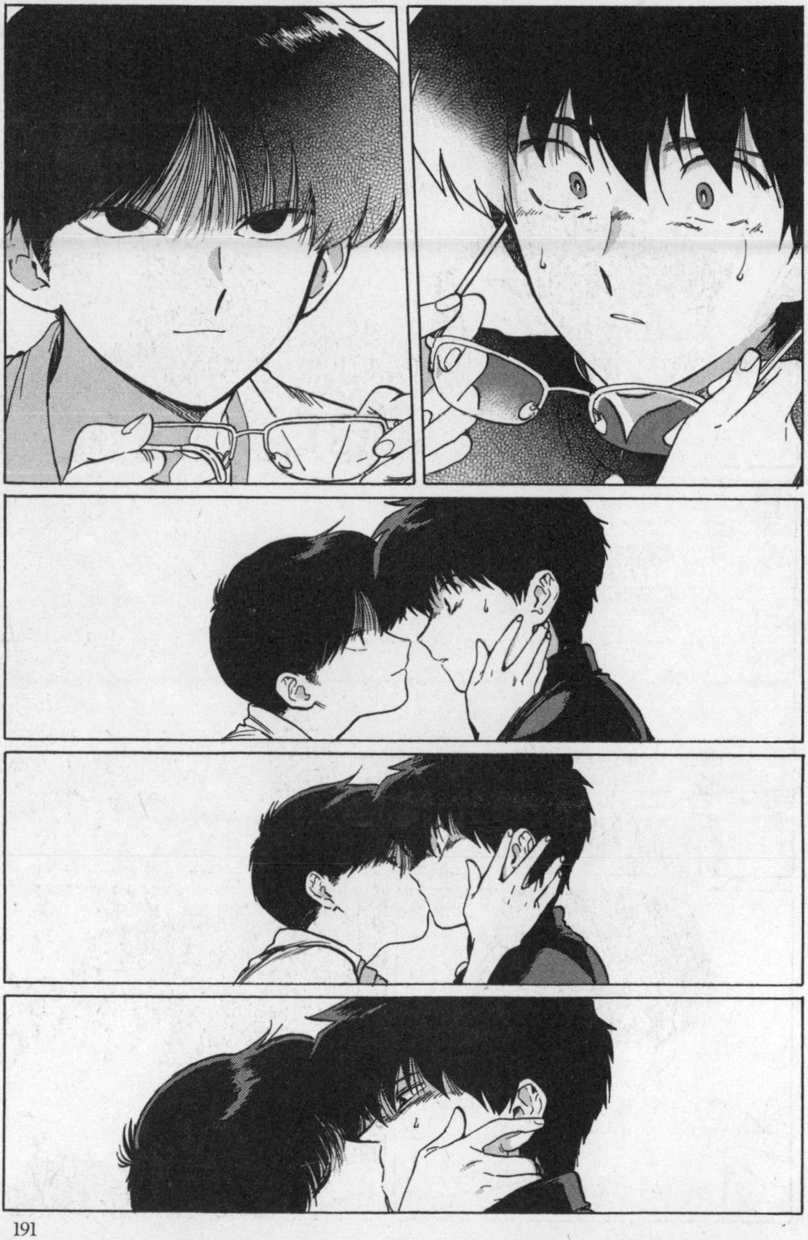

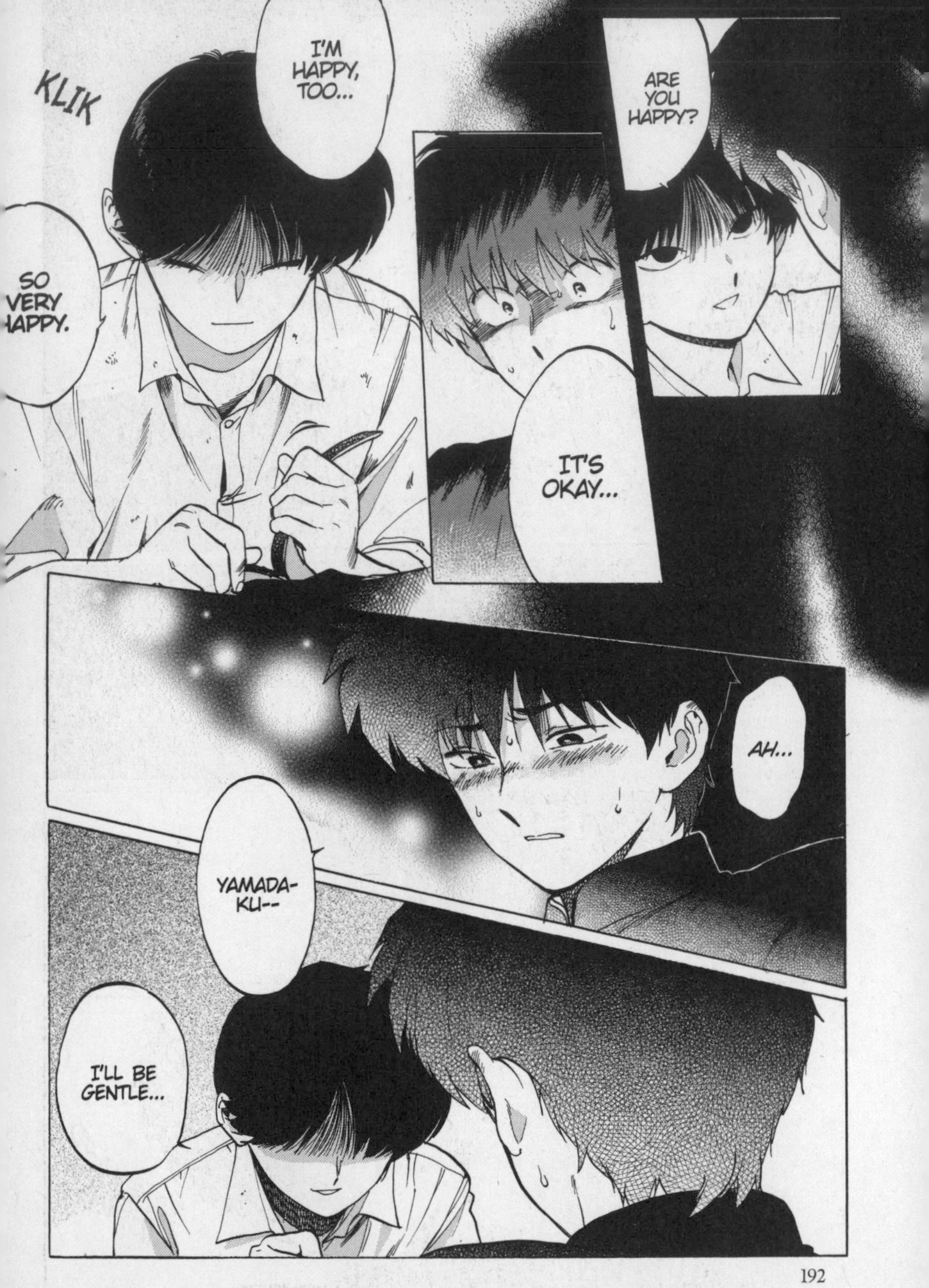
ARE YOU HAPPY?
IT'S OKAY...
I'M HAPPY, TOO...
KLIK
SO VERY HAPPY.
AH...
YAMADA-KU--
I'LL BE GENTLE...

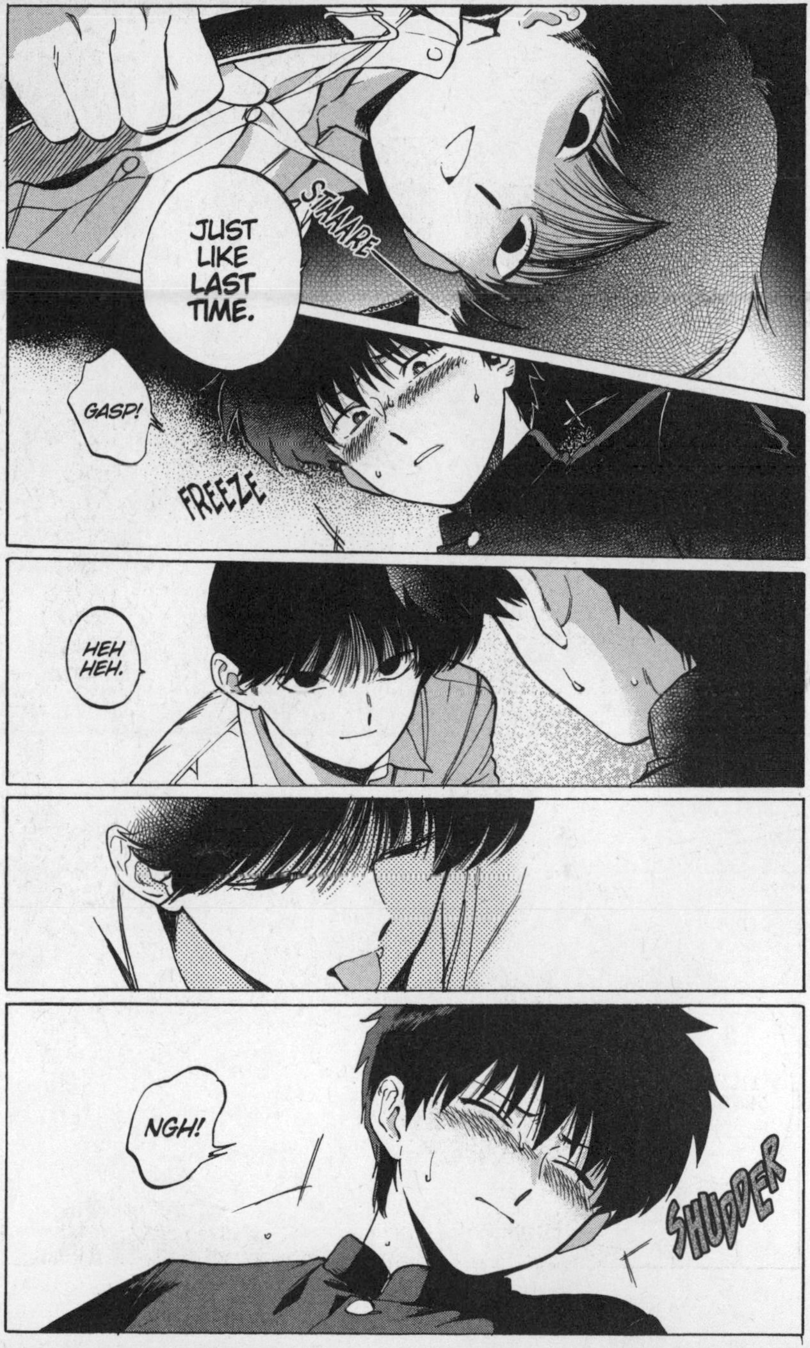
STAAARE
JUST LIKE LAST TIME.
GASP!
FREEZE
HEH HEH.
NGH!
SHUDDER

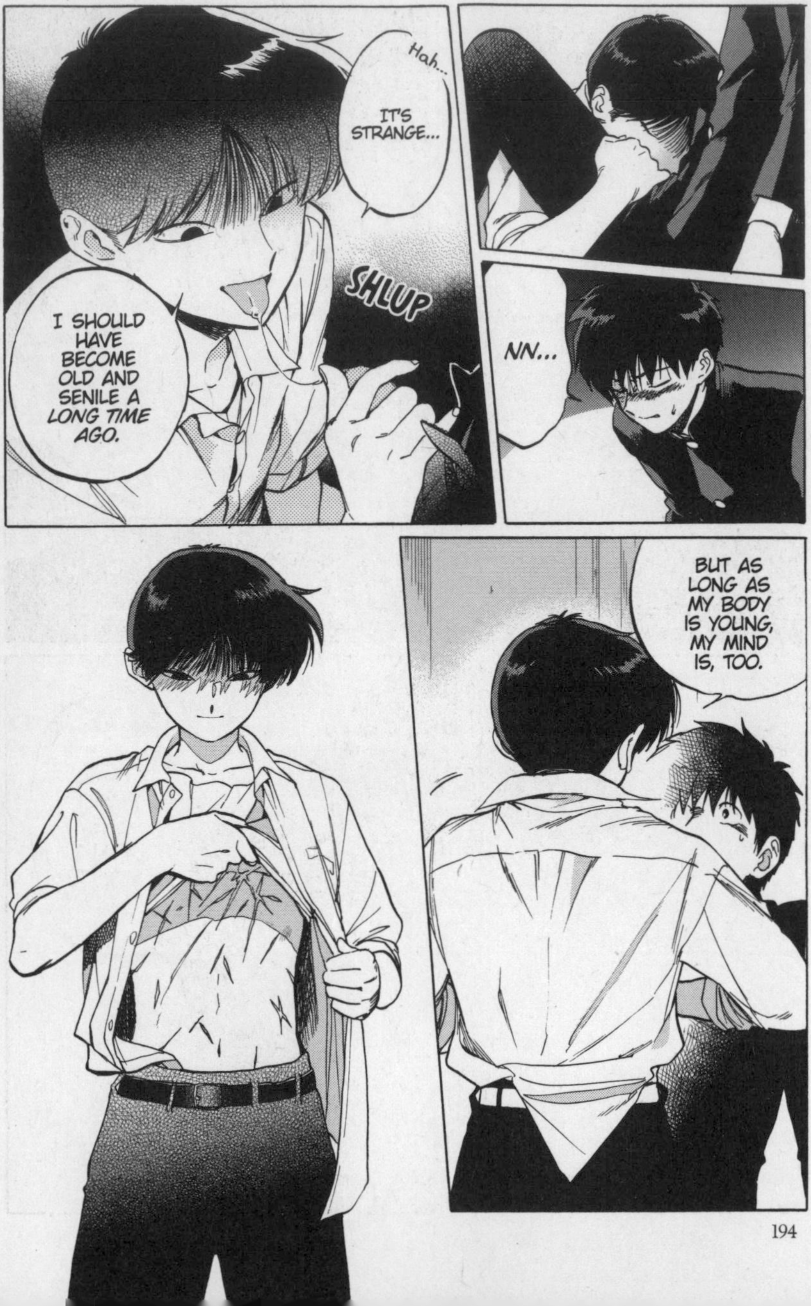
NN...
Hah...
IT'S STRANGE...
SHLUP
I SHOULD HAVE BECOME OLD AND SENILE A LONG TIME AGO.
BUT AS LONG AS MY BODY IS YOUNG, MY MIND IS, TOO.

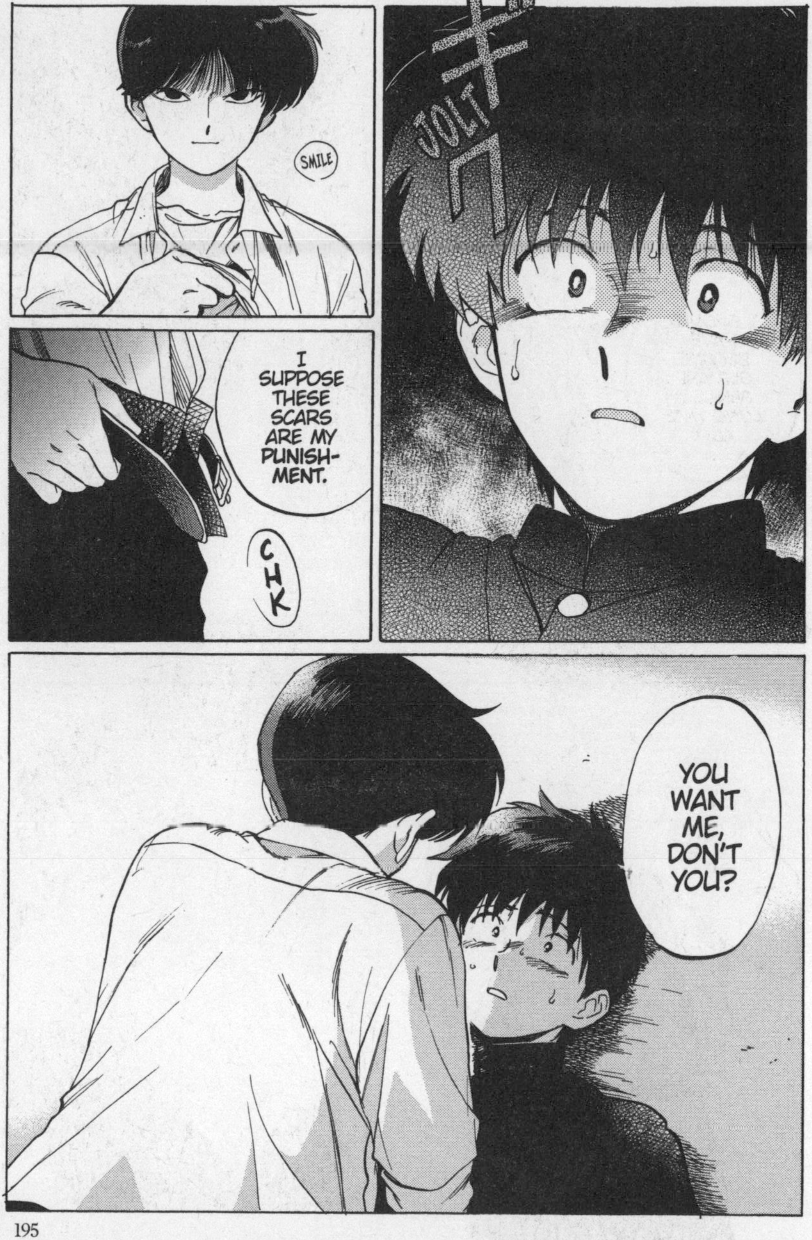
JOLT
SMILE
I SUPPOSE THESE SCARS ARE MY PUNISHMENT.
CHK
YOU WANT ME, DON'T YOU?

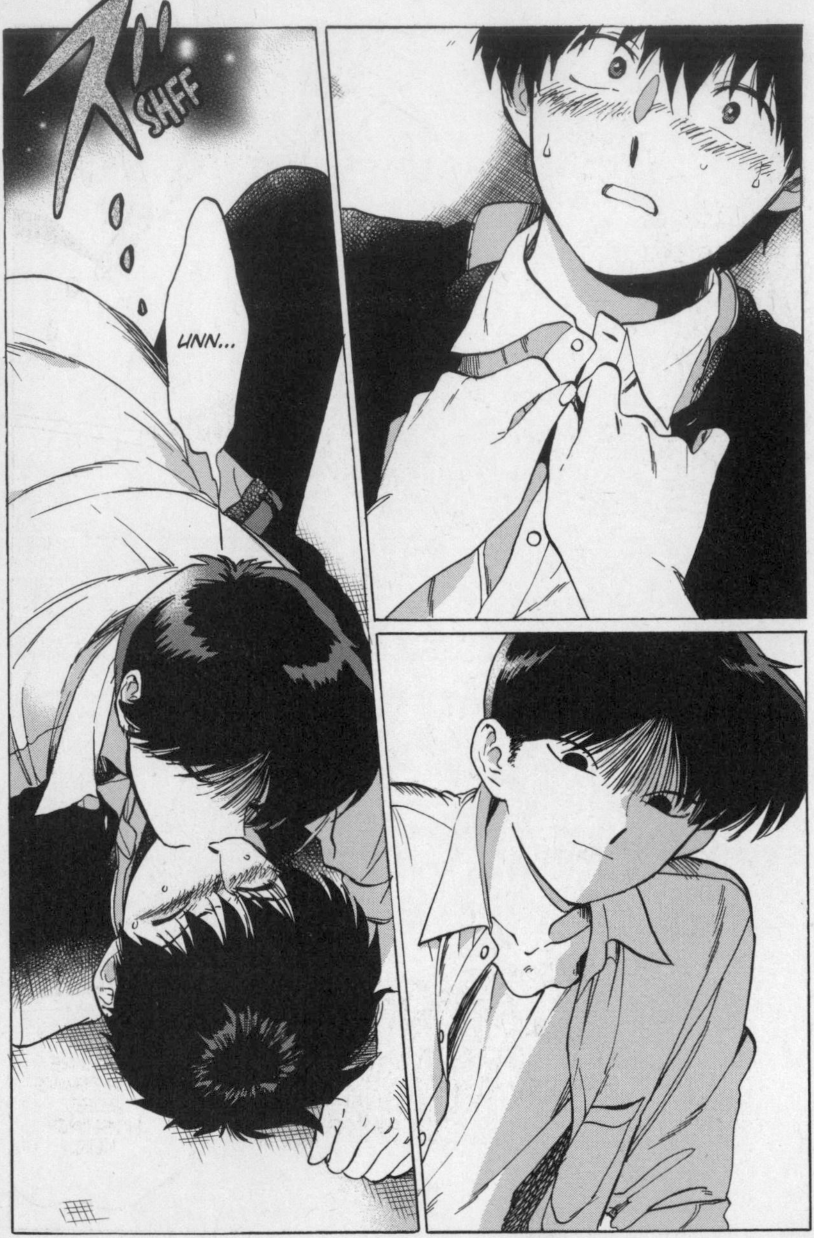
SHFF
UNN...

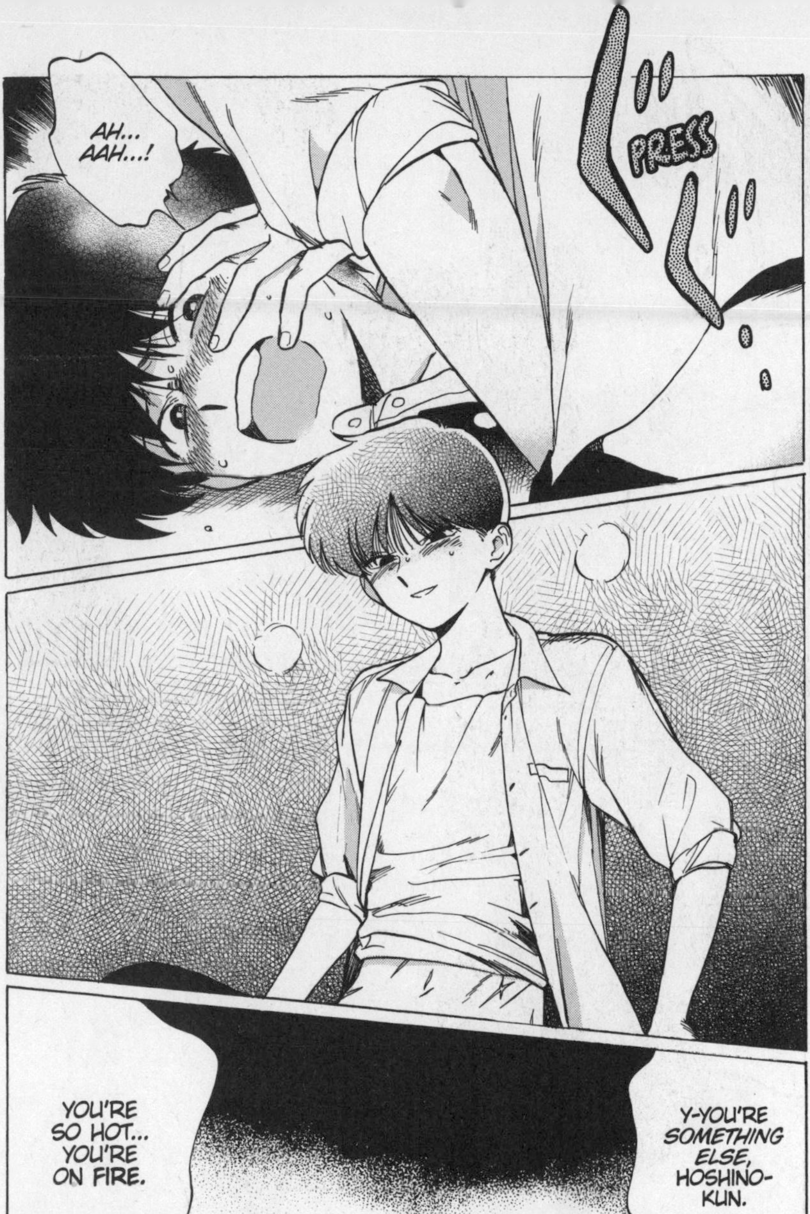
PRESS
AH... AAH...!
Y-YOU'RE SOMETHING ELSE, HOSHINO-KUN.
YOU'RE SO HOT... YOU'RE ON FIRE.

JUST LIKE BEFORE...
HOLD ME CLOSER...
IF I DIE WITH YAMADA-KUN...
WE REALLY WILL BE BOUND TOGETHER.

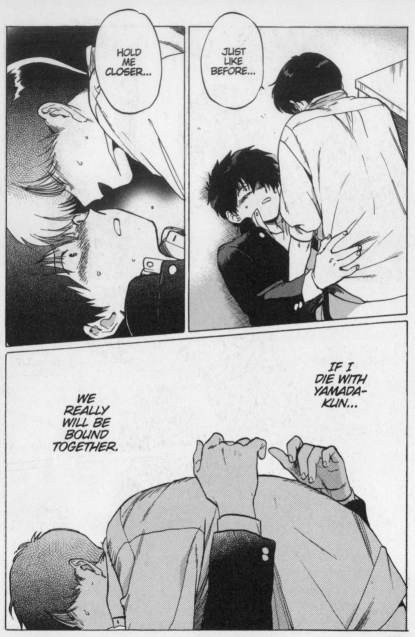

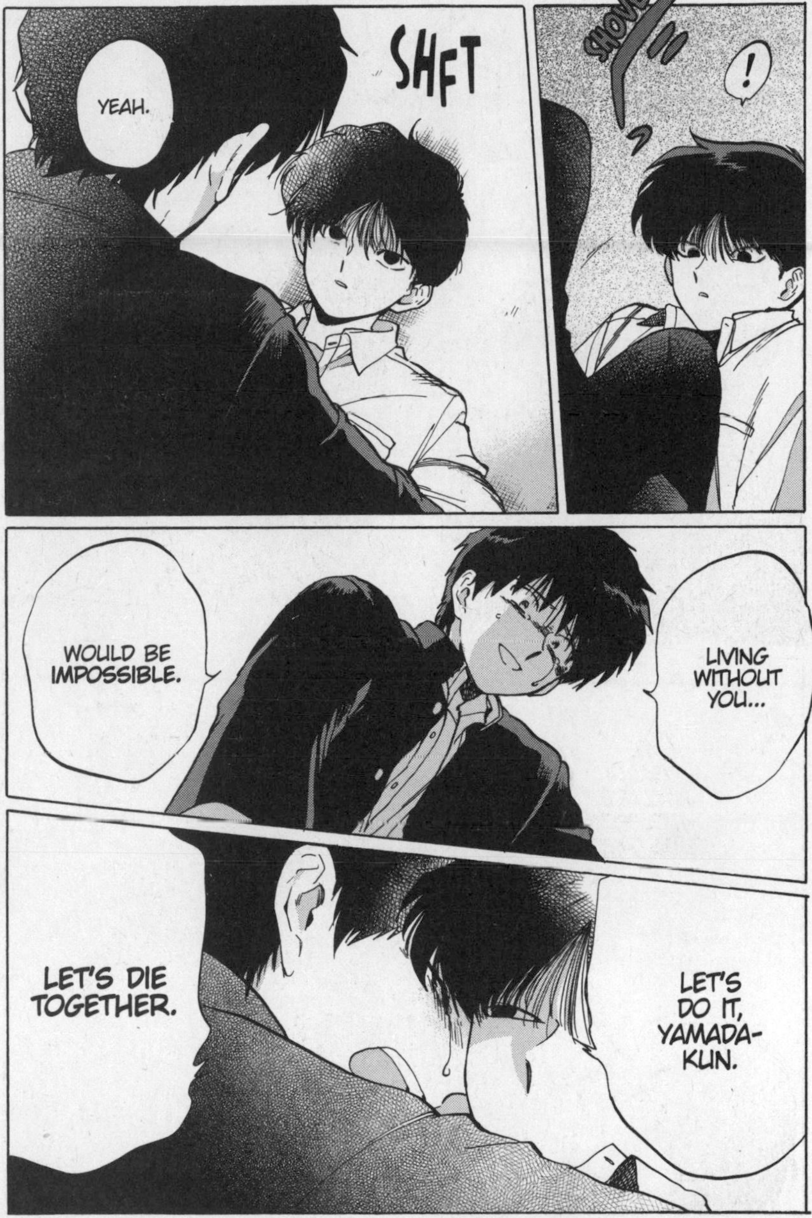
SHOVE
!
SHFT
YEAH.
LIVING WITHOUT YOU...
WOULD BE IMPOSSIBLE.
LET'S DO IT, YAMADA-KUN.
LET'S DIE TOGETHER.

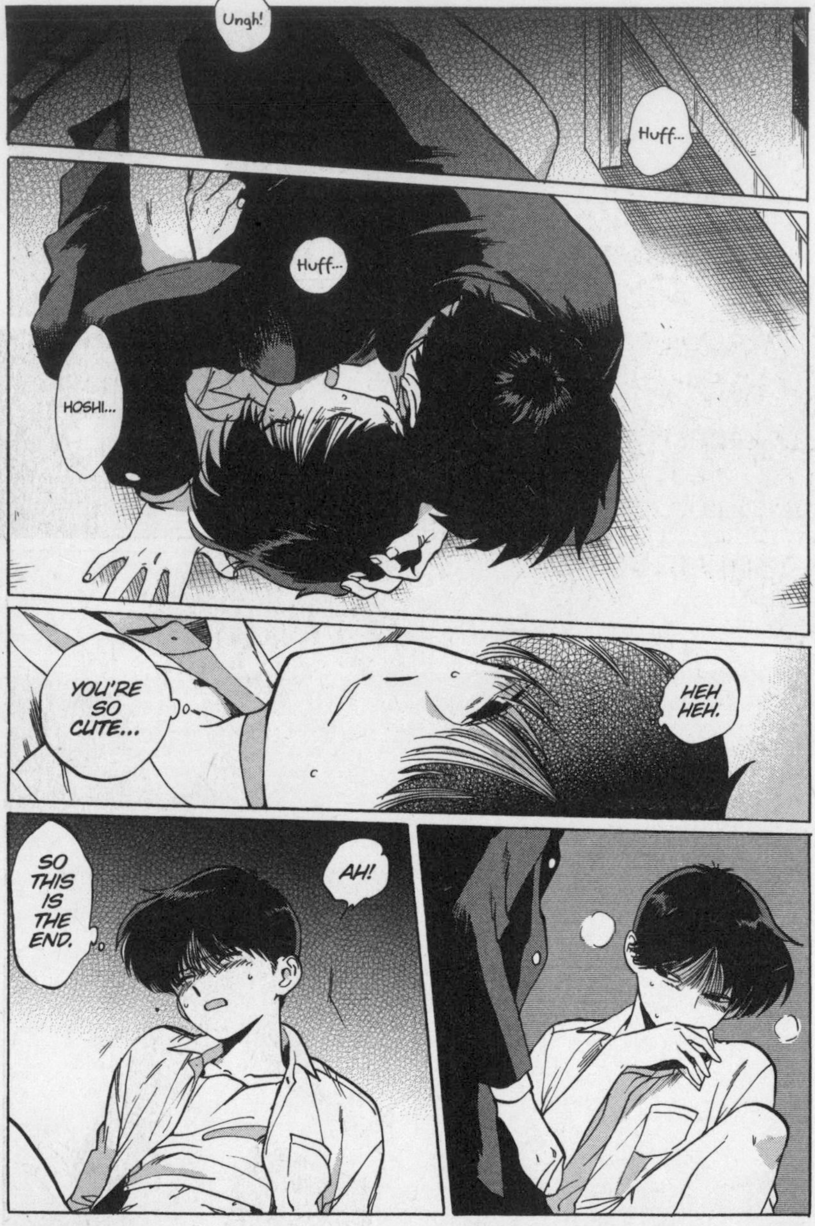
Ungh!
Huff...
Huff...
HOSHI...
HEH HEH.
YOU'RE SO CUTE...
AH!
SO THIS IS THE END.

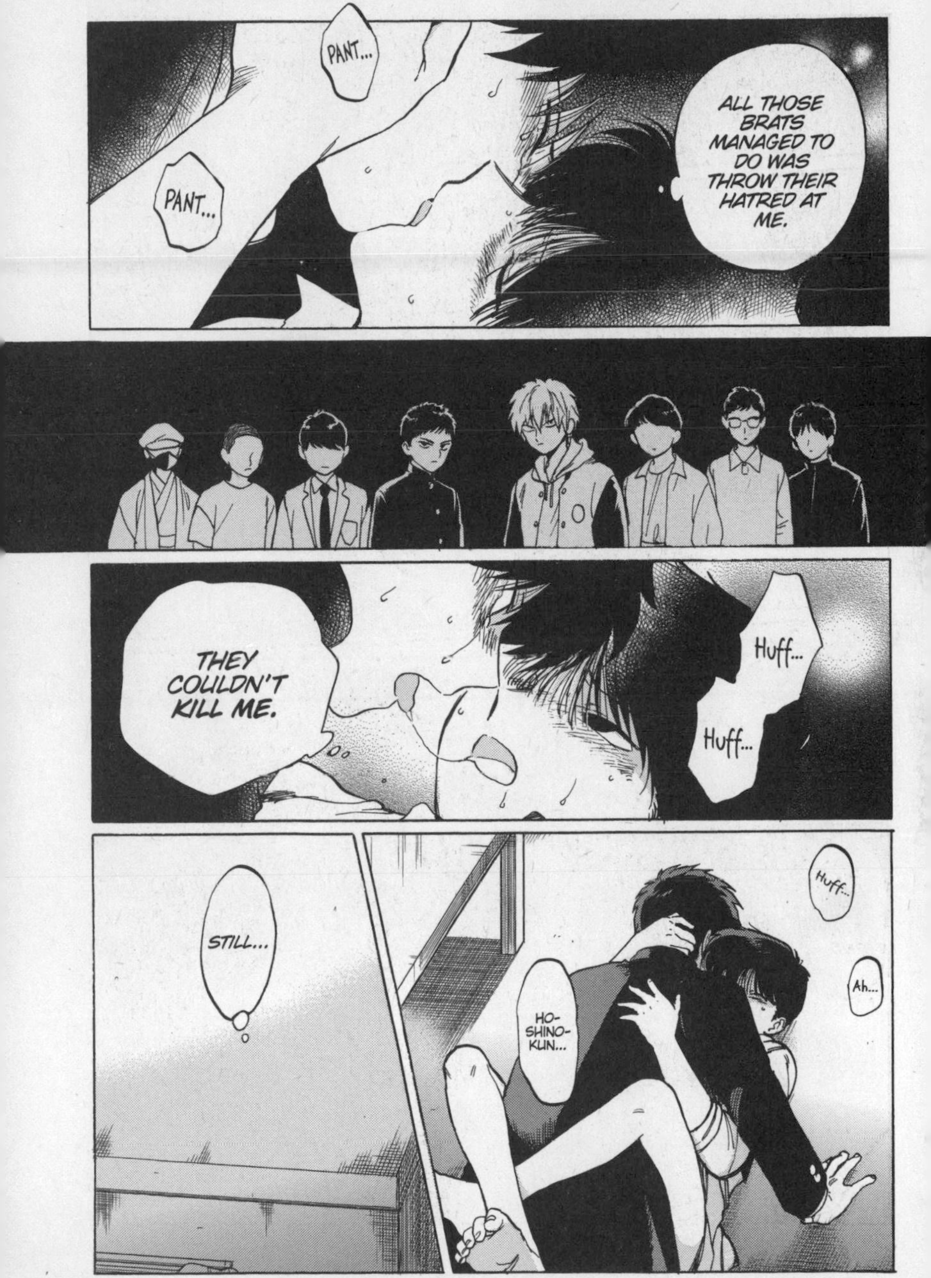
ALL THOSE BRATS MANAGED TO DO WAS THROW THEIR HATRED AT ME.
PANT...
PANT...
Huff...
Huff...
THEY COULDN'T KILL ME.
Huff...
Ah...
HO-SHINO-KUN...
STILL...

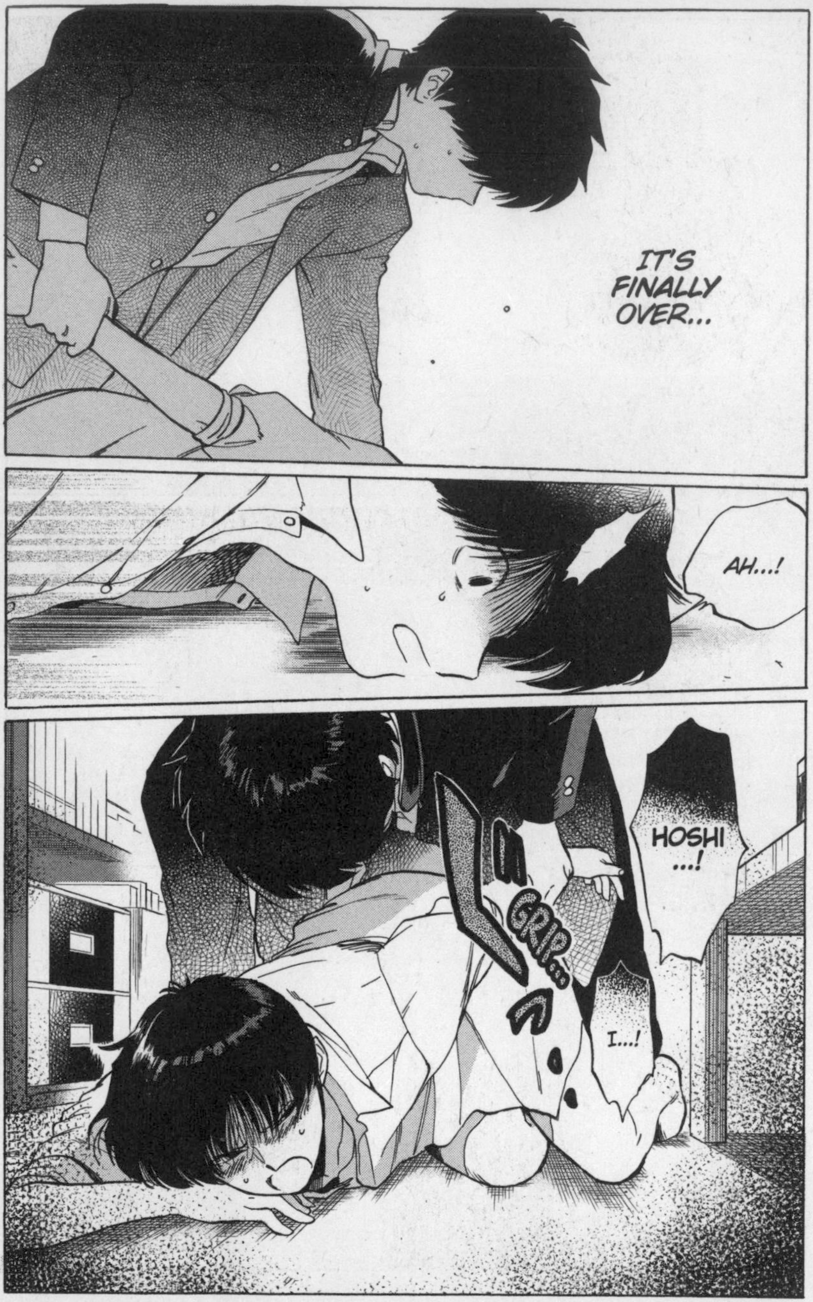
IT'S FINALLY OVER...
AH...!
HOSHI ...!
GRIP...
I...!

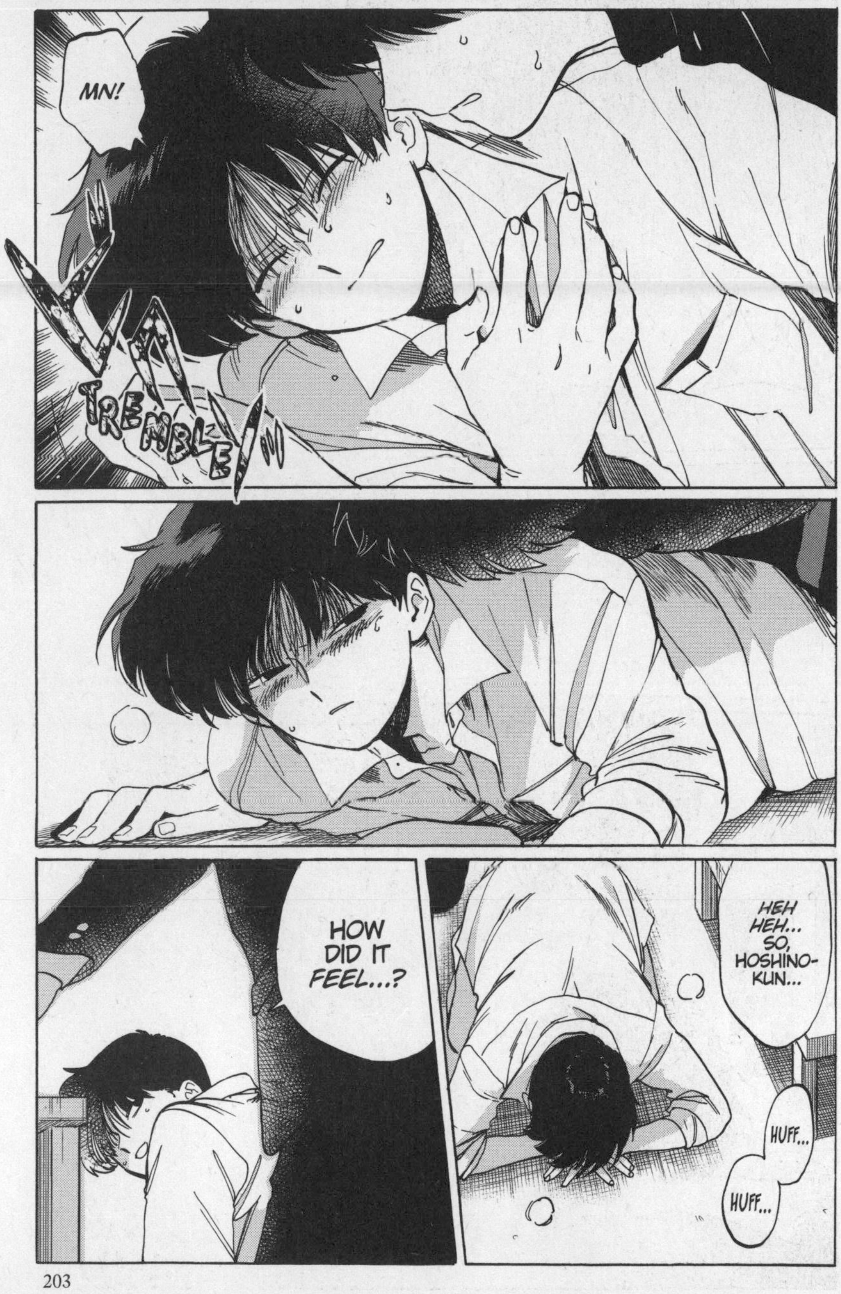
MN!
TREMBLE
HEH HEH... SO, HOSHINO-KUN...
HUFF...
HUFF...
HOW DID IT FEEL...?

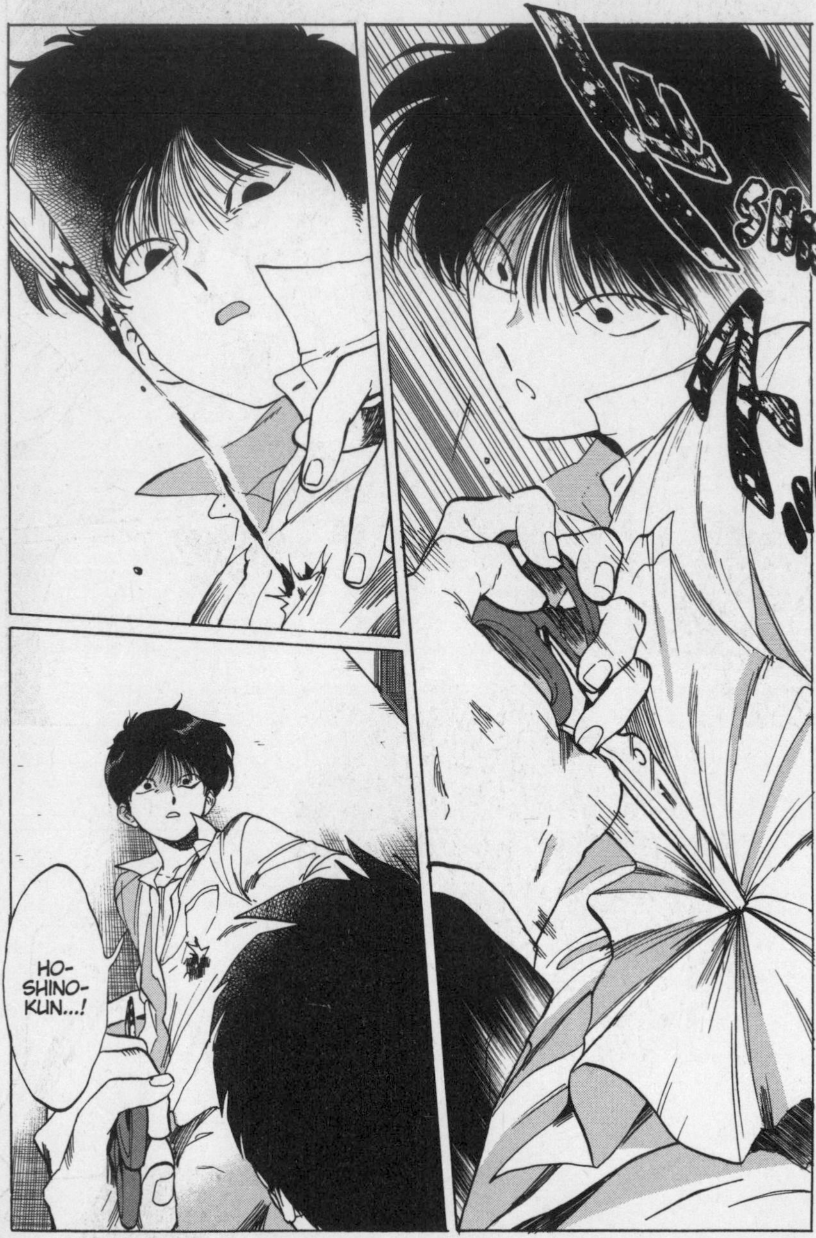
SHK
HO-SHINO-KUN...!

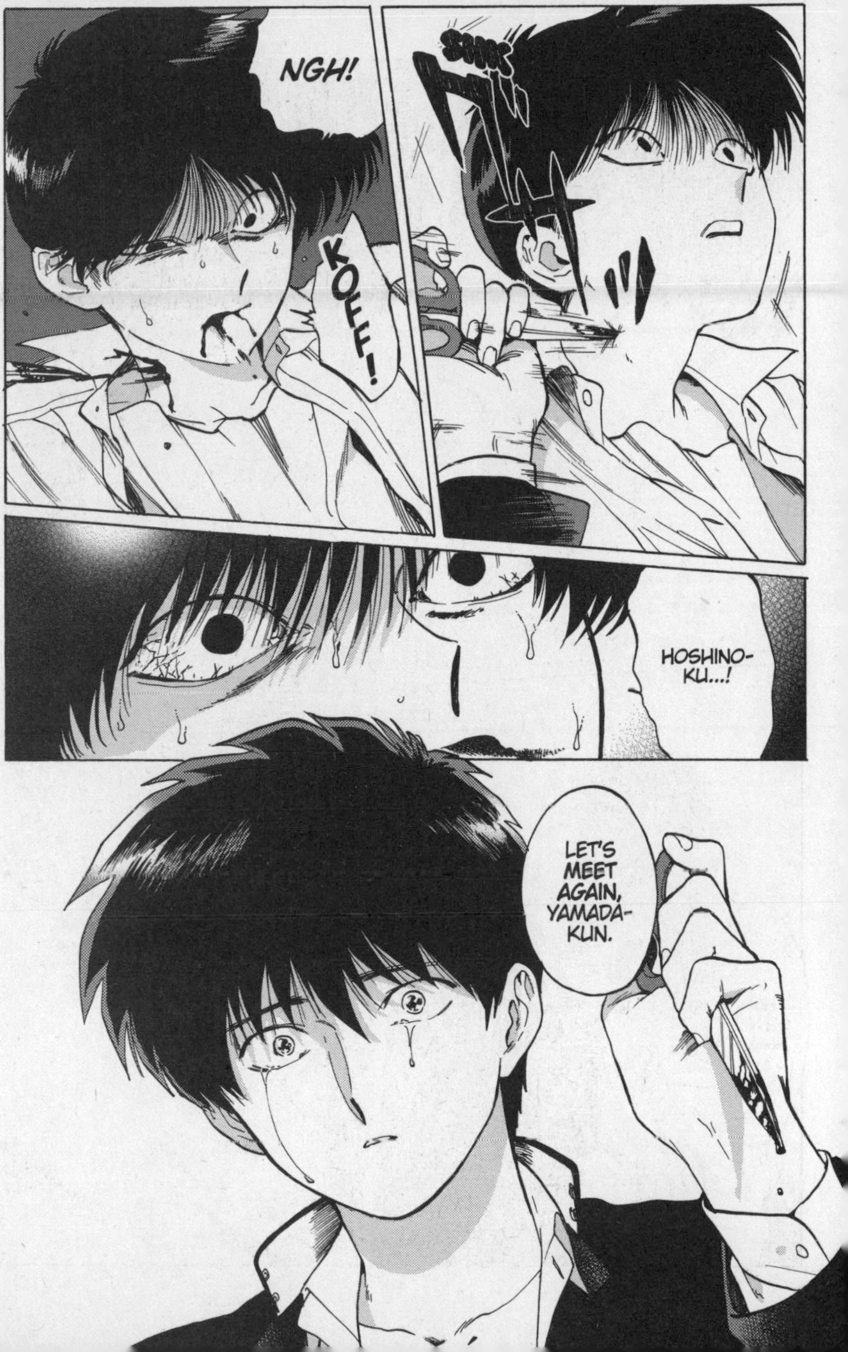

NGH!
KOFF!
HOSHINO-KU...!
LET'S MEET AGAIN, YAMADA-KUN.

STAB
UNGH ...!
STAB
AAGH ...!

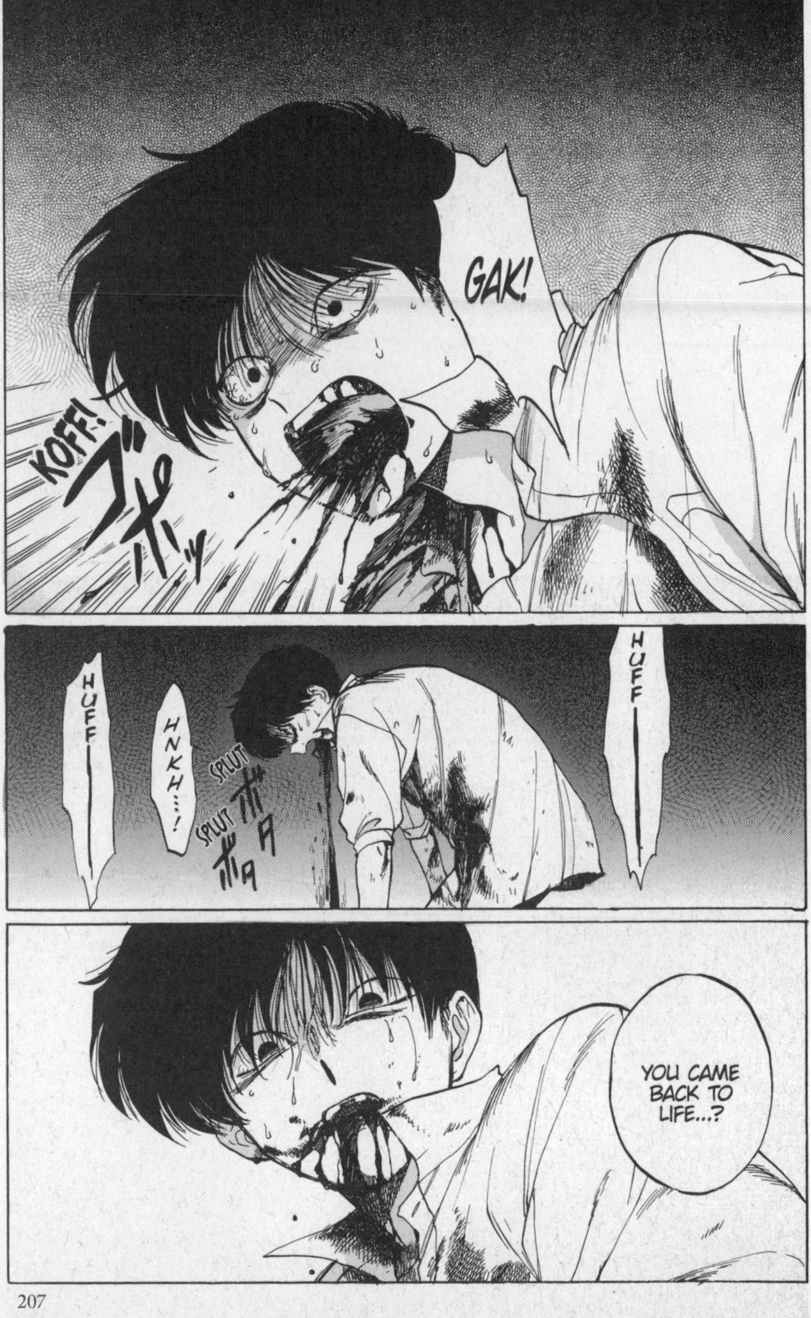
GAK!
KOFF!
ゴポッ
HUFF—
HNKH...!
SPLUT
SPLUT
ボタボタ
HUFF—
YOU CAME BACK TO LIFE...?

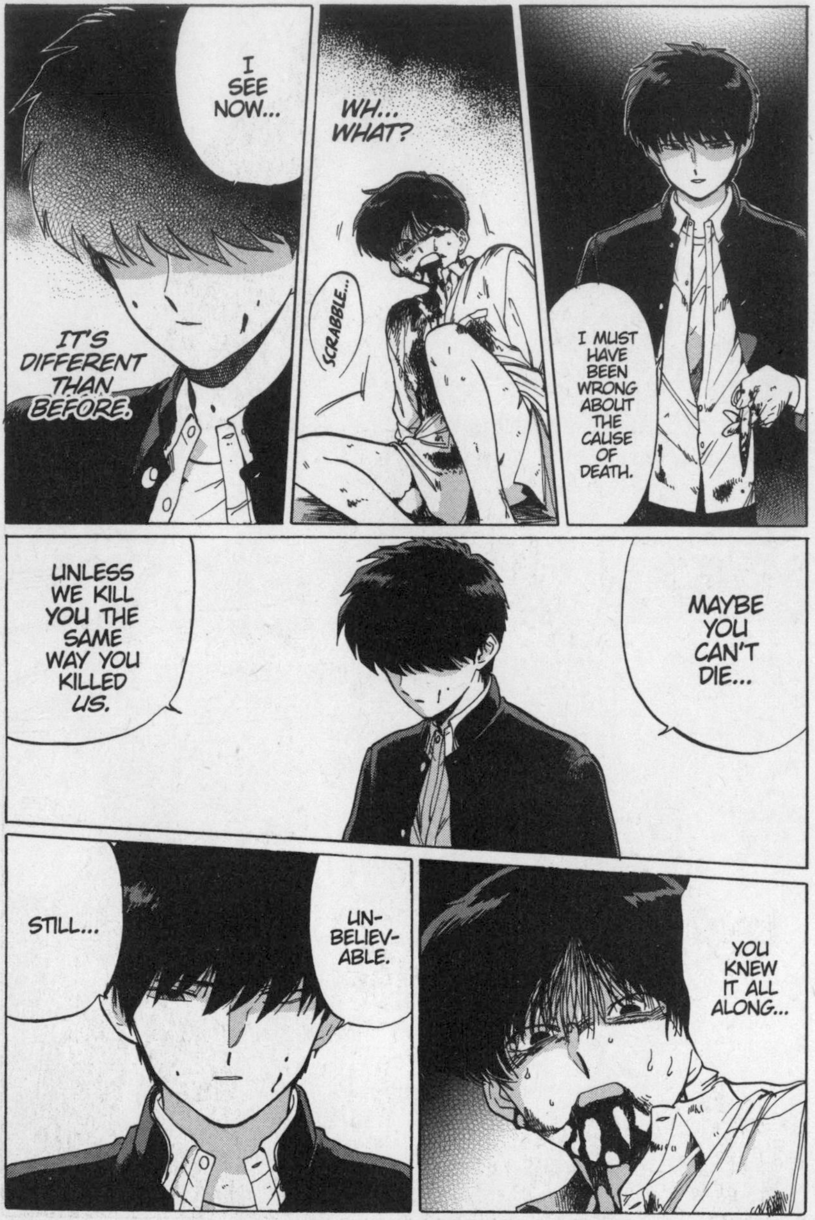
I MUST HAVE BEEN WRONG ABOUT THE CAUSE OF DEATH.
WH... WHAT?
SCRABBLE...
I SEE NOW...
IT'S DIFFERENT THAN BEFORE.
MAYBE YOU CAN'T DIE...
UNLESS WE KILL YOU THE SAME WAY YOU KILLED US.
YOU KNEW IT ALL ALONG...
UN-BELIEV-ABLE.
STILL...

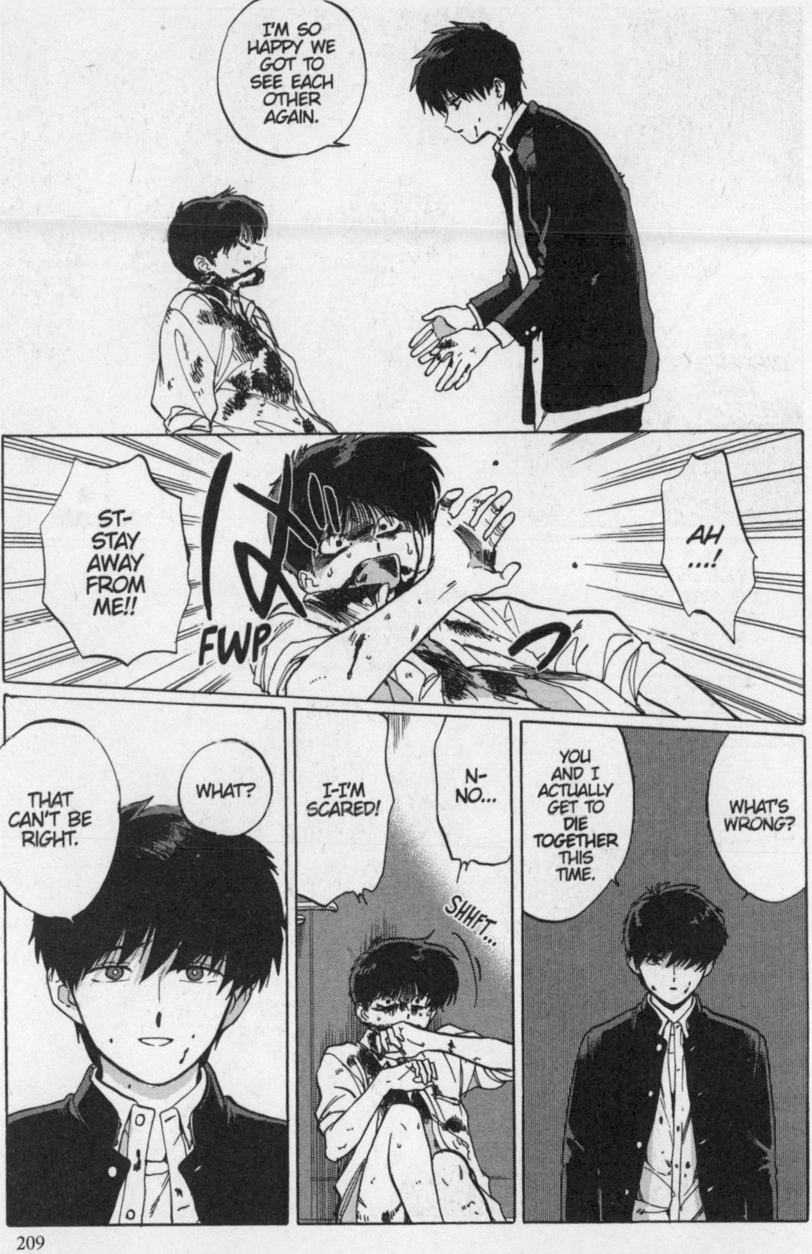
I'M SO HAPPY WE GOT TO SEE EACH OTHER AGAIN.
AH ...!
ST- STAY AWAY FROM ME!!
FWP
WHAT'S WRONG?
YOU AND I ACTUALLY GET TO DIE TOGETHER THIS TIME.
N- NO...
I-I'M SCARED!
SHHFT...
WHAT?
THAT CAN'T BE RIGHT.

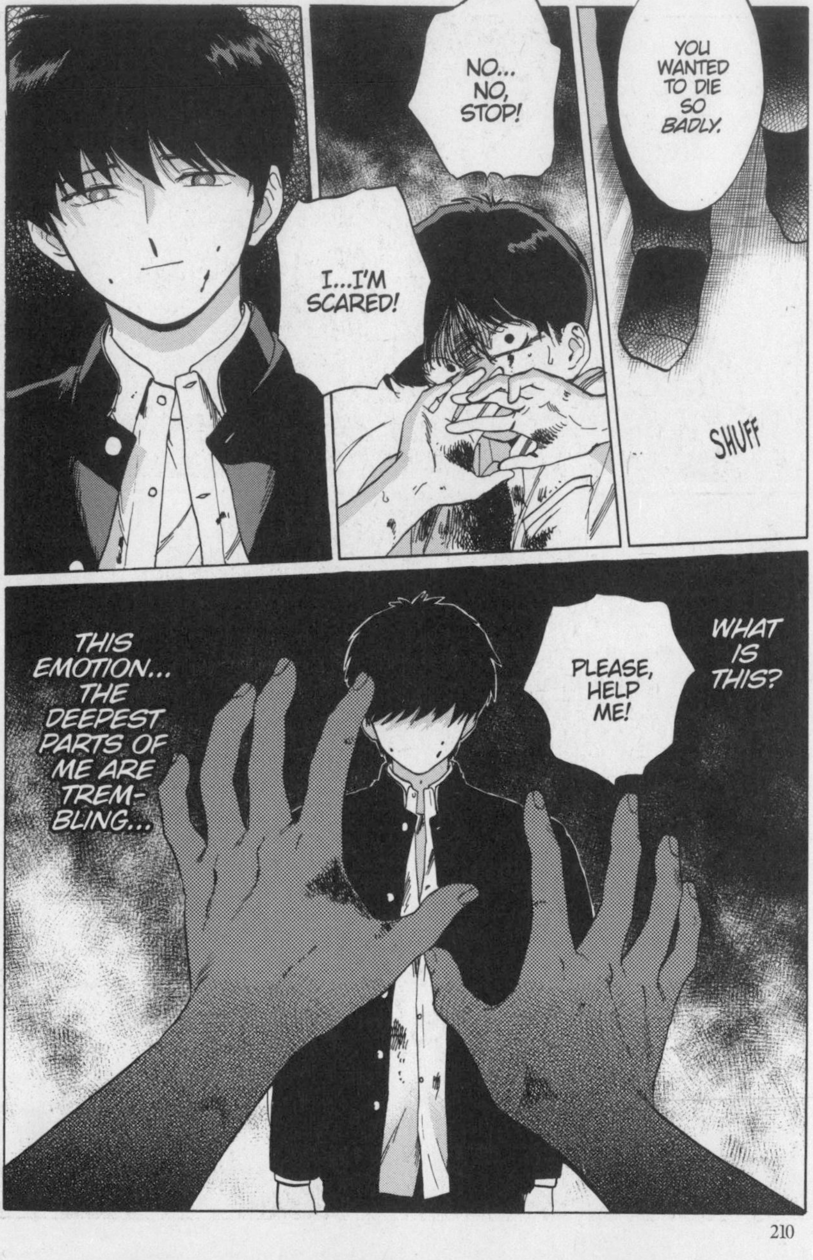
YOU WANTED TO DIE SO BADLY.
SHUFF
NO... NO, STOP!
I...I'M SCARED!
WHAT IS THIS?
PLEASE, HELP ME!
THIS EMOTION... THE DEEPEST PARTS OF ME ARE TREM-BLING...

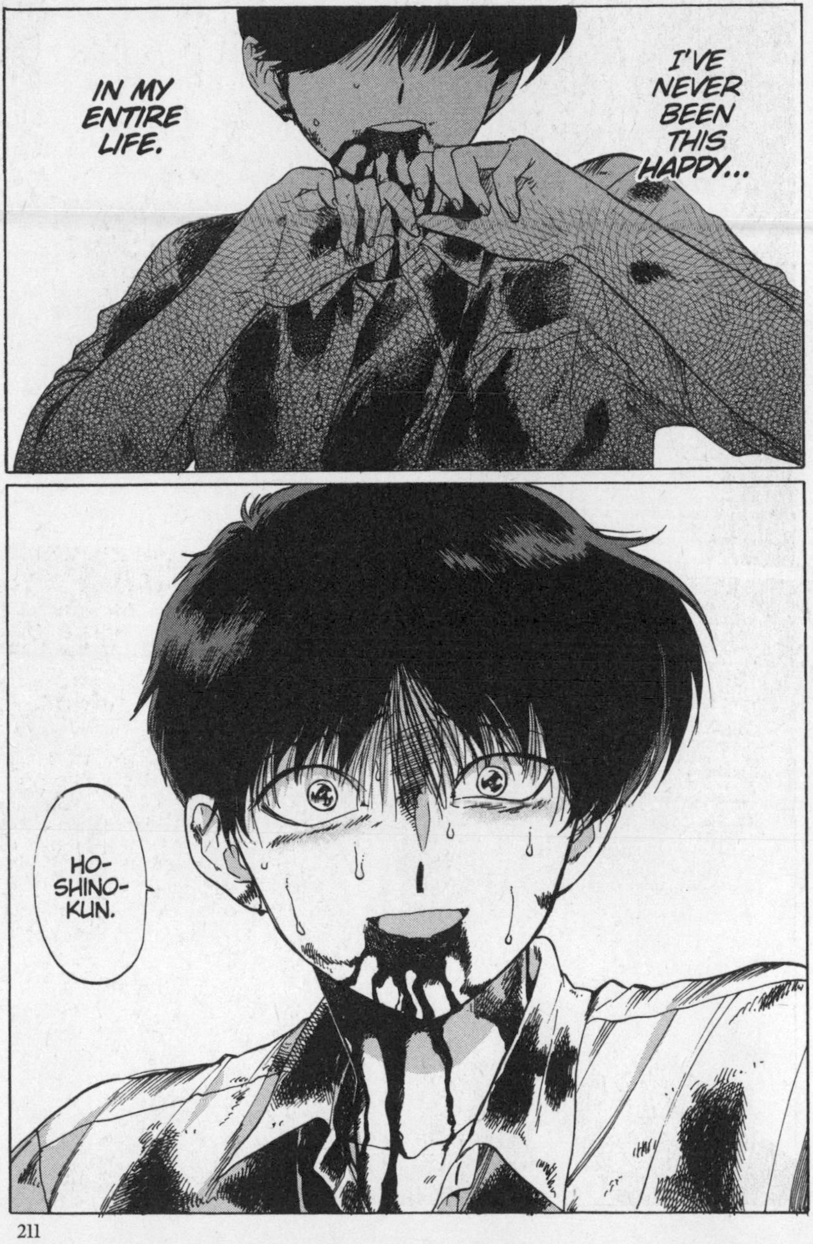
I'VE NEVER BEEN THIS HAPPY...
IN MY ENTIRE LIFE.
HO-SHINO-KUN.

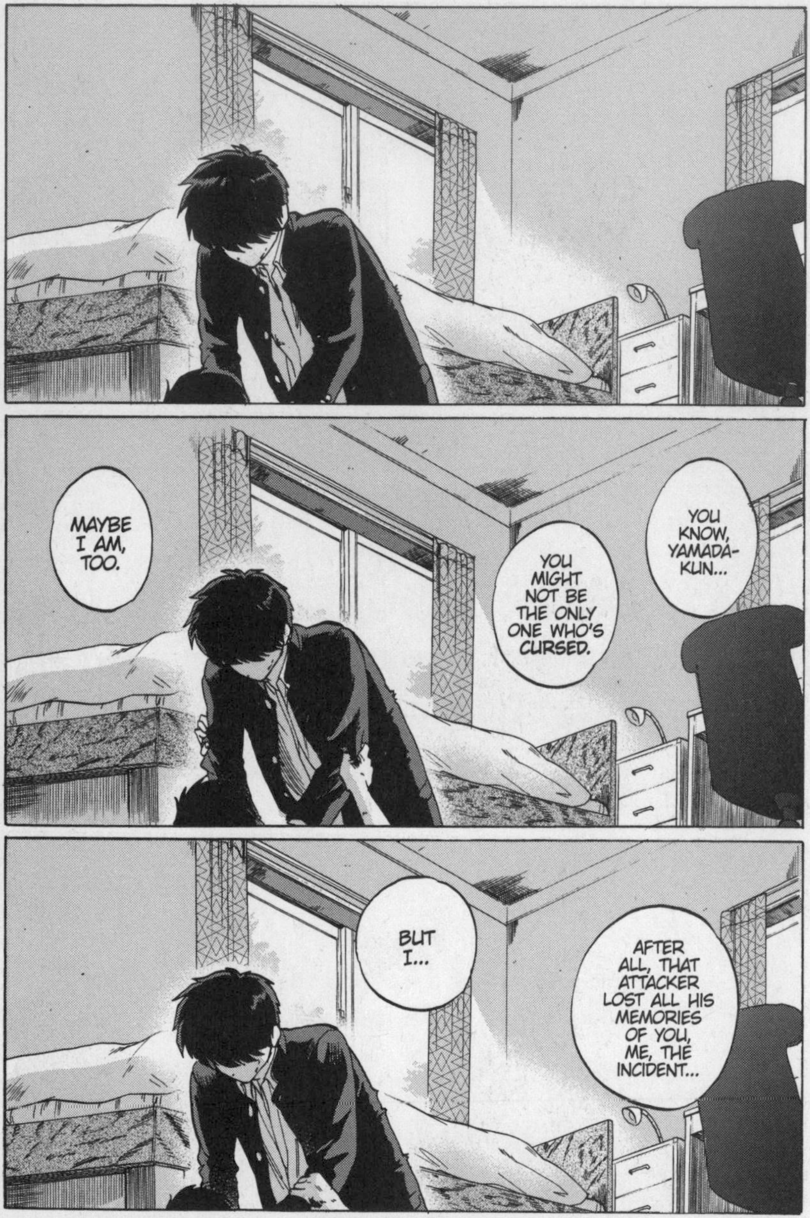
YOU KNOW, YAMADA-KUN...
YOU MIGHT NOT BE THE ONLY ONE WHO'S CURSED.
MAYBE I AM, TOO.
AFTER ALL, THAT ATTACKER LOST ALL HIS MEMORIES OF YOU, ME, THE INCIDENT...
BUT I...

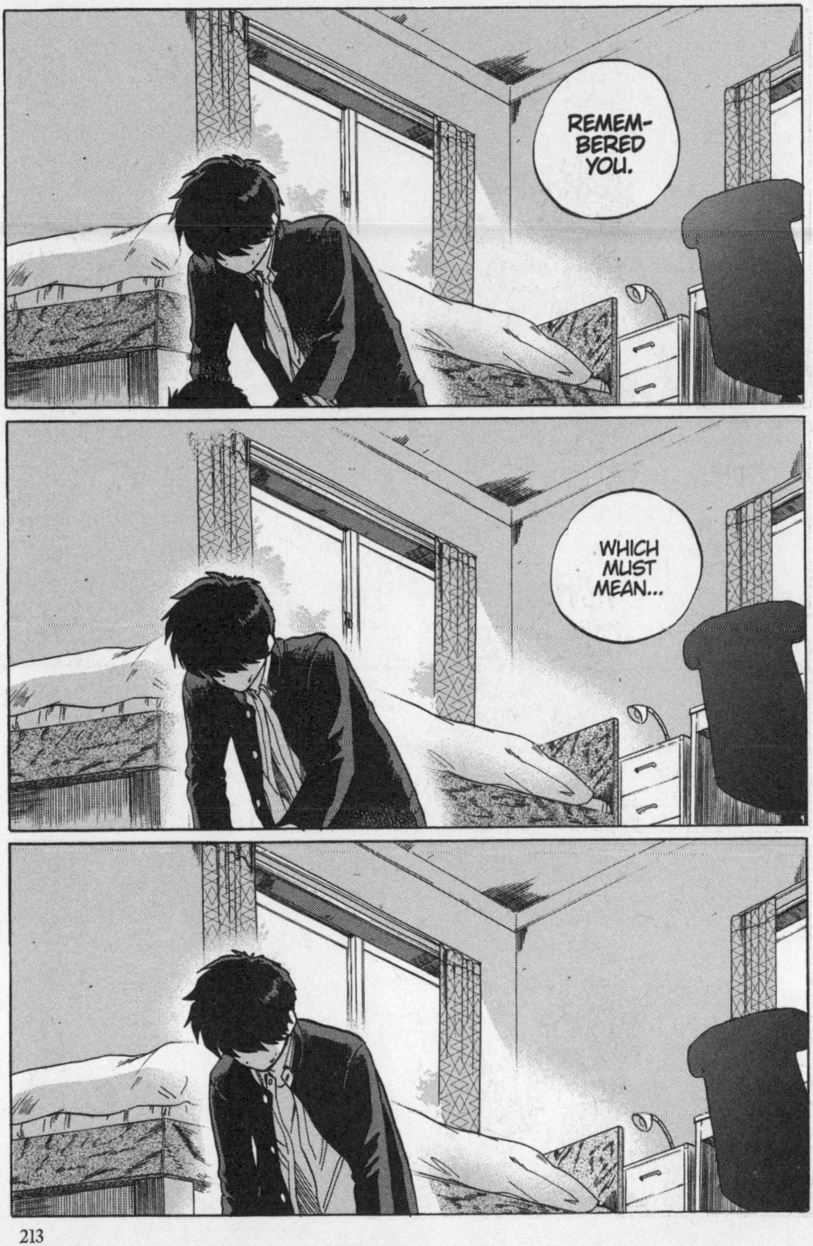
REMEM-
BERED
YOU.
WHICH
MUST
MEAN...

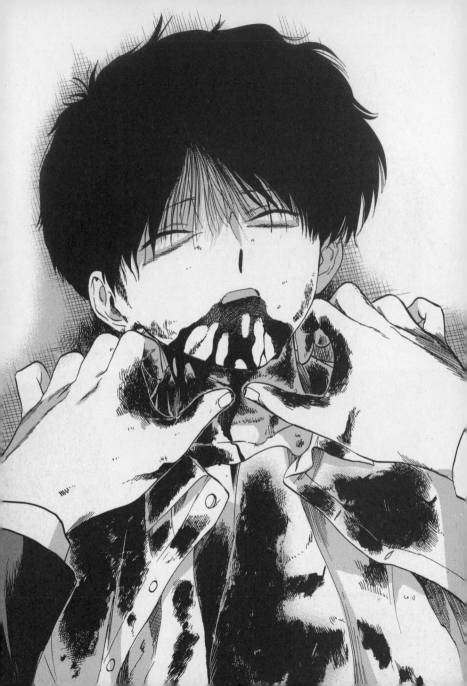

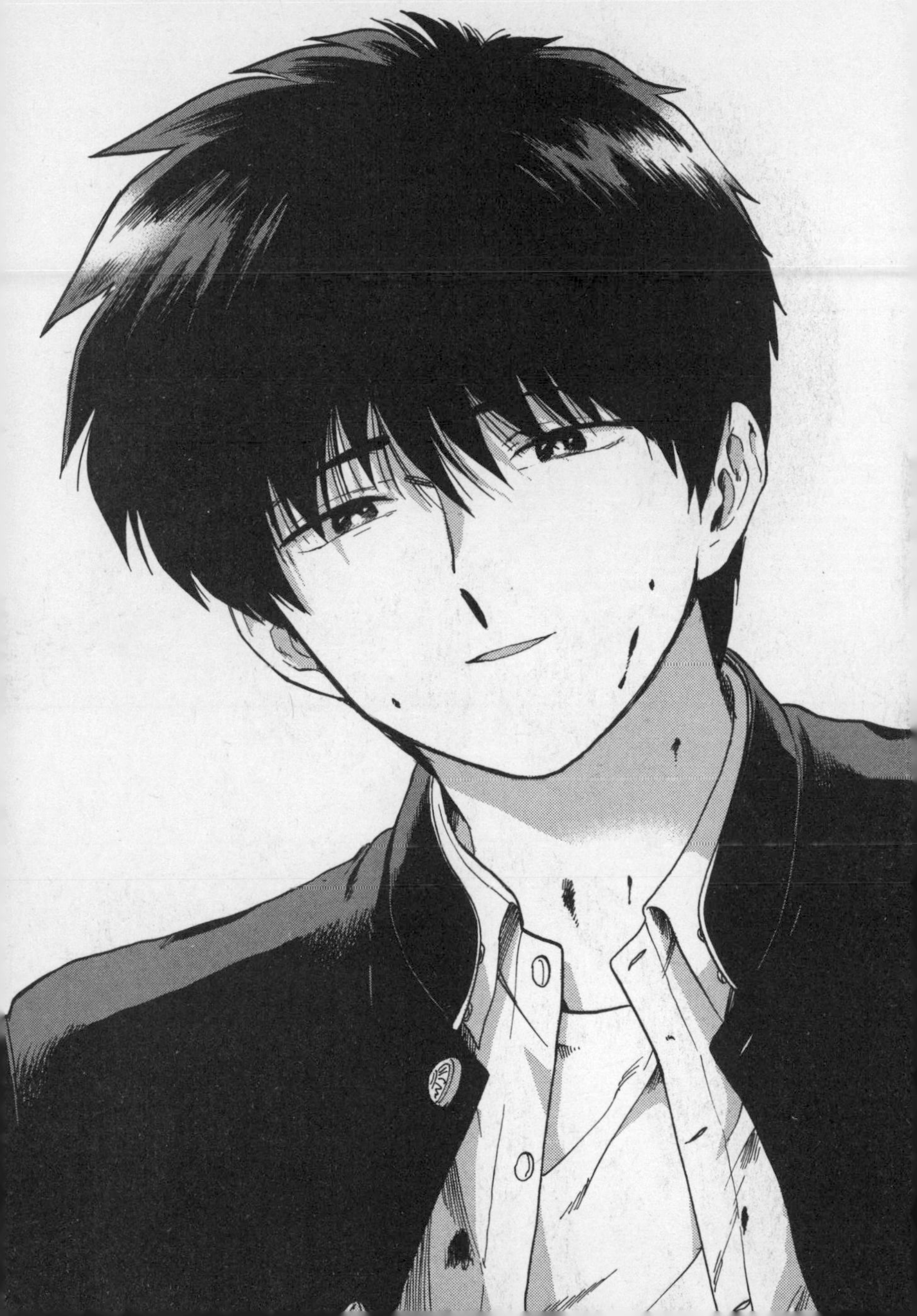

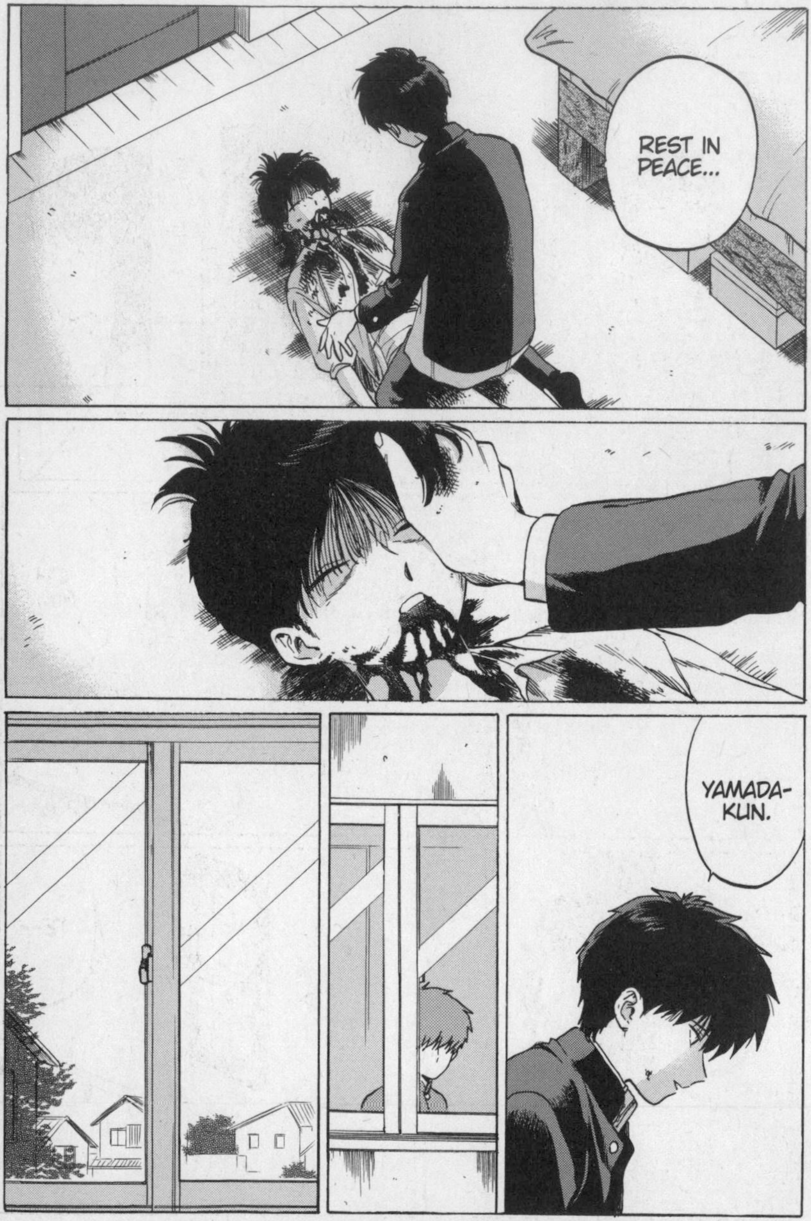
REST IN PEACE...
YAMADA-KUN.

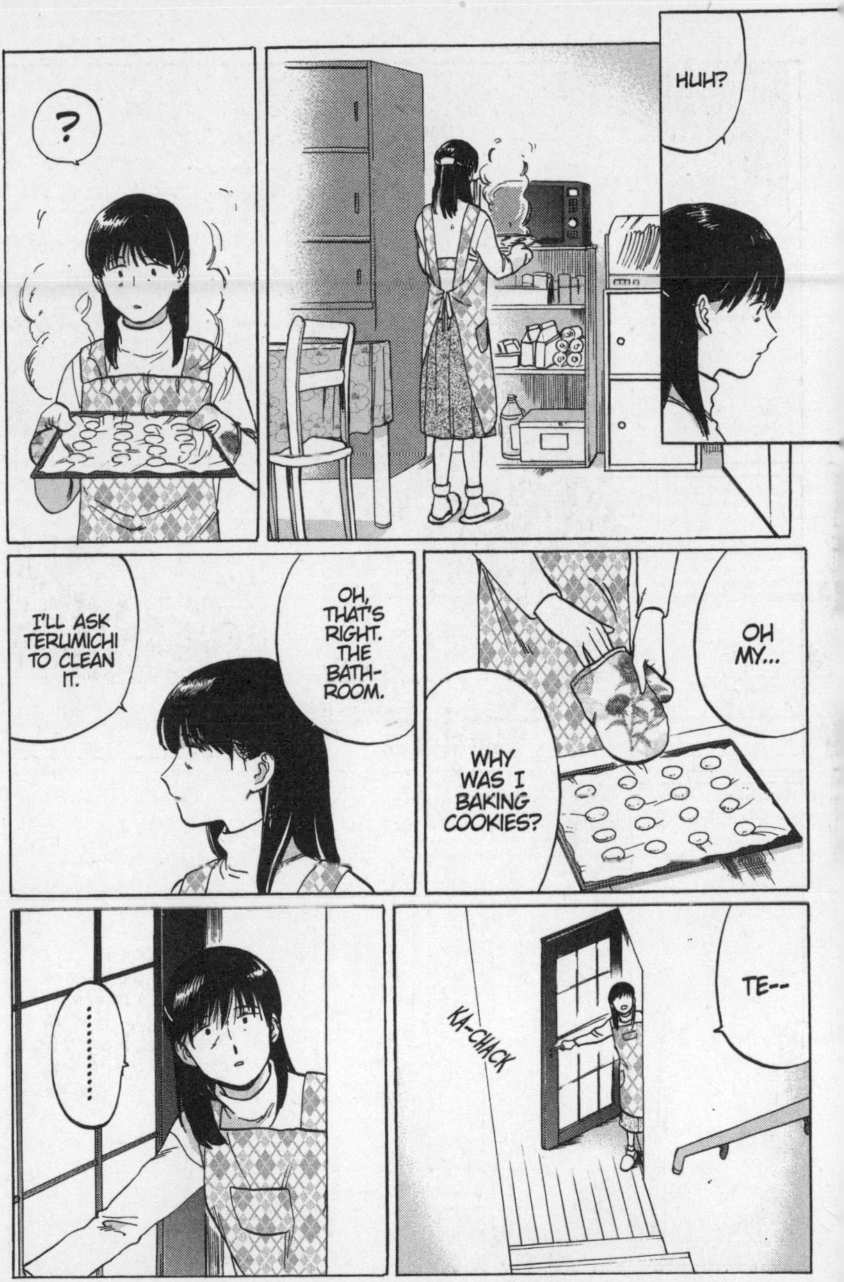
HUH?
?
OH MY...
WHY WAS I BAKING COOKIES?
OH, THAT'S RIGHT. THE BATH-ROOM.
I'LL ASK TERUMICHI TO CLEAN IT.
TE--
KA-CHACK
....

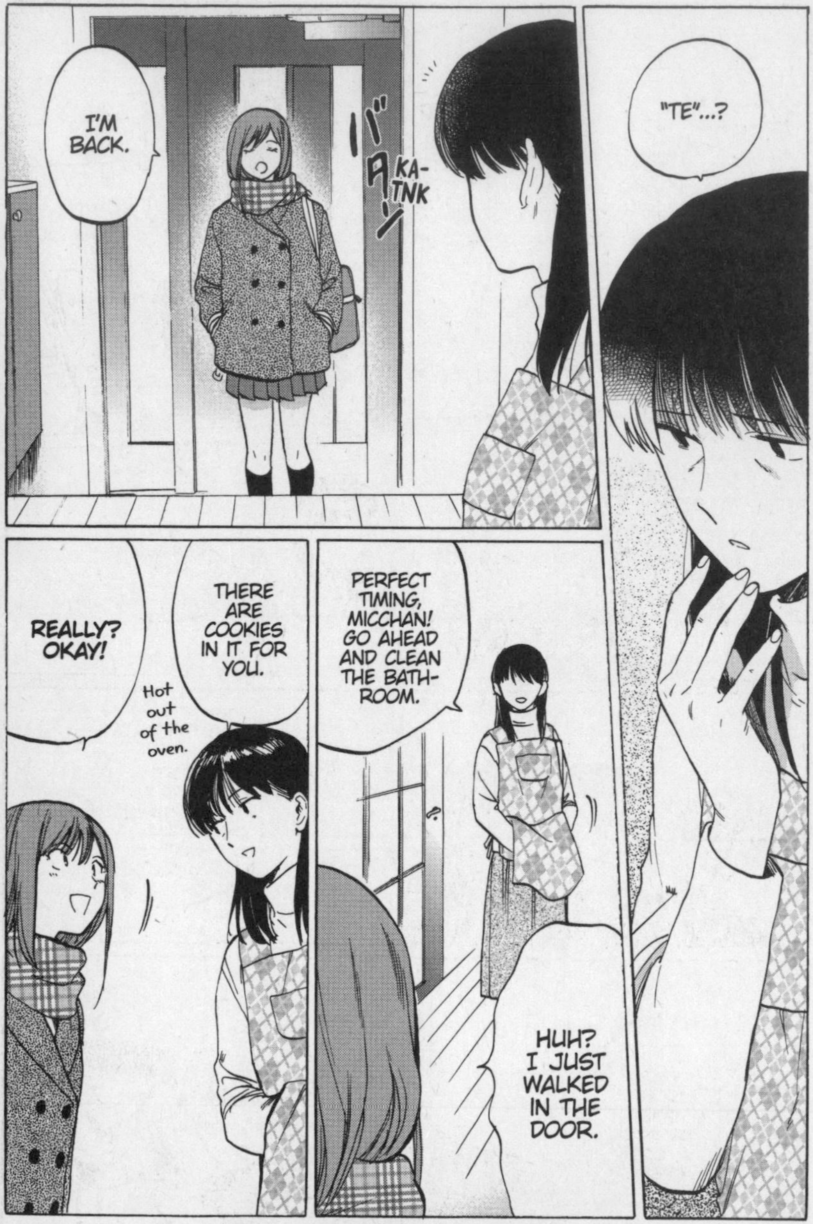
"TE"...?
KA-TNK
I'M BACK.
PERFECT TIMING, MICCHAN! GO AHEAD AND CLEAN THE BATH-ROOM.
HUH? I JUST WALKED IN THE DOOR.
THERE ARE COOKIES IN IT FOR YOU.
Hot out of the oven.
REALLY? OKAY!

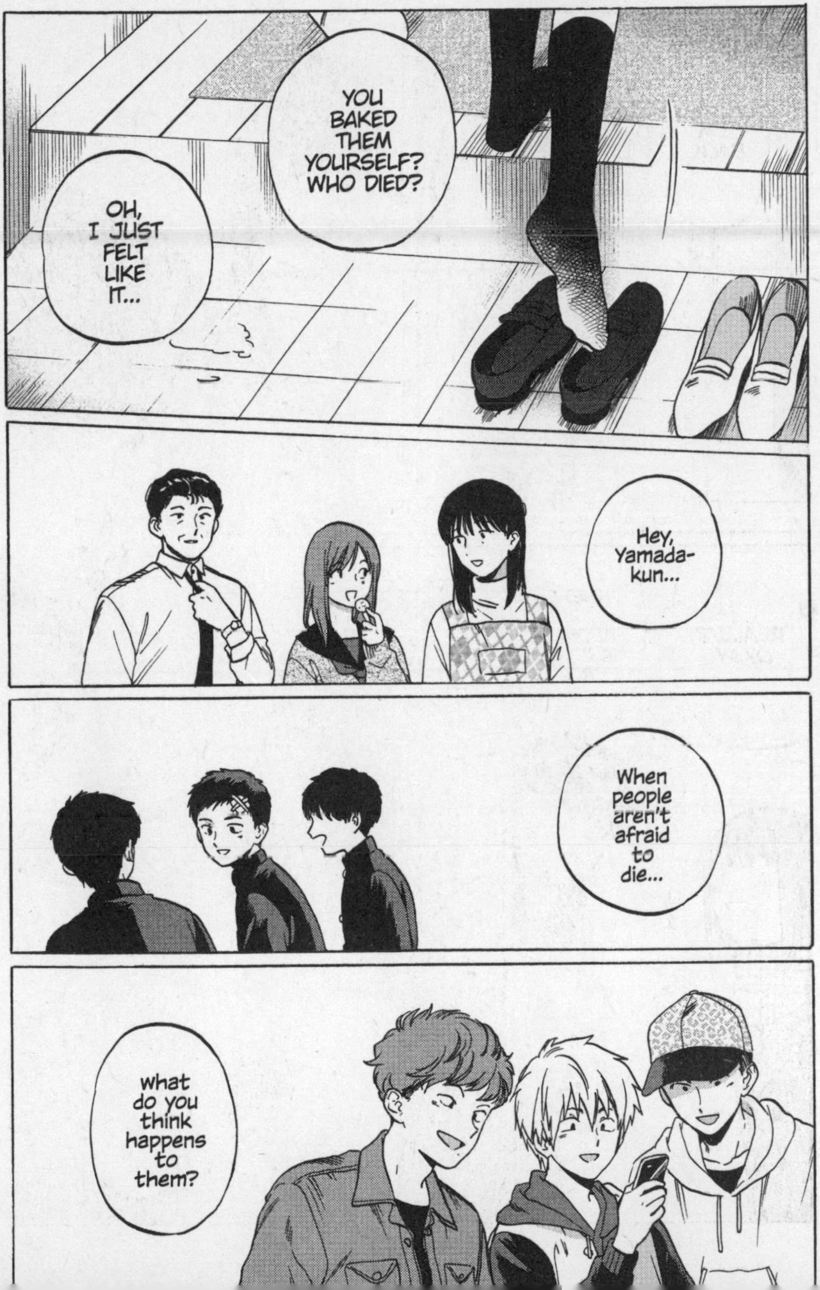
YOU BAKED THEM YOURSELF? WHO DIED?
OH, I JUST FELT LIKE IT...
Hey, Yamada-kun...
When people aren't afraid to die...
what do you think happens to them?

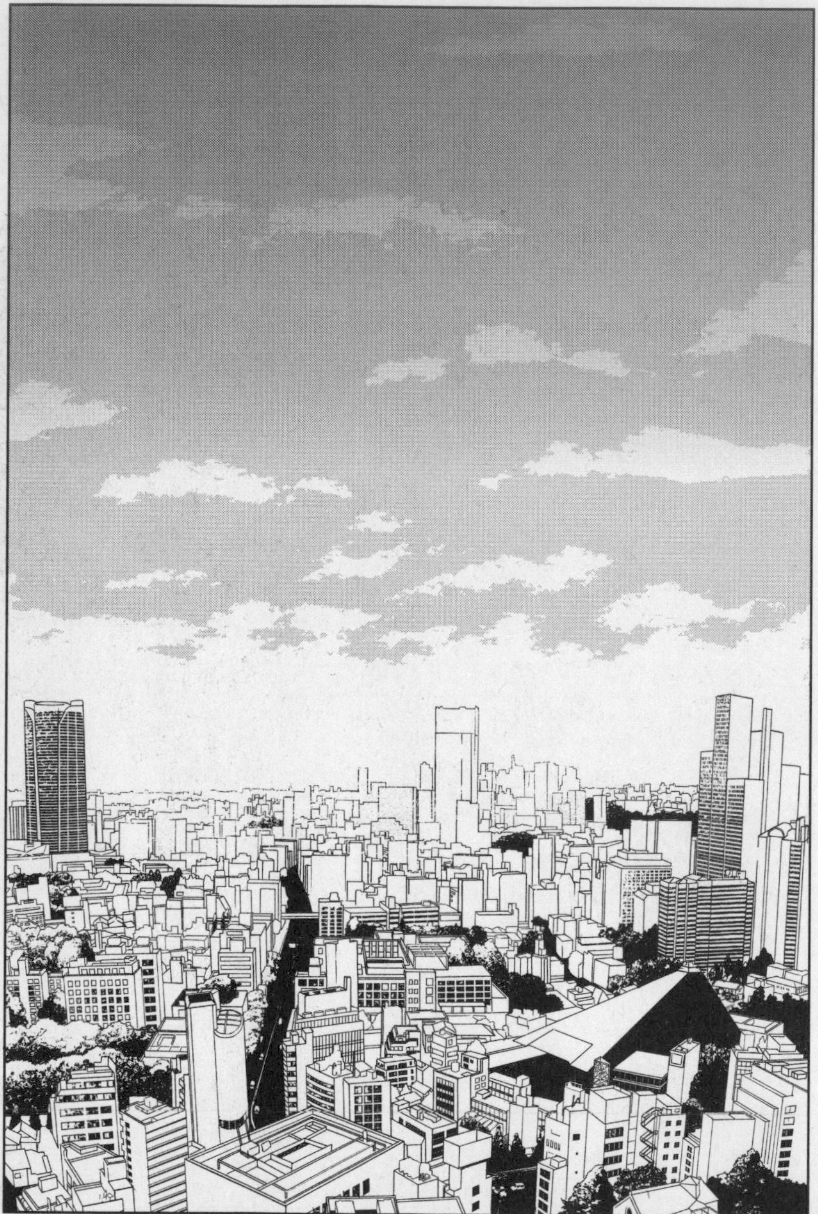

【 Final Chapter 】END

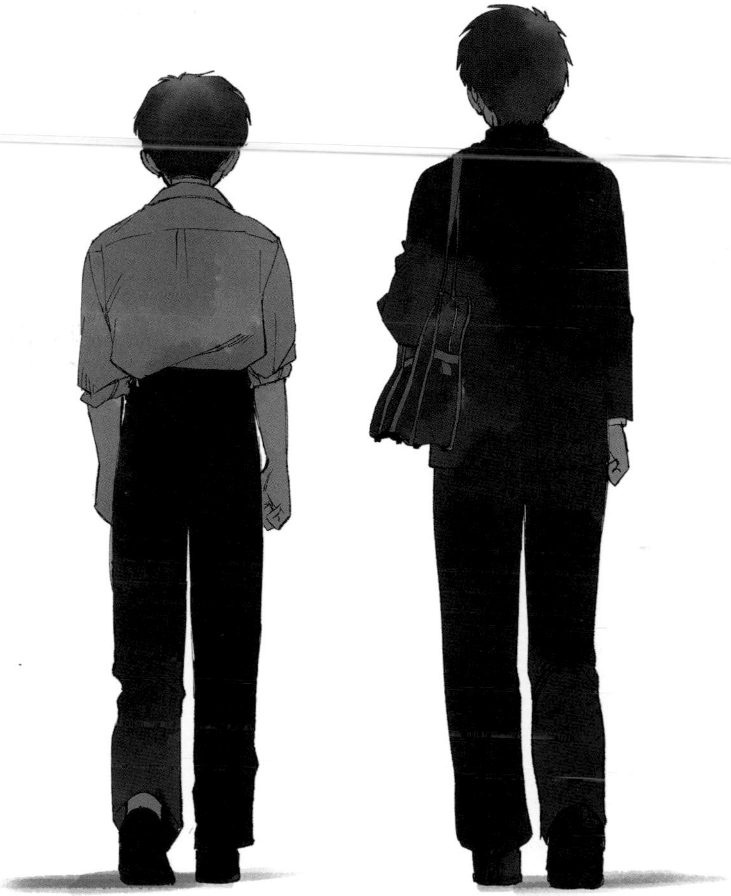

TOTAL ECLIPSE OF THE ETERNAL HEART

【 The End 】

SPECIAL THANKS:
Yumeno Rui

SEVEN SEAS ENTERTAINMENT PRESENTS

TOTAL ECLIPSE OF THE ETERNAL HEART

story and art by SYUNDEI

TRANSLATION
Amber Tamosaitis

ADAPTATION
Lora Gray

LETTERING AND LAYOUT
Kaitlyn Wiley

COVER DESIGN
KC Fabellon

PROOFREADER
Cae Hawksmoor
Shanti Whitesides

EDITOR
Jenn Grunigen

PRODUCTION MANAGER
Lissa Pattillo

EDITOR IN CHIEF
Adam Arnold

PUBLISHER
Jason DeAngelis

GESSHOKU KITAN
©Syundei 2017
Originally published in Japan in 2017 by AKANESHINSHA, Tokyo.
English translation rights arranged with COMIC HOUSE, Tokyo,
through TOHAN CORPORATION, Tokyo.

Seven Seas books may be purchased in bulk for promotional, educational, or
business use. Please contact your local bookseller or the Macmillan Corporate
and Premium Sales Department at 1-800-221-7945, extension 5442, or by
e-mail at MacmillanSpecialMarkets@macmillan.com.

Seven Seas and the Seven Seas logo are trademarks of
Seven Seas Entertainment, LLC. All rights reserved.

ISBN: 978-1-64275-040-9

Printed in Canada

First Printing: March 2019

10 9 8 7 6 5 4 3 2 1

FOLLOW US ONLINE: *www.sevenseasentertainment.com*

READING DIRECTIONS

This book reads from *right to left*, Japanese style.
If this is your first time reading manga, you start
reading from the top right panel on each page and
take it from there. If you get lost, just follow the
numbered diagram here. It may seem backwards at
first, but you'll get the hang of it! Have fun!!

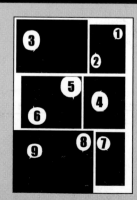